THE BUBBLE
AND THE BEAR

How Nortel Burst the Canadian Dream

Douglas Hunter

DOUBLEDAY CANADA

In memory of David Ricardo (1772–1823)

Copyright © Douglas Hunter 2002

Doubleday Canada and colophon are trademarks.

National Library of Canada Cataloguing in Publication Data

Hunter, Douglas, 1959–
    The bubble and the bear : how Nortel burst the Canadian dream /
    Douglas Hunter

ISBN 0-385-65918-0

1. Nortel Networks—History.   2. Northern Telecom Limited—History.
I. Title.

Jacket design: CS Richardson
Printed and bound in the USA

Published in Canada by
Doubleday Canada, a division of
Random House of Canada Limited

Visit Random House of Canada Limited's website: www.randomhouse.ca

BVG   10   9   8   7   6   5   4   3   2   1

Contents

Preface

For the past few years, it has been well nigh impossible for Canadians to contemplate the stock market or read the business pages of the newspaper without confronting Nortel Networks. It was the engine that drove the TSE 300 composite index to record heights, the stock that did the heavy lifting in the equities portfolios of pension and mutual funds and that crammed innumerable RRSPs to the bursting point. Nortel's common shares were more than just a hot stock. The company was a major claim to fame for the country in global communications, and in high tech in general. Nortel's successes helped encourage politicians to seek more successes like it, to prioritize growth in the tech sector, to convince the next generation of university students that they should seriously consider becoming software and electrical engineers. It gave Nortel's celebrated chief executive, John Roth, a podium from which to speak out regularly on the role of Canadian taxation in the so-called brain drain of knowledge workers to the United States.

We may eventually discover that the company's penchant for buying new technology through acquisitions of American firms, rather than developing proprietary technology itself, will have a profound effect on the quantity and quality of innovation in this country. But what Nortel mainly did was cause a lot of people to lose a lot of money. As a writer, I wanted to understand and explain how this came to pass. Consequently, *The Bubble and the Bear* is fundamentally a book about investing in Nortel, as opposed to being about Nortel itself.

I'm not dismissing the importance of the story of Nortel as an enterprise, and it does figure prominently in the telling of this tale. But from the perspective of exploring the sad story of Nortel's common shares and the damage they inflicted on so many portfolios, we all have to be aware of what filmmaker Alfred Hitchcock called the "maguffin": the object that sets the plot rolling. Its exact nature isn't as important as its purpose—to provide motivation for the characters.

The Nortel stock story's maguffin was the revolution in networking technology that erupted in the 1990s. Nortel pursued dominance of that technology the way Humphrey Bogart pursued a stone bird called the Maltese falcon, and this maguffin provided impetus for the actions of the leading character, John Roth, and dramatic tension between Nortel and its main rivals, Cisco Systems and Lucent Technologies. But it's still just a maguffin. If this story was a film script, global networking supremacy could have been easily replaced by a desire to build the next-generation, hydrogen-powered automobile, or to create the perfect seedless tangerine. As long as the audience buys into the maguffin, the plot can unfold.

This might not sit well with people who still firmly believe that Nortel's recent history begins and ends with the Internet—that, like Sister Mary Ignatius, IP networking can explain it all for you. On the contrary, you will encounter in this book ample evidence of how the new communications phenomenon figured in Nortel's corporate strategy. But in the course of investing in Nortel, it was routinely possible for people to get lost in the intricacies of the maguffin. The details of Nortel's core strength in fibre optics—ring topologies and mesh architecture, dense wave division multiplexing and synchronous optical networking—are beyond the ken of most people, but that didn't stop people from trying to understand it all. Many investment professionals will still insist, oh, but anyone with money riding on this company should have tried to understand it. To a degree, that is true, but it is perhaps a surprisingly small degree. The downfall of so many investors and analysts who received their comeuppance from Nortel lay in the fact that they were blinded by the hype of new technology and distracted by debates over which networking company had the edge in one sector or another: digital wireless, enterprise IP networks, ultra-long-haul optical carrier backbones. In the end, none of it would matter nearly as much as it had seemed in the heat of the investing moment. The whole sector was overhyped and the shares in participating companies were seriously overvalued. Having a firm opinion on which company was going to gain the most market share in terabit-speed IP routers wasn't going to save you.

I confess that I too was dazzled by the maguffin at first. I devoted much energy to understanding optical networking technology before recognizing it for the maguffin it was. I benefited from boning up on it, but I also realized that approaching the story from the predictable angle of "who had the coolest technology and what did that mean to their market fortunes?" would lead in an ultimately pointless direction.

There are certain aspects of the technology revolution that must be grasped—ATM versus TCP/IP switching, the evolution from analog to digital telephone switching, SONET versus DWDM optical networks, for example. But even where I've found it important to explain some aspect of the maguffin, I've presented it on a need-to-know level for the reader. You don't need to be an expert on the maguffin's intricacies. Every expert who believed that the sky was the limit for Nortel revenue growth and share value was utterly wrong. That field of experts included the company's management, the directors who approved their actions and oversaw their escalating compensation packages, the research companies that produced data on networking industry growth (which was seriously discredited in 2001), the analysts who produced twelve-month valuation targets for the stock in late 2000 and early 2001 that proved to be overstated by about 95 percent, and the journalists who took the experts at their word and broadcast the received wisdom to the world. Think of the Nortel maguffin as the big fish in Hemingway's *The Old Man and the Sea*. You need to appreciate the presence of that fish, what it means to the old man, and how it attracts the sharks. But a degree in marine biology is not required.

If technology is important to this story as a maguffin rather than as a core issue, what is left? Merely the plain old question of how much a company's stock should actually be worth, based not on what the company itself and the technology gurus were predicting for the future, but on the basic information contained within the company's financial statements. The most important fact to realize about the technology maguffin is that it convinced people that the so-called New Economy required new ways to think about corporate profitability and stock values. But, to paraphrase John Kenneth Galbraith, the moment you hear someone saying that they have a different way of evaluating earnings, run in the opposite direction. The New Economy delusion is an old one. It was around during the 1920s, before the 1929 crash showed up, and appears with tiresome regularity in the history of investment. While I give the subject some consideration, it is too broad to be dealt with extensively in this book. If you want to know more, read Edward Chancellor's *Devil Take the Hindmost* or Robert Shiller's *Irrational Exuberance*.

Nortel's valuation implosion didn't just happen. There were abundant signs that it would happen, one way or another, about a year before the shock of February 15, 2001, when Nortel unexpectedly revised its guidance for its first-quarter 2001 performance. This book's narrative stretches back to Nortel's birth in 1895 as the Northern Electric and Manufacturing Co. in Montreal, but the bulk of the story transpires between February 1997, when John Roth took command of the company, and that traumatic day in February 2001, when Nortel abruptly ran out of growth and began the steady descent that continues to unfold even as I write. In the spring of 2002, it seemed I couldn't open a newspaper without encountering some new milestone in the Nortel story: the resignation of the chief financial officer after insider-trading misbehaviour; regular downward revisions in earnings and revenue estimates; the company's debt reaching junk-bond status; the shares dropping below $4 Canadian and $2.50 American. The persistent unravelling of Nortel over the year that followed the February 15, 2001, revelation was a secondary matter for me. It was far more important to understand how the company and its shareholders got themselves into that sorry state, which is why six chapters of this book are dedicated just to the first six weeks of 2001. As a shell-shocked member of the Nortel bulletin board at RagingBull.com posted at 5:39 P.M. on February 15: "What happened from 1/18 to 2/15? Does anyone know?" As it turns out, a lot happened, and this book's narrative is structured to build toward that bewildering, crucial period.

The February 15 guidance revision and the immediate crash in Nortel's share price caused more than a dozen class-action shareholder lawsuits to be launched in Canada and the United States, which as I write have yet to be certified in any court. Statements of claim always make for fun reading, but nothing in them is proven, and Nortel has said it will defend itself vigorously against them. (I discuss the various suits at the end of the book.)

I confess that these lawsuits trouble me—not because I am in any way opposed to allegedly wronged investors having their deserved day in court, but because in the post-Enron investing environment, it is all too easy to become obsessed with identifying fraudulent activities as the root cause of investor misery. On the contrary, investors in a broad swath of companies have been made miserable by activities that are completely legal, carried out in broad daylight, and, for the most part, with their consent and even their active participation. Nortel does not require allegations of revenue inflation in a particular quarter, for example, to explain the mess that its stock became. They might prove to be a contributing factor in how the implosion of share values played out, should they ever be proven true, but they would not alter the underlying reality of how Nortel's shares climbed so high, then fell so far and so fast. Revenue recognition problems have nothing to do with the price distortions of index investing or how receivables are treated on balance sheets, for example. The indisputable tragedy in the Nortel case is how surprised investors were when their investment began to slither toward the floor.

The lessons to be gleaned from Nortel are not about the foibles of the networking revolution. They're about how a company presents its investment attractiveness to the public, how the public embraces the company's message, how the press and financial professionals too often aid and abet the corporate spin. Above all, it's about how the rules of financial reporting, even when followed to the letter, can warp perceptions of profitability and even lead to serious problems in a company's operations. While I did not embrace this project as an educational crusade, the more research I did beyond the maguffin, the more I came to believe that Nortel represents a cautionary tale of how little the average investor truly understands about a stock that is pinned in the thousand-watt headlights of investor and media enthusiasm.

Midway through researching this book, I spoke with *Globe and Mail* business columnist Eric Reguly, with whom I worked at the old *Financial Post* back in 1987. "It's an accounting story," Eric said of

Nortel, which may seem beyond obvious, but is absolutely true—
and critically so. By that, Eric meant that the technology was indeed
the maguffin. The tale was in the numbers. And in studying the
numbers in financial reports stretching back to the mid-1970s, it
was clear that pretty well everything a judicious investor needed to
know about Nortel was there in front of them all along, if only they
had the ability to read a financial statement properly, or had an
investment adviser who could (or was inclined to) do the same for
them. Sometimes the answer took the form of a troubling question
that a statement could not satisfy, but that kind of answer is often the
most important kind of all. With Nortel, knowing what you didn't
know was as important as knowing what you did.

Not all information is of equal merit in the Nortel story. If you
understood the difference between speed and channel count in dense
wave division multiplexing switches, good for you. But as an investor
during Nortel's heyday, it would have been a whole lot more useful
to have understood how Nortel (with perfect legality) capitalized
long-term receivables, isolated them from current assets, and in the
process improved the appearance of its operating cash flow and day-
sales rate. It also would have been useful to know that Nortel (with
perfect legality) could enter into long-term supply contracts in which
it agreed to provide products that might not yet even exist in a
market-ready form, then book the revenues on the basis of costs it had
incurred, not on the basis of money it had actually collected. It also
would have been useful to know that Nortel's "earnings from operations" figures, which indicated the company was profitable, were a
major departure from generally accepted accounting principles and
managed to mask the fact that Nortel did not have a single profitable
year between 1997 and 2001. Despite this, these were the figures cited
in Nortel's press releases and used as the basis for earnings guidance.
It also would have been useful to know that by year-end 2000, Nortel
was creating a retained earning deficit that measured in the billions as
it continued to pay dividends on common shares, despite the fact that
it was actually losing money. It also would have been useful to know
that John Roth's salary and bonuses (including stock options) were
awarded based on a measure of corporate performance that ignored

the acquisition-related costs of the company's expansion spree. And once you knew all that, it would have been useful to know how measuring corporate performance without regard to legitimate accounting costs locked Nortel into a pattern of increasing its revenues by acquiring companies and their coveted technologies with its treasury shares, thereby placing Nortel on an escalator of revenue growth that was powered by a steady dilution of each share's claim on earnings— which would all come to a clattering halt if the networking industry overall couldn't deliver on its promises of massive year-over-year global sales growth.

Investors were failed badly by the architects of Nortel's late-1990s' expansion into Internet-based networking and their self-serving earnings calculations. But they were also failed badly by the chattering classes in the media and the investment community. The voices that strove to warn investors about the serious risks in this alleged blue-chip stock and the illogic in its share value were drowned out by the analysts who went along with whatever financial figures Nortel supplied them and at the same time followed the gung-ho projections from research companies that forecast incredible rates of growth in networking sectors for the next quarter-century. Analysts have been thoroughly roasted for their ridiculous cheerleading of stocks during the recent tech boom, and shots have also been taken at business news programs like CNBC for giving these analysts free air time with which to tout their favourite picks to the unquestioning masses. But the problems did not begin and end with CNBC. Though I am indebted to the many writers who filled in the broader timeline for me, it must also be said that some writers from North America's financial press did their own bits to keep the Nortel balloon aloft, by passing along the received wisdom, by actively counselling readers not to worry about their Nortel holdings when trouble surfaced, by tuning out the credible objectors to Nortel's numbers when canvassing for expert opinions, and (in at least one case) by ignoring the problematic evidence when it was shoved right in their faces.

As a writer, I am preternaturally hesitant to dump all over the media in this tale. Business journalists have to keep pace with a lot of companies and issues simultaneously, and they come to depend

on the expertise of professionals (as I have). That often means looking to analysts for wisdom, but with many news organizations it also
means just reporting what the analysts say. And if many analysts are
just saying what the company in question has fed them, there's been
no real analysis at all performed for the reader or viewer. I was also
troubled by the widespread lack of disclosure in the media. Investors
typically have no idea how much money a columnist, commentator,
or reporter has invested, directly or indirectly, in a particular stock
being covered. The media regularly champions the cause of transparency in governments and businesses, but the Nortel debacle suggests that we need far more transparency in the media itself. (For the
record, I owned no shares in Nortel, its associated companies, or its
competitors at any time.)

My main goal in shaping the narrative of this book was to
approach Nortel from the perspective of what was known or, more
importantly, knowable, about the company and its stock during the
investing heyday. I stepped into the investor time machine, reading
the continuous disclosure documents like any investor or analyst
would have or should have and tried to make sense of them. The
information being presented in the business and technology press
was also important to recreating the landscape of information. In this
way, I recreated the timeline by drawing as much as possible on information that was actually available during those crucial years: what
might be called the "on-the-record" record. I wanted Nortel to
remain exactly as investors found it: a bright and shiny object, like
Jupiter in the night sky, that they could see but not touch. The
Nortel that I presented would be the Nortel that investors saw—or
that was there to be seen, in particular by reading the fine print in
the company's filings (and the filings of other companies) with
securities regulators, absorbing the public comments of senior executives, and questioning the logic of how the earnings, balance sheet,
and cash flow statements of Nortel and its main competitors were
constructed. No secret storehouse of information that had only come
to light after the shares fell to single-digit value was required to
explain what had gone wrong.

I had a huge amount of help from the people I call the contrarians—

Al and Mark Rosen, Ross Healy, and Paul Sagawa—investment and accounting professionals whose analysis had run counter to the received wisdom on Nortel. They provided copies of the analysis they distributed to clients during Nortel's brightest days on the stock market and answered my questions. They became for me the Cassandras of the Nortel story—the respectable, rational contrarians who by and large couldn't get people—even their own clients—to listen to them as the stock steamed *Titanic*-like toward its appointment with an iceberg. Because of them, and because of the abundant information contained within the rest of the "on-the-record record," the story I came to tell was one of a clear and present danger.

Back in 1987, I completed the Canadian Securities Course as part of my employment as a staff writer with the *Financial Post*. It taught me the basics of market and investment theory, and how to read financial statements. It didn't teach me how to take apart a financial statement by using the idiosyncrasies of Generally Accepted Accounting Principles (GAAP) as a pry bar. I had to learn this, in part, from the Rosens, and in part from ploughing through the accounting regulations of the standards boards of Canada and the United States.

It must be emphasized that nothing I came across in Nortel's financial statements, accepted at face value, was in any way illegal. Yet within the vagaries of GAAP, there is plenty of room for financial information to be managed to a company's advantage. That's what good accountants do. Good analysts should be able to take apart a set of financial statements and pinpoint areas of concern and detect trends that bode ill for the shareholder. The number of analysts among the many covering Nortel who were actually doing this when the stock was an investment darling was pitiably small.

The Nortel saga should teach us that the financial figures on which forecasts of stock performances are built are shot through with hazards and incongruities. Back in 1979, when he was a vice-president of the Toronto Blue Jays, Paul Beeston famously told the *Wall Street Journal*: "Under generally accepted accounting principles, I can turn a $4 million profit into a $2 million loss and I could get every national accounting firm to agree with me." Nortel went one better. In creating its own supplementary performance measurements, it turned annual losses that came to exceed one billion dollars into multimillion-dollar profits by throwing out costs that were recognized under GAAP. Not only that; Nortel got pretty well every major investment analysis operation to agree that this was a smart thing to do, whether or not they agreed that Nortel was a good investment (although virtually all of them did).

The tech stock boom of the late 1990s, and the greater bull market in general, demonstrated a lopsidedness in the knowledge of typical investors. They knew (or thought they knew) a lot about the products of their favourite investments, their competitors, their market sectors. They were well versed in the maguffin. What they knew very little about was the accounting that was the basis of the dollar figures in revenues and earnings that got everyone so excited, or whether or not departing from GAAP in producing customized earnings numbers, the way Nortel did, made any fiscal sense.

Buying or selling a particular stock on the basis of how a company measures up to a quarterly earnings forecast of 17 cents per share is absurd, unless you understand how those earnings were calculated, and how the revenues that produced those earnings were recognized. The most salient question that can be asked of an earnings forecast is: Where'd this thing come from? Yet with Nortel, sadly, it was seldom asked. Not asking represented a widespread failure of prudent investing and analysis. The departures from GAAP made by innumerable companies with their customized earnings numbers I will argue created more problems than they solved. In addition, it must be noted that within GAAP itself, simply because of the way accrual accounting principles function, there is plenty of opportunity for revenues to go in one direction while cash flow is going in an entirely different one, and for cash flow and earnings figures to be spruced up by the way costs and assets are allocated. And unless an investor clearly understands how revenues are actually being recognized by a company, how it presents its earnings, and how it treats assets on the balance sheet, there's no reasonable way of knowing what a company means when it says it sells a particular amount, earns a particular amount, or shows a particular amount of operating cash flow. If those things aren't known, predictions of earnings, revenues, and share value are utterly meaningless.

I'm still wondering about how it came to pass that investors were rendered so oblivious to the realities of corporate reporting. The pathologies of the analyst industry are so vast that they deserve a book of their own and are certain to receive many. In another case of "even as I write," the attorney general's office of the State of New York was pursuing some of Wall Street's most famous tech stock cheerleaders for their relentlessly positive spin on stocks that they apparently knew were going down the drain. Suffice to say that investors were largely on their own during Nortel's investing glory years. But there was already widespread skepticism of analysts, long before Nortel delivered its forecast shocker on February 15, 2001, in large part because the NASDAQ had already suffered its flameout almost a year earlier. Many investors were doing their own due diligence as they traded through discount on-line brokerage accounts. But as I will explain in this book, judging by the exchanges of opinions on investment bulletin boards, the process of do-it-yourself due diligence was deeply flawed. It tended to reinforce the investment decision already made rather than question the underlying value of the stock or the risks the company faced. Accounting was never a subject of much interest or concern to these investors. I think the general perception that accounting rules are impenetrably dense (and dull) served to turn away inquisitive minds. But I think a larger factor was that people simply accepted the numbers presented to them by companies like Nortel as some kind of absolute value, as if "earnings" could be measured with as much certainty as the temperature of a liquid could be with a thermometer. Investors by and large failed to look beyond the maguffin and confront the real issues with Nortel: those that were lurking in the financial statements.

I won't lie to you. Accounting is, by and large, damned dull. My own accountant, when I told him I was looking at pooling and purchase method acquisitions in this book, responded with: "Where's the sex and violence in that?" But accounting is nothing more than a way of organizing numbers, and when you start to see how the numbers are in fact organized, narrative suddenly emerges: a company comes alive; assumptions are challenged; trends are revealed; dangers rear their ugly heads.

A critical aspect of the reconstructive effort I attempted with Nortel was to stay "in the moment," as it were, as much as possible. Interviews with the above-mentioned contrarians as well as investors were informative, but it was important not to be led astray by the possibility of post-event rationalization and wishful recollection. Collecting the private reports to investors from my contrarians and placing them within the narrative timeline at the appropriate points emphasized what was known, and being said, at a particular moment. The reader can also see the convictions and suspicions of these contrarians, particularly Healy and the Rosens, evolve as more information became available, or in some cases in the absence of information that would have been useful to them at that moment. I have occasionally made my own elaborations on their arguments which go beyond what they were capable of making, or were inclined to present, at the time. I must also thank Al and Mark Rosen for considering and commenting on some of my theories on what was going on in Nortel's books, although those theories ultimately are mine to defend.

With investors, I am grateful for the frank cooperation I received from people who lost tens of thousands of dollars, and their efforts to recollect their motivations at particular points in their investing activity. I cannot say enough about the assistance I received from David Chmelnitsky, and must also thank Terry Blackman for sharing his experiences. A number of other former Nortel investors, stretching from Vancouver to Montreal, spoke to me about their experiences, and while I did not make specific use of their recollections the way I did with David Chmelnitsky and Terry Blackman, they nonetheless contributed to my impressions of investor experience.

At the same time, I found a priceless resource for assessing the perceptions of investors at precise moments in Nortel's trading history in the on-line investor bulletin boards that preserve the real-time comments of their pseudonymous members. Two members of the Raging Bull board, Wayne Schmengrum and Michael Hollander, agreed to come out from behind their on-line aliases and answer questions about their investing experiences, but the preserved record of their on-line comments, in addition to those of other board members, provided a fascinating window into how active and fairly knowledgeable investors responded in real time to the events unfolding around them. The electronic bulletin boards, whose archived postings sometimes stretch back several years, offer an unprecedented glimpse of the way ardent investors actually think, and how they react to information gleaned from analysts, the media, and a company like Nortel. I chose the Nortel board at Raging Bull in particular as a means of exploring what investors thought of the company and its stock, especially in the six-week period at the beginning of 2001. The postings also provided the most visceral responses imaginable to the news that Nortel was drastically revising its guidance on February 15. Most of the board's participants are as anonymous to me as they are to each other, but I thank them all for making such valuable postings to a public forum, and for their pack-rat–like dedication to collecting information and posting it on the board. And Teletruth, wherever and whoever you are: you are the man.

In addition to the individuals mentioned above, I would like to thank several others who contributed in their own ways. My wife, Debbie Christmas, was a telecom professional at a major investment bank in another life, and pitched in by contributing research on Cisco and Lucent. Steve Bochner, a university lecturer and securities lawyer specializing in technology companies at the Silicon Valley law firm Wilson Sonsini Goodrich & Rosati, was a big help in sorting out the SEC's Regulation FD and "safe harbour" initiatives. University of Toronto law professor Jeffery Macintosh entertained my questions about statutory liability for continuous-disclosure documents in Canada and replied with clarity. Susan Wolbergh Jenah, general counsel of the Ontario Securities Commission, filled me in on the status of efforts to bring statutory liability to those documents in Canada. Joel Rochon of the Toronto law firm Rochon Genova spoke with me about the shareholder class-action suits against Nortel in Canada and the United States. Mel Calder, a retired Bell engineer, provided some pointers on early Nortel switching technology. Kirsten Watson spoke fondly and frankly to me about her experiences being both hired and fired by Nortel, while a present Nortel marketing executive I refer to as John Richards also spoke at length with me about his experiences inside the company. "John Richards" had no axe to grind with his employer—in fact, he emphasized how much he enjoys working there—but on my suggestion he has been identified by a pseudonym.

1

Warning Bells

At Nortel, we are committed to growing profitably and to both creating and investing in long-term shareholder value. We are, and must remain, a growth company, but that growth must not result from simply striving to be the biggest.
—Letter to shareholders, 1996 Nortel Annual Report

The New York Stock Exchange trading day used to begin with the percussive flourish of a Chinese gong, but in 1903 the gong was replaced by the Yankee sobriety of a brass bell. There are now actually four bells, positioned in each corner of the Lower Manhattan trading floor on Broad Street, controlled by a single switch in a VIP balcony. The clean tones of the urgent, staccato ringing suggest a locomotive departing the station: *All aboard,* it announces. If the movement of money could make noise, the deals that immediately begin coursing through the trading posts would roar like a fleet of bullet trains fanning out across the land. On a raw dollar basis, half of the world's securities transactions pass through what amounts to the world's greatest auction house. It is the Grand Central Station of the global economy.

The bells are more than a quaint tradition. An institution concerned like no other with profit and loss naturally has figured out how to commercialize them. There is both an Opening Bell and a Closing Bell, which are proprietary features of the exchange. When the trading day begins at 9:30 A.M. and ends at 4:00 P.M., a guest of the NYSE gets to ring the bells. The appropriate corporate logos are slapped up on the balcony as the senior executive of the moment gets a hit of publicity, usually for something to do with his or her (Martha Stewart has done the honour) company and the NYSE—a new listing, a stock split, a merger. There are rare exceptions. When the exchange resumed trading on September 17, 2001, after the attack on the nearby World Trade Center six days earlier, American flags replaced the normal corporate logos on the balcony, which was crowded with public figures, led by Mayor Rudolph Giuliani. For more than two weeks thereafter, the balcony was host to nothing but patriotic bell ringings. It took until October 10, when David O'Reilly, chairman and CEO of Chevron, and Glen Tilton, vice-chairman of Texaco, appeared on the balcony to celebrate the merger of their firms, for the bells to return to their normal routine.

The prospect of money to be made or lost could not have a more bracing forewarning than the NYSE's Opening Bell. Unlike the nearby NASDAQ exchange or the Toronto Stock Exchange, which are virtual marketplaces where deals are marshalled by computers (the TSE[1] closed its trading floor in 1997), the NYSE remains at its heart an auction pit, where traders mill and match up buy and sell orders. The panic and euphoria of the pursuit of personal gain is still palpable here.

On November 30, 2000, John Roth appeared like Caesar on the balcony before the gladiators of the trading floor to ring the Opening Bell. The honour was granted to the president and CEO of Nortel Networks to celebrate the twenty-fifth anniversary of Nortel listing its common shares on the NYSE on Monday, November 10, 1975. The shares had already been listed on the Toronto Stock Exchange in 1973, and while the stock acquired an enormously important role in the fortunes of Canadian investors large and small, New York had come to be where the action was for Nortel. It was where most of the Nortel shares changed hands on any given day—usually twice as many on the NYSE as on the TSE. For Wall Street was where Nortel's reputations both as a global leader in communications technology and as a hot stock were most aggressively cultivated.

At times it had seemed that Nortel faced a hopeless battle against the myopia of American analysts and investors, who were inclined to think first of domestic companies like Cisco Systems and Lucent Technologies when it came to communications networking. Back on September 8, 1998, the widely read Internet investment site TheStreet.com ran a story on networking companies in a special series called "Ten Things to Watch in Tech." The article surveyed the activities of a broad spectrum of players in the business: Cisco, Lucent, Ciena, Ascend, Avici, Juniper Networks, Nexabit, Qwest, Uniphase. Not a word about Nortel, even though it had made equity investments in both Avici and Juniper. Completely overlooked was the fact that, in August 1998, Nortel had executed a $9.1 billion acquisition of San Francisco's Bay Networks Inc., vaulting Nortel, theretofore best known as a giant in the world of telephony, into the leading ranks of Internet Protocol (IP) data networking companies. With one multibillion-dollar acquisition, John Roth had turned Nortel into a major player in both voice and data. With a sales presence already established in more than 150 countries, Nortel stood to challenge the expansionary ambitions of telephony rival Lucent (a spinoff of AT&T in 1996) and data network rival Cisco (which had gone public on NASDAQ the same year).

Under Roth's leadership as president since February 1997 and as chief executive officer as well since October 1997, Nortel had dedicated itself to becoming the leading international networking systems provider, transcending telephone equipment and switches in a quest to conquer the Internet, e-commerce, and wireless applications, focusing in particular on the broadband potential of the new fibre-optic networks. As a business plan, Nortel's rapid growth and diversification scenario were both audacious and, many believed, necessary.

The old communications order had begun to wither in the early 1990s, as established revenue sectors like voice and data switches for phone companies and corporations began to lose momentum and new high-growth areas like wireless technology took priority. Nortel had been well positioned in the main networking sectors—traditional digital switching, fibre optics, and wireless. But then along came the Internet in earnest in the mid-nineties, with new opportunities for new companies and new dangers for old ones that didn't adapt, just as the telecom carriers themselves in the United States were confronting massive deregulation that opened up their business to new competitors and opportunities. The new opportunities for competition poured unprecedented amounts of capital into startup technology firms and fuelled a rapid development of increasingly sophisticated products. The old distinctions between voice and PC-based data traffic, between conversation and information, were evaporating the way Nortel had hoped, but not in the way that it had planned.

The phone companies were carrying voice and data on traditional copper wires using digital selective line (DSL) technology, but they and their new competitors were rapidly building fibre-optic networks to use light to move far more traffic at blistering speeds. Cable companies, no longer content to carry just television programs, were muscling in with the high-speed bandwidth of their coaxial cables, to compete with the phone companies for Internet business. And the data crowd was trying to make off with the conversation business. Using a new trick called Voice Over Internet Protocol (VOIP), they were developing a way to allow the human voice to be broken down into data packets for the Internet and transmitted through computer networks, obviating the need for an account with a traditional telephone carrier. So lucrative was the new age of information haulage that electrical utilities were even experimenting with ways of transmitting voice and data through their power lines and residential and business wiring.

John Roth had made a vivid corporate impression as the head of Nortel's high-growth mobile wireless division, which led to him being promoted to president of North American operations in 1995 and then president and CEO of the entire company in 1997. Wireless communication was being lashed into the converging networks, as a standard known as Wireless Applications Protocol (WAP) was used to move data through the ether to e-mail-enabled cell phones, to laptop computers, and to e-mail and Web-enabled personal digital assistants (PDAs) such as PalmPilots. To make this new communications regime truly practical and provide the bandwidth proper Web browsing required, the new third-generation (3G) digital wireless standard was about to take transmission speeds from 14 kilobits to 2 megabits per second, an increase of 140 times. So promising was the new service considered to be that in Europe in the summer of 2000, 3G radio licences auctioned by various governments generated $190 billion (U.S.) from carriers, which was more than the capitalization of all the stock markets in Europe—and France and Belgium hadn't even conducted their auctions yet.

With the rapid adoption of the Internet by businesses and the population at large, the new field of e-commerce was opening up. A host of new on-line retailers such as Amazon.com and E*Bay were being joined by traditional brick-and-mortar enterprises who were tempted to conduct some of their business via the Internet, or at least develop a more sophisticated customer service presence in which the consumer could interact with the company by telephone, e-mail, and the World Wide Web. To knit these different services together on one desk at a call centre and fully integrate them with the company's established systems in marketing, sales, and inventory management, businesses began to look to networking companies to provide a one-stop solution. Moreover, all the new traffic generated by e-commerce was projected to require massive amounts of fresh bandwidth.

With the Net and digital communication becoming the focal point of the new information age, it was vital for companies like Nortel to establish themselves at the forefront of the data networking world. Nortel was in danger of being marginalized by a company like Cisco, the leading IP networking firm whose routers—the devices that steer packets of IP data to their destinations—were at the heart of the Internet. Thanks to the convergence of the voice and data worlds, Cisco was now a prime competitor in the rush to build the new integrated global information infrastructure. Nortel also had to contend with Lucent Technologies, its main (and larger) rival in traditional voice switching systems, which had its own expansionist ambitions, and to a lesser degree Alcatel of France. Finally, the new technology firms popping up on the NASDAQ were driving forward development of next-generation products, some of which were competing directly with those of Nortel.

A company once known mainly as the unglamorous nuts and bolts subsidiary of Bell Canada, making telephone handsets and mainly voice-based switching products, Nortel had repositioned itself as the brainy tech monolith that would help the world wire (and wireless) itself together. Microsoft had asked consumers, "Where do you want to go today?" in the advertising for its Web browsing software, having already licensed the rights to the Rolling Stones' "Start Me Up" to promote the release of its Windows 95 operating system. Nortel tagged along by asking, "What do you want the Internet to be?" and licensing the rights to the Beatles' "Come Together," to drive home its fundamental message that the new Nortel was a Net-focused networking company.

Nortel had resolved to defeat its new rivals and rule the intertwined networking world, providing the hardware and software that made those networks function, that allowed individuals and corporations to communicate in whatever way they wanted—voice, data, graphics, and video—within corporations; along traditional copper telephone, coaxial cable, and new fibre-optic lines; across empty space by wireless transmission. It even participated in experiments in Britain to make voice and data move through electrical utility wires.

Yet Nortel had come perilously close to missing out on the convergence of conversation and information, by pushing its own vision of how content should be moved around on fibre-optic networks while ignoring the rise of the Internet and IP-based switching. By the time Roth took over Nortel, it was clear the company had seriously misread the Internet's momentum. Nortel's R&D labs and product development efforts had bet the farm on an alternate switching technology, called ATM, and the company had persisted with its commitment to ATM long past the point where the ascent of IP should have been obvious. Nortel under Roth had been forced to turn to acquisitions to gain a presence in the IP world, and so the Bay Networks purchase, and many more, transpired. Nortel scrambled to keep pace with the similar acquisition binges of Cisco and Lucent as they strove to build their own multifaceted arsenals of products and services. The major players had resolved that to quickly develop broad product portfolios and build market share, it was more practical to swallow new companies and their emerging technologies than to develop the technologies themselves.

Between January 1998 and October 2000, Nortel had bought eighteen companies in deals worth more than $30 billion (U.S.), and except for about $450 million-worth, almost all of them had been paid for with Nortel stock. The most recent, Alteon WebSystems, had been announced on October 19; its $8 billion price tag was met with an issue of 81.9 million shares. At the end of 1996, there were about 260 million Nortel common shares outstanding, but because Bell Canada Enterprises (BCE) owned 51.6 percent of them, only 126 million were actually available for trading. Through splits, BCE's divestment of all but 2 percent of the outstanding shares in May 2000, the exercise of employee stock options, and issues from the treasury to pay for acquisitions, the Nortel float available on the open market had grown to more than three billion by the end of 2000. More than 900 million of the additional shares were directly due to acquisitions. The stock options held by employees of acquired companies, which had been converted into Nortel options, could cause further dilution of as many as 159 million shares. Without even considering the additional options, the shares issued in the acquisitions had acquired a market capitalization of more than $110 billion at the height of the stock's value in the summer of 2000. That was about what the company had booked in revenues between 1994 and 2000—seven years of sales. It was as if Nortel's primary product in the Roth years was not networking systems, but common shares that retail and institutional investors couldn't buy enough of.

Roth was fashioning a pricey colossus with a presence in all the major market segments: broadband wireless; data networking; e-business solutions; integrated voice, video, and data; call centres; Web switching; management software for application service providers (an emerging industry in which computer programs and other software services are offered to client firms over the Internet on a dial-in basis); high-speed Internet service over traditional copper telephone lines (DSL); and, in particular, optical switching and components. The Bay Networks acquisition alone had made Nortel a leading player in IP data networking, as Bay (along with 3Com) had been Cisco's main rival in the sector. At the same time, Nortel divested or outsourced the responsibilities for manufacturing the less complex products, keeping the finicky optical components in-house, and in the process drove its percentage of capital expenditures to sales below that of both Lucent and Cisco. And by being first to market with high-speed optical equipment in late 1998, Nortel had left Lucent standing still in the race to supply a critical segment of the ferocious fibre-optic networks boom. For almost two years, Nortel had no competitors whatsoever for its high-speed, 10-gigabit per second (10-gbps) optical switch. By the fall of 2000, Nortel commanded over half the market share in global optical networking.

Nortel's stature on the NYSE had just been reaffirmed that October, as the NYSE had included it in its list of the top twenty non-American listed stocks. Three other Canadian firms joined Nortel, all from the natural resources industry: Barrick Gold Corporation, Alcan Aluminum, and Placer Dome. The prominent non-American stocks were a mix of the old economy and the new: oil and mining companies alongside high-technology firms, and the tech firms, in addition to including Nortel rival Alcatel of France and Finland's cell-phone success, Nokia, were dominated by telecommunications companies (or "telcos"), many of whom were Nortel customers. There was China Unicom, Germany's Deutsche Telekom, Spain's Telefónica, Telefonos de Mexico, Brazil's Telecomunicações de São Paulo, and the U.K.'s Vodafone Group. The NASDAQ may have been where the American Internet and communications hardware companies flourished, but it was on the NYSE that most of the big foreign network and associated hardware and software companies had come to play.

Back in Canada, Nortel was a huge success story dear to the hearts—or, more precisely, the wallets—of many citizens. Like its northern boreal cousins of Sweden, which was home to Ericsson, and Finland, which had Nokia, Canada had produced a telecommunications powerhouse in Nortel, and each dominated its country's stock exchanges. While it was true that trading was heaviest for Nortel in New York, in Canada the stock had turned into an 800-pound equity gorilla; at the height of its value in July 2000, more than 37 percent of the TSE 300 composite index's value was attributed solely to Nortel, and the majority of the index's growth in the now-jittery bull market had been driven by Nortel and its former parent, BCE. Nortel had attracted a disproportionate share of Canadian investment capital, becoming the stock of choice for pension funds, mutual funds, and RRSPs. A nation's retirement plans were riding on Roth's ability to drive Nortel's share price ever higher. As Nortel enthusiasm threatened to turn Canada into an investment monoculture, the giddy glee of easy money earned by the rapid ascent of the stock in particular and the index in general began to give way to concerns that the financial security of Canadians was at risk.

But for all the economic sway Nortel enjoyed in Canada, it wasn't hard to argue the case that the company deserved to be treated as an honorary American multinational. The company was much less "Canadian" than the National Hockey League. Most of its employees (nearly 100,000 by the end of 2000), its 32 manufacturing sites, and its 20 R&D labs, not to mention its 370 international offices, along with the bulk of its customers, competitors, and shareholders, were outside of Canada. Most of its revenues also came from outside Canada, and the home country's share of those revenues was rapidly diminishing. In 1991, Canada had contributed about one out of every five dollars Nortel generated in sales. By 2000, that proportion was down to one in twenty. Nortel had long issued its financial statements exclusively in U.S. dollars and, beginning with its 1999 annual report, began compiling its numbers in accordance with U.S. as well as Canadian Generally Accepted Accounting Principles (GAAP) to satisfy American investors. It contributed far more dollars to American political parties than to Canadian ones. And as Roth's public profile rose with Nortel's share price, Roth began throwing his weight around in the Canadian public policy arena, arguing for lower American-style income taxes to stave off the "brain drain" of the Canadian tech-savvy workforce heading south, and even darkly suggested that Nortel would have to move its head office stateside, where it already had a large corporate presence in Raleigh, North Carolina, and in the Dallas, Texas, suburb of Richardson.

While Nortel was routinely hailed at home as a great Canadian success story and lorded over the TSE, the fact remained that the enthusiasm of the American-dominated shareholder ranks had been critical to providing the market capitalization that allowed Roth to use Nortel shares as currency in acquiring a string of American companies. And it was this American technology that allowed Nortel to compete in the American market (which provided 60 percent of its revenues), primarily against American competitors. Getting the message out to American analysts and investors that Nortel was a major networking player had been the motivating force behind a retooled corporate communications strategy for Nortel in 2000—a strategy so successful that the U.S. industry publication *PRWeek* named Nortel Networks Global Communications, the company's in-house shill factory, its PR Corporate Team of the Year in February 2001.

The company flaks had been given the job of making American investors and analysts pay more attention to Nortel, in part to draw more investment capital to the shares and deliver prices that made acquisitions as inexpensive as possible on a per-share basis, in part to allow Nortel to stand on its own in the market's mind, and not have its shares blindly move up and down on the basis of what the NASDAQ, Cisco, or a sector index was doing. Nortel was a star at home, but to become that star it had to make it big on Wall Street. It had to get big enough to make the market pay attention, and then it had to dance its way into the hearts of the great American investment community, where the predominant thoughts of Canada concerned mining stocks and some ghastly mess called Bre-X.

When Roth took over as president in early 1997, Nortel was coming off a solid year in which revenues had increased 20 percent, reaching $12.85 billion. Thanks to the slew of acquisitions, revenue had since more than doubled; in 2000, Nortel marked its first $30 billion sales year. And the stock price, which had been so fundamental to the company's acquisition binge . . . Well, the stock price was a bit of an issue as Roth appeared on the NYSE balcony.

Back in November 1975, Nortel was Northern Electric Company Ltd., and Roth was a 32-year-old engineer, a western Canadian, and a McGill graduate who had already been with the company for six years. Northern Electric had finished its first day on the NYSE at $24³/₄.[2] Over the next twenty-five years, splits diluted the common shares by a factor of 48. The three billion shares of 2000, projected back in time, had a split-adjusted value of about fifty-one and a half cents on the day of the stock's NYSE trading debut. As Roth rang the bells on November 30, 2000, Nortel shares opened at $34^{13}/$_{16}$. In real, inflation-corrected 1975 dollars, the Nortel stock Roth ushered into the trading day was worth $10.85. But that was still about twenty times what a split-adjusted share commanded back in 1975. With an annual real rate of return of 80 percent before dividends, Northern Electric shares circa 1975 had proved to be not a bad buy.

Trouble was, the vast majority of Nortel investors hadn't loaded up back in 1975. Most shares had been accumulated since Roth took over, with hundreds of millions of shares having changed hands in the first few months of 2000 as the stock headed for a historic high that summer. Many people had just come aboard for the long haul and weren't expecting a precipitous drop. About one billion Nortel shares had been spun off by BCE to its shareholders in the May 2000 divestment, but the capital gains taxes on any subsequent sale were so punitive that few Canadian investors could see their way to unloading them when the shares were at their peak. There were also thousands of Nortel employees who had invested chunks of their pay in shares for their retirement funds under the company's long-term investment plans and were now watching the equity for their golden years dwindle away. Unlike the senior executive ranks, not all employees had been able to exercise stock options to acquire shares at a fraction of their market value and then sell them for a quick profit.

After BCE had spun off most of its interest in Nortel in a $70 billion (Canadian) divestment that also included a Nortel stock split, Nortel had soared to its delirious midsummer heights. On July 25, it reached an all-time high in New York of $89 before closing at $87; in Toronto on July 26, the all-time TSE high of $124.50 was set, with a close of $123.10. With Nortel having begun the year in Toronto at a pre-split $137.35, investors had almost doubled their money in about seven months. After the July high, Nortel closed above $80 on the NYSE as late as September 5, before settling back to earth in the $70 range, then slid into the sixties.

On September 28, analyst Paul Sagawa of Sanford C. Bernstein & Co. released a controversial report on the networking sector. Having surveyed the capital expenditure plans of 59 telecom carriers in North America and Europe, he had come to the unavoidable conclusion that their infrastructure spending was going to tank in 2001, which was very bad news for Nortel. Sagawa was, for the most part, dismissed as a crank. Then came October 24, when Nortel missed the consensus earnings forecast of analysts by a penny and revealed lower than expected sales in the critical optical equipment market. No longer satisfied by promises of ever-increasing revenues, the market hammered Nortel for its earnings performance, shearing away $17 in one trading day on the NYSE as the stock was massively dumped. Volumes overwhelmed the TSE and forced the exchange to cease trading in Nortel at noon on the twenty-fifth. At the beginning of November, Nortel was in the $45 (U.S.) range, but another month of being punted around by disillusioned or nervous investors had cleaved away an additional $10.

But even after the October 24 debacle, confidence remained high, not only among average investors who didn't know dense wave division multiplexing from synchronous optical networking, but also among the analysts, the media pundits, and the managers in charge of mutual fund and pension plan portfolios.

With the share price in descent, the many private investors and fund managers who remained committed to Nortel reassured one another with standard-issue platitudes about doing the right thing and holding for the long term, even diving into the market to scoop up "undervalued" Nortel shares. They continued to believe in Roth's vision, in the acumen that led to his being chosen the country's CEO of the year and (in its December 25 issue) as *Time* Canada's Newsmaker of the Year. And the analysts were still overwhelmingly backing the company.

The "buy" recommendations were proving remarkably resilient. In the looking-glass world of most Bay Street and Wall Street analysts, there seemed to be almost no market conditions any more that warranted a "sell" recommendation. When a stock seemed overvalued, no one was told to offload it, as the analysts had usually talked the thing into the stratosphere in the first place. And when a price started dropping, the bargain-hunting logic kicked in and investors were supposed to start accumulating before the stock recovered. After the third-quarter results disaster, Wall Street analysts could not bring themselves to recommend selling the stock. There were a few downgrades, but these were from "strong buy" to "buy," and from "buy" to "market outperform." Although downgrades were always a worrying sign, and in some cases they were the equivalent of a third-base coach's cryptic signal to the batter to walk, nobody was flat-out saying "sell," and some analysts were upgrading Nortel and urging investors to accumulate. The analysts and some members of the press, particularly in Canada, were rallying to Nortel's cause, as if sticking with Nortel was a motherhood issue.

The pension funds were steering toward their year-end loaded to the gunwales with Nortel stock. The oft-spouted industry wisdom about the need for diversification in the quest for long-term incremental growth had been cast aside by many fund managers eager to capture double-digit asset growth by betting heavily on the TSE's strongest performer. Some had been forced to take big risks on Nortel because their own asset management performance was being measured by the yardstick of the TSE 300.

The great unknown was how exposed the average Canadian was to a Nortel flameout, above and beyond the shares in their pension plans. Most pension plans in Canada were still "defined benefit," with the assets managed on behalf of the pension plan enrollees. But as the bull market gathered steam in the 1990s, direct-contribution plans, in which enrollees made their own decisions about how their pension funds should be invested, became increasingly popular, and even Nortel had introduced a direct-contribution option for its employees in 2000. There was no data on how much Nortel stock had been squirrelled away in the nation's direct-contribution accounts, never mind how much was lurking in the RRSPs of individual Canadians. But as the 1990s unfolded, Canadians, like their American neighbours, had come to embrace the securities markets as being literally secure, the source of their own long-term security. Canadians, through their RRSPs, and Americans, through their IRAs, were diverting income away from their tax departments and into shelters that were supposed to allow them to get to their golden years more quickly, with a small fortune awaiting them on their arrival. In a raging bull market, stocks were seen by taxpayers as the sure-fire way to rapidly grow their retirement funds. In Canada, regulations for RRSPs, mutual funds, and pension funds that limited foreign investment, along with less attractive returns on bonds and the dominance of Nortel in the hot TSE 300—which posted the largest growth of any broad market index in the world in 1999—unquestionably funnelled hundreds of millions in retirement savings into the common shares of John Roth's company. Many used mutual funds to do their investing for them, and fund managers (like their pension fund counterparts), in hoping to outperform the benchmark TSE 300, inevitably took especially large positions in Nortel, the index's undisputed star.

Roth himself had purchased 33,000 shares on the TSE at $60.45 on October 30 at a cost of nearly $2 million (Canadian). Roth lost about $100,000 on the purchase over the next month, but this was a small-change setback for him. On August 9, he exercised stock options to buy 450,000 shares at an average price of $8.57 (U.S.), then immediately sold them all that day at an average price of $81.02. His pre-tax gain on the day was $32.6 million. Come November, Roth still directly owned 493,000 shares and had about 65,500 shares in the company's long-term investment plan. There were also 171,600 shares held by Morningview Inc., a company Roth controlled. Another 12,800 shares were in his wife's name. In total, Roth claimed beneficial ownership of about 742,900 shares. Every dollar of downward movement in Nortel common on the NYSE was personally costing Roth more than a cool million Canadian. Since the stock's vertiginous midsummer ascent, the market capitalization of Roth's company had plunged almost 60 percent, a sickening $150 billion (U.S.). That was more than a decade of sales by McDonald's, and most of it had vanished since the first week of September.

While the company had faithfully been paying dividends (and a two-cent dividend was declared on the day Roth appeared on the NYSE balcony), it hadn't actually turned an annual after-tax profit since fiscal 1997, despite the impressive growth in raw revenues under Roth's direction. The stupendous ascent of the stock in 1999 and especially in 2000 had made a lot of people rich, including Roth and other company insiders. But now the stock was losing altitude at a rate of $12 (U.S.) a month, with every dollar evaporating $3 billion in shareholder equity. When Roth assumed the presidency, the stock had a split adjusted value on the TSE of about $12. Inflation meant purchasing these 1997 dollars would cost $13.31 in 2001. This was the John A. Roth Loss Threshold, the point at which, if the stock sank below it in 2001, he would make the company less valuable than he had found it. Unless the slide could be arrested, the threshold would be crossed some time in February 2001, as Roth marked his fourth anniversary in command.

During their first day on the NYSE, 864,000 Northern Electric shares had changed hands. Roth's bell ringing on November 30 propelled more than 21 million Nortel shares through the NYSE trading system over the course of the day, while another 11.5 million tagged along at the TSE. Roth's presence on the NYSE balcony may have brought good fortune, but an announcement that day by AT&T that it had chosen Nortel as a supplier for its new 3G wireless network worked more pragmatic magic. When the Closing Bell halted trading, Nortel was up to $37³/₄ in New York, a gain of almost $3 in just six and a half hours, while an improvement of more than $4 (Canadian) had been logged on the TSE. About $9 billion (U.S.) had just been restored to the company's capital value. Maybe this was the end of the slide, or the beginning of the rebound.

Roth held a press conference in conjunction with his appearance on the NYSE balcony, accompanied by Nortel's president of e-business, Bill Conner, and chief technology officer, Bill Hawe. Despite the shock of the third-quarter surprise, the downward trend in the stock price, and a gathering gloom concerning the future of the networking industry, Roth was defiantly upbeat, not wavering from the optimism he had demonstrated nine days earlier, when he appeared before an audience of analysts and investors in Boston. Nortel had provided revenue and earnings guidance for the remainder of 2000 and for 2001 when the third-quarter results were released, and in Boston Roth had confidently reaffirmed it. Revenues for the final quarter of 2000 would come in between $8.5 and $8.8 billion

(U.S.), with earnings per share of 26 cents. Optical revenues for the year 2000 would exceed $10 billion, and overall Nortel's revenues and earnings for the year would be up by more than 40 percent. Roth was promising less robust growth for 2001, of 30 to 35 percent, but that was still an impressive prediction, given that Nortel was only calling for the market for its products to grow "in excess of 20 percent." In other words, Nortel was predicting that it would continue to grow while increasing market share. The first quarter of 2001, traditionally the slow one for the networking companies, would bring revenues of between $8.1 and $8.3 billion with earnings per share of 16 cents. Rumours of Nortel losing optical systems market share to Ciena Corp. of Maryland, a NASDAQ favourite, were dismissed, as was a buzz that layoffs were coming. On the contrary, more hirings were promised. Roth's reassurances in Boston had given Nortel a nice bounce of $2³/₁₆ on the NYSE that day, but the gains drifted off as the month drew to a close, and it had taken Roth's NYSE balcony appearance and the AT&T announcement to restore it.

By the time Roth came to speak at the press conference in New York on November 30, he and his management team had achieved something even more wondrous than double-digit revenue growth, year after year. They had also managed to convince the general investing community, most analysts, and the press that Nortel actually made money. They had achieved this coup by dreaming up a supplementary earnings calculation called "earnings from operations," which had made its debut in early 1999. To calculate it, Nortel simply threw away all the acquisition costs related to the companies it had been acquiring since the Bay Networks deal in the summer of 1998. There was no basis in GAAP accounting for the figure, beyond Nortel's desire to have investors ignore the billions in amortization charges generated by these ongoing acquisitions. It was a sad comment on the state of the stock market that not only uninformed private investors, but market professionals—particularly analysts—went along with Nortel's "earnings from operations." They were the basis of Nortel's assertion that it would "earn" 26 cents per share in the fourth quarter of 2000 and 16 cents per share in the first quarter of 2001.

Nortel in truth was losing money and heading for even greater problems. It wasn't just the Sagawa forecast alone that cast the shadow. Nortel's own financial statements contained evidence of a company in trouble. By the time Nortel's 1999 annual report had been released in late March 2000, anyone with the patience and skill to read a balance sheet and a cash flow statement could have seen that a worrying trend was developing. Its revenues under GAAP were going in one direction, but its operating cash flow was heading in an altogether different one. And the puzzling way Nortel was booking long-term receivables was making that cash flow look even better than it was, compared to the way its main competitors booked similar receivables. Nortel's business plan had chained the company to a treadmill of perpetual revenue growth through acquisition. The moment revenues slowed down, or the company could no longer grow them through acquisitions, the impact on the value of those three billion outstanding shares—shares on which so many people had bet their long-term financial security—would be devastating.

At the New York press conference on November 30, Roth displayed an arrogant confidence. "We grew 40 percent this year," said Roth. "We'll grow 30 to 35 percent next year. A lot of people would like to have that problem. Nortel does not have a problem." And he took swipes at the main competition, qualifying Cisco as a "good router company" whose strategy for the optical market was "random." As for the threat posed by Lucent's Bell Labs division, Roth quipped that it would provide competition "as soon as Bell Labs Innovations finishes innovating."

Lucent was almost too easy to kick while it was down. Caught flat-footed by Nortel's masterful domination of the high-speed optical market, Lucent was stumbling from one self-inflicted disaster to another, missing revenue and earnings targets, taking huge write-offs for bad debts resulting from its vendor financing activities, being forced to restate revenues after reporting sales too aggressively. Five weeks earlier, Lucent had fired its chairman and chief executive officer, Richard McGinn.

John Roth could not have imagined for whom the bell was now tolling.

2

Irrational Exuberance

They all went in. Jim Eliot mortgaged the inside of the drug store and jammed it into Twin Tamagami. Pete Glover at the hardware store bought Nippewa stock at thirteen cents and sold it to his brother at seventeen and bought it back in less than a week at nineteen. They didn't care! They took a chance. Judge Pepperleigh put the rest of his wife's money into Temiskaming Common, and Lawyer Macartney got the fever, too, and put every cent his sister possessed into Tulip Preferred.

And even when young Fizzlechip shot himself in the back room of the Mariposa House, Mr. Gingham buried him in a casket with silver handles and it was felt that there was a Monte Carlo touch about the whole thing.

—Stephen Leacock, *Sunshine Sketches of a Little Town*

On December 5, 1996, Alan Greenspan, chairman of the U.S. Federal Reserve Board, delivered the Francis Boyer Lecture at the annual dinner of the American Enterprise Institute for Public Policy Research in Washington, D.C. The title of his 4,300-word chat, "The Challenge of Central Banking in a Democratic Society," was hardly a scintillating forewarning of the contribution Greenspan was about to make to the popular lexicon.

The fact that Greenspan's first real job had been playing saxophone in a jazz band, combined with his purported preference for writing his speeches in the bathtub, conjures the image of a naked seventy-year-old economist adrift in bubble bath, employing a mind familiar with the noodlings of Coltrane to craft reflections on the state of the greenback. The general public wasn't setting aside evening hours for contemplating the dry prose that emerged from the suds, nevertheless Greenspan was guaranteed a rapt audience, not only within the ranks of the adulatory neo-con American Enterprise Institute, but wherever people who worried about prosperity gathered to ponder his carefully measured phrases.

Since his initial appointment as chairman of the Fed by President Ronald Reagan nine years earlier, replacing the beleaguered Paul Volcker, Greenspan had become the most powerful non-elected figure in America. He had outlasted the administrations of both Reagan and George Bush, and when Bill Clinton's second term ended in January 2001, Greenspan would continue on with the approval of his fourth president, Bush the younger. His essential job was to manage the American money supply. While he was expected to help carry out the economic policy of the current White House administration and was required to report on his activities twice annually to the Senate Committee on Banking, Housing, and Urban Affairs, Greenspan nonetheless enjoyed a fair measure of operational independence.

In the post-recession nineties, Greenspan's reputation had become so exalted that he had transmogrified into a hybrid super-hero/monetary warlord. When the American economy hinted at trouble, the quavering populace could shine a giant "G" on the clouds of the night sky over Washington, and Greenspan would roar out of the Fed-Cave and rout the arch-villains who were ratcheting up the Consumer Price Index. At the same time, Greenspan was a feared oligarch whose power to direct the economy was imagined to be unrestrained and unpredictable, beyond the reach of the political norms of Capitol Hill arm-twisting. If you bet heavily on bonds and Greenspan decided one afternoon that interest rates had to go up, complaining to your congressman was about as productive as screaming into a pillow.

Greenspan had gained the trust of a succession of presidents in part because there wasn't much he hadn't experienced in the economy's arsenal of surprises. The son of a New York stockbroker, Greenspan was three when the crash of '29 ushered in the Great

Depression. Trained as an economist at New York University, his first brush with public life came when he served as Richard Nixon's director of policy research in the 1968 presidential campaign. President Gerald Ford appointed him to his Council of Economic Advisors, and as a card-carrying Republican there wasn't any call for his opinions when Jimmy Carter took to the White House after defeating Ford in 1976. Greenspan ran a successful economic consulting firm, Townsend-Greenspan & Co. Inc. (which he formed with bond trader William Townsend), and got to watch the economy perform all sorts of unlikely gyrations in the seventies and eighties—inflation, stagflation, an energy crisis, a bad recession in 1981–82, followed by a Wall Street bull market, juiced by the leveraged buyouts of a mergers and acquisition craze. In 1987, when Reagan nominated him to the chair of the Fed, he agreeably dissolved his consulting partnership and that October reported to Washington—just in time for the worst market crash since 1929, then another severe correction two Octobers later, then an especially tough recession in 1991–92. And then, back roared the bulls as Bush gave way to Clinton and Greenspan's second term at the Fed was confirmed under a Democrat administration.

Greenspan had a been-there, seen-that, done-that aura when he was embraced by the ideologically flexible Clintonites. Regardless of whether or not he was the brightest economist in the land, he was certainly the most influential—the village elder who had gone through pretty well everything you could think of when it came to money and its skittish place in the American public interest—and was empowered as no one else in his fractious profession to put theories into practice. His stature was unprecedented in the republic's history, greater than that of the office he occupied, as vaunted as it was. His vast experience was abetted by an admired penchant for understatement and sobriety, for not making any sudden moves that might spook the economy; in short, for unflashy moderation.

As chairman of the Federal Reserve Board, Greenspan was where the buck literally stopped in America. The board, as its name indicates, runs the Federal Reserve, the central bank of the United States, which was founded in 1913 (twenty years and one enormous market crash before Canada established a central bank of its own). The board's duties are multifold, but its primary mission is to conduct the country's monetary policy by (in the words of the Fed itself) "influencing the money and credit conditions in the economy in pursuit of full employment and stable prices." Those are ridiculous rules of engagement, because full employment (i.e., zero unemployment) and price stability (i.e., no inflation) are simultaneously (and probably individually) unachievable. The essence of Greenspan's job lay in the "pursuit" of those conditions. The best that could be expected of him and his board was that both employment and inflation remain low, somewhere deep down in the single digits, while the economy continued to grow.

Inflation, which monetarists had generally come to agree was the Great Satan of free markets, erodes the purchasing power of the dollar that Greenspan was sworn to defend. His only significant weapon was the Fed's influence on short-term interest rates, but the central bank's ability to monkey with the economy is surprisingly limited. Acting on the guidance of its Federal Open Market Committee (FOMC), the Fed routinely ventures into the open market to buy and sell government money instruments in an effort to regulate the size of the money supply, but its sole tool in directly influencing short-term rates is its own discount rate—the rate the Fed charges commercial banks that participate in the Federal Reserve system to draw additional reserves to maintain minimum levels of liquidity. The discount rate directly involves only a fraction of the American money supply, a fact the Fed itself readily acknowledges. Only federally chartered banks are required to participate in the reserve system, for example—state banks and other financial institutions are free to opt in or out—and even for those participating banks, discount borrowing from the Fed is considered a reserve management tool of last resort. The volume of funds affected by the discount rate is hardly sufficient to force across-the-board changes in commercial lending (and deposit) rates. The true influence of the bank rate is more one of moral suasion. As the Fed changes its discount rate, it expects the reserve system's participating banks to move in sympathy with their far more important "Fed rate," which is the rate at which they lend one another money to maintain minimum reserves. From the Fed rate, all other significant lending rates take their cue.

From the perspective of the discount rate, Greenspan hadn't been up to much lately. During the dark days of the previous recession, as a stimulative measure the weekly discount rate had dropped to 3.0 percent in August 1992—a rate not seen since 1963—and had remained there until beginning an upward trend in May 1994 as the economy finally rebounded. Since January 31, 1996, the rate had been parked at 5.0 percent. Almost a year of inactivity from the Fed on the discount rate, with inflation running around 3 percent, contributed considerably to Greenspan's steady-as-she-goes persona as he prepared to deliver his speech, but it also left market watchers with a pent-up curiosity as to what Greenspan's next move would be, and when it would come.

Greenspan's every public utterance was carefully parsed and analyzed by those interested in where the economy was headed, because no individual was invested (or at least credited) with more control over it than Greenspan. His words were of particular interest to professional and amateur gamblers—the people betting on the future values of securities, from stocks to bonds to derivatives, which is to say just about anyone who owned some. Any tip of the hand Greenspan might make as to the intentions of the Fed was a spur to action, to capitalize on the impending changes before they actually occurred. Basically, any indication that Greenspan was worried about inflation was a bad sign—if the economy was overheating as consumers and businesses became overly enamoured of credit and as cost-of-living increases placed upward pressure on wages. Fighting inflation meant a rise in interest rates. Higher rates meant lower values for existing bonds (because new bonds would have a higher yield). Consumer spending would be throttled as credit became dearer, and so would corporate spending as demand fell for products and the cost of borrowing increased. Higher bond rates also made them a more attractive investment relative to stocks, and as investment capital shifted away from stocks into bonds, stock prices would tend to fall.

Greenspan of course was more than aware of how the most casual comment from him could send market indices careening in new directions. And so his words were never off the cuff and never blunt. If he did have some concern about the state of the economy, he was careful to state it in a way that was, to put it mildly, less than emphatic. Greenspan watchers were guaranteed at least two major pronouncements a year, in addition to the minutes released from FOMC meetings, as he made his requisite testimony before the Senate Committee on Banking, Housing, and Urban Affairs. His next scheduled appearance was February 26, 1997, and so his speech to the American Enterprise Institute on December 5 was a bonus opportunity for a Greenspanian foreshadowing of some critical shift in Fed policy. It would also be the first major statement from Greenspan since the triumphant re-election of Bill Clinton in November.

The speech was no barn-burner. Greenspan walked his audience through the history of central banking in the United States, segueing into a discussion of the rise to prominence of inflation reduction as a primary goal of the FRB in the 1970s. He confessed to the difficulty of accurately measuring inflation when the economy had evolved so profoundly from its basis of industrial production in the first two-thirds of the century. "Pricing a pound of electrolytic copper presented few definitional problems," he noted. "The price of a ton of cold rolled steel sheet, or a linear yard of cotton broad woven fabrics, could be reasonably compared over a period of years. But as the century draws to a close, the simple notion of price has turned decidedly ambiguous. What is the price of a unit of software or a legal opinion? How does one evaluate the price change of a cataract operation over a ten-year period when the nature of the procedure and its impact on the patient changes so radically?"

Good questions, but not the kind that keep people other than central bankers and statisticians up at night. Greenspan, however, was stalking bigger game than statistical puzzles. You could almost imagine him moving the history of central banking ahead of him like a duck blind, creeping through the weeds closer to his quarry. Pontificating on the nature of inflation allowed him to make the point that "sustained low inflation implies less uncertainty about the future, and lower risk premiums imply higher prices of stocks and other earning assets." Suddenly Greenspan had his blind set up in lower Manhattan, with the front doors of both the New York Stock Exchange and NASDAQ in range of his buckshot. Without warning, Greenspan was allowing his thoughts to wander in broad daylight into the state of the stock market. This was something new. The audience members who had nodded off during the bits about the history of the Federal Reserve Board scarcely had the chance to jerk heads in his direction as he loaded both barrels for bull.

Greenspan made note of "the inverse relationship exhibited by price/earnings ratios and the rate of inflation in the past." He didn't have to fill in all the blanks for this audience, but what he was saying was that, in times of low inflation, investors are so confident of asset values not seriously eroding that they are willing to pay more for stocks than their underlying earnings would normally dictate. Dividend yields can drop because inflation is at bay. And as he spoke, dividend/price ratios on American markets were challenging historic lows.

"But how do we know when irrational exuberance has unduly escalated asset values, which then become subject to unexpected and prolonged contractions as they have in Japan over the past decade?" he asked. "And how do we factor that assessment into monetary policy? We as central bankers need not be concerned if a collapsing financial asset bubble does not threaten to impair the real economy, its production, jobs, and price stability. Indeed, the sharp stock market break of 1987 had few negative consequences for the economy. But we should not underestimate or become complacent about the complexity of the interactions of asset markets and the economy. Thus, evaluating shifts in balance sheets generally, and in asset prices particularly, must be an integral part of the development of monetary policy."

It was an amazing burst of forewarning from Greenspan. He had all but announced that the FRB, in its evolving battle to defend the American dollar, had followed the trail of inflation to the gates of Wall Street and discovered a fresh threat it had every intention of addressing. Greenspan had served notice that his board wasn't going to act primarily against inflation any more. Just because inflation, as defined by the rising prices of consumer goods and services, was under relatively tight wraps and the discount rate hadn't moved in almost a year, didn't mean the Fed had lost all incentive to change its lending rates. It was now prepared to take on the stock market when it felt overvaluation threatened the economy. Greenspan had in effect identified a dangerous new kind of inflation: of capital assets rather than goods and services. Stockbrokers were accustomed to the Fed's actions affecting equities, but customarily the Fed had treated the consequences as a sideshow. Now Greenspan was promising to act in direct response to equity values.

The question was, did Greenspan think the markets were over-valued *now*. The speech was classic Greenspan. The only market he directly mentioned was the Japanese one, which had been spiralling downward since the beginning of the decade. Rather than saying out-right that he thought the NASDAQ or NYSE was overvalued (and with time the myth would develop that Greenspan had specifically criticized the NASDAQ index in this speech), he simply posed through a series of questions the possibility of overvaluation and its consequences. But in the process, he had used some mightily provocative phrasing: *unduly escalated asset values, collapsing financial asset bubble,* and—most memorably—*irrational exuberance.*

In the midst of an otherwise mundane beltway black-tie speech, Greenspan contributed a fresh colloquialism to the popular lexicon. "Irrational exuberance" became a rallying cry for those who felt the nineties' bull was going to treat the economy like a china shop, ram-paging through asset values as the inevitable crash followed.

Interpreting Greenspan's statements is a bit like reading the wall posters in Maoist China, searching for the root meaning in the careful phrasing. Chairman Al had asked when we would know that irra-tional exuberance had "unduly escalated asset values." Thus, while he didn't say outright that asset values were already unduly escalated, he did imply that the markets might already be irrationally exuberant. In essence, the market mechanics of irrational investor behaviour were already in place: it was just a matter of determining when their deranged trading habits forced the markets into dangerous highs that invited the Fed to act. And the ultimate conclusion that Greenspan left to be drawn was that when the Fed decided the markets were in fact dangerously high, it *would* act.

Were they already dangerously high? An immediate dip in market values has been attributed by some (including the American Enterprise Institute) to Greenspan's comments, although this seems like more mythologizing of his omnipotent influence. The S&P 500 index had hit a daily high of 761.75 on December 3 and was already in a downward trend when Greenspan made his speech; it would finish the day at 720.98 on December 16 before beginning another climb. Nevertheless, Greenspan's remarks caused such a stir that he was compelled to return more explicitly to his opinions of stock market valuations on February 26, 1997, in his semiannual monetary policy report to the Senate Committee on Banking, Housing, and Urban Affairs.

Overall, Greenspan was upbeat about the U.S. economy, but unable to shake an unease about the markets. "History demonstrates that participants in financial markets are susceptible to waves of optimism, which can in turn foster a general process of asset-price inflation that can feed through into markets for goods and services," he remarked. "Excessive optimism sows the seeds of its own reversal in the form of imbalances that tend to grow over time. When unwarranted expectations ultimately are not realized, the unwinding of these financial excesses can act to amplify a downturn in economic activity, much as they can amplify the upswing. As you know, last December I put the question this way: 'How do we know when irrational exuberance has unduly escalated asset values, which then become subject to unexpected and prolonged contractions?'"

Congress waited for the other shoe to drop. "We have not been able, as yet, to provide a satisfying answer to this question," Greenspan advised, "but there are reasons in the current environment to keep this question on the table.

"Clearly, when people are exposed to long periods of relative economic tranquillity, they seem inevitably prone to complacency about the future. This is understandable. We have had fifteen years of economic expansion interrupted by only one recession—and that was six years ago. As the memory of such past events fades, it naturally seems ever less sensible to keep up one's guard against an adverse event in the future. Thus, it should come as no surprise that, after such a long period of balanced expansion, risk premiums for advancing funds to businesses in virtually all financial markets have declined to near-record lows.

"Is it possible that there is something fundamentally new about this current period that would warrant such complacency?" Greenspan posed. "Yes, it is possible. Markets may have become more efficient, competition is more global, and information technology has doubtless enhanced the stability of business operations. But, regrettably, history is strewn with visions of such 'new eras' that, in the end, have proven to be a mirage. In short, history counsels caution."

And so Greenspan resolved to remain cautious, but not pessimistic. He was watching the markets but not, for now, acting. He gave the economy a thumbs-up, and the stock markets breathed a collective sigh of relief. The discount rate, still stuck at 5 percent, would not change for almost eighteen months, when the Fed cut it by a quarter point on October 15, 1998, moving in the opposite direction of inflation fighting[3] as the Asian economic crisis kicked in. Whatever worries about irrationally exuberant markets Greenspan had expressed at the American Enterprise Institute and repeated before the Senate Committee appeared to be rapidly fading.

But if Greenspan had resisted taking action against the accelerating bull market, others were deeply concerned. Indeed, Greenspan's own concerns may have been due to the joint testimony before the Federal Reserve Board by two economics professors, John Campbell of Harvard and Robert Shiller of Yale on December 3—just two days before Greenspan made his American Enterprise Institute Speech.

John Campbell and Robert Shiller were like detectives trying to prevent, rather than solve, a crime, sifting through more than a century of market data in a quest to find a signature forecast of the next downturn. In the midst of such an explosion of wealth and contentment, these Ivy League profs were prophets of doomed profits. Their testimony before the Federal Reserve Board substantially informed their subsequent joint article, "Valuation Ratios and the Long-Run Stock Market Outlook," published in the Winter 1998 issue of *The Journal of Portfolio Management*.

Campbell and Shiller's research took aim at the central premise of how stock markets behave. The efficient markets theory, which had first been proposed by E.L. Smith in 1925 and had come to dominate academic opinion in the 1980s, presumes that at the heart of the market is a rational "everyman" investor making informed decisions on buying and selling, with prices determined substantially by a company's future earning power. Prices moved in a "random walk," rather than in predictable patterns, because the information on which rational trading decisions are made by nature appears randomly. Fundamentally, the market is anticipatory, with price movements forecasting profitability rather than reflecting present circumstances. Implicit in this theory is that the market is always right, that assets cannot be undervalued or overvalued because rational decisions by investors maintain a pricing equilibrium. But despite the hubris of efficiency and rationality, trading based entirely on anticipating what a company's future earnings might be is the very definition of speculation.

Campbell and Shiller were interested to know whether this speculation was at all measurably rational. After all, if the market was truly efficient, fluctuations should have some quantifiable, predictive logic. Despite the fact that the efficient markets theory demanded a random walk in prices, the changes could not be truly random. Trading based on anticipated future earnings should actually predict those increased earnings. If trading didn't, the price changes were wrong and the market was behaving irrationally. And one might conclude that when prices rose far higher than dividend growth warranted, the market was irrational in a noticeably exuberant way.

They decided to test the theory by assessing its central tenet: that when share values rose, dividends should logically follow—and conversely, when share values dropped, dividends should then come down as well. According to the efficient markets theory, as the market anticipates higher earnings, the price of a stock is bid up, momentarily decreasing the relative value of the dividend, as measured by the dividend/price ratio (D/P). Prescient investors begin bidding up the share price because they are confident increased earnings are going to boost the dividend.

Proving (or disproving) this theory would seem straightforward.

Rather than wade through decades of price and earnings values for individual stocks, you just had to pick consistent representatives of the overall market's historic values and shareholder earnings, and see how they played out. After all, if the efficient markets theory was to hold up, the entire market had to behave itself. A researcher then need only look for points in the market's history when the value of dividends relative to price moved beyond the mean, signifying a widely held anticipation of a dividend change for the market in general, and then see what happened next. If the efficient markets theory was correct, when the D/P was low, prices would remain high and dividends would rise as the market had predicted and move the D/P back to the historic mean. But if the market's speculation was unfounded, then prices would collapse to return D/P back to the mean.

Campbell and Shiller selected the Standard & Poor's 500 index for the New York Stock Exchange to represent the trading price, developing a data set that extended the modern S&P 500 index back to 1872. The S&P 500 was used rather than the Dow Jones Industrial Average (DJIA) because it is a float-weighted index: its value is based on the total market value of actual shares traded in the tracked stocks, essentially by multiplying their outstanding shares by their share price (although the precise methodology is more complicated). A weighted index thus better reflects market activity than the DJIA, which is a non-weighted assembly of key industrial stocks. To arrive at a D/P figure, the average dividend paid for the previous year by the index's stocks (the trailing dividend) was divided by the S&P 500 value for January of each year.

Campbell and Shiller arrived at a historic D/P mean of 4.73 percent, and found that the ratio had crossed the mean twenty-nine times since 1872. The D/P for the index for each January was then plotted against both the real growth rate of dividends and the real growth rate of the S&P 500 in an effort to assess how accurately stock price changes forecast the wandering of the D/P above and below the mean.

Campbell and Shiller's results were formidably distressing from the perspective of the rational market. They observed that "only one-quarter of 1% of the variation of dividend growth is explained by the initial dividend/price ratio." In other words, only a microscopic proportion of the movement in dividend growth, whether up or down, was actually forecast, as the efficient markets theory held, by movements in the value of the S&P 500. Further analysis showed that on a short-term (one-year) measure, the dividend/price ratio could explain about 15 percent of dividend growth, but thereafter failed miserably, falling below 1 percent. Thus, a higher than normal D/P for the S&P 500 almost never meant that dividends were about to fall, and a lower than normal D/P almost never meant that dividends were about to rise.

In examining the historic trends of the world's largest equities market, Campbell and Shiller had proved mathematically that when market prices in general grow to the point that the D/P drops below the historic mean, the market is not rationally forecasting a rise in dividends. In fact, it's the price—the denominator—that drops, to return the ratio to the historic norm. Improving corporate earnings might ignite a bull market, as it did in the 1990s, but if a bull market was carrying forward with noticeably low dividend yields, prices had got ahead of themselves and the market was wrong. The shareholder's claim on earnings was not going to increase at the predicted rate. Prices were going to have to retreat.

And there was more bad news. Their analysis of movement in prices relative to D/P ended in 1983, because that year the D/P dipped below the historic mean of 4.73 percent and hadn't returned since. Over time, they found that the D/P generally moved between 3 percent and 7 percent, sometimes going as high as 10 percent. But since 1983, D/P had become unusually suppressed, and in January 1997, the last data point in their 1998 article, it was down to 1.9 percent. They had also examined trends in the relationship between share price and corporate earnings, and noted that the price/earnings ratio (P/E) of 28 for the market in January 1997 was seriously out of whack with the historic mean of 15.3. In fact, the only time the ratio had been so high before in their data was in January 1929, ten months before the market nose-dived into its great crash.

Examining the extreme values for D/P and P/E, they concluded that "these ratios are extraordinarily bearish for the U.S. stock market." Their scatter plots suggested that the real value of the market would be 40 percent lower in ten years, and that the cumulative, compounded real return on stocks (that is, including reinvested dividends and factoring in inflation) would fall by 15 percent.

Their analysis didn't end with the S&P 500. They also produced scatter plots for D/P and price and earnings growth in foreign markets, and while the data sets for these markets extended back to only about 1970, they did find a curious parallel to the S&P's behaviour in English-speaking countries. Irrational exuberance appeared to be an Anglo-Saxon disease. They found that France, Germany, and Italy actually behaved consistently with the efficient markets theory. But Australia, Canada, and the United Kingdom, as well as the Netherlands, Spain, Sweden, and Switzerland, showed a similar pattern to the U.S. data. In these markets, low D/P values just weren't accurately forecasting subsequent dividend growth.

It was a heroic effort to disprove the efficient markets theory with the heavy artillery of historic statistics. But Campbell and Shiller's results were actually old news that had never got through to modern investors. Sir John Bowring would recollect in his memoirs how the esteemed nineteenth-century British economist and highly successful stock market investor David Ricardo essentially profited from the fact that markets overestimated growth of company profits on the way up, and overestimated the decline of those profits on the way down. He wrote how Ricardo "made money by observing that people in general exaggerated the importance of events. If, therefore, dealing as he dealt in stocks, there was reason for a small advance, he bought, because he was certain the unreasonable advance would enable him to realise; so when stocks were falling, he sold in the conviction that alarm and panic would produce a decline not warranted by circumstances." It was one of Ricardo's golden rules of investing and proved to be exactly true of the Roaring Twenties and the crash that followed. Ricardo understood precisely the essential psychological, rather than rational, nature of stock markets. There was no reason to doubt that his general wisdom still applied as another millennium approached.

Campbell and Shiller's conclusions would not be published until about two years after their testimony before the Federal Reserve Board, but the substance of their conclusions was already on the table before Greenspan. It should have been headline-making in investment communities, as Campbell and Shiller had shown convincingly that the market, historically, was inefficiently speculative. Rather than acting as an accurate forecast of earnings growth, markets that showed an unusually low D/P and an unusually high P/E such as the NYSE and the TSE were actually on course for a major correction. And for the past thirteen years, according to Campbell and Shiller's data, historic means indicated these markets had been overestimating shareholder returns. Rather than being efficient and rational, these stock markets were inefficient and nuts.

Further proof came in the fact that no perceptible attention was paid to Campbell and Shiller's dire testimony in December 1996. The major markets the academics judged to be prone to irrational exuberance just kept on climbing, racking up ever more improbable levels of D/P and P/E in the process. When Campbell and Shiller testified before Greenspan and the Federal Reserve Board, the S&P ended the day at 748.28. When their article was published about two years later, the index was above 1,100. By the summer of 2000, the index had doubled its level at the time of the two professors' pessimistic testimony before Greenspan and his board. On Thursday, November 28, 1996, right before Campbell and Shiller testified before the FRB, the TSE 300 index broke through the magical 6,000 barrier, closing at 6,018.70. In just one month, it had climbed about 400 points; one year earlier, the index had been at 4,674. In March 1998, the index breached the 7,500 mark. Campbell and Shiller appeared doomed to share the fate of Priam's daughter Cassandra, whose prophecies Apollo proclaimed would be true, but never believed.

Two months after Campbell and Shiller demolished the efficient markets theory for the Federal Reserve Board and warned of serious overvaluation in the unfolding bull market, and just days before Alan Greenspan was moved to elaborate on "irrational exuberance" for the Senate Committee on Banking, Housing, and Urban Affairs, John

Roth assumed the presidency of Nortel. The company's stock price was about to grow more than ninefold over the next enormously exuberant three and a half years.

3

Phones and Switches

"We don't care.
"We don't have to.
(snort)
"We're the phone company."
— signature motto of Ernestine, the telephone operator,
created by comedian Lily Tomlin

In reading Nortel's history on its Web site—the timelines of achievements and senior executives—you can't help but gather the impression that the company has been a perpetual renovation project for the better part of half a century. One executive after another is congratulated for having turned the company around or revamped its corporate culture. This is partly symptomatic of the widespread PR practice of freely dispensing kudos to each successive senior executive without paying any attention to the collective narrative—everyone is a turnaround specialist, yet no one is the cause of the problems for the turnaround specialist who succeeds him. Still, with Nortel, there never seems to be a true golden age: repeatedly, there are shakeups of some kind to be initiated, an ossification of ambition to be surmounted. In the 1990s alone, the ambitious (and largely forgotten) restructuring under Jean Monty leads to the celebrated "hard right turn" under John Roth beginning in 1997—only to segue into another (ongoing) rebuilding era under his unlikely successor of 2001, former finance man Frank Dunn. The story resembles the Escher drawing of a perpetually ascending staircase, each flight leading to the next in a series of hard right turns until the staircase has turned back upon itself, rejoining the base of the first flight. At every landing, Escher's manipulation of perspective leaves you unsure of whether you are at the top—or at the bottom.

Perhaps this is evidence of some essential corporate pathology: an enterprise too large and too bureaucratic to ever be sufficiently nimble to succeed in a fast-moving industry without regular interventions from the senior-most management ranks—and even then, the work of the outgoing top gun must be built upon, overcome, rehashed, or rescued. That may well be true, but it is also true that Nortel has striven to grow and prosper in an industry that has experienced successive shocks in ownership, government regulation, and technology. The U.S. Telecom Act of 1996 set the pace of those shocks at fast forward. No senior executive of Nortel has ever faced the diversity of challenges (or the rapidity with which they appeared) as John Roth did, and at the same time, no executive had a more capable centre snapping him the ball, as Monty did when he turned the company over to Roth in 1997.

Nortel is one of Canada's oldest industrial and engineering companies. It celebrated its centennial in 1995, but its true heritage as an innovative, high-tech communications firm with a global reputation stretches back perhaps only thirty years. To understand the company's recent, rapid ascent (and all that corporate re-engineering) and even more rapid comeuppance, you have to first appreciate its heritage.

The company has been around almost as long as the telephone. Alexander Graham Bell invented the device for transmitting the human voice across electrical wires in his parents' house in Brantford, Ontario, in 1874, and patented it two years later in the United States. When he secured the Canadian patent in 1877, he assigned 75 percent of it to his father, Melville. The elder Bell shortly sold his patent right to the National Bell Telephone Company of Boston, the original American telephone company co-founded by his inventor son. Thus, when the Bell Telephone Company of Canada was established in Montreal in 1880 by a former New England sea captain named Charles Fleetford Sise, the Canadian venture was set up as a licensee of the proprietary technology of American Bell and thereafter operated as an honorary member of the American Bell family. AT&T, which became the parent company of the American Bell system in 1899, even acquired equity in Bell Canada (as the company became known in 1968), still holding a 2 percent interest in 1972.

In 1882, Bell Canada (the name we will use for the Canadian Bell hereafter) moved its ad hoc mechanical department into its own workspace in Montreal. The mechanical department was incorporated as the Northern Electric and Manufacturing Company Ltd. in 1895, and at this point Nortel's history officially begins. In 1914, the company was merged with another Bell Canada property, Imperial Wire and Cable, to create the Northern Electric Company Ltd., known to telecom history buffs as NECO.

Northern Electric provided the hardware required to make the Bell Canada system work, but its manufacturing capabilities allowed it to churn out all manner of electrical devices, such as radios, phonographs, motion picture projection equipment, and, in the early 1950s, televisions. No technology transfer was too arcane, it seemed. Being experts in making bells for telephones, for example, Northern Electric also made sleigh bells at one point. It even founded an AM radio station, CHYC, in Sudbury, Ontario, in 1923.[4]

Northern Electric might have carried on in perpetuity, turning out products that required wires, tubes, and bells, were it not for a major hard right turn in 1956, when the Western Electric Company shed its 40 percent equity interest. The event looms within Nortel's official on-line history resources as a monumental, but entirely unexplained, event. Nortel used to provide an on-line historic overview, but for some reason has ditched it, leaving Western Electric as a ghostly presence.[5]

Western Electric is mentioned not at all in its achievements timeline, but is referred to several times, shorn of all context or explanation, in the short bios of top executives. And so, Dr. A. Brewer Hunt, we are told, "headed Northern's Research and Development division in the 1950s, during the difficult transition away from Western Electric's support." Similarly, H. Holley Keefler was promoted from within Bell Canada in the 1960s, having been "selected to smooth

relations between Bell Canada and Northern Electric. To help
Northern pull through a tough adjustment period during which it
learned to get on without the support of Western Electric, Keefler
restructured the company's executive hierarchy. . ."

The fact was, Nortel had operated for decades as a northern
branch plant of the American telecommunications manufacturing
giant, the Western Electric Company, relying on Western Electric's
technical expertise and product designs for its own wares. "As a col-
lector of nostalgic mid-20th Century telephones, I know that NECO
equipment was 'virtually identical' to that of WECO," wrote Mark
Cuccia in an informative 1996 contribution to *Telecom Digest,*
archived by MIT's Lab for Computer Science.[6]

"Both used the same model numbers for telephones and
parts. Even NECO's old three-slot payphones looked just like
WECO's. In Canada, NECO phones had the stamp 'Northern
Electric–Made in Canada,' written in the same 'lightning-bolt'
script used by Western Electric."

Western Electric was the manufacturing subsidiary of AT&T,
owner of the American Bell system. Its co-founder, Elisha Gray, had
been beaten to the U.S. patent for the telephone by Alexander
Graham Bell by mere hours in 1876, and in 1882 Western Electric
became part of the growing American Bell empire, which, as previ-
ously noted, came under the ultimate ownership of AT&T in 1899.
In 1914, Western Electric had a manufacturing presence in
Antwerp, London, Berlin, Milan, Paris, Vienna, St. Petersburg,
Budapest, Tokyo, Buenos Aires, Sydney—and Montreal, where
Western Electric took a 44 percent interest in the new Northern
Electric when Bell Canada merged Northern Electric and Imperial
Wire and Cable that year.

In 1925, AT&T decided to concentrate on the U.S. market and
sold what was known as the International Western Electric Co. to a
new outfit, International Telephone and Telegraph (ITT), but
retained its interest in Northern Electric. Canada thus was the only
foreign manufacturing market in which AT&T kept a hand,
although the great white north had never been that foreign to the
American Bell system. In 1925, when AT&T got rid of its

International Western Electric holdings, save Northern Electric, it also spun off the R&D efforts of Western Electric into a new entity called Bell Telephone Laboratories, known informally as Bell Labs; in 1934, the R&D department of AT&T was folded into Bell Labs as well. Through licensing agreements and the cozy relations of the ownership umbrella, Northern Electric enjoyed access to the product designs and expertise of both Western Electric and Bell Labs.

Northern Electric was also a licensee of the switching technology of Western Electric's main equipment rival, the Automatic Electric Co., whose automatic Strowger switch was the basis of most telephone exchange equipment until digital technology came along in the 1960s. The original automatic switch had been invented in 1888 by a Kansas City undertaker named Almon Brown Strowger. Tradition has it he was motivated to create the industry's fundamental switching technique by his conviction that an operator at the local exchange was either mistakenly or deliberately routing calls to one of his competitors. The clincher may have come when a close friend of his died, yet his body somehow ended up with a rival mortician. If the operator was on the take, Strowger needed to remove her from the process of placing a telephone call. His step-by-step (SXS) system, using a rotary dialler, allowed a local call to be made automatically, without having to be patched through by an operator. It was a huge hit with independent telephone companies, but American Bell wanted nothing to do with a technology whose patent it didn't own, and was even known to tear out Strowger switches when it purchased independents that were lucky enough to have them. Only in 1919 did Bell relent and begin using Strowger switches itself.

By the mid-1920s, 80 percent of the world's automatic telephone equipment was being produced under licence from Automatic Electric, which had been formed in 1901 and had the right to exploit the Strowger technology. That technology came very early to Canada, with Strowger switches being installed in Regina, Edmonton, and Saskatoon soon after Automatic Electric's incorporation.

The success of the Strowger technology is a reminder that the phone business in North America was not an absolute monopoly controlled by AT&T and its licensees. Although AT&T owned the

American long-distance business (service from New York to Chicago by 1892, finally reaching San Francisco in 1915), there were many independent local and regional phone companies. In fact, in 1903, the number of telephones in service with the independents outnumbered those in the Bell system by about 2 million to less than 1.3 million. North of the border, Bell Canada operated mainly in Ontario, the Maritimes, and western Quebec. Lower British Columbia had its own phone company, and after World War I, Bell operations in Alberta, Saskatchewan, and Manitoba were bought up and turned into publicly owned utilities, which became, respectively, AGT (now Telus), Sasktel, and MTS.

Thanks to the Strowger technology and the generally better service it afforded, in the early 1900s the independents were outperforming the Bells. But the very independence of the many companies caused service problems, as customers with one company couldn't call someone serviced by a different one. It took the robber-baron instincts of the ruthless financier J.P. Morgan to turn Bell into the dominant (albeit not the sole) local phone service. Under Morgan's direction, AT&T swallowed every independent it could to create the AT&T monolith, which by 1911 had settled into the collection of regional holding companies that endured until 1984.

The antagonism between the AT&T empire and the independents provided sales opportunities for Northern Electric. Because AT&T refused to sell Western Electric equipment to the non-Bells, Northern Electric was able to rack up sales of telephone equipment to many North American independents by providing de facto access to Western Electric products whose technology it licensed.

In the mid-1950s, the phone business experienced two major changes. The first, in 1955, saw Automatic Electric acquired by General Telephone, which changed its name to General Telephone and Electric (GTE) in 1959. In 1919, Automatic Electric had been acquired by American financier Theodore Gary, who also owned the British Columbia Telephone Company and the Eugene F. Phillips Electrical Works in Canada. In acquiring Automatic Electric, General Telephone also got its hands on the phone service in lower British Columbia (now BC Tel), and, through another purchase the same year, Quebec-Telephone, the phone service in lower and eastern Quebec—both of which GTE still owns.

But the biggest change came in 1956, when AT&T signed a consent decree with the U.S. Department of Justice to settle an antitrust suit that had been festering since 1949—a suit that ended up serving as a preamble to the 1974 justice department suit that led to the breakup of AT&T in 1984. Because the 1956 decree limited Western Electric to manufacturing only phone equipment, and phone equipment only for the Bell system and the U.S. government, it could not hold on to its interest in Northern Electric, and so it sold its then 40 percent stake to Bell Canada. Suddenly, the umbilical cord was cut, and while the licensing agreements with Western Electric and Bell Labs did not end overnight, Northern Electric now was essentially on its own.

It was a profound break, because in addition to the engineering expertise and product designs of Western Electric, Northern Electric had enjoyed a close proximity to the blazing brains of Bell Labs, which had established itself as one of the premium research facilities in the world. In addition to coming up with new communications gizmos, Bell Labs pursued avenues of pure research, in pursuit of scientific wisdom that could be exploited commercially. The quest to build a better phone system literally took Bell Labs to the birth of the universe, and most points beyond.

The first of eleven Nobel prizes to have been awarded to Bell Labs staffers was conferred upon Clinton J. Davisson in 1937 (in physics) for demonstrating the wave nature of matter, which was a feat a little more challenging than making sleigh bells. The Labs' innovations in the 1930s included stereophonic sound (as well as LP and stereo records), the first electrical digital computer (using switches and electromechanical relays borrowed from telephone technology), and the science of radio astronomy.

In the 1940s came a slew of achievements. Most famously, three Bell Labs scientists won the Nobel in 1947 for inventing the transit resistor (better known as the transistor), but the Labs also produced the first demonstration of speech patterns with a spectrograph, created the closed space triode (a microwave tube that made possible transcontinental television broadcasting), came up with the concept of information theory, and invented pulse code modulation, which allowed the transmission of numerous telephone conversations over the same wire.

The 1950s saw Bell Labs dive into superconductor research, the physics of imperfect crystals and their role in electric conduction in magnetic materials (which led to a Nobel prize in 1977), and other technological wonders, finding time to come up with the principle of the laser in 1958. In 1962, Bell Labs developed Telstar, the world's first orbiting international communications satellite. In 1964, researchers Arno Penzias and Robert Wilson were using a horn antenna (a Bell Labs invention in 1942) to investigate atmospheric noise when they stumbled upon the background radiation of the universe, which provided powerful evidence for the Big Bang—an achievement that netted them a Nobel prize in physics in 1978. (In 1977, another Bell Labs scientist, Philip Anderson, had shared the physics Nobel for developing an improved understanding of the electronic structure of glass and magnetic materials.)

Without Western Electric and the science champs over at Bell Labs, Northern Electric was little more than a producer of telephone equipment and assorted wired appliances mainly for the Canadian market, with no innovation of its own to speak of, and no reliable source of new technology. Northern Electric was issued 788 patents in Canada between 1920 and 1956 (American Electric secured 393 Canadian patents during the same period), but these were essentially technology transfers from Western Electric. As Dr. A. Brewer Hunt, who ran the Northern Electric R&D labs in the 1950s conceded (in a quote forthrightly reproduced by Nortel on its Web site), the break from Western Electric "was a tough situation for us to consider at the time and we moved slowly. It had been so seductively easy for us to pick up the phone and ask someone in Western Electric what to do about this or that, so that we didn't have to think for ourselves. Having lost that crutch, it now threw the responsibility back on our own scientific people. We had to find the answers ourselves." The answers were a long time coming, and "finding the answers ourselves" has been the single most important factor in Nortel's successes and travails since the break with the mother company in 1956.

Northern Electric's problems, it could be argued, were under-standable in the North American telecommunications business, where the carriers enjoyed virtual (or in most cases, actual) monop-olies and owned the main R&D and manufacturing interests. There wouldn't necessarily be a whole lot of pressure to move the technology forward. Customers could hardly turn elsewhere for their local or long-distance services, and if the phone company wasn't under competitive pressure to ramp up the development and deployment of new technologies, the R&D and manufacturing subsidiaries weren't going to be feeling any pressure from above to come up with them. At the same time, the R&D and manufactur-ing subsidiaries weren't going to be taking the initiative to press into new frontiers if the parent telcos felt no obligation to spend the money on the resulting technologies.

But it would be wrong to suggest that the telecom world was moving at a snail's pace because of monopolies, and by extension that Northern Electric was doing no better, innovation-wise, than one could have expected. A lot was going on with phones and phone lines in the 1960s. There was the first transcontinental picture phone call in 1962, and touch-tone dialling in 1964. There were the first microwave relays for long-distance transcontinental calling, transatlantic telephone cables (before which, radiotelephone placed the overseas calls), and the first steps toward a digital, rather than analog, network.

Multiplexing—the ability to send more than one phone call down a single wire—had already been made possible in the 1940s by the invention of pulse code modulation, but this was based on the use of different analog channels operating at distinct frequencies. In 1963, Bell Labs came up with T1, a new multiplexing scheme that turned calls into binary (i.e., digital) information for transmission. Adopted for use in long-distance transmissions and the movement of calls between phone company central offices, T1 (which is still in use today) ushered in the digital communications age.

In 1963, the 101 ESS, an electronic office switch that was partly digital, came out of Bell Labs' Essex Project. It was the forerunner of the modern private branch exchange, or PBX, which provides switching services on a customer site, generally within one building. In 1965, the first phone company electronic central office switch, the 1ESS, was built by Western Electric. While it wasn't truly digital, the 1ESS did have memory capabilities that would allow it to offer features such as call forwarding and speed dialling. Essex Project had been on the job of coming up with digital switching for a decade, burning through $500 million (U.S.). This massive, expensive push for a new telecommunications system, based on digital switches, satellites, and microwave relays, was unfolding in the United States right after AT&T cut Northern Electric loose— stranding it just as the really exciting stuff was brewing in the labs.

Northern Electric was not left entirely in the technological dust. R&D facilities were established in Belleville in 1957; Northern Electric Research and Development Laboratories followed in 1959, with a new facility opened in Ottawa in 1961. It built the world's longest microwave system, the 3,800-mile-long Trans Canada Skyway, which went into service in 1958. It also produced the Precision Satellite Tracking Antenna in 1966. Forty-two engineers began working at the company's new R&D lab in Ottawa in 1961, and by 1966 the facility had 800 employees. However, between 1957 and 1965, Northern Electric averaged less than twenty patents a year in Canada, and in 1964, only 1 percent of Northern products were of its own design, a proportion that rose to just 6 percent in 1969. It was a humbling time. Down at Bell Labs, the science champs were building satellites, unlocking the secrets of the universe, and lining their rec room shelves with the big Swedish award.

Meanwhile, the American telephone monolith, as represented most vividly by AT&T and its various regional and local Bell operating companies, doomed itself to an eventual breakup by building an impressive reputation for impassive arrogance to the needs of its captive customers. In 1969, just as the FCC handed down a landmark ruling that non-AT&T equipment could be attached to the Bell network by consumers and businesses, Microwave Communications International (MCI) began carrying business calls over their private service between St. Louis and Chicago. At the time, MCI's customers had to conduct their calls entirely within the MCI network, but there was a showdown looming over MCI's attempts to connect to the Bell system and make its alternative long-distance service widely accessible.

It so happened that, as the FCC ruled on non-Bell equipment connectivity and MCI's alternative long-distance service made its debut, the comedian Lily Tomlin joined the cast of the television show *Laugh-In*. Soon thereafter, she unveiled one of her most enduring characters: the snorting, sexually repressed, misanthropic telephone operator, Ernestine. The character could have been born only when the monopoly was at its alienating nadir. Ernestine didn't work for AT&T or any particular subsidiary (and service, it must be said, may have been worse in the GTE phone empire): she worked for "the Phone Company," and the gleeful maltreatment she doled out was appreciated by "phone company" customers just about anywhere in the world. Among her more memorable bon mots were "$12.50 a month doesn't buy perfection," and "Look it up yourself, I've got better things to do."

An appearance on *Saturday Night Live* distilled Ernestine's personal mantra into one devastating salvo:

> (*snort*) Here at the Phone Company we handle eighty-four billion calls a year. Serving everyone from presidents and kings to scum of the earth. (*snort*) We realize that every so often you can't get an operator, for no apparent reason your phone goes out of order [*plucks plug out of switchboard*], or perhaps you get charged for a call you didn't make. We don't care. Watch this—[*bangs on a switch panel like a cheap piano*] just lost Peoria. (*snort*) You see, this phone system consists of a multibillion-dollar matrix of space-age technology that is so sophisticated, even we can't handle it. But that's your problem, isn't it? Next time you complain about your phone service, why don't you try using two Dixie cups with a string. We don't care. We don't have to. (*snort*) We're the Phone Company.[7]

Ernestine was a deadly accurate portrait of a corporate minion with stupefying abilities to inflict pain on thousands of unsuspecting consumers. But she was also a perplexing anachronism, with her 1940s hairstyle and clothing and jack-equipped switchboard. Down at Bell Labs, the digital revolution was marching forward. The science champs had come up with the Unix operating system for minicomputers in 1969 and the "C" programming language in 1973. And while Bell Labs was off innovating in all directions and winning more Nobel prizes, Northern Electric was setting its eye on the prize of producing a fully digital product line. The number of Canadian patents Northern Electric was awarded jumped from nineteen in 1965 to forty-two in 1966, and reached a high of fifty-five in 1968.

Northern's efforts to produce its own line of switches had begun in 1963 and grew out of its experiences adapting AT&T's 1ESS for the Canadian market. The 1ESS was built for major urban markets; Northern was determined to develop a smaller switch that could help it break into the more rural U.S. markets not controlled by AT&T. In 1969, Northern Electric brought out the prototype of its first notable product of the emerging digital age, a switch called the SP-1. It was a "stored program controlled switching system," which meant it wasn't a truly digital switch—a dedicated control computer (which Nortel had to design and program) oversaw the switching functions and would be more properly described as "electronic" or "predigital." What matters is that, after six years and $60 million in initial R&D, Northern Electric had a product that could give it a presence in the transitional U.S. telecom market. The first one went into operation in 1971. It was a small switch that worked on principles similar to those of an AT&T's Bell Labs design, the ESS-101, and was tailor-made for the needs of independent phone companies in rural America who didn't want to buy from AT&T. In 1983, Northern would report that total R&D costs for the SP-1 were $104 million, but they produced cumulative sales of $1.08 billion.

Despite the achievement of the SP-1, Northern Electric had a long way to go before being considered a player in the global telecom market. Nortel describes itself circa 1971 as "sleepy." Indeed, 1970 had been a pretty awful year. While revenues had increased from $482.5 to $563.6 million, earnings had slid from $11 to $4.1 million, and earnings per share from 52 to 17 cents. In 1971, the company underwent the shakeup that the Western Electric selloff of 1956 had begged for. The R&D efforts of Northern Electric and Bell Canada were spun off into their own entity, Bell Northern Research (BNR), jointly owned by Northern and Bell, which held 51 percent. Don Chisholm was put in charge at BNR, creating what Nortel would call "a graduate university campus atmosphere that nurtures creative thought and esprit de corps." A turnaround specialist, John C. Lobb, was brought in to serve as Northern Electric's president—the first outsider to run the company. According to corporate folklore, when he asked an employee what it was Northern Electric made, Lobb would reply, "We don't make switching, goddamn it. We make money." Lobb drove Northern Electric's profits from $4.1 million in 1970 to $20.1 million in 1972 to $32 million in 1973. At the same time, earnings per share rose to $1.35. It was a fairly remarkable performance, considering that overall revenues increased less than 9 percent during the same period.

Northern's emerging business strategy was founded on three important principles. First (and in no particular order of priority), R&D was critical, and that meant attracting top talent, treating them well, and getting marketable results out of them. Second, the digital revolution was under way, and Northern needed to be at its forefront. Third, the U.S. telecom market beckoned, but under AT&T much of it was a closed shop for new technology. Northern needed to make inroads on the margins, with the phone companies outside the AT&T umbrella and the business customers. Thus there were two distinct streams of product development: customer premises equipment (CPE) for businesses, which produced PBX systems, and central office (CO), which produced switches for the phone companies.

The SP-1 had served to get Northern in the door of the independent telcos with a not-quite cutting-edge product. It got the job done, but other companies were beginning to produce true digital switches. In 1970, AT&T and the Bell Labs can-do crowd produced the 4ESS for telephone offices, while the same year Rolm, which specialized in military computers (and subsequently was bought by IBM, and later Siemens), came out of left field with a digital PBX.

In late 1972, Northern brought out a PBX, the SG-1, which it also called the Pulse. The first, the Pulse-80, was addressed at the 100-line market, and a larger Pulse-120 followed. Like the central office SP-1, this new switch was electronic, rather than fully digital, but it stood out for using integrated circuits rather than electro-mechanical switches, and also employed time-division multiplexing, which meant that more than one call could be handled on one transmission line. Northern would claim that it was the first commercially successful, fully electronic, time-division PBX. Within three years Northern had sold almost 6,000 of them, mainly south of the border, but in about twenty countries in all. That same year, Northern opened its first American manufacturing operation, in Port Huron, Michigan—an American operating subsidiary, which became Northern Telecom Inc., had already been established in Waltham, Massachusetts, in 1971.

In 1973, the company arranged to list 10 percent of its shares on the Toronto Stock Exchange, and they also began to trade in Montreal and London. The listing on the NYSE followed in 1975, after Lobb gave way to a Bell Canada veteran, Walter Frederick Light. Northern Electric was poised for a spectacular success.

The company had made a great stride forward in 1974. In one year, revenues jumped from $612.8 to $970.7 million, earnings from $32 to $53.8 million, and earnings per share from $1.35 to $2.05. "Digital" became the company's raison d'être. The SP-1 and Pulse switches were computer controlled, but the calls were still in analog form. Nortel publicly aimed to have a line of digital switching equipment for all new central office applications by 1980. A Semiconductor Standards Engineering Group was established to investigate nothing but integrated circuits (IC). By now, Northern was having to compete with a domestic startup that had embraced IC. In 1973 a former BNR engineer named Michael Cowpland had co-founded Mitel in Kanata, Ottawa's emerging high-tech suburb. In 1975, Mitel produced the first tone-to-pulse converter, which allowed phone companies with old electromechanical switches (rotary-dial pulse) to offer service for touch-tone phones, thereby delaying a costly upgrade to the full digital switching Northern was aiming to exploit.

By 1975, in addition to twenty-four plants in Canada, Northern had manufacturing operations in Butler, North Carolina; Concord, New Hampshire; Mountain View, California; Nashville, Tennessee; Port Huron, Michigan; and West Palm Beach, Florida. BNR was also operating a distinct research facility in Palo Alto (BNR Inc.) in association with the Mountain View plant. Both were in the heart of the San Francisco Bay area's celebrated Silicon Valley, and they provided Northern with its first product of the digital revolution.

In 1975, Northern unveiled a stunner of a product: a PBX called the SL-1, which had been in the works since the summer of 1973. Electromechanical workings were completely banished in this true digital switch. Its sublime beauty is best appreciated by a telecom engineer, but there were a number of noteworthy features. Large-scale integrated circuits were used to code and decode analog signals so that all the switching functions could be fully digital. From the user's point of view, perhaps its most impressive characteristic was the way the SL-1 managed its programmable features. A separate signalling channel between the handset on the office desk and the PBX was a design breakthrough that set the standard for the PBXs that followed from all manufacturers.

Its modular architecture meant that Northern could continually refine and expand it, making the SL-1 the basis of a family of SL switches that evolved right through the 1980s. It was also the basis for the designs of two other switching lines—the central office switch family, called DMS, and a data-only switch, the SL-10. By 1975, Northern could proudly say that half its product line was based on its own technology; that proportion would increase to 71 percent by 1977.

After the SL-1's introduction, Northern Electric still had more surprises in store and positioned itself accordingly. The company name was changed to Northern Telecom in 1976, in part because a company named Northern Electric, which produced consumer appliances, already existed in the United States. And it launched a new product-defining promotion called Digital World. The company was promising a full suite of digital switching products and practically begged customers not to consider any purchases until the new stuff was rolled out.

In 1976, Northern increased its ownership of BNR to 70 percent and began unveiling the new line of central office switches called Digital Multiplex Subscriber, or DMS. These were the first fully digital central office switches from any company. The DMS-1, which had remote switching capabilities, was aimed at the non-AT&T American phone companies looking to upgrade rural service and eliminate party lines. These rural markets also generally didn't have the corporate customers to support orders for the SL-1 PBX, and so Northern came up with a central office switch that could provide its switching capabilities. The DMS-10 was a small digital central office switch that could handle anywhere from a few hundred to six thousand lines. Both DMS models were being field-tested, with orders being taken for 1977. Nortel reported in 1976 that it had significant orders and commitments for the DMS-10 from five of the ten largest independent telcos in the United States. By year-end, General Electric Co. had licensed the SL-1 for the United Kingdom and other overseas markets.

Nortel had undergone an enormous transformation. It recorded its first $1 billion sales year in 1975, which was more than double its revenues of 1969. Between 1974 and 1976, earnings per share increased almost 50 percent, reaching $2.91. It had increased its earnings per revenue dollar from six-tenths of a cent in 1967 to about seven cents in 1976. And R&D spending had virtually doubled since 1973, reaching $61.5 million in 1976. By 1981, those 1976 R&D dollars would triple.

Northern's American ambitions increased, and it began buying companies in a foreshadowing of its late 1990s expansion binge. In December 1976, it acquired Cook Electric Co. of Chicago for about $30 million. With more than 1,100 employees in seven plants (including one in Winnipeg), Cook Electric delivered sales of $30.5 million and more manufacturing capacity. That same month, Northern paid an undisclosed amount in cash for Telecommunications Systems of America to boost its sales efforts. In 1977, Northern spent $11.6 million to acquire 24 percent of Intersil Inc. of Cupertino, California, which produced large-scale integrated circuits (LSIs) and computer components and subsystems.

In 1977, Northern underwent a restructuring. Northern Telecom Canada Ltd. was created to manage the company's Canadian manufacturing and marketing efforts, with a new headquarters in the Toronto suburb of Islington. The division had more than 15,000 employees, and more than 80 percent of the company's manufacturing space was contained in the twenty-six plants located in nine provinces. The U.S. division, Northern Telecom Inc., whose headquarters had been moved to Nashville, employed about 4,000. BNR, headquartered in Ottawa, had about 2,200 employees. Another research joint venture with Bell Canada, B-N Software Research in Toronto, employed 114. Northern also owned Nedco Ltd. (a contraction of Northern Electric Distribution Co.), a holdover from the old Northern Electric days, which was the largest distributor of electric, electronic, industrial, and telecommunications products in Canada. Fewer and fewer of these products, though, were actually made by Northern, and in 1979 the company sold this division. Northern's foreign operations outside North America were organized under Northern Telecom International Ltd., with headquarters in Montreal. About 2,300 employees worked in Northern's subsidiaries in Turkey, Switzerland, the Republic of Ireland, Singapore, and Malaysia, as well as at the Florida headquarters of Northern Telecom CALA (for Central and Latin America). Northern also incorporated its first finance subsidiary, to handle vendor financing for customers, in 1978.

Northern also made four significant acquisitions in the United States in 1978: Sycor Inc., DATA 100 Corp., Eastern Data Industries Inc. (Spectron), and Danray Inc. Altogether, Northern committed $277 million in cash, notes, and common shares to these purchases.

Several aspects of these early Northern deals stand out. In the case of Sycor, the entire acquisition was completed with shares, as Northern agreed to swap nine-tenths of a Northern common share for every share of Sycor. The purchases generated a large amount of goodwill—the amount the price exceeded the net asset value. With the four 1978 acquisitions, $108.4 million in goodwill—almost 40 percent of the total expenditure—had to be booked and amortized against revenues. And in the case of DATA 100 Corp., which made remote job entry terminals, and Sycor Inc., which specialized in intelligent terminals for distributed data processing, Northern was determined to branch into a new technology area where it lacked expertise. Sycor and DATA 100 were combined in a new business unit called Electronic Office Systems (EOS), which was dedicated to the design, manufacture, and marketing of computer terminals and peripheral equipment. Acquisitions through share swaps, large amounts of goodwill, breaking into a new business territory by buying companies that were already there—all were harbingers of Nortel's expansion strategy in the late 1990s.

By agreeing to pay $23 million for Danray of Richardson, Texas, Northern made an early appearance in an emerging communications hotbed that would become known as Telecom Corridor. Richardson is a suburb of Dallas and home to the University of Texas (at Dallas) campus. The town's high-tech fortunes had been building since the end of World War II. The arrival of freeway U.S. 75 along with the Cold War defence contracting boom fostered the growth of electronics firms around Richardson. In the 1950s, Texas Instruments established its new headquarters just south of Richardson proper. Then came Collins Radio later that decade, compelled to relocate from Cedar Rapids, Iowa, by a Pentagon preference that its defence spending spread the wealth around the nation. In 1958, a newly hired engineer at Texas Instruments named Jack Kilby was stuck at work in July because he didn't have enough time in to qualify for a holiday. With nothing better to do, he invented the integrated circuit. In California, at startup Fairchild Semiconductor, Robert Noyce was working on the very same idea. It was Bell versus Gray all over again. In 1961, the U.S. patent office awarded the integrated circuit patent to Noyce, but this core feature of the electronic revolution has generally been regarded as a co-discovery. It changed the landscape around Richardson. By 1970, Texas Instruments was employing 20,000, Collins Radio another 3,000.

In the early 1970s, the Richardson area (then known as Electronic City) was going through some major shifts. Defence spending cutbacks were causing layoffs at Texas Instruments; Collins

Radio hit some rough spots and was bought by Rockwell International. Some of the engineers struck out on their own with startups, and a couple of them from Texas Instruments launched Danray, whose main claim to fame was making all the toll switches for long-distance upstart MCI. Northern was destined to become a major employer in the Richardson telecom boom; by the mid-1990s, it would be a leader among the 500 firms that formed the Telecom Corridor at that time.[8]

Northern's purchase of Danray appeared well timed. Completed in January 1978, it anticipated the FCC ruling that year that AT&T had to allow long-distance rivals like MCI to connect to the local Bells. It was yet another important step toward creating a monopoly-free communications environment and helped spur the development of networks that were both competitive and cost-effective.

In 1979, Northern introduced the DMS-100, which could handle both local and long-distance (toll) calls, with support for up to 100,000 lines. The technological gains in the DMS central office switches spurred on the development of a large PBX, the SL-100. These were the first in a series of significant digital switches that made Nortel a major player in telecom switching, not only in North America, but around the world, as Northern would become the first non-Japanese supplier to Nippon Telephone and Telegraph.

In 1980, however, Northern hit a financial wall. While revenues had increased from $1.5 to $1.9 billion between 1978 and 1979, they only edged forward to $2.05 billion in 1980. At the same time, acquisition expenses were gnawing away at revenues. R&D expenses, which were less than $50 million in 1975, reached $140.9 million in 1980. Interest charges had zoomed from $6.6 million in 1977 to $44.9 million as long-term debt had grown from $52.4 to $321.7 million. Depreciation on plant and equipment was up from less than $24 million in 1975 to $112.7 million. Earnings had increased from $85.3 to $113.5 million between 1977 and 1979, but earnings per revenue dollar had decreased from seven to six cents.

Nortel had begun to face stiff competition in its own backyard. In 1978, Mitel introduced the SX-200 Super Switch, an analog PBX with a microprocessor control. Compact, with low power requirements, the

SX-200 became "the most successful PBX ever," according to Mitel's successor company, Zarlink Semiconductor. Mitel went public on the TSE in 1979 with an issue of 1.1 million shares, then joined Northern on the NYSE in 1981.[9]

But the main culprit in Northern's financial woes was its prototypic expansion spree in the United States in 1977 and 1978. The EOS division had become a serious burden. Northern was unhappy with the way revenues were earned from leases on EOS equipment sold by third parties, and moved in mid-1980 to cut off these lease efforts and try to replace them with direct sales. With the arrival of a tough recession and the additional problem of aging technology at EOS, the division suffered a revenue collapse. In one year, the division's sales fell from $350 to $259 million.

In December 1980, Northern's board approved what amounted to a full retreat from the acquisition-driven expansion of the late 1970s. All the remaining goodwill and the value of technology associated with the EOS division—$97.9 million in all—were written off. Another $8.5 million was struck off for Danray technology. In 1981, Northern's interest in Intersil would be dumped for $16 million. The EOS and Danray write-downs produced a hit of $106.4 million, and another $113 million was shouldered for plant closings, employee terminations, inventory write-downs, potential equipment repurchases and uncollectible receivables. To make matters worse, Northern still had to meet obligations under the existing leases for EOS products. For 1980, Northern reported a loss of $185.2 million, or 63 cents per share (before extraordinary items), a grim reversal from the historic high of $3.70 per share of the previous year. The company had never lost money before, and the stock was pounded when the write-downs were revealed. Having traded as high as 55\frac{1}{2}$ in the first quarter of 1980, Northern common shares fell to a low of 29\frac{3}{4}$ in the fourth quarter.

This misadventure would be quickly forgotten as Northern's digital switching products racked up huge revenue increases and quickly restored profitability. In 1981, Northern stock exceeded $60 for the first time. The EOS division was absorbed by a new operating division, Integrated Office Systems, in 1982, and haunted investors no more. The investors attracted to Nortel in the late 1990s, attracted by its grand expansion plans into an exciting new area of business, would exhibit no knowledge of how badly the company's last attempt to grow through acquisitions, twenty years earlier, had turned out.

Northern Telecom would never have enjoyed its spectacular growth in the 1980s without its first-class technology, but its ability to capitalize on this technology was made possible by two hugely important factors in the all-important U.S. market, both related to AT&T. Bell Labs had been so busy winning Nobel prizes that it had allowed Northern to beat it to the market with the DMS-100. A fully digital version of AT&T's 5ESS didn't come out until 1982, giving Nortel a solid head start in large central office switches. At the same time, AT&T was under siege from the justice department. The latest antitrust suit had been grinding ahead since 1974, and by 1980 it was clear that AT&T would have to capitulate. The Bell system was astonishingly large, employing about one million people, and Lily Tomlin's Ernestine was as popular as ever. Even before the Baby Bells were cut loose in 1984, there was considerable concern among them that if they kept on buying equipment from AT&T, more antitrust action would be around the corner. The compulsion to behave like good corporate citizens helped drive AT&T and the Baby Bells into the arms of Northern salespeople.

The breakthrough came in 1980, when AT&T signed a DMS-10 supply agreement with Northern and also installed the DMS-100 for trial in Ticonderoga, New York. A new Northern Telecom DMS manufacturing facility was already under construction in Research Triangle Park, near Raleigh, North Carolina. The 250,000-square-foot facility opened in May 1981, but the success of the DMS line prompted an immediate expansion of 76,000 square feet for mid-1982. Meanwhile, in 1981, Northern made its first U.S. data network sale based on the SL-10 switch to the Federal Reserve Board, which had turned to Nortel to link its fourteen reserve banks. In July 1981, AT&T completed an evaluation of a toll switch, the DMS-200, and signed a four-year supply agreement in January 1982. In October 1982, a four-year contract was signed with New York

Telephone for the DMS-100 after a successful trial in Ticonderoga. It was Northern's first contract with a Baby Bell. Soon, twenty-one of the twenty-two local exchange carriers owned by the Baby Bells were shopping at Northern Telecom for their switches.

In 1982, Northern's U.S. revenues surpassed its Canadian revenues for the first time as domestic sales began to flag. That year, AT&T and its operating companies became Northern's single largest customer. The $161 million in revenues they provided in 1982 represented a 49 percent leap over 1981. The SL-1 was the world's most successful PBX, with 5,687 sold since its introduction in 1975.

U.S. sales continued to increase as the AT&T breakup approached. Total sales to AT&T and its soon-to-be-independent operating companies reached $343 million in 1983, then more than doubled to $699.3 million in 1984. By the end of 1984, Northern Telecom was the second-largest domestic telecommunications equipment manufacturer in the United States. It had almost 20,000 employees (just behind the 23,700 in Canada) at fifteen plants and fifteen R&D labs in eleven states. It was also pushing hard in the international markets. Its first DMS switch in South America, a DMS-10, went into service in Peru that year, and another DMS-10 marked the debut of Northern's DMS line in the People's Republic of China.

Northern Telecom's success was part of a wholesale transformation of the telecommunications industry. For decades, large companies had employed dedicated staff on-site to deal with their phone systems and the phone company. With blistering speed, the knowledge base of these workers was rewritten. An entirely new breed of telecom expert had to be trained, and Nortel was instrumental in encouraging educational institutions to produce at top speed the next generation of technicians, analysts, and managers who could cope with the software-driven features of its products. Sheridan College of Applied Arts and Technology in Oakville, Ontario, rolled out a new program in 1984 specifically to train the new Northern-savvy telecom professionals.

At the same time, the information technology (IT) industry was taking shape. IBM unveiled its first PC in 1982, having been goaded into exploiting the desktop market by the success of pioneering startups like Commodore and Apple. Since 1956, there had been an unnatural divergence between computers and telecommunications, owing partly to the fact that in settling the previous antitrust case in 1956, AT&T promised that Western Electric and Bell Labs would keep their hands off the computer and office machine businesses, leaving IBM alone to build its own monopoly and eventually attract its own antitrust investigation by the justice department.

As computers and microelectronics were used to drive electromechanical and analog phone switches, and fully digital switches came into being, software became a fundamental part of the telecom business. Northern had even been building its own switching computers right through the 1970s, because there was nothing off the shelf that would do the job. But with the arrival of the PC in the early 1980s, information technology began to blaze its own trails. "Voice" and "data" were evolving on parallel paths, with analysts, technicians, and their managers working in distinct departments within large corporations—the voice people concerned with software-driven switch features like call forwarding and voice messaging, the data people worrying about databases, software tools, and desktop computers linked by networks within buildings and across wide geographic areas. Both departments were in the business of communicating, but weren't necessarily communicating with each other any more than their respective industries were.

The 1984 antitrust settlement with AT&T removed the 1956 restriction on the company getting into the computer business. But the telecommunication world's efforts to dominate the data market focused on the technology necessary to move data around. Individual PCs were being linked in networks to share files or a common device like a printer. Small networks, which generally operated within a building, were called local-area networks, or LANs. Larger ones, which linked these LANs together, were called wide-area networks, or WANs.

LANs came in various physical configurations, called topologies. One of the simplest and cheapest was a bus topology, in which the computers and devices were joined along a central cable, or bus. This was the topology commonly used by the Ethernet, a LAN architecture developed by Xerox in association with DEC and Intel in 1976. The Ethernet could also be employed in star topologies, in which a central hub serviced the various connected devices. The star configuration made the Ethernet a direct competitor to Northern Telecom's ambitions to dominate not just voice but data traffic as well on the private networks within institutional and corporate environments. A powerful on-site switching device like a PBX was a natural contender for the hub role in a star topology LAN.

The PBX-based LAN had two important advantages over its Ethernet counterpart. Ethernet at the time could only handle data traffic, not voice, and its bandwidth was only 10 megabits per second (mbps). Northern began introducing voice and data switching capability to its PBX line as PCs began to proliferate. In February 1985, it launched a new line of SL-model PBXs, called Meridian, along with a proprietary LAN architecture called LANSTAR in conjunction with its SL-1 and SL-100 products. It also offered upgrades to existing SL-model PBXs to give them data capability. Through a Meridian PBX, Northern was promising bandwidth of up to 40 mbps. Its Meridian M4020, equipped with its own terminal screen, offered a suite of applications and services, including voice and text messaging, e-mail, spreadsheets, database management, word processing, and an electronic calendar.

Northern sold plenty of Meridian product as its revenues grew from $2.7 billion in 1983 to $8.2 billion in 1991, along the way becoming the largest supplier of digital PBXs in the world. But in the long run, PBX-based switching was not going to supplant the slower, data-only Ethernet. For PC computing and networking was marching to its own drummer, and while the phone system proved to be a vital communications backbone, phone system products were unable to dictate how computer networks evolved and interconnected.

This was due in part to the fact that the phone companies were unable to produce a compelling data product for the public networks, not just for the private networks within an organization that used something like Meridian. When phone companies traditionally thought about bandwidth demands, they had in mind the old dream of videophones—circuit-switched connections with network infrastructure robust enough to handle the heavy lifting of both voice and video in one go. Their answer to accommodating robust traffic in data along lines already handling voice was the Integrated Services Digital Network (ISDN), a high bandwidth switched public network service that provided end-to-end digital connectivity over standard phone lines for simultaneous transmission of voice and data. Northern was heavily involved in the development and testing of ISDN. The first commercial long-distance ISDN service was introduced in the United States in 1988, and the first dial-up transmission of video using ISDN followed in 1990. But the ISDN service for high-speed simultaneous voice and data service was not aggressively pursued by the telcos, and the needs of institutional and business customers for efficient data communications were neglected by the carriers.

An alternative communications system was growing up in the telephone's shadow, one based on the convergence of a multiplicity of emerging computer networks, ranging from the simple Ethernet LAN of a company or university department, in which a couple of desktop computers might share a file server and a printer, to Ethernet clusters, to cable networks at the university campus level, all the way to an entire corporate linked network that operated on a multinational basis. As they became interconnected in a network of networks—LANS becoming WANS, WANS interconnecting to create the biggest WAN of all—by using telephone lines to bridge the gaps between them, the Internet took shape.

In 1984, as Northern Telecom's new switches were helping remake the world's phone systems and AT&T was being cut down to size, a new company, dedicated to making data networks function, arose in the San Francisco Bay area. It was called Cisco Systems. At that moment, the Internet was beginning to coalesce around vital communications standards. The Internet did not yet exist in its modern sense. It had begun with a pioneering computer network, based on data switching, called ARPANET, created by the Advanced Research Projects Agency (ARPA) of the U.S defence department. ARPANET was fundamentally a defence research tool that linked academics working on Pentagon-funded projects. By the early 1980s, it was clear that this network could benefit not just defence research, but academia in general, and the movement began to split the service into military and civilian networks.

The key to the Internet's growth was a robust communications protocol suite called TCP/IP—Transmission Control Protocol over Internet Protocol. The TCP part dealt with service features of the network, while IP took care of the addressing and forwarding of individual packets of data. One of the contracts let out by the Defense Advanced Research Projects Agency (DARPA) for the development of TCP/IP went to Stanford University, from which Cisco sprang forth. On January 1, 1983, ARPANET cut over from the old Network Computer Protocol to TCP/IP, and ARPANET spun off its military component into MILNET. Desktop workstations began to appear, many of them running the Berkeley version of Bell Labs' invention, Unix, which included IP networking software. The Domain Name System (DNS) came into being in 1984. The Internet was on its way.

Be that as it may, it was still almost impossible to imagine that a little startup like Cisco, conceived by four Stanford University professors around the debuts of then-obscure networking entities like TCP/IP and DNS, would come to represent one of Nortel's main competitive hurdles in the last years of the millennium.

4

Missed Connections

enable end-to-end niches
morph 24/365 initiatives
grow turn-key relationships
orchestrate back-end synergies
transition collaborative e-business
revolutionize efficient deliverables
empower interactive experiences
deploy one-to-one metrics

—Tech industry phrases produced
by the Web Bullshit Generator

On February 8, 1996, Bill Clinton gave his blessing to the Telecommunications Act (or Telecom Act 1996) in a ceremony at the Library of Congress in Washington, D.C. It was the first time an American president had signed a bill into law at the Library, which signalled that this law was intended to be a cornerstone of the new information age so enthusiastically promoted by the vice-president, Al Gore. While there were provisions to benefit services to schools and libraries, the act's main goal was to increase competition in the telecommunications field in order to lower costs for consumers and promote technology advances.

The overhaul was long overdue, as the existing Telecom Act had been passed in 1934. "Telecommunications" encompasses any service that electronically conveys content between a sender and a receiver, without altering the content along the way. Cable TV is an example of a one-way conveyance in sending programming into households. The telephone is the definitive example of two-way conveyance, and in the United States, the single largest market in the world, the new Telecom Act meant the phone system was about to undergo another major transformation.

Already, on January 1, 1984, the local phone monopoly, which had endured for a century, had been addressed by breaking up AT&T into what became seven Regional Bell Operating Companies—the so-called "Baby Bells" (Ameritech, Bell Atlantic, Bell South, Nynex, Pacific Telesis Group, Southwestern Bell, and US West). With the exception of a precious few independent operators, AT&T had pretty well owned the local phone business in America since the dawn of electronic conversation. The Department of Justice, which had been in pursuit of AT&T with its antitrust suit since 1974, went along with the creation of the local Bells because continuing the regulated monopoly service for the local exchange carriers was still seen as okay, while it was felt competition should be encouraged for long-distance service (which already existed, thanks to companies like Sprint and MCI), manufacturing, and research and development.

Now, however, the Clinton administration wanted to foster competition all through the telecom world: by permitting long-distance companies to enter the local exchange business, and vice versa; by having new local exchange carriers start up; by permitting other utilities, such as electrical and gas, to use their established rights-of-way to businesses and households to get in on the communications game if they so wished; and especially by encouraging the cable TV business, subscribed to by 60 percent of American households and available to another 30 percent, to go beyond one-way transmission and use its infrastructure to develop two-way services. At the same time, cross-ownership would be permitted between telephone and cable companies, to allow companies in one domain to expand into the other. (Participation of Regional Bell Operating Companies in cable companies had already been permitted by the Federal Communications Commission in 1993.)

Changes in the United States were mirrored in Canada and Europe. In August 1996, the Canadian government released its policy framework on convergence that would permit cable and phone companies to offer each other's services; deregulation in telecommunications services came to Europe in 1998. But from the perspective of business opportunities, the American initiative was the most significant.

The U.S. Telecom Act laid bare a wealth of opportunities for existing telecom ventures and startups; for suppliers of equipment, software, and other services; and for acronym-happy tech wonks. The Regional Bell Operating Companies were known as RBOCs, among which were Regional Bell Holding Companies, or RBHCs, whose collections of local operations crossed state lines. The RBOCs and RBHCs in turn owned a total of twenty-two Bell Operating Companies, or BOCs, the carriers that provided service at the local level. Under the Telecom Act, companies that provided local telephone service were known as Local Exchange Carriers, or LECs. LECs that weren't part of the AT&T spinoff family were called Independent Telephone Companies, or ITCs, or sometimes ICOs. With the passage of the Telecom Act, the existing LECs were labelled Incumbent Local Exchange Carriers, or ILECS (eye-lecks), while their startup adversaries were Competitive Local Exchange Carriers, or CLECs (see-lecks).

The RBOCs, RBHCs, BOCs, LECS, ITC/ICOs, ILECs, and CLECs were just the first few flaky hints of the blizzard of seemingly impenetrable terminology that was about to be dumped on the investment community. At times, the blizzard would approach whiteout conditions. The acronyms came so thick and fast that the average person couldn't see beyond his own fingertips, and for many what appeared to be an investing paradise turned into a kill zone. Assaulted by jargon and technological concepts they could not understand, or lured into thinking that mastering the buzzwords somehow brought clarity to the situation, investors in the communications technology boom that followed the Telecom Act would not only be snowed under—they would come to wonder if they hadn't been conned in a Wall Street snow job. In 1996, there were 110 federal securities fraud class-action cases. In 2001, thanks to the fallout from the bursting of the overall tech bubble of which the telecom business was a major part, there were 487. One of the unquestioned competitive spinoffs of the Telecom Act was the rivalry between law firms lining up to sue companies and their senior executives on behalf of impoverished shareholders.

By the time Bill Clinton signed the Telecom Act, the single largest revolution in communications history was well under way. The Internet was growing so quickly that it would shortly fuel the vast majority of changes in the communications landscape fostered by the Telecom Act.

It took the better part of a century for the telephone, though now virtually ubiquitous, to conquer the United States. Alexander Graham Bell had patented the device in 1876, and while it rapidly gained popularity, it took until the end of World War II for half the households in America to get phone service. Another quarter-century passed before households with phones reached 90 percent in 1969, then another quarter-century and change for the percentage to inch up to 94 by 1996.

In comparison, the rise of the global Internet was astonishingly quick. Between 1989 and 1994, total annual traffic (as measured by data packets) on the Internet rose from less than 12 million to 21 billion; between 1984 and 1998, the number of hosts—computers that allow users to communicate with other host computers on a network—rose from 1,000 to more than 40 million, while during the same period the number of global Internet accounts increased from 30 million to 150 million. "No other technology has taken hold of America so quickly," Larry Irving, Assistant Secretary for Communications and Information at the U.S. Department of Commerce's National Telecommunications and Information Administration, told his audience at the Voice on the Net (VON) Conference in Washington, D.C., on September 17, 1998. "It took radio 25 years to become a household fixture, broadcast TV about 20 years, and the World Wide Web about 5 years."

The Internet may be a decentralized network of smaller computer networks, but its information must cross space through some communications medium, and when the Telecom Act became law, the favoured medium overwhelmingly was the telephone system. Simply by collectively owning the public switched telephone network (PSTN), which was the most pervasive, most reliable communication system around, the phone companies (aka the telcos) were the default choice of conveyance for the digital information revolution. Market penetration of households by telephone lines was all but complete: when household income reached $30,000, as research by the Consumer Federation of America and the Benton Foundation showed prior to the Telecom Act's passage, telephone subscribership stabilized at 99 percent. The decades of building the phone system to the point where virtually everyone in America had one made possible the rapid proliferation of Internet hookups. The resulting change in the way the phone network was being used was profound. A system built for telephony—the electronic transmission of the human voice—was now being asked to convey vast amounts of data at the same time that people were still talking to each other.

Thanks to the Internet, the proliferation of total subscriber line accounts didn't have to end. As the Net caught on among home users, demand for separate dedicated phone lines for computer modem hookups rose. Corporations made their own considerable demands on traffic, as regional operations stayed in touch with one another and their customers, clients, and suppliers via e-mail, and as a new phenomenon known as e-commerce arose. Thus traffic increased in both the absolute numbers of subscribers and the volume of traffic they generated. Internet-based communications developed a ravenous appetite for bandwidth, as simple e-mail messages began to sprout megabyte-sized file attachments and the Internet found its true calling for middle America with the rise of the graphic-intensive World Wide Web browser.

In the early 1990s, the Internet was promising to make its great leap forward with the Web. To surf the Web, you needed a browser (or a client), and a number were being made available, mainly on a nonprofit basis, from academic sources. Amazingly, none of the big software companies, such as IBM or Microsoft, had a Web browser in its product line. Cornell Law had Cello, while the University of Kansas had a purely text-based browser called Lynx. But the most impressive was Mosaic, developed by the National Center for Supercomputer Applications (NCSA) at the University of Illinois, which came in both Windows and Macintosh versions, and first became available to the public in February 1993. From Mosaic arose the first potent commercial Web surfing tool.

On April 11, 1994, Netscape Communications was formed in Mountainview, California, as a partnership between Jim Clark, the founder of Silicon Graphics in 1982 and a former Stanford professor, and Marc Andreessen, a grad student at NCSA who had worked on Mosaic before graduating in December 1993. The first version of Netscape was released in October 1994. On August 9, 1995, Netscape Communications made its initial public offering on the NASDAQ.

Microsoft had allowed the upstart Netscape to beat it to the commercial browser market. The software giant didn't release its own browser, Explorer, until the fall of 1995, when it also unveiled Windows 95. In November that year, Netscape had 78 percent of the market, while Microsoft Explorer had just 3 percent. Clawing back market share from Netscape became a focal point of Microsoft's marketing activities, and its controversial bundling of Explorer (and the e-mail program Outlook Express) with the Windows operating system triggered the antitrust case filed against it by the Department of Justice. In hindsight, it seems astonishing that a software company as dominant as Microsoft could find itself playing catch-up (and risking its existence in jousting with the DOJ) in the market sector that defined consumer and corporate software communications needs in the unfolding decade.

Netscape's debut on the NASDAQ is considered by many to be the first signal event in the commercialization of the Internet. Coming six months before the passage of the Telecom Act, the arrival of Netscape was punctuated by a parallel development in the telco world. AT&T, having lost its regional operating companies and local exchange carriers in 1984 under pressure from the Department of Justice, announced on September 20, 1995, that it was now voluntarily breaking itself up into three separate companies. A communications services company would carry on as AT&T. NCR, the computer manufacturer it had acquired in 1991 in a $7.3 billion deal, was going to be turned loose again. And a new systems and equipment company, including the longstanding R&D operation known as Bell Labs, would stand on its own under the name Lucent Technologies. On September 30, 1995, Lucent officially came into being, and on Thursday, April 4, 1996, it began trading on the NYSE.

Lucent was the American version of Nortel: a research and man-ufacturing arm of the dominant telephone company in its country. Where newly minted Lucent was now on its own, Nortel was still majority-owned by Bell Canada Enterprises. But unlike Lucent, the established Nortel had a long history of selling its products and serv-ices in the international market, including the United States. For the past three years, the percentage of Nortel's revenues from the United States had hovered between 50 and 55 percent and were increasing in absolute figures, from $4.85 billion in 1994 to $6.86 billion in 1996.

In the race to service the new communications order, Nortel seemed to have a potent new competitor in Lucent, but Nortel did-n't see it that way. In its 1996 annual report, Nortel noted that, prior to AT&T's self-directed breakup, the communications giant was already its biggest competitor in the U.S. market for equipment sales. Now that AT&T's equipment and R&D business had been spun off as Lucent, Nortel wasn't admitting to losing any sleep. "Nortel does not expect that the establishment of Lucent will have a material impact on Nortel's overall operations," it asserted.

Certainly, in addition to the quality of its products and services and its global reputation, Nortel had a major advantage in the new deregulated U.S. market. For the startup competitors to the Baby Bells and former parent AT&T, Lucent was stained by its previous association with the phone monopoly. Indeed, the Baby Bells immediately became Lucent's main customers, and their needs helped shape Lucent's product development priorities. But regardless of what Nortel thought of the threat posed by Lucent, the two companies now shared a major adversary from the other side of the communications tracks, the data networking champion called Cisco. The voice and data worlds were con-verging through the Internet, and so were their sales territories.

And the impending collision caught Nortel completely unprepared.

If a giant like Microsoft could allow an upstart like Netscape to beat it to the market with a Web browser, the fact that Nortel could have so badly misread the ascent of the Internet should not be surprising. But Nortel's failure to prepare for the ascent of IP-based networking is nevertheless astounding and, more important, was the basis for much of its share-based acquisitions from 1998 onward. Nortel had simply missed the next big thing and began paying for the error by massively diluting its share base.

Nortel had begun the early nineties in rough shape. It had built a global reputation in the 1980s for its digital switching products, but the company was falling into an earnings and innovations slump. While revenues had continued to grow, from $4.3 billion in 1985 to $5.4 billion in 1988, net earnings dropped from $328.8 million to $165.6 million between 1987 and 1988. In 1989, the company was consigned to the care of Paul Stern—the first outsider to run Nortel since John Lobb. Sometimes described simply as a former IBM executive, Stern in fact was an electronics engineer who also held a doctorate in physics and had been a senior physicist at E.I. du Pont. He had once worked for IBM (in addition to Rockwell International and Braun), but he had been named president and CEO of Burroughs Corporation in 1982, and when Burroughs took over Sperry Corporation in 1986 and created Unisys, Stern carried on as CEO of the new company until December 1987.

Stern had then moved over to Nortel, becoming a paid consultant and joining the board and the executive committee in April 1988. Nortel was coming off its disappointing 1988 earnings performance when it announced in January 1989 that Stern would become vice-chairman, president, and CEO in March. By April 1990, with the retirement of Edmund Fitzgerald as chairman of the board, Stern held all three key senior positions—president, CEO, and chairman of the board.

The best Nortel can say about him in its official history of senior executives is that Stern "refocused the company to prioritize meeting the marketing needs of customers in the global marketplace." What he was actually accused of doing was prioritizing sales while costs, particularly research and development, were cut to maximize profits. Revenues increased from $6.1 to $8.4 billion from 1989 to 1992, and earnings per share grew from the low of 70 cents in 1988 to $2.17 in 1992. He has been blamed for downgrading the importance of R&D, and it is true that R&D spending increased only 6 percent in his first year on the job, which when inflation is considered was no real increase at all, but it must be noted that R&D spending actually increased by 22 percent between 1989 and 1992. A new 600,000-square-foot lab opened in Ottawa in 1992, and a new R&D and marketing centre was also established in Richardson, Texas, that year. The focus of R&D at Richardson originally was the DMS switching software, but it became redirected at wireless technology, the networking segment that allowed John Roth to make his mark.

Nevertheless, Stern's reputation at Nortel was that of a cost cutter who was focused on maximizing profits. Restructuring and cost-reduction programs had already been announced in December 1988, before he formally took control, and in fact 1988 would have turned out much better had a $200 million restructuring provision not appeared on the books that year, as the company shut down some manufacturing operations, streamlined operations, and reorganized sales and marketing.

Initially, investors loved what Stern was doing. In 1989, sales surpassed $6 billion, earnings per share more than doubled, and dividends per share increased by two cents. The company also looked like it had a technology game plan after wandering in the ISDN wilderness for several years, by unveiling a new strategy called FiberWorld, based on optical networking.

But there is no question that customer dissatisfaction, triggered in part by Nortel's sluggish response to the need for updates in switching software, helped precipitate a full-blown crisis. In mid-1991, a rattled Nortel unveiled its "Excellence!" initiative to (in the company's words) "focus on customer satisfaction and continuously improve the company's operations worldwide." It set a goal of "re-engineering" the company's major business processes, including product introduction, planning, and sales and order flow. But with a brutal recession hovering over the company, Nortel's parent, BCE, engineered a management change. In September 1992, Jean Monty, chairman and CEO of BCE subsidiary Bell Canada, came aboard as a director. Monty took over from Stern as chief operating officer and president in October; he then moved up to president and CEO in March 1993.

Monty's first year was painful. Nortel recorded a net loss of $884 million ($3.47 per share) in fiscal 1993 as revenues fell 3 percent and Monty (still running Bell Canada) began overhauling the business. Some investors were sufficiently displeased with the downturn in 1993 that they filed class-action suits in New York alleging that the company and a number of its senior officers (in Nortel's own words) "made material misstatements of, or omit[ted] to state, material facts relating to the business operations and prospects and financial condition of the Corporation." These suits, in their subsequent amended states, were finally dismissed in 2000.

For all the trauma surrounding Stern's departure and the arrival of Monty, Nortel was doing a few things right. It was developing and exhibiting a world-class expertise in what would prove to be two of the high-growth communications technologies of the new decade: wireless and optical networking.

Wireless technology was proving to be enormously lucrative. U.S. cell-phone subscriptions were growing at a rate of more than 30 percent a year, and in developing countries, wireless could quickly provide telephone service, rather than waiting around for traditional wires to be strung on poles through uncooperative terrain. As John Roth noted in one annual report in the early 1990s, wireless acted like a foot in the door for Nortel's other communications technologies. When these developing countries were ready for complex wired phone systems, Nortel would already be known to them through its wireless work.

Nortel was not the biggest wireless company in the world—in total sales it trailed firms like Ericsson, Siemens, Nokia, and Motorola. And a joint venture formed with Motorola in 1991, called Motorola-Nortel Communications Co., headquartered in Chicago, had been a bust. Set up to service North, Central, and South America, it began operating in May 1992, but was shut down in August 1993. But Nortel's strength in wireless was that it had a much more diverse product line than its competitors, who tended to be specialists. In addition to analog service, for example, in 1992 Nortel boasted of having the world's highest-capacity digital cellular switch and was also the only company with a dual-mode base-station radio system, which it said offered three times the capacity and half the cost per channel of analog systems. This "DualMode" cellular base station could operate in digital or analog on a per-call basis. And in June 1992, Alberta's AGT Cellular introduced the world's first commercial digital cellular service using Nortel technology.

Despite strong growth in revenues, which reached $12.8 billion by 1996, Monty was facing a major problem in how the company had chosen to exploit its technological strengths. It would turn out that Nortel had the right stuff, but the wrong idea.

As noted, in 1989, Nortel introduced FiberWorld, the company's "vision for a wideband, optical fiber network for the high speed telecommunications services of the 21st century." Nortel wouldn't have to wait for another century to arrive for optical networking to start delivering huge revenues.

Fibre-optic communications had been around in theory since the mid-1960s. (For that matter, Alexander Graham Bell's initial concept for the telephone considered using light, rather than electricity, as the communications medium.) However, there were many technical hurdles to overcome in using glass fibres the width of a human hair, bundled into cables, to transmit the human voice and, later, data, by turning content into photons. There was also the hurdle of a minuscule market demand. Corning Glass Works of Corning, New York—which had manufactured the first light bulbs for Thomas Edison in the 1890s and given the world Pyrex in 1914—was able to market fibre-optic cable for the first time in 1973, but the phone companies were getting along fine with traditional copper wire and didn't see a tremendous need for the high-traffic capacity of glass. Global fibre-optic sales totalled a mere $2.5 million in 1975, and most of that money ($1.78 million) was spent on cable rather than components.

For Corning and the fibre-optic business in general, the decision of upstart long-distance company MCI to place a major order for fibre-optic cable in 1982 was a major turning point. But Nortel was already seriously involved in fibre-optics by then. Its optoelectronics research arm had begun trials on a fibre-optic system in the late 1970s, and signed a $22 million contract with Sasktel to provide a 3,200-kilometre system, which Nortel claimed was the longest digital integrated telecommunications network in the world. A similar network was provided for Manitoba Telephone in Elie, and as part of the Sasktel deal, Nortel opened an optoelectronics facility in Saskatoon in 1982. (Monty would close it as part of his restructuring efforts.) By 1982, Nortel had 115 optical systems either sold or on order around the world and had doubled its optical revenues to more than $37 million that year. In 1983, Nortel signed a contract to supply up to 62,000 miles of fibre-optic cable to MCI, its first major optical contract in the United States.

In 1988, the Synchronous Optical Networking, or SONET, standard was established by Bellcore, a division of AT&T concerned with research into and creation of communications standards. (Bellcore was spun off by AT&T in 1996 and later became Telcordia Technologies.) The international standards equivalent was Synchronous Digital Hierarchy, or SDH. Nortel made a strong R&D commitment to SONET, and its expertise allowed it to participate in the buildout of optical networks as it gained momentum in the 1990s. Two Nortel sales stood out in 1991. Southern New England Telephone in Connecticut became the first major phone company in the U.S. northeast to commit to upgrading its statewide interoffice transmission to SONET-based fibre optics, and MCI that year became the first U.S. long-distance carrier to transport live traffic over a long-haul (long-distance) SONET backbone on a 150-mile stretch between Dallas and Longview.

In 1992, Nortel announced that to date it had shipped worldwide more than 3,400 SONET systems. It also announced that BNR's global optoelectronics group had demonstrated a 10-gigabit-per-second (gbps) transmission system that could span 120 kilometres on land or under the ocean without having to use signal amplifiers to push the light along. This was a significant accomplishment. Optical bandwidth is defined by Optical Carrier, or OC, levels. The basic transmission rate is 51.84 megabits per second; a level-one SONET network, known as OC-1, thus has a bandwidth of 51.84 mbps. OC levels increase thereon with multiples of the base transmission rate. OC-48, with a bandwidth of 2.5 gbps, was the top of the operational bandwidth scale in the early 1990s. As Nortel noted in 1992, a typical OC-48 system required amplifiers every seventy kilometres. Nortel's experimental system could carry the signal farther, without amps, at four times that speed. It was, in effect, an OC-192 system and was a harbinger of the huge advantage Nortel would enjoy over its networking rivals when the optical market went into hyperdrive around 1998.

Before it could get to the golden opportunity presented by its OC-192 expertise, Nortel had to negotiate a precarious dead zone in its corporate strategy. Its optical expertise was getting way ahead of an already lagging customer base. Nortel might as well have built a speedway that could handle Formula One racers when the average user of the public switched network was getting around by horse and buggy. Nortel had to identify and promote a need for its high-speed networking technology. This was, to be sure, laudable strategic thinking, but it had a fatal flaw. It was based on what Nortel thought it could sell, and not on what the market was actually demanding. It was vendor-driven planning that could not have come at a worse time in the history of networking. It caused Nortel to strategically think its way right past the Internet.

In an interview with *National Post Business* magazine, published after he was selected Canada's CEO of the Year in 2000, John Roth candidly addressed the schism between the world of Nortel circa the mid-1990s, in which its main customers were the telcos (and its majority owner was BCE), and the world of data networking, which had given rise to the Internet. "The data world creates the traffic, and telcos carry it," Roth explained. "The telephone company world had its sense of how it would like to run the network and carry the traffic. We'd make the data world conform because it's our network and they'll have to meet us on our terms. The data guys had a very different plan. They said, 'We're just going to rent capacity and put out what we want. We can just get raw capacity and we'll run our protocols over it and we don't care what the telephone company does.'"

Behaving as a subsidiary of a telco, Nortel exhibited what can only be categorized as a wilful blindness toward the Internet. By the early 1990s, the Internet could not be dismissed as some fringe communications phenomenon. Nevertheless, Nortel managed to ignore it completely as it restructured its business units and unveiled its strategy for an integrated world of voice, data, and video. It came down to what you thought networks were good for, and the best way to leverage their potential. Nortel's vision was essentially an old and enduring one for the telephone world. The company wanted to move voice and video simultaneously, in real time, using a protocol called asynchronous transfer mode, or ATM, and also use this protocol for hauling around large amounts of data.

Nortel was coming out of the traditional telephone world of circuit switching, which is as old as Alexander Graham Bell. Circuit switching means that the sender and the receiver of a message are connected along a single, dedicated circuit—you dial your friend Norman, and a telephone switching system links your phone with his via a dedicated circuit path for the duration of the call. It works the same way when data are transferred through modems from one fax machine to another.

TCP/IP (which we'll refer to hereafter simply as IP) is the best-known form of packet switching, and it works in an entirely different way from circuit switching. The computer of the sender breaks the message down into discrete packets of data, and these are individually sent on their way to their destination. The Internet is a decentralized network of networks; information moves through it by way of computers called routers, which in older Net lingo were also known as gateways. A router's job is to stay in touch with other routers, to keep tabs on how traffic is flowing through the Internet, and as it receives a data packet, to send it on to the next router that promises the quickest transmission to the next router, and on and on until the packet reaches its destination. If the message is broken into, say, ten packets, it's entirely possible that the packets will get to their

ultimate address by ten different routes. Once they're at their destination, the packets are reassembled into the original message.

It would be wrong to think that Nortel missed the IP bandwag-
on because it didn't have a feel for packet switching. On the contrary,
Nortel had a long and productive relationship with IP-type packets.
Back in 1976, the X.25 packet standard had been established, and
Nortel had almost immediately put it to use with its data-switching
products in 1977 and used it for its data switches in the 1980s.

ATM is a form of packet switching but can be considered a close
cousin of circuit switching. While there is not a dedicated circuit in
the traditional sense, ATM does establish a fixed channel, or route—
a linear path between sender and receiver. ATM is a "cell relay" standard. Content is broken into regular, 53-bit cells (or packets) for
transmission and sent off in a constantly moving conveyor of cells.
The best analogy asks you to think of ATM as being like an infinite
moving train. The content of your message, be it voice, video, or
data, is broken into the standard 53-bit cells and put aboard each
available empty rail car as the train goes by. Then all the cells in your
message get off at their destination. It's fast, it's extremely reliable,
and all the cells ride along the same track. ATM can also rank messages, giving a quicker lift to video, for example.

One of IP's perceived strengths was that it optimized network
capacity by sending each packet along the most efficient path. This
contrasted with ATM's possible vulnerability to sudden surges in network traffic, as the relay method insisted on sending all the packets
along a single route. ATM's greatest strength was said to be its reliability in meeting the telco world's extremely high standards of quality of service. It was a top-to-bottom protocol, handling the message
at all levels of transit, whereas IP was simply a "top-layer" protocol.
IP could not promise anywhere near ATM's reliability. And because
ATM didn't have to go through the hassle of routing and reassem-
bling all the individual packets, it was better suited to real-time content like voice and video. Its "latency"—the delay in transmission
and reception—was far lower than IP. And it had been designed
specifically to work with the telco world's high-speed networks, like
SONET and T3. Besides, even if Internet messages were being

shipped using IP, when they entered a SONET high-speed backbone, it was ATM that delivered the packets.

But there was another advantage to ATM, at least from a phone company's perspective. The linear nature of cell travel made it easy to track and bill traffic on an ATM network. From this perspective, maybe Nortel wasn't really blind to the IP-based Internet at all. Having a phone company as its majority owner, it may have been enamoured with ATM's traffic-billing friendliness.

If you were a networking company circa 1993, dreaming of the future of your business, and that dream involved leveraging your strengths in fibre-optic technology to bring real-time voice and video communication to your customers, ATM was the way to go. So that was the way Nortel went. Nortel exhibited a fervent (some called it a religious) commitment to ATM. The problem was, Nortel was so convinced of the superiority of ATM that it had no time at all for IP.

Looking back and watching Nortel not get the Internet in the early to mid-1990s is like watching the railways not get the coming of the automobile. It wasn't so much the fact that railways would necessarily become obsolete or stop evolving—it was the fact that automobiles were a whole new system of transportation that opened fresh vistas of profitability. Cars (or trucks) would never be as efficient at moving large bulk commodities like grain or coal. On the other hand, trains would never deliver the versatility and independence of motor vehicles. Nortel circa 1990 was criticized as being arrogant and out of touch with its customers, but by the time Jean Monty took charge and launched the restructuring, the company was already riding the ATM rails.

In 1992, Nortel introduced the VISIT, for VISual Interactive Technology—or, as that year's annual report put it, the "first in a family of personal multimedia communications products that will create powerful new capabilities for anyone using phones and computers." The report showed off VISIT running on a Macintosh IIci. It was the videophone dream of the 1960s, which never seemed to die in telecom engineering circles, welded to the only brand of personal computer with a decent graphical user interface. Nortel said that its VISIT video product "delivers real-time video, screen-sharing, and file transfer capabilities." This persistent dream would crop up eerily in Nortel's advertising in 2001, when a tech-savvy dweeb who couldn't find a copy of his speech has his assistant dictate to him in real-time via a video feed on his wireless personal digital assistant.

Richard Faletti, president of Nortel's private networks division, boasted that VISIT was "a collaborative desktop computing application, and no one has that kind of package on the market today." Nortel crowed that VISIT products "are being tested by businesses and universities throughout the United States and Canada, including California's Jet Propulsion Laboratory and the University of Michigan."

The envisioned VISIT product line sank without a trace, but it was around long enough to illuminate one of the essential weaknesses of Nortel's networking strategy. Nortel's main customers fell into two categories: in the public networks sector, there were the telcos, to which it could sell central office switches and networking gear like carrier backbones; in the private networks sector, there were institutions, governments, and corporations that were buying PBXs and data switches and operating LANs and WANs carrying primarily voice and data. There was a marketing symbiosis between the two groups for Nortel. It was trying to sell technology to the private network customers that made economic sense to the telcos, and sell technology to the telcos that made economic sense to the private network customers. Being majority-owned by a telco, Nortel's planning tended to tilt in the favour of what a telco could get excited about. Nortel was not going to back a technology that appeared to have little obvious benefit to a telephone company. Like ISDN, ATM was a networking concept that promised easily billable usage by customers.

The Internet, using a communications technology Nortel declined to embrace, was coming together with the industry and enthusiasm of individual users. It was a decentralized "passive" network. Nobody owned it. There was nobody ultimately in charge to whom a salesman could sell something in the way that Nortel was trying to push ATM as the world's networking solution. While universities had played a large role in developing the Internet, the enthusiasm of individuals, signing up for accounts with service providers, was fuelling its growth. And as the Internet grew, the institutions, governments, and corporations that made up Nortel's private network customers were being forced to respond, both to the information demands of those individuals and to the commercial opportunities they represented.

ATM made sense in a world that wanted to use a product like VISIT, but the world wasn't clamouring for VISIT. Internet users generally were trying to get by with slow modems running on copper phone wires, which made real-time simultaneous voice and video laughably impossible. But that didn't matter, because the Internet's growth, except for chat rooms in which people typed each other messages, was not based on real-time communication between two or more circuit-switched parties. People sent and retrieved e-mail, participated in newsgroups, downloaded files, and browsed Web pages. They were thrilled with what the Internet could do already and were largely patient with its teething pains. The whole thing was a bit of a technocultural adventure. Browsers crashed, e-mail attachments arrived corrupted, and viruses destroyed their hard drives, but the average Net user put up with quality-of-service standards they would never tolerate from the phone company in placing and receiving calls. Besides, the bugs were getting worked out. And with the graphic interface of the World Wide Web coming to the fore, there was no compelling reason to abandon it for something one networking company was insisting represented the real future. As the technology evolved, the Internet would close in on delivering the real-time services of voice and video.

Nortel was determined to press on with a networking vision that could only have been hatched by a phone company. In 1993, Nortel's first full year under Jean Monty, the company dramatically articulated its vision of where the networking business was headed by creating a new business unit called Multimedia Communications Systems (MCS). It had begun developing a family of ATM and enterprise switching systems, called Magellan, for broadband multimedia networks that were enterprise-wide, community, residential, and carrier-backbone in scope. The unit was also given the development of

DPN-100 data networking equipment and Meridian PBXs, among other things, to oversee.

Nortel's networking strategy was based on three technologies: high-speed fibre-optic transmission, ATM switching, and wireless communications. By 1994, Nortel was in overdrive. It claimed to have set up the largest number of ATM enterprise networks in the world, which, in the face of the exploding Internet, was a bit like claiming to have built the most cars with Wankel rotary engines. It hired celebrated thinkers James Burke, Douglas Coupland and John Polanyi, among others, to contribute essays to its 1994 annual report, which brashly celebrated the "World of Networks" Nortel was creating, just as a lot of other uncelebrated thinkers were jumping into the business of creating the software, Ethernet hubs, and routers of IP-based networks.

Nortel's vision, as elucidated in its 1994 annual report, was a mellifluous marvel. "We see a world of dynamically evolving networks, weaving paths across the globe, delivering high-value services in different ways. Networks that advertise, announce, and automate; clarify, classify, and co-ordinate; teach, televise, and translate. Networks that offer conversations, continuing education, a credit check, or a cross-examination. Networks that permit data processing, desktop publishing, or directory assistance; an electronic funds transfer or an emergency broadcast; a press conference or a public opinion poll. Networks for people at home, at work, and on the move—empowering education, employment and entertainment opportunities as we become an information-based society."

Nortel asserted that its technologies were "vastly increasing the value of networked computers. This is particularly evident in enterprise networks, which serve the burgeoning knowledge-sharing that characterizes the global networking of business, its customers, and its suppliers. Enterprise networks transfer voice, data, and images—the raw ingredients of knowledge—on a worldwide scale through a hierarchy of local area networks, metropolitan area networks, and wide area networks. These networks are the most advanced in existence today."

Nortel was *describing the Internet* in its essential concept, its current state, and its imminent fluorescence, while denying its very existence in favour of Nortel's alternative reality. "We are working closely with our customers to evolve these sometimes different networks into an 'infostructure' in which the boundaries between networks will essentially become seamless to the end user," Nortel promised. "This infostructure will carry any type of communications—voice, data, or full-motion video—anywhere, at very high speed. We will achieve this goal in evolutionary steps using revolutionary technologies that are available today—technologies like wireless, fiber optics, ATM switching and SONET/SDH standards."

The *infostructure?* Nortel achieved the pinnacle of hubris when it coughed up that stillborn concept. It was ATM versus IP taken to an absurd extreme. And by 1994, when Nortel came up with *infostructure* as the inelegant label for its anti-Internet, there was no longer any reasonable excuse for Nortel having missed the boat entirely on the greatest communications revolution of the 20th century.

The *infostructure* sounded like a bad idea that had escaped from Disney's Epcot Center aboard a wayward monorail. Nortel's 1994 vision ranks as one of the most wrongheaded in the history of technology. It radiates obstinacy, refusing to even acknowledge the Internet by name, although the insistence that this *infostructure* was going to be built "using revolutionary technologies that are available today" was a clear signal that Nortel didn't think the evolving IP world was worth the attention of the company or its customers. Nortel was just going to go out and build a far better global network. In a way, this was a throwback to Nortel's experience with X.25 in the late 1970s and 1980s. By its own admission, it had helped make X.25 a broadly accepted standard by building its data switching products around it. Whatever you gave the customer was what the customer had to work with. The persistent belief in ATM recalled the years when the phone company got to decide how everybody communicated. But it defied a prime directive Nortel itself had spelled out back in the mid-1980s in a customer service philosophy it called the "five C's"—control, cost-effectiveness, congeniality, continuity, and compatibility. Under "control," Nortel declared: "An organization—not its supplier—must be able to determine the optimum use and configuration of its information management system." But because the *infostructure* would be so superior to that other I-thingie, Nortel didn't have to pay any attention to it—except when explaining to customers the superiority of ATM.

Which, as people now know, if they didn't already know it then, was a bit of an oversight. It was as if Nortel had been lovingly watering and weeding its patch of carrots, only to wake up one morning to find that a giant beanstalk called the Internet had sprouted overnight in the yard—and that the communications networking customer base was lined up around the block, its members climbing the beanstalk as fast as they could find handholds.

Yes, in many ways, ATM was much better than TCP/IP. But ATM's main weakness was that Nortel was fighting a losing battle in trying to make it migrate from the telephone world into the enterprise networking world, because IP was already there, running on Ethernet-linked PCs. The demonstration of VISIT on a Mac IIci sadly foreshadowed the coming showdown between ATM and IP. In a rational comparison between graphic-based operating systems, the Mac OS beat Windows hands down. But that didn't prevent Windows from commanding a PC market share of more than 90 percent. A dominant technology, even an arguably inferior one, is very difficult to displace.

Networked customers had time, money, and expertise invested in their existing PC-based LANs, which were overwhelmingly configured with Ethernet technology, which in turn used IP protocols. With a standard speed of just 10 mbps, Ethernet could not compete with ATM in bandwidth, but Ethernet was getting increasingly faster, achieving 100 mbps, 1 gpbs, and 10 gbps. It did not make overwhelming sense to many network managers to scrap their existing networks and start over with ATM. With Ethernet already in place, managers could grow with it, realizing incremental improvements, without committing to a far more expensive cut-over to something entirely different. And that kept them rooted in IP at the same time.

ATM versus IP had all the hallmarks of the mind-numbing tech-geek debate over VHS versus Betamax in the videotape world. Ultimately, however, one network standard was not going to obliterate the other, and there would be room in the new communications environment for both. But if Nortel really wanted to build a new world of networks, it had to stop flogging the ATM horse exclusively and get with the IP program.

Nortel had come tantalizingly close to getting all the pieces of the new communications order lined up in its favour. It had world-class optical networking. It had ATM, which was still an important technology. It had wireless communications. It had digital switching for the traditional phone system. It just didn't have this IP stuff. And not only did it not have it, it had shown no inclination of wanting to get it, preferring instead to try to pile-drive its love of ATM into the market instead of realizing that IP was developing a tenacious grip on PC networking, and that it was fast becoming the dominant basis for linking one network to another, via—of all things—the telephone networks Nortel had so ably developed.

In 1995, a series of horrifying events came to pass for Nortel's strategic plan. Netscape went public on NASDAQ, igniting the Internet IPO firestorm. It may have all been one big bubble, but the Internet investment mania meant that billions of dollars of capital were handed over to tech upstarts that were committed to exploiting and refining the IP-based Internet. Microsoft released Windows 95 (and with it, the Explorer browser), a big leap forward from Windows 3.X in bringing a serviceable graphics operating system to the majority of PCs. The dominant PC operating system had been significantly improved and had buttressed the IP basis of networking communications.

Ironically, the first identifiably Internet-related product from Nortel, the Rapport Dialup Switch, was introduced in 1995 to help the phone companies cope with the overwhelming amounts of data traffic that Internet users were pouring onto the telephone network. "Growth of functional networks such as the Internet has created a need for networking solutions that can help people roam information highways with greater ease," Nortel explained in the 1995 annual report in discussing the Rapport switch.

There. It had finally said it. The Internet. Still, the Internet was apparently just one of an unspecified number of "functional networks," one information highway among many, not the communications behemoth that was pounding Nortel's business plan to flinders. But at least the thing had been acknowledged to exist. And the *infostructure,* that magnificently wrongheaded telecommunications paradise, was banished from the Nortel vocabulary. Having acknowledged that the Internet might be something to contend with, Nortel now had to figure out how to capitalize on it. Nortel had squandered several precious years hustling exclusively its ATM dream, watching its switching product sales flatline, while agile upstarts brought to market the IP routers and Ethernet-based enterprise networks that were actually wiring together a new global communications order.

Nortel's 1996 annual report, released in early 1997 as John Roth prepared to take command of the company, is an intriguing artifact, revealing how the company articulated its strengths and opportunities for investors and customers alike around the first anniversary of the passage of the Telecom Act. The document is laden with references to the firm's wireless capabilities and successes, reflecting in part the background of the new boss. Even though the document opens with a lengthy spiel about Nortel's networking know-how, with an unprecedented amount of attention paid to the Internet, the network it is talking about is still one largely rooted in the established telecommunications world.

Nortel's favourite buzzwords in the report were "digital," "wireless," and "network." The company was striving heroically to distance itself from its past, from its reputation as a supplier of powerful telephone switches to phone company central offices and corporate environments. "We're still a leader in traditional digital switching solutions," read the copy in an imaginary conversation between a Nortel rep and a customer. "We've simply added new digital solutions to meet the needs of the day. We no longer think in terms of switching; *we think networks.*"

Yes, but the mother of all networks, the Internet, was taking shape around Nortel, and Nortel was in danger of walling itself in, cut off from the high-growth opportunities. While Nortel wasn't about to admit as much in its annual report, the company had a huge hole in its skill set if it intended to live up to its claim *"We're here to stay*—building networks for enterprises, telephone companies, wireless network operators, and alternate carriers."

By now, Nortel was well aware of the impact of the Internet on carrier traffic and demands for new network infrastructure, which it was only too happy to provide. Nortel had also created a separate company, Entrust Technologies Inc., to address on-line security issues for enterprise customers (in December 1996) and had sold 27 percent of its stake with a public share offering at year-end. But like so many technology companies, Nortel had not anticipated the sheer scale of the coming change in the communications sector and the speed with which it was unfolding. Even considering the move to digital switching, the telecommunications business had evolved at a fairly leisurely pace, technology-wise, until the Internet and the Telecom Act unleashed a torrent of new technologies, many of them developed by completely new companies. One of the other "C's" in Nortel's 1985 customer-service philosophy, "continuity," prescribed that the customer wouldn't be stuck with orphaned technology. Nortel intended for its product lines to evolve, and for customers to be able to adapt and upgrade without scrapping what they already owned. The IP world was delivering Nortel a rude dose of near-obsolescence in its own marketing and product lines.

Soon after the passage of the Telecom Act, it became clear that IP was destined to become the networking standard of the information revolution, serving as the communications basis for all sorts of network devices, including wireless tools such as cell phones, personal digital assistants, and laptop computers. Most threatening to a company like Nortel, the first steps had already been taken to adapt IP to the task of moving voice traffic through packet-based computer networks. This meant that the old circuit-switched conversation, enabled and billed by the phone company, could migrate into the world of desktop computers. The first software program employing Voice over IP (VoIP) technology had appeared in 1995. In August 1998, a California Internet service provider, A+Net, began offering IP-based telephony to its customers on an introductory one-cent-a-minute basis.

"It's absolutely true that Internet telephony is poised to become a potential competitor to traditional telephone service," the Commerce Department's Larry Irving observed at the Voice on the Net (VON) Conference in 1998. While acknowledging that the $157 million expected to be generated by Internet telephony in 1998 was only two-tenths of a percent of the $55 billion raked in by the carriers on the telephone network, he nonetheless cited the prediction that one-third to one-half of all voice communications would be carried over the Internet early in the next century, noting that long-distance giants like AT&T, British Telecom, and Deutsche Telekom had begun experimenting with VoIP.

The world wasn't quite ready for VoIP. There were many technical hurdles still to be cleared, as well as sound quality issues, and a considerable resistance from corporations to move their voice traffic from the highly reliable telephone network onto their own internal data networks, which had a tendency to regularly go down. A 1998 survey of readers of the U.S. publication *Network Computing*, which was favourite reading of corporate network managers, found that less than 1 percent were employing VoIP and only 13.5 percent were either evaluating equipment or participating in field trials. But the next survey, in 1999, revealed that 61 percent of readers intended to deploy VoIP in the next 12 months. (Another 16 percent had plans to deploy the alternate voice packet technologies known as Voice over ATM and Voice over Frame Relay.) As publisher Fritz Nelson commented in the October 18, 1999, issue, "Either you were lying last year, or there's change afoot."

The switches, routers, hubs, software, hardware, wireless gear, and transmission lines were all going to answer to the demands of computer-based packet-switched communication networks. Whether or not the world rapidly embraced something like IP telephony, there was no denying the fact that the coming explosion in communications as a high-growth, high-margin commercial opportunity was going to be driven by the Internet and the underlying expertise in IP-based packet-switched networking.

And as businesses woke up to the commercial potential of the Net, the computer networking crowd was poised to hijack the emerging e-commerce phenomenon right out from under the telephone types like Nortel. Call centres, which were at the heart of customer relationship management (CRM), were no longer going to be glorified warehouses with rows of desks and telephone handsets. The new communications order would integrate a multitude of communications channels—traditional telephone, e-mail, the Web—on a computer screen in front of the CRM agent and link it all to the "back office" programs that tracked inventory, accounting, and customer accounts. The old suite of services offered by a telecom supplier like Nortel wasn't going to cut it in this new environment.

To hear Nortel tell it in its 1996 annual report, the Internet was suddenly a slam dunk for any enterprise that bought its products. "We've removed Internet traffic congestion and security concerns from the equation," it claimed. "Nortel offers a full Internet/intranet solution set that won't get bogged down, and it's a solution that will grow with you. In a nutshell, we take fear out of conducting business on the Web. The result is better services for both you and your customers."

Promising a "full solution" to the Internet was a brave assertion. The fact was, the Internet was evolving so quickly that no single company could keep up with it. Its potential and its challenges were constantly being redefined, and at this point Nortel was a long way from drawing an accurate bead on this moving target.

"Our R&D people are thriving in this new environment," gushed the annual report. "They're out in the trenches with our customers, learning what they really need and finding ways to deliver it. Everything is changing—not just technology, but the marketplace and entire ways of doing business." There was a tinge of desperation in this assertion, a tacit admission that things were moving so quickly that Nortel didn't yet have all the answers, and that it had stopped hyping ATM and was now listening to what customers actually wanted to do with IP. Nortel was asking customers to trust its track record as a solutions provider to come up with the proper solutions for them. The main thrust of its marketing message was that Nortel was big, had been around a long time, and thus wasn't going to disappear in the middle of the night, had a lot of experience in a lot of international markets with a lot of communications technologies, and could be trusted to stay abreast of technological change.

Out in the trenches, they were certainly learning. Soon they would learn that Nortel did some things exceptionally well, but there were a lot of other things in which the company was way behind the learning curve, or not even on the curve, and that if the company was serious about being a total networking solutions provider, it was going to have to adapt far more rapidly than it had to date. This wasn't unique to Nortel. All networking businesses were going through the same process of coming to terms with the transformative rise of the Internet and the plethora of opportunities unleashed by the Telecom Act. They would have to make some fairly bold decisions about the directions they would choose, and at the same time would be praying that they had already done the necessary R&D to offer the technology that carriers and individual enterprises needed at that moment. And if they hadn't, they would have to figure out how to get it.

"A World of Networks is Nortel's vision for the global communications environment: networks serving many different customers, operated by many different entities, and carrying many different kinds of traffic—voice, video, and data—for information, communication, entertainment, education, and commerce." That was a fairly ambitious pledge to make in early 1997. The next four years would witness an extraordinary effort from Nortel to make good on the promise.

5

The World According to GAAP

Dilbert was a doodle long before he had a name. He was a composite of my co-workers at Crocker Bank and Pacific Bell. I worked with a lot of technical people and noted that many of them had potato-shaped bodies and glasses.

—cartoonist Scott Adams

In the mid-1970s, Henry Dortmans, fresh out of university, was working at Bell Canada in Toronto when he crossed paths with an operator services manager for Bell in London, Ontario, named Clarence Chandran. They would meet regularly on the road, and their own roads were headed in different directions. Dortmans would become one of the country's leading telecommunications consultants, a principal in Angus TeleManagement in Ajax, Ontario. Clarence Chandran would end up as the heir apparent to John Roth at Nortel in the late 1990s. Chandran's ascent amazed Dortmans. "I never would have guessed, twenty-five years ago, that he would end up at the top of Nortel."

It's a remarkably consistent theme in the careers of the seniormost people in the Nortel story. Time and again, people have expressed surprise that the people they knew decades earlier—John Roth, Frank Dunn, Clarence Chandran—could ever end up running a company with tens of billions of American dollars in annual revenues. Only Chandran actually came up short, and Dunn only got the job when Roth required a successor other than Chandran. But it was Roth who started this unusual chain of successions, and Roth whose performance continues to define the Nortel investors have been left to lament.

John Andrew Roth was not a Central Casting example of a bold tech company CEO in the 1990s. He didn't, for example, have the testosterone overdrive of Oracle's Larry Ellison, who duelled in the world's greatest ocean races in his custom eighty-foot yacht *Sayanora*—and in 2000 agreed to bankroll the San Francisco Yacht Club's 2002–03 America's Cup challenge—when Ellison wasn't taking jabs at software rival Bill Gates. Nor was Roth an über-geek like Gates, a hands-on inventor who played a major role in crafting the first BASIC computer language for microcomputers while still at Harvard in the mid-1970s. And when Gates got bored with being the world's richest man in the late 1990s, he was capable of going back to writing code at Microsoft for fun. While Roth joined Northern Electric as a design engineer in 1969, he never contributed his name to a single patent among the thousands filed by the company. As a corporate lifer, his strengths were in managing, and he has been widely regarded for boosting the importance of R&D and for shaking up an internal creative culture that moved at the speed of molasses, producing too few marketable products. When he finally did contribute something truly novel to the company, however, it was making Nortel grow through a spree of acquisitions that were supposed to fill the gaps in its technology tool kit.

Fifty-three years old when he assumed command of Northern Telecom in 1997, Roth bore a passing resemblance to the Cigarette Smoking Man played by Canadian actor William B. Davis in the X-Files. An approving profile of Roth in *BusinessWeek* on October 29, 1999, described him thus: "Partial to funereal dark suits and soft-spoken enough to be mistaken for a modest librarian, he hardly looks the part of an Internet swashbuckler." When Roth wasn't at work, shaping a networking supercompany, he unwound at his fifty-acre hobby farm in Orangeville, Ontario, making stained glass and tooling around on his tractor. But *BusinessWeek* was quick to provide him with Ellisonesque cachet, pointing out his love of fast cars (which included a 1966 Jaguar, a 1967 Corvette, and a new Chrysler Prowler) and that he liked to rip down a local speedway for fun at 160 mph. He even took forty Nortel customers out to Pennsylvania's Pocono Speedway in the fall of 1998 so that they could put the pedal to the metal, as Roth was doing at Nortel. Whatever his charisma, it steadily won over the business press in both Canada and the United States. Roth was the hard-driving visionary who was retooling the sluggish corporate culture of Nortel and finally moving the company onto the information superhighway at breakneck speed.

Roth had first breached the senior ranks of Nortel management in 1978, when he became an officer of the company as vice-president of manufacturing operations, a newly created post. In 1981, he shifted over to the research arm, becoming executive vice-president of Bell-Northern Research Ltd. in Ottawa and chairman of the board of BNR Inc., its Palo Alto unit. In 1982, the forty-year-old Roth was made president of Bell-Northern Research and remained in command through some of its greatest years, when Northern Telecom was conquering the United States and foreign markets with a series of trail-blazing digital switches, and when R&D spending grew handsomely. (This growth was abetted by the creation of a separate entity which gathered money from investors and issued them tax receipts under the Canadian government's scientific research incentive program.) Roth left BNR in 1986 to become an executive vice-president responsible for product line management, and in 1991 he was named president of Northern's wireless systems division.

Under Roth, wireless networks became the company's hottest product sector as traditional switching sales began to recede into single-digit percentage growth. He was promoted to an executive vice-presidency in 1993 as he became president of Nortel North America, and during his tenure, wireless revenues, driven by strong consumer demand in the United States, continued to climb. In 1994, wireless revenues were $893 million, or 10 percent of Northern's total sales. They increased 74 percent in 1995, to $1.55 billion, or 15 percent of sales, and leapt another 60 percent in 1996, to $2.49 billion, or 19 percent of sales. During these same years, Canada continued to recede in importance as a place of business for Nortel when measured on percentage of sales. Although the company's headquarters were in Canada and most of its shareholders (including Bell Canada Enterprises) were located there, in 1996 customer revenues from Canada were just 10 percent of sales. On July 1, 1995, Roth was named the company's chief operating officer as well as president of Nortel North America, thus steepening his learning curve as he prepared to assume control from Monty. A directorship with Nortel came in April 1996; in July 1996 he relinquished the North American presidency for an executive vice-presidency while continuing as chief operating officer.

For all the praise Roth would receive in the coming years, none of his achievements, alleged and otherwise, would have been possible without the overhaul that took place under Monty's command. As a ranking senior executive in those years, Roth certainly deserves some of the credit, but Monty was the one who set the agenda. Shareholders (except the ones suing the company in New York) were mollified, customers were assured that their needs would be met, especially when it came to switching software, and Monty went about reshaping the company, selling off chunks that were under-utilized, under-performing, or didn't fit the mix of the new priority on networking.

Data systems cried out for exploitation because other long-standing sources of revenue for Northern were withering or no longer capable of providing double-digit growth with high margins. Sales of software for traditional switching products experienced an actual decline in revenues in 1996. Tech companies with a commitment to R&D investment need to avoid "commoditization," the process by which products lose their patentable uniqueness and profit margins begin to fall as competitors undercut the pricing of the once-dominant suppliers. Cutting-edge products, protected by patents and unmatched by rival operations, come with high profit margins and, with technologies being rapidly and widely adopted, tremendous year-over-year growth in sales. The recipe for success in the networking business is basic: come up with new things that everyone wants before anyone else does. Reap high margins and explosive revenue increases. And because networking is a field of interdependence, offer top-flight products and services in as many product areas and customer groups as possible: wireless, broadband, switching, voice and data; corporate environments, local and long-distance telecom carriers, wireless networks, call centre operators.

Under Monty, Nortel made several small acquisitions to increase its presence, in particular in data. But as Roth assumed control in 1997, Nortel was facing the profound sea change in the networking world created by the Internet boom and deregulation in the United States—the market that produced more than half the company's revenues. Nortel revenues increased from $12.8 to $15.4 billion in 1997, Roth's first year; profits also rose, from $619 to $812 million. Earnings per common share, which had been 92 cents in 1995, were $1.56 for 1997. Investors eagerly came aboard as the general bull market and enthusiasm for dot-com and networking companies gathered steam. Beginning the year at $85 in Toronto, Nortel was trading above $150 in October before finishing the year at $127.15. The stock was split two-for-one on January 12, 1998. In just two months, the stock appreciated about 50 percent. Nortel was on its way to replacing bank stocks as the favourite investment of Canadians. And as the market surged into Nortel, investors were providing John Roth with a war chest to go shopping for synergies.

Few investors probably suspected—although many fearful companies did—that the fate of the nineties bull market might lie in the hands not of the celebrated dollarcrat Alan Greenspan, but of a bunch of bean counters far from the New Economy limelight. They were the members of the Financial Accounting Standards Board (FASB), an independent, private, nonprofit organization charged with setting the rules known as Generally Accepted Accounting Principles (GAAP) used in the grand game of reporting corporate results for public companies in the United States.

In a boom in which many investors paid little attention to fiscal intricacies of stocks—and sometimes paid no attention at all, either through indifference, ignorance, or having left it to mutual fund managers to do their picking for them—the FASB's power was easily overlooked. In part, this was because this power wasn't exercised in time to have the effect it well could have had: of deflating much of the energy of that bull market, even avoiding the runaway valuations in the Internet economy. Analyst cheerleaders liked to crow about the new era of profitability and technological convergence that were going to change our lives as they touted the improbable stock prices of the decade. In truth, those bubble valuations owed a profound debt to the persistent distortions of profitability made possible by the fun-house mirror known as Opinion 16.

The FASB had been worried about Opinion 16 for quite a while. "The opinion"—accountant-speak for a regulation—had been handed down to the FASB by its standards predecessor, the Accounting Principles Board (APB) of the American Institute of Certified Public Accountants, which drew it up in 1970. Opinion 16 was dragged out for inspection later in the same decade, after the FASB was created in 1973, but nothing came of this early probing. It was returned to the shelf, where it awaited exploitation in the dot-com revolution. And by the time the FASB and concerned financial professionals saw what fresh hell was being shaped with it, they could not act quickly enough to prevent the consequences. They were impeded not only by their own cautious processes, but by rearguard actions, fought through members of Congress and New Economy businesses that had exploited Opinion 16 to spectacular self-benefit.

It all had to do with how corporate takeovers were reported in financial statements. The customary strategy was to use the purchase method, in which one company simply bought another and acquired all its assets and liabilities. The alternative, which was spelled out in Opinion 16, was to use pooling of interest, in which the assets and liabilities of purchaser and purchasee were melded at historic costs rather than present value.

The difference sounds subtle, but there were important distinctions. With the purchase method, the company doing the purchasing had to contend with a critical consequence of most takeovers: the price paid is usually in excess of the net asset (book) value of the acquisition. The difference between the purchase price and the book value is known as goodwill. It's a premium that theoretically reflects all sorts of intangibles worth owning such as market share, the costs incurred in building asset value, customer satisfaction, reputation, the wisdom of management, and potential future earnings. These are all valuable things to possess, and that being the case, accounting standards demanded that this goodwill be dealt with in financial statements. Accounting, as well as nature, abhors a vacuum. Goodwill might be intangible, but it was not ethereal. If you paid ten dollars for something, you could not just put down three dollars for it in your list of assets.

Thus, under the purchase method, as spelled out by the APB in Opinion 17, goodwill had to be reported not only as a kind of asset, but as a "wasting" one and be written off over time like any other depreciating possession. If a company bought another firm for $200 million, and its book value was $140 million, then the $60 million of goodwill had to be steadily amortized over a reasonable period of time, although Opinion 17 permitted a period as long as 40 years. And as anyone who has ever read a financial statement knows, amortization shows up as a charge against revenues. A lot of intangible goodwill can have a tangible effect on earnings per share—the measure of corporate performance so dear to analysts and investors, and to corporate executives whose bonuses are based on them.

In the Internet economy, the purchase method was a big headache. Investors were bidding up shares of startups based on their purported phenomenal future earnings power. The massive discounting of future dividends was creating share values that hadn't the slightest relationship to the company's book value. These startups had little in the way of traditional assets: they were often still in the R&D stage; even the startups that were actually making and marketing something might not have production facilities, having chosen to outsource the responsibility. Bulky assets like real estate, raw materials, or machinery were Old Economy encumbrances. The New Economy was about ideas, innovation, and how many nights your employees were willing to work without sleep to write killer code—in other words, intangibles.

The New Economy was also about making a personal fortune on your own terms, about going solo to develop a new product rather than slaving away for some monolithic enterprise. Straight out of graduate school Marc Andreesson co-founded Netscape rather than go to work for an established software giant. He became an almost instant paper multimegamillionaire, thanks to the enthusiasm of NASDAQ investors. As such startups began to produce results (or at least results that appeared promising), they became highly desirable to larger companies, some of them old-timers like Nortel—others former startups themselves like Cisco. These larger companies realized that technology was evolving so quickly that it was simpler to buy a lot of it, entire companies at a time, rather than spend years trying to develop it themselves. The result was an economy based on startups, rapid stock appreciation, and acquisitions that often had very little in the way of conventional assets.

Let us imagine that in the late 1990s the delirious enthusiasm of investors propelled the market capitalization of an immensely desirable enterprise to $2 billion. To beat competitors to purchasing it, you had to pay $3 billion. You now had a bit of an accounting problem if the acquired company's identifiable assets amounted to only $100 million. Under the purchase method, you were left facing $2.9 billion in goodwill, which had to be amortized over a relatively short period, because in the go-go tech world, the latest breakthrough router switch or revolutionary software application was going to be on the trash heap in a couple of years. So you had to start writing down the goodwill at a brisk clip—say three to five years—and that had a punishing impact on your bottom line, because your own pre-purchase profitability might not have been all that spectacular—which was why you were so keen to buy this enterprise in the first place. Goodwill write-downs could destroy any hope of reporting anything in the way of positive earnings. Your share value would be hopelessly depressed (or, as critics would point out, hopelessly accurate), and without net earnings, you would have a hard time justifying dividend payments. Valued employees would view their stock options as worthless and go to work elsewhere. Your brilliant quest for synergy and profitability would melt before your eyes.

Lucky for you, there was another way to do this deal: pooling.

The assets of the purchaser and purchasee were thrown together in one big pile in the middle of the boardroom floor, in what was in effect a merger. All the shares in the company being taken over were swapped for an agreed equivalent in shares of the company doing the swallowing. In the case of your aggressively visionary takeover, you agree to provide the original shareholders two of your shares for every three of theirs, based on an agreed price for the enterprise and the market price of your own shares on a date just before the closing of the deal. This kind of swap was going to create another New Economy sub-industry: shareholder class-action lawsuits over the valuations of the exchanged shares. But we'll get to that later.

Because nothing had been literally purchased by the purchaser, there was no reason to worry about goodwill. At all. You could pay $3 billion for a company worth $100 million in book value by using shares from the company treasury and never have to account for the $2.9 billion difference. It was as if it had never been spent, which defenders of this practice would agree with. After all, you had used stock, not actual cash. Mind you, the individual shareholder's equity had just been diluted a little or a lot, but that was another problem altogether. So long as the acquisition contributed to revenues—either actual ones or the ones to come in the future that the market so adored—the share dilution problem might never crop up.

It should have been hard to ignore the possibility that it would crop up, particularly when the purchaser was swapping its sky-high shares for the sky-high shares in a takeover target, which raised the goodwill even higher. But from a number-crunching point of view, this was a whole lot better than seeing the bottom line crushed by intangibles that stuffy old accounting processes demanded be charged against earnings if the traditional purchase method were used.

And there were bonus benefits once the company doing the acquiring got to add the acquired company's precious assets to its own. Let's say these assets included $30 million in real estate. In four years, this property might be sold for $70 million. The company got to record a one-time profit of $40 million, without ever having to account for the fact that, to get that property, it had paid $1 billion over book value for the company that owned it. And over the ensuing four years, the acquired company might have become all but valueless. Better yet, the entire acquired company could be sold at some future date. The original $1 billion purchase was only on the books at net asset value of $100 million. So if the company managed to get $400 million for it, it was able to report the sale as a $300 million profit—not a $600 million loss on the original acquisition.

You don't need to be a CPA to recognize how sublimely ridiculous this kind of accounting was. According to FASB chairman Edmund L. Jenkins in his testimony on May 4, 2000, before the federal government's wonderfully incongruous Subcommittee on Finance and Hazardous Materials of the Committee on Commerce, the failure to properly recognize goodwill under the pooling method meant that "the future earnings of the newly combined company are artificially inflated." One commentator has more bluntly called the result "earnings on steroids." Nevertheless, it actually served as the fiscal foundation for much of the New Economy.

Pooling was never intended to be a clever bookkeeping alternative to the purchase method. It was expected that pooling would serve (as the title of Opinion 16 implies) "business combinations," in which the companies were of roughly equal size and the idea of one of them actually buying the other was impractical or unreasonable. Indeed, pooling has been used in some of the best-known mergers of recent years, including Daimler and Chrysler, Bell Atlantic and GTE, Citicorp and Travellers, Exxon and Mobil, and SBC and Ameritech.

As the New Economy gathered steam, it became evident that pooling was an extremely handy bookkeeping strategy that perfectly suited the highly speculative share valuations of the companies involved. When America Online acquired Netscape in 1998, it wisely chose the pooling method to avoid having to account for $9 billion in goodwill. Pooling legitimized the market's extreme valuations of tech companies by allowing shares to be used as money, without companies ever having to account for the expense of using them that way. Presto: one minute shares are money so that something can be purchased, and the next minute, they're not. And it also had a debilitating effect on the quality of stock analysis.

This was because pooling wasn't for everybody. Under U.S.

GAAP, the two companies involved had to meet all twelve of the criteria laid down under Opinion 16, and if they couldn't, they had to use the purchase method. That set up an accounting universe of pooling haves and have-nots: on the one hand, firms that could go on an acquisition spree without ever having to account for goodwill; on the other hand, firms that basically had to punch themselves in the head over and over again with amortization charges after they made a purchase. Analysts attempting to compare the performances of two companies in the same industry, one using pooling and the other using the purchase method, faced incompatible bottom lines. There was no fair way to compare the earnings per share of these companies if one was amortizing goodwill and the other wasn't.

Well, it turned out there was a way: ignore amortization altogether to level the playing field. After all, what was amortization but some mouldy accounting concept? It's not like you balance your chequebook by pencilling in a charge for the depreciation of your car. Resolving the pooling-or-purchase method dilemma in revenue statements helped grease a slippery slope in financial reporting. The quality of the numbers coming from companies was unquestionably going downhill.

Analysts were enablers in the degradation of corporate reporting. Companies found analysts either eager to promote the use of funny numbers or at least willing to go along with the crowd. Whichever way it came about, the credibility of earnings figures became seriously undermined just when their infallibility was most demanded: in the midst of a raging bull market.

In the 1990s, companies began to find it useful to ignore altogether all sorts of annoying charges against revenues. They effectively began to keep two sets of books. One set adhered to the accounting standards and logged all the charges. While these were faithfully released to shareholders, companies had another set of books to show off. The earnings figures they produced went by a variety of labels. "Pro forma" was a popular term, which, being Latin, sounded serious. It most commonly cropped up as earnings before interest, taxes, depreciation, and amortization, better known by the acronym EBITDA. A more contemptuous term was EBS earnings—"everything but the bad stuff."

Pooling became an insidious factor in the perceived profitability of tech companies. For it wasn't just the companies actually using pooling that benefited from it: analysts extended honorary pooling status to companies using the purchase method by basically throwing away the amortization charges (and often a lot of other charges) in the quest for measuring apples against apples. Not that the analysts were solely to blame. Companies were more than willing to issue quarterly results and guidance in every format imaginable. Just like Burger King, companies were happy for analysts and investors to Have It Your Way. If they didn't want amortization, they could just hold the goodwill pickle.

For analysts, companies, and investors, it sounded like a win-win situation. Everybody looked more profitable. True costs of acquisitions either weren't being reported in pooling or were being de facto ignored in analysis of purchase-method companies that employed EBITDA, pro forma, or just tossed away amortization of goodwill as if it had never happened and no one should worry about it. And the more charges against revenues you scrapped in an effort to make a "fair" valuation, the more justified the bubbly share prices seemed. These alternate or supplementary accounting methods could in no way replace GAAP, and public companies were supposed to make clear the unofficial nature of the pro forma results. But companies, analysts, and investors much preferred the customized numbers. They paid about as much attention to GAAP as many smokers do to health warnings on cigarette packs.

It didn't take long for the FASB to start worrying about pooling. The New Economy revolution had scarcely started when the board put pooling on its to-do list in 1996 and created a business combinations task force. Its first public meeting was held in February 1997, and that June it published a special report that looked at the project's scope, direction, and content. It invited comment and got a grand total of fifty-four letters. Considering the thousands of e-mails the Securities and Exchange Commission would shortly receive regarding its new fair disclosure initiative, it is evident that accounting of business combinations was scarcely registering in the minds of average investors. Yet it was probably the single most important issue facing the investment community as the tech boom gathered momentum. Everything would have turned out very differently had the FASB been in a position to move immediately on reforms.

The FASB didn't like pooling and wanted to get rid of it altogether. However, doing so would have completely undermined the essence of the New Economy. Investors were becoming excited about stocks in companies whose earnings potential often seemed as distant as a manned Mars mission. Pooling was justifying those inflated prices when measured by old standards like dividend/price and price/earnings ratios. Companies that employed pooling were using stock with inflated prices to buy companies with inflated stock prices of their own, without ever having to record the cost of the purchase above and beyond net asset value. At the same time, companies that employed the purchase method were using the incompatibility of pooling and purchase-method accounting as a reason or excuse to ignore amortization and, while we're at it, interest, depreciation, and taxes, in showing off their earnings power with pro forma type reportage. Kick away the pooling method support, and the New Economy dropped like a circus tent.

It's easy to understand why there was widespread investor disinterest in reforming the accounting rules for business combinations, no matter how much it was argued that shareholders would be the ultimate beneficiaries as accounting "transparency" was improved. With pooling alive and well, stock values could continue to run riot. But the FASB's plans certainly raised concerns among companies that had based their business plan on pooling, and this concern inevitably found its way to Washington. By 1998, the FASB was facing a lot of heat over its plans to replace Opinions 16 and 17 with a whole new set of regulations, because by 1998, the tech sector had begun to throw its weight around with political campaign contributions.

In 1990, companies and employees in the computer and Internet sector contributed just $1.26 million to Republicans and Democrats, leaving them fifty-fifth in sector rankings. By 1999, contributions were up to $9.48 million and the sector had climbed to twenty-fifth. In 2000, the sector's contributions went supernova, totalling $39.98 million and moving the computer and Internet companies to seventh overall. The telecom services and equipment sector had undergone a similar political awakening. In 1990, the sector sent a paltry $762,747 to the Republicans and Democrats, giving it an industry ranking of 64. By 1998, the cash contribution was up to $5.3 million and the ranking to 45th. Like the computer and Internet sector, 2000 was the breakthrough year: donations reached $18.29 million and the ranking went to twenty-first.

These companies wanted a lot of things out of Washington, but what a lot of them especially wanted was for the FASB to give up its quest to get rid of pooling. In 1998, there was talk that the FASB might not have the stamina or muscle to push ahead with its replacement of Opinions 16 and 17, but as it turns out, it did—albeit at a cautiously measured pace. An exposure draft was released on the proposed changes in September 1999, and in February 2000 the FASB held public consultation meetings in San Francisco and New York. The anti-pooling juggernaut appeared unstoppable, although there was considerable resistance from its greatest beneficiaries: tech companies that employed it, and law firms and investment banks that profited from the merger binge. The increasing inevitability of the approaching loss of the pooling strategy doubtless cranked up the urgency to complete as many such deals as possible before the accounting rules were rewritten.

Opinions 16 and 17 were central to Nortel's quest to become the leading global networking company, because it didn't qualify for pooling. As a Canadian company, it still kept its books according to Canadian GAAP standards, and under Canadian GAAP, pooling was seldom seen, tolerated only for mergers between companies of comparable size. The combination of Telus and BC Tel in 1998 was a rare example of pooling in this country. And if Nortel had followed U.S. GAAP instead (as it intended to do by its 1999 annual report), of the dozen tests a company participating in pooling had to meet, Nortel would have failed at least one: it had to be an independent company, and with BCE owning such a large block of shares and appointing members of the board of directors, Nortel most certainly wasn't.

In February 1997, as John Roth took command of Nortel, Opinion 16 greatly defined the opportunities and strategies available to Nortel and its main competitors. The FASB was holding its first public meeting that month on getting rid of pooling, but the acquisition strategy was far from dead. Nortel could not use pooling, while Cisco could, and did at every opportunity. Lucent was in a transitional state. AT&T had distributed to its shareholders the shares in the spun-off Lucent on September 30, 1996. Pooling criteria stated that there could be no change in equity ownership of a participating company for two years leading up to a deal; that meant Lucent wouldn't be able to enter into any pooling deals until after September 30, 1998. As a result, the first eighteen months of John Roth's reign were especially significant. Although he couldn't use pooling to keep pace with Cisco's acquisitions, for the moment, neither could Lucent, and Lucent was expected to hold off on making any big acquisitions until it could resort to pooling. This gave Nortel a narrow window of opportunity to get the jump on Lucent.

Confined to the purchase method, Nortel could still use its own shares to make acquisitions, but in the process it was going to load up its assets with goodwill whose amortization could lower its earnings. So long as analysts kept throwing away amortization in doing their share valuations, this might not matter much. But if the FASB carried through on its plans and drew up a new set of purchase-method rules, Nortel would be the most disadvantaged. Any acquisitions made by Cisco and Lucent using pooling would never have a bottom-line day of reckoning, no matter how badly the deals turned out. Nortel, on the other hand, would amass a mountain of goodwill that could bury the company's profitability in the first serious downturn. If revenues associated with a particular acquired asset, tangible or intangible, slowed to the point that the asset's value was impaired, Nortel would have to write it all off in one go rather than continue to amortize it. At the end of 2000, better than half the value of non-current assets on Nortel's balance sheet was represented by goodwill. In other words, more than half of Nortel's non-current assets were nothing more than the excess price it paid for various companies, above and beyond their net asset values.

The implications of this accounting debacle scarcely registered. The New Economy was in overdrive; in many minds, the Old

Economy was dead, in the sense that even the traditional business cycle of expansion and recession was over. To the armies of true believers, it was impossible to imagine that, only four years after taking command of Nortel and committing it to more than $30 billion (U.S.) worth of acquisitions, paid for mostly with stock, John Roth would be forced to abruptly write off about a third of it as worthless.

The Telecom Act of 1996 was supposed to encourage greater competition in the local and long-distance telephone and the cable television markets by opening these fiefdoms to competition. To encourage competition, it permitted cross-ownership. But for many members of corporate America, the natural reaction was not to launch new ventures in direct competition with incumbent operations, but to buy itself an incumbent operation in order to grow more communications tentacles without having to go through the bother of competition. Mergers and acquisitions, rather than new ventures, became a dominant characteristic of the new communications environment.

The ink was barely dry on the Telecom Act when the deals started. The act was passed in February 1996. In April, two Baby Bells, Bell Atlantic and Nynex, announced their merger plans. In August, WorldCom agreed to buy MFS Communications, and in November 1997, it outbid British Telecom for MCI. A plan by WorldCom to merge with Sprint was called off in 2000 in the face of growing regulatory concerns over industry consolidation.

On June 30, 1999, Gene Kimmelman, co-director of the Washington Office of the Consumer's Union, testified before the House Judiciary Committee on the Internet Freedom Act and the Internet Growth and Development Act. Kimmelman argued that the Telecom Act had not delivered as promised on its benefits to consumers. Since its passage, cable rates had increased about 23 percent, more than three times the rate of inflation, while changes in local and long-distance rate structures meant that customers who made less than 30 minutes of interstate long-distance calls per month had seen their rates double. He also took the justice department to task for not using its antitrust powers to prevent an ongoing convergence of the eight major local telephone companies (the Baby Bells and

GTE), which were turning into "two giant super-regional monopolies." When it was finished acquiring Pacific Telesis and Ameritech, SBC Communications would control about one-third of all household accounts. Another third would be within the domain of Bell Atlantic when it got through swallowing Nynex and GTE. Meanwhile, AT&T's acquisitions spree was about to give it about 60 percent of the country's cable service, including the leading high-speed Internet access providers, @Home and Roadrunner.

In this acquisition-oriented climate, it was inevitable that when the leading networking companies confronted the opportunities in the converging worlds of voice and data that coincided with the passage of the Telecom Act, they would look to each other as potential partners or takeover targets, rather than as mortal enemies. Over on the IP data networking side was Cisco Systems, by far the dominant force in Internet routers and corporate computer networks. And over on the telecom side were the two offspring of AT&T—Nortel and Lucent. The blurring of the voice and data worlds was becoming obvious. The Internet was putting increasing volumes of data traffic over the telephone system. A big jump in traffic was being promised, once a standards bun fight could be settled for the 56-kbps analog modem. U.S. Robotics and its "x2" 56K technology was up against the "flex" technology championed by Lucent, Motorola, and Rockwell Semiconductor. The International Telecommunications Union created an expert group in March 1997 to recommend a universal standard, and this finally came about in January 1998. Most Internet users had been labouring with 9600-bps and 14.4-kbps modems. Sorting out the 56K mess meant that Internet traffic, already growing when measured by users, could make a significant leap in volumes of data, as users could better handle larger file downloads and more complex Web page designs. A broader adaptation of higher modem speeds was fundamental to the Internet's commercial future.

In the months following Lucent's spinoff from AT&T in September 1996, Cisco held exploratory talks with both Lucent and Nortel over a possible partnership. The idea was to seek synergies of products and technologies—which would also avoid the expense of making themselves competitive on each other's turf. Cisco's first choice of a partner appears to have been Lucent, a widely admired tech company, which, in having its shares distributed to AT&T shareholders and then enthusiastically traded on the NYSE, quickly became America's most widely held stock. The choice may have been encouraged by the fact that Lucent had a bone to pick with Cisco. Lucent felt Cisco had violated data-networking technology patents held by Bell Labs. Lucent would subsequently allege that it had been approached by Cisco over the winter of 1996–97 with the idea of negotiating a settlement, which might include a technology licensing agreement. But a deal was never struck, and while Cisco CEO John Chambers would later say that there was too much overlap in their product lines to allow them to pursue a partnership, an irresolvable dispute over patents must have played a significant role in partnership talks being broken off in the spring of 1998. By the summer of 1998, Lucent and Cisco were suing each other over alleged patent infringements.

Thus Cisco also considered Nortel as a possible partner. Nortel stood at a corporate crossroads. It could strike a partnership deal with the largest data networking company around and create a spectacular synergy with its own telecom products. Or it could branch out aggressively into data networking and try to beat Cisco at its own game, and at the same time leave Lucent in the dust.

The world might have turned out to be a very different place for investors had Nortel been able to—or been inclined to—strike a strategic alliance with Cisco. Instead, John Roth decided to build a networking colossus of his own. In May 1998, news broke that Nortel was about to buy one of Cisco's largest data networking rivals, Bay Networks of Santa Clara, California. The price was $9.1 billion (U.S.). It was the most expensive integration of telecom equipment and data networking companies yet seen.

6

Bay Watch

The stock-market may be likened to a withered old harridan, enameled, painted, and decked in the latest mode, which leers on the speculator, and points to golden prizes, that like the desert mirage, fades away and leaves him to his ruin.
—William Fowler, *Ten Years on Wall Street* (1870)

By 1997, Nortel had seen the future, and it was high-speed optical networking, wireless—and the Internet. The mission to bring ATM to the barbarians of the PC networking world was called off. How this came about is not entirely clear, but John Roth, the new head of the company, usually gets the credit.

CBC News would relate the story that the power of the Internet sunk in to Roth in 1997, when he went on-line looking for parts for his vintage Jaguar XKE and found a supplier in England on the Web. This was a surprisingly delayed reaction to the possibilities of the Internet by the head of a leading international networking company. In an interview with *National Post Business,* Roth would confirm the details of this epiphany. "I went looking for a glove box for my 1966 XKE, but then I also found a few other parts. But what got me about the glove box thing was that it was so profound. The vintage car business doesn't strike you as one where you'd find a bunch of guys on the Web. And the U.K. is one of the last spots I'd ever expect to find people on the Web. Here was a guy selling antique parts for XKEs out of England on the Web, and I thought, This really is pervasive."

There is an almost charming ingenuousness to this recollection.

Nortel was already selling Web security services through Entrust when its new president discovered what millions of people already knew: that the Web was an amazing virtual library of information, an unprecedented means to personal interaction, and a monstrous commercial opportunity.

To be fair, 1997 was the year the Internet experienced a breakthrough with large numbers of users. But you would have thought that an enterprise committed to creating a World of Networks would have had a better handle on the Internet boom. The way Roth recalled it, the summer of 1997 was an educational experience for a man running one of the largest networking companies in the world. He said that when he took charge, he knew his vision of the company's direction "had to be around the Internet. But the trouble was crystallizing exactly what it was going to be. There was a lot of discussion at the time about different technologies that would play on the Internet. At Nortel, we were coming at it from the point of view of a certain set of standards that we in the telephone industry had invented. We thought they were the right ones."

This was an obvious reference to Nortel's ATM obsession. Roth seemed to be suggesting that Nortel had thought the Internet, as a concept, could be reworked as an ATM network—as the *infostructure* of Nortel's surreal 1994 annual report. But then Roth asserted he hadn't been part of the ATM crowd. "I was skeptical, because the telephone industry had been consistently wrong in picking data standards over the years. So in the summer of 1997, I spent a lot of time talking to people in the data world and listening carefully to what they were using. In our world, it wasn't decided at all, but in theirs, this was all decided; it was a fait accompli."

The fait accompli was IP. Let us remember that the TCP/IP protocol had been in use for more than fourteen years when Roth conducted his fact-finding mission. Roth's professed skepticism about ATM must be taken with a grain of salt. After all, he had become president of Nortel North America, which presided over most of its business operations, in 1995, giving him several years of opportunity to recognize IP and persuade the company to take it seriously. Not everyone is sure that he was such a visionary. "Roth got the credit for

Nortel doing IP," says a Nortel insider, "but it was people in R&D who convinced him and got the money to look into it." And it should also be remembered that Roth was in charge of BNR back in the halcyon days of the early to mid-eighties, when Nortel created switches with data capability based on the X.25 protocol, which Nortel helped make a widely employed standard just by deciding to use it. Embracing ATM for the new generation of Magellan switches had a similar kind of "if we build it, they will have to use it" logic.

Nortel's prolonged insistence on the suitability of ATM for desktop environments is at least consistent with an engineer's adamant view that, like Betamax and VHS, ATM was just way better than TCP/IP. At some point, the salesman in Roth had to take command and realize that, engineering convictions be damned, the customers wanted TCP/IP, because that's what they'd already spent their money on. And with that in mind, Roth wrote a famous e-mail to employees after assuming the CEO's role in October 1997, in which he announced Nortel's "hard right turn" into IP and the Internet.

Nortel's decision to drop more than $9 billion on Bay Networks, a company highly proficient in IP, in June 1998 is widely seen as the turning point in its business strategy. In fact, Nortel had already begun moving into the IP world through much quieter deals. Although the information in its own financial statements was thin to nonexistent, Nortel had secured equity positions in two startup firms: Juniper Networks Inc. of Mountain View, California, and Avici Systems Inc. in the Boston suburb of North Billerica.

Founded in February 1996 with an initial round of $16 million in venture capital, Juniper was bent on creating hardware and software products for high-speed IP optical routing. Juniper was developing an Internet "backbone" router called the M40, which it would declare market-ready in September 1998 and begin shipping that October. The company was expecting the Internet to evolve into the next-generation public communications network, "superceding and expanding upon many of the functions provided by the traditional telephone network," according to its IPO in April 1999. On September 2, 1997, Nortel joined with Ericsson, 3Com, the Siemens/Newbridge Alliance, and WorldCom subsidiary UUNet

Technologies Inc. in providing a total of $40 million in equity financing, according to a Juniper press release. Nortel made no mention of the Juniper investment in its own financial reporting, and so there is no record of how much of this $40 million was invested by Nortel, or when and how Nortel got it back. And no mention was made of Nortel's 1997 investment in Juniper in the IPO that Juniper released some eighteen months later.

A few months after participating in the Juniper financing, Nortel started shovelling far more money at Avici. Founded in 1996, Avici was developing a terabit-speed optical router called the TSR, which it would pitch at the telecom carriers as a "scalable" solution to their increasing optical traffic. (This meant the router's capacity could be incrementally improved without having to be ripped out and replaced.) On January 28, 1998, Avici conducted its first round of financing using preferred shares. Nortel signed on for that round and the next five, investing a total of $32.5 million through the financing rounds extending into 1999. In the process, it acquired 6.46 million common shares (registered to Nortel Networks Inc. in Tennessee) and a seat on the board of directors. With the first round, Nortel also entered into distribution, technology licence, and assistance agreements with Avici. Nortel provided no information about this investment or the various agreements in its own financial reporting; in its 1998 annual report, Nortel simply noted in its "year in review section" that it had taken "minority interests in companies such as Avici Systems, Inc." and never provided any further details.

Some word from Nortel would have been helpful to investors in understanding why the company felt it necessary to take these equity positions. The level of detail expected from management discussion and analysis (MD&A) and notes to financial statements allowed Nortel to leave them unexplained and unexplored, but for that one sentence in the 1998 annual report. Companies like Nortel could carry hundreds of millions of dollars in accounting categories like "other assets" and "other investments" without explaining what any of it was devoted to. The Juniper and Avici deals were, in hindsight, among the earliest signs that Nortel knew it would have to look beyond its own R&D efforts for the technology it needed to compete in the new communications order. For if Juniper was right, and the Internet proved to be the basis for the next-generation public network, the implications for Nortel were frightening. Unless it developed IP ability and products quickly, Nortel was risking irrelevancy.

The sums Nortel quietly invested in these two startups were not large—in addition to the $32.5 million sunk into Avici, Nortel we might guess chipped in $8 million (based on five investors contributing a total of $40 million) to Juniper. This was small change, unworthy of elaboration or even specific recognition in Nortel's financials, compared to the billions it dropped on Bay Networks. But that was precisely the point. Avici would not amount to much in the Nortel game plan, but a major shortcoming in the expensive Bay acquisition would eventually bring Nortel back to Juniper's door. When the optical Internet router market came alive in 2000, Juniper's M160, introduced that March, would prove to be a giant killer. The OC-192 backbone router was four times faster than anything Cisco had to offer, and Nortel, after the huge expense of Bay, would have nothing to offer at all, despite repeated promises that a high-speed Bay router was on the way. Perhaps the great "what-if" of Nortel's expensive plunge into IP networking was this: what if it had instead bought Juniper, which, at the time the Bay deal was announced, was only three months away from unveiling a market-ready product, the OC-48 M40? Granted, Juniper would not have delivered Nortel an instant, broad presence in IP networking. But it sure wouldn't have cost over $9 billion.

Bay Networks of Santa Clara, California, had been created in 1994 by merging SynOptics Communications Inc., a company that produced Ethernet hubs, and Wellfleet Communications, Inc., which built IP routers. The company established a data-networking product line that include switches, routers, hubs, remote and Internet access systems, and configuration software. When 1998 rolled around, Bay was struggling, but with 7,000 employees, a global marketing presence, and annual sales of $2.4 billion, it was still considered enough of a player in Cisco's business to make it a likely purchase for Nortel or Lucent if they wanted to hit the ground running in the enterprise PC networking and IP router game.

"Data has a growth rate of 30 to 40 percent per year, and it's driven by the Web," Roth explained when the Bay Networks acquisition was announced. "The IP component is growing more like 70 percent per year. That's really the segment we're focusing on." Looking back on the deal, Roth would remark that if there were any doubts within Nortel that he was serious about changing the company's direction, "the acquisition of Bay ended any of that. This was a 'you bet the farm' kind of decision."

The acquisition of Bay Networks was actually treated as a merger. Bay Networks, it was announced, was to continue operating as a wholly owned subsidiary of Nortel, and Bay's chairman of the board, chief executive officer and president, Dave House, would assume the presidency of Nortel from Roth and join the board of directors, while John Roth continued as CEO and vice-chairman of the board. It didn't end up working out that way. While Bay products remained distinctly labelled, the operation would be swallowed up by Nortel, and after a year of working to bring the two companies together, House would take his leave and Roth would resume the presidency.

The merger resembled a pooling deal, with Nortel shares being used as the currency, except that Nortel wasn't able to use pooling accounting and so would have to swallow enormous goodwill costs. Under the merger agreement, dated Monday, June 15, 1998, Bay Networks shareholders received 0.6 Nortel shares for every one of their Bay shares.

Just how much the deal "cost" depended on how you measured the value of Nortel's shares. Nortel itself put the total estimated cost of the deal when it was announced at $9.1 billion (U.S.), based on Nortel's closing price of $63^{11}/$_{16}$ in New York on Friday, June 12. But when the deal was actually consummated on August 28, Nortel was down to $50^{1}/$_{8}$. Canadian GAAP dictated that the cost be booked using the price of the stock at the deal's closing, rather than at its announcement as under U.S. GAAP. This brought the price down to $6.9 billion and saved the company $2.2 billion in intangibles under Canadian GAAP. However you added it up, it was a colossal deal for the networking industry. It placed about 20 percent of Nortel's outstanding common shares in the hands of Bay shareholders and reduced BCE's interest in Nortel from about 52 to 42 percent.

This reduction in BCE's interest was far more important than was generally acknowledged. Although the acquisition could not have been undertaken without the approval of Nortel's BCE-controlled board, it allowed Nortel to wiggle out from under the thumb of its longstanding parent and made it inevitable that some-day BCE would sell its remaining interest rather than continue as a minority shareholder. Nine billion dollars evidently was a price worth paying if it also bought corporate freedom, and meant that Nortel's strategic planning—the kind of planning that had led to the ATM debacle—would no longer have to satisfy the interests of a telephone company.

Not having to answer to BCE also meant that Nortel could now pursue a series of stock-based acquisitions. "Nortel in the past did not use all its resources," Roth would reflect. "We used our R&D program and marketing, but we never used acquisitions. And we didn't do that for one major reason: Bell Canada owned 52 percent of Nortel and every time we wanted to do an acquisition, Bell would encourage us to use cash rather than stock, because if we used cash, they'd ante up nothing. If we did use shares, we'd have to then buy back an equivalent amount of stock so we wouldn't dilute BCE's position."

This time, BCE had gone along with the dilution. And reducing BCE's interest to a minority position also granted John Roth some precious room in which to manoeuvre—room that he knew Paul Stern never had. Citing Stern's ouster in 1992, Roth would tell *Financial Post* Business that "if BCE's at 52 percent and Paul Stern is not doing well at Nortel, Red Wilson [then CEO of BCE] can go and tap him on the shoulder and say it's time to bring in Jean Monty. . . . But if BCE was at 30 percent, Stern could say, 'Who are you, Red? I don't agree; I'm staying.' You're going to have to consolidate your 30 percent of this thing that you're not happy with, but which you can't do anything about." It would require a major disaster for the Nortel board to summon up the nerve to tap John Roth on the shoulder.

Up until the day of the Bay announcement, Nortel and its shareholders had been having a pretty good year. As already noted, after adjusting their value for a stock split in January, shares had appreciated about 50 percent in the first six months of 1998. The company had achieved revenues of $15.4 billion in 1997, up from $12.8 billion. An estimated 70 percent of Internet traffic was flowing on optical backbones of telecom carriers that were created with Nortel products. But with the Bay Networks deal, Nortel began to encounter a series of setbacks.

First, the markets generally hated the Bay deal. Even though the acquisition had been anticipated for a month, many analysts didn't like the move. Bay was dismissed by some as a company that had already peaked and whose best people had moved on. Nortel's willingness to pay a 35 percent premium on Bay's share price seemed pretty steep for a mature technology company. Under U.S. GAAP, Nortel would show that it only acquired $665 million in net tangible assets for the $9.06 billion price. Another $1 billion was assigned to the value of in-process research and development, and about $2 billion for acquired technology. That left almost $5.4 billion in goodwill. The acquisition differed greatly from the modus operandi of Cisco, for example, which made a point of targeting young companies with emerging technologies that often had not yet made it to market.

When the deal was announced on June 15, investors stampeded to unload Nortel stock. Nortel routinely traded at volumes well under a million shares on the NYSE; on June 12, when the stock finished at $63^{11}/$_{16}$, only 436,700 shares changed hands. But after the news of the Bay merger was released on Monday the fifteenth, investors aggressively bailed from Nortel. Almost 8.6 million shares were moved on the fifteenth as the price plunged to $54. In all, about 20 million shares moved through the NYSE between June 15 and 17 as the price dropped further, to $52^{1}/$_{2}$. The stock subsequently rebounded to its June 12 closing of $63^{11}/$_{16}$ with its daily high on July 21, but then fell away again. On August 27, the day before the acquisition was to be consummated, Nortel got as low as $47^{7}/$_{8}$ before pulling back up above $50 in time for the deal to be wrapped.

In hindsight, one might wonder whether Nortel could not have accomplished its growth goals by striking a licensing or joint marketing deal with Bay Networks, rather than swallowing the entire company and loading up its income statement with punitive amortization charges. But that option would not have had the strategic advantage of an acquisition. Since 1995, Bay had supplied infrastructure items such as Ethernet hubs and IP routers to Nortel's chief telecom sector rival, Lucent. Lucent needed Bay's products for its multivendor network installations of LAN and WAN networks. Thus, Nortel's Bay acquisition has to be appreciated as a strategic move against a major opponent. Nortel's purchase of Bay cut Lucent off from an important source of data product. Without Bay, Lucent had nothing and likely would be forced to buy a data-networking company of its own. Biding its time on large acquisitions until pooling became available to it, Lucent had missed out on Bay and lost a key supplier in the process.

Nortel's troubles were far from over after the deal closed. The wisdom of the Bay purchase was still a hard sell to many analysts and investors, and the overall economic picture was deteriorating. Malaise had been spreading through the heretofore celebrated "tiger" economies of South Asia since 1997, and Russia's twin default and devaluation in August 1998 helped trip a hedge fund crisis on Wall Street. On September 14, Nortel announced that it was eliminating 3,500 jobs, about 4.5 percent of its workforce, in order to cut costs. The market responded by taking Nortel down from $47^{5}/$_{8}$ at the opening on the fourteenth to $43^{3}/$_{4}$ at the close the next day.

On September 29, Nortel was scheduled to make a crucial presentation at New York's Essex House, a grand hotel overlooking south Central Park, between Sixth and Seventh avenues. For this year's dog and pony show before Wall Street analysts, Nortel was positioning itself as a total-solutions networking monster. It was getting ready to unveil its new marketing program, featuring the rebranding of the company as Nortel Networks—although the actual company, for now, was still legally called Northern Telecom.

Nortel was broadcasting its enhanced global presence, while assuring analysts that the integration of Bay's IP technology into

Nortel's existing product lines was chugging right along. The company had a new logo to show off, featuring a stylized globe, and a new title—executive vice-president of Global Marketing—for Bill Conner, the former president of its Enterprise Data Networks business. Hill/Holliday Advertising had come up with a new advertising campaign built around the theme "How the World Shares Ideas."

The analyst show was supposed to be a good-news, ready-to-conquer-the-planet sort of affair. But the Nortel bandwagon went in the ditch when Nortel released earnings figures that failed to include any numbers from Bay Networks, which had officially been part of Nortel for more than a month. James Kedersha, an analyst with SG Cowen, later described for *Forbes* magazine the ensuing mayhem as he and fellow analysts tried to get some consistent numbers out of the Nortel suits: "We went down with about four people. I went after Clarence [Chandran] who runs the carrier/IP effort; somebody else went after the wireless guy. The executives milling around were all saying the business sucked. It culminated with Wes Scott, who was chief financial officer, getting up on stage and saying 'Here's our expectations for the year, but that second-half ramp up we were looking for ain't happening, and a couple of other things aren't going quite right.' Then he got offstage and he was just descended upon. I don't think we ever saw him again. A few phones flipped open and within 30 seconds the stock was trading down."

Roth would recall how "my CFO told the analysts and investors, 'You know, you folks were expecting a little revenue pop in the fourth quarter. Well, right now, it looks like it's not going to happen.' Wes Scott didn't even finish the sentence and we were looking at a nearly empty room. The second before, we could have sworn there were 470 people sitting there. They were all gone."

Wes Scott is the typical goat in recollections of this harrowing ordeal, but it's clear from Kedersha's recollection that the presentation was already in trouble by the time Scott suffered an ill-timed attack of brutal frankness. Maybe it had all been too much too soon for Nortel—the Bay purchase barely wrapped, a disintegrating economic picture provoking forecasting jitters inside the company. Whatever the case, it was a harsh lesson in the folly of trying to carry off a presentation with style rather than substance in this town. And it showed that, contrary to the received wisdom, analysts were not patsies for every company broadcasting an aggressive enthusiasm for the Internet.

There is surely some irony in a gang of analysts turning to the wireless technology in which Nortel was one of the world's foremost providers to flambé the company's stock. How the world shares ideas, indeed. These analysts turned to their cell phones to share the idea that everyone should get the hell out of Nortel common. Nortel had opened on the NYSE at $41³/₈, up ⁵/₈ from the previous day's close, and was up to $41⁵/₈ when word of the chaos inside Essex House hit the market. The stock shed more than $6 before recovering slightly to finish at $35⁷/₈. The volume increase over the twenty-eighth, from 2.4 to 3.9 million shares, was just the beginning. The next day, almost 13 million Nortel shares blew through the exchange as the stock dropped to $30¹/₁₆; on October 8, it fell through $28. Since announcing the Bay acquisition less than four months earlier, Nortel's stock had lost more than half its value.

Nortel's performance before that unforgiving crowd of analysts seriously damaged the company's reputation, just as the Bay Networks deal put one-fifth of its shares into the hands of a new block of largely American investors. From that day forward, Nortel paid careful attention to getting all the suits singing from the same song sheet, crafting the corporate message carefully, and making sure the numbers were presented in a way analysts could appreciate.

And they wouldn't come to New York again with Wes Scott. On January 28, 1999, it was announced that Scott had moved over to Bell Canada to serve as vice-chairman, responsible for all corporate staff functions. In his stead as Nortel's chief financial officer came forty-five-year-old Frank Dunn, who had been serving as senior vice-president, finance and planning. Like Roth, Dunn was an old Nortel hand, having joined the company in 1976. Like Roth, he'd also gone to McGill. And like Roth, people who knew him way back when never imagined him having the type A corporate moxie that was supposedly required to get to the top of a major enterprise.

Meanwhile, over at the headquarters of Lucent Technologies in

Murray Hill, New Jersey, America's number-one telecom networking company was preparing to celebrate the happy day when pooling became available to it, which happened to be September 30, the day after Nortel's big spiel to Wall Street analysts turned into a near-death experience for the company. Lord knows exactly what Lucent might have had in mind at this point, but here's a telling clue to what some people thought could happen.

On October 5, news broke that the Federal Trade Commission had initiated an investigation of Cisco's partnering ambitions. Cisco confirmed that, the previous week—that is, the week in which Lucent's restriction on pooling expired—the company had received a letter from the FTC, inquiring about exactly what it had discussed with Lucent and Nortel in the past year. The letter felt like a shot across Cisco's bow with respect to Lucent, since Nortel had already staked out its own territory in data networking with the Bay acquisition.

The FTC appeared concerned that Cisco and Lucent might execute a pooling merger, put their patent suits behind them, and conquer the networking universe. U.S. courts as a rule consider any market share greater than 70 percent by a single entity to be a monopoly, a situation the FTC likes to discourage. The FTC was being criticized for not standing in the way of the rash of telecom and cable mergers, but it was watching the networking equipment companies warily, just as it was concerned about collusion in the computer, software, and chip-making industries. If keeping Lucent and Cisco away from each other was the FTC's intent, the investigation was successful. The FTC's queries left Cisco dangling for about eight months. On June 2, 1999, Cisco announced it had received notice from the FTC that the agency had determined that nothing in Cisco's discussions with Lucent and Nortel "warranted further examination."

Nortel's acquisition of Bay may not have single-handedly set off the shopping binge among networking companies, but the Bay deal unquestionably meant that there would be no turning back. Nortel made it clear it intended to compete on Cisco's turf, in IP switching and data networking, and by snatching Bay, it forced Lucent to go find a Bay of its own—which it did, in a pooling merger with Ascend Communications, announced on January 13, 1999. The

WAN specialty firm, once one of the NASDAQ's most highly tout-ed tech stocks, had fallen so far by then that analysts and brokers had taken to calling it Ass-End.

"I think there have always been discussions of working together and dividing up the markets," Ray Keneipp, an analyst with Current Analysis, told CNET News.com on the day Cisco confirmed the FTC was asking questions about its 1997 discussions with Nortel and Lucent. "In the past, though, these networking companies were not that large, so the dynamics of changing the markets was not that great. But now these companies are much larger and, with the con-solidation of the market, these kinds of deals can change the market."

Cisco had already begun expanding through acquisitions in 1993, when it made a single purchase. Three more followed in 1994, four in 1995, seven in 1996, six in 1997, nine in 1998. In 1999, Cisco went into M&A overdrive, swallowing eighteen companies. In the summer of 1996, Therese Mrozuk joined the Palo Alto office of the San Francisco law firm Brobeck, Phleger & Harrison, and quick-ly was named Cisco's outside counsel. By the summer of 2000, Mrozuk had helped Cisco acquire sixty-four different companies in deals totalling $32 billion, paid for with Cisco stock. Mrozuk was overseeing a team of ten lawyers in Palo Alto, Dallas, Austin, and New York that did almost nothing but vet Cisco acquisitions. No networking company matched Cisco's zeal for acquisitions, but they gave it the college try. And investment banks eagerly drew up lists of potential takeover targets for all three major networking players.

While Nortel lagged behind Cisco in the total number of acqui-sitions, it nonetheless would assemble an impressive portfolio between 1998 and 2000—eighteen in all, totalling $30.6 billion (U.S. GAAP), almost as much as Cisco spent in the course of mak-ing four times as many deals. Nortel had made acquisitions prior to the Bay Networks deal, but it was by far the most important. Not only was the Bay deal much larger than anything even Cisco attempt-ed—it started Nortel down the road to creative earnings figures. Without access to pooling, Nortel had to account for every dollar of goodwill and other intangible assets generated by every stock-fuelled acquisition. By the end of 2000, the accumulated goodwill alone would amount to more than \$22 billion (U.S. GAAP), dragging at Nortel's GAAP earnings like a boat anchor tied to the bumper of John Roth's vintage Jag. The only way to deal with it was to convince people to ignore it. And by and large, they did. Until a steep decline in the networking business would make it impossible for even Nortel to overlook it any more.

The indignities for Nortel rolled in during the fall of 1998. On October 14 came a shareholder class-action lawsuit, filed by the firm Wolf Haldenstein Adler Freeman & Herz, in the Southern District court of New York. The firm represented Bay shareholders who felt they'd been hosed by Nortel in general and specifically by Roth and Scott. The crux of their complaint was that the registration statement and prospectus for the Bay acquisition

> was materially false and misleading because it failed to disclose that: (a) Nortel was suffering a significant decline in its business and revenue growth and that the decline was so severe that it would negatively impact its business for the balance of 1998; (b) a significant amount of Nortel's workforce would have to be laid off because of the declines in business and revenue growth; and (c) the demand for Nortel's products was substantially diminishing in Asia and Europe.

The suit basically complained that the plaintiffs had been blowing nonstop sunshine when they knew better, that since filing its year-end 1997 results, the company had been downplaying its exposure to the Asian downturn.

The class-action suit was practically a boilerplate document for every shareholder suit alleging improprieties during an acquisition. In the standard-issue sob story, shares are swapped at a ratio dependent on the market value of the acquiring company. The deal gets done, and then, whoops, the acquiring company hits financial turbulence it didn't warn anyone about and was probably hiding knowledge of the whole time. The share price crashes. The shareholders from the acquired company see their payment—the acquiring company's stock—turn to Weimar Republic deutschemarks that can be exchanged by the wheelbarrow for a loaf of bread. They round up some lawyers and cry foul. Or, conversely, some lawyers smell a possible injustice and round up some shareholders.

And Nortel, like most every company before it and since, pronounced the suit without merit and vowed to defend itself vigorously—which it did successfully, with the suit being dismissed in January 2000. Even so, plagued by the Bay shareholder lawsuit, the raspberries aimed at the Bay deal, and the fallout from its Essex House performance, Nortel clawed its way to the end of 1998. Revenues had improved year over year by about $2 billion, to $17.5 billion, but largely because of its acquisitions, the $812 million net earnings of 1997 had become a $569 million loss, and in the process, earnings per share of $1.56 had crashed to a per-share loss of 99 cents.

The 1998 fiscal year had truly been Nortel's and Roth's *annus horribilus*. Nineteen ninety-nine would turn out far better, not only because of a major triumph for Nortel in optical networking, but because of a whole new approach to presenting its financial performance, which bore no resemblance to GAAP, but which Nortel was able to get investors and analysts to happily accept. The next few years would never have unfolded the way they did for John Roth and other executives, who scored millions of dollars in stock-option profits, had they not been able to market so successfully an invention that was as impressive and as mysterious in its inner workings as the old SL-1: a simple number that Nortel liked to call *earnings from operations*.

7

Cold-Fusion Economics

Adam Anderson, a former cashier of the South Sea Company, later claimed that many purchasers of shares in the South Sea and other promotions bought knowing that their long-term prospects were hopeless, since they aimed to get "rid of them in the crowded alley to others more credulous than themselves."
—Edward Chancellor, writing on the South Sea Bubble of 1720 in *Devil Take the Hindmost* (1999)

On March 23, 1989, two chemists at the University of Utah named Stanley Pons and Martin Fleischmann made an incredible announcement: they had discovered a way to produce energy by fusing atoms at room temperature in a laboratory apparatus so simple that a high school student could build it.

By the standard of everything then known by physicists, the "cold fusion" of Pons and Fleischmann was impossible. Fusing atoms on planet Earth was supposed to require temperatures many times greater than those generated on the sun and stupendously complex machinery. Creating energy through fusion was both dangerous and hideously expensive. The market value of the energy generated could never overcome the enormous costs of creating it. But then along came the Utah chemists, producing limitless, nonpolluting energy from a ridiculously basic contraption.

A palladium cathode was inserted into a test tube of heavy water, in which normal hydrogen atoms of H_2O had been replaced by "heavy" hydrogen atoms (containing a neutron as well as a proton in the nucleus), called deuterium. When a current was introduced to the cathode, according to these chemists, more heat was generated than normal chemical processes could account for. The excess energy, they concluded, could only be due to the fusion of the heavy hydrogen atoms in the palladium cathode. You didn't need a monster facility and fantastic temperatures. Pons and Fleischmann had done the job essentially with pressure, not heat, as they argued that the deuterium was fused by being packed tightly together in the cathode. Simple electrolysis had created nuclear energy on a desktop.

It took years for the cold-fusion hubbub to die down, for Pons and Fleischmann to be proved utterly, shamefully wrong, and even at that, a Toyota subsidiary continued to fund cold-fusion research in the hope there might actually be something to the chemists' discredited claims.

What does cold fusion have to do with Nortel Networks and the bull market it rode? Everything. The cold-fusion junk science of Pons and Fleischmann was the operative model for the junk economics of the late 1990s tech economy. For a while, Pons and Fleischmann were able to persuade a lot of people that there was a whole different way to make energy with very little effort. All people had to do was ditch everything they knew about physics and fail to ask some startlingly fundamental questions. In hindsight, it seems amazing that the junk science of Pons and Fleischmann got as far (and attracted as much public and private research dollars) as it did. No less remarkable is the fact that cold-fusion economics managed to captivate the minds and wallets of legions of investors and financial professionals who should have known better.

The cold fusion of Pons and Fleischmann was the star witness in a lucidly argued exposé of the history of bad science by physicist Robert Park. Park called bad science "voodoo science" (which provided the title for his book, published in 2000).

Park was most certainly inspired by George H. Bush's memorable dismissal of Ronald Reagan's supply-side fiscal policies as "voodoo economics" during the 1980 primaries for the Republican presidential nomination. (Bush then found himself sufficiently comfortable with voodoo economics to accept the vice-presidential ticket from

Reagan and enter the White House with him.) The field of economics is a font of voodoo, because for all its scientific trappings, it is not science, occupying a strange terrain between mathematics, political science, and sociology. Very little, if anything, in economics is absolutely testable in a strict, scientific sense. Theories abound, and the evidence is pliable. Truths are no more than widely held assumptions. Beyond the roles of supply and demand in pricing, there's not much for people to agree on. Alan Greenspan himself has confessed, "There is, regrettably, no simple model of the American economy that can effectively explain the levels of output, employment, and inflation. In principle, there may be some unbelievably complex set of equations that does that. But we have not been able to find them and do not believe anyone else has either."

And so it is not only inevitable that voodoo science should have parallels in voodoo economics, but that voodoo economics be the more common of the two phenomena. Voodoo economics is far more difficult to expose and defeat, because there are no absolute tests that can be constructed on laboratory apparatus. The only way economic theories are tested is by actually turning them loose on economies, and with economies being as complex and as imprecisely understood as the weather, there's no guarantee that such theories can be irrefutably proved or disproved.

Because economics relies on the observation of past events to come up with ideas and answers to vexing problems, the stock market and its mountains of data are a theorist's gold mine. The actual data, unfortunately, as voluminous as they might appear, are spotty. While virtually all the basic stock market instruments (including derivatives) existed by the dawn of the eighteenth century, the modern free-market economy is a relatively recent invention, and with stock markets, there are legitimate questions about whether the time line is long enough to validate patterns or norms. Since the 1870s, there have been only four major periods of bull market activity. Are those enough to provoke absolute standards on issues like overvaluation and "normal" dividend/price ratios? A more pressing question is whether the data collected is even reliable. As admirable as the work of researchers like Robert Shiller and John Campbell might be, there is some doubt that long-term trends can be accepted, for the simple reason that the stock market has been subject to so much manipulation (particularly before the Securities and Exchange Act of 1934). Unlike a hydrogen atom, which always has one proton, a particular stock does not have an absolute value.

When it comes to stock markets, the best that theorists can do is examine the past and see if there are general patterns worth paying attention to—if not purely out of intellectual curiosity, then because anything that allows you to predict the market's course will make you money. On the subject of repetition, science and economics diverge. Good science depends upon the repeatability of experimental results, which is why cold fusion was such a bust. In economics, repeatability is an entirely different matter. Believing that something will happen because something like it has happened before is a deductive trap, just as believing that the law of averages demands that a flipped coin must come up heads if it has just come up tails. On the other hand, it would seem foolish to overlook the patterns in statistics with a reasonable relationship to equities values that consistently crop up in advance of severe market corrections. And it is surely prudent to employ statistical analysis to see whether prevailing economic theories have any basis in reality. At the same time, capitalism has spent several centuries refining basic principles of corporate profitability. There are not only ways to achieve profitability, but ways to measure an investment's performance in the best interest of the shareholder.

Every now and then, however, the essential uncertainties of economics allow contrary ideas to emerge about the measurement and achievement of prosperity. Revolutions in thought are trademarks of good science. Ideas like the theory of relativity have relegated once widely accepted concepts to the waste bin, but only by meeting rigorous tests of logic. Furthermore, there is a big difference between rewriting or disproving a fundamental truth and simply ignoring it. With Pons and Fleischmann, a seeming impossibility of their experiment was that, if fusion truly was responsible for the excess energy they observed, where was the massive amount of radiation that should accompany it? Why weren't the scientists and their assistants robustly nuked?[10]

The conclusion of Pons and Fleischmann was that some other fusion process, as yet undiscovered, was at work that didn't involve radiation. This was hubris at its best: a complete rejection of the broad and rigorously tested knowledge of modern physics, rather than considering that perhaps the very small amount of surplus heat allegedly detected was in fact due to something as mundane as poor instrument calibration. The cold-fusion economics of the late nineties bull market would have its own moments of missing radiation, and Nortel investors and analysts who failed to explain the absence adequately would find themselves at the core of the meltdown.

To understand how cold-fusion economics came to rule the equities markets, first imagine our typical public company as a magic box. Companies have four main sources of cash: they can earn it, borrow it, sell an asset, or sell treasury shares. By far the most important source is revenues from sales. In the old-fashioned, time-tested blueprint of profitability, a pipe carries all these revenues into the box from one end. After costs are deducted for various expenses—including labour, debts, taxes, leases, depreciation, marketing, and costs of raw materials—whatever is left over is a pool of profit called net earnings. From this pool a reasonable portion is fed into a pipe exiting from the other end of the box. This pipe delivers to the ownership ranks—the common shareholders—their slice of the annual profits in the form of dividends, paid out on a per-share basis.

It's a simple process with discrete roles for all involved. The shareholders—the people who own the company—are outside the box. The employees—the people who actually do all the work that earns the revenues—are inside the box. To manage the box, the shareholders elect a board of directors, led by a chairman of the board. The board members may or may not have an interest in the company's equity; some may be significant shareholders, or senior executives with the company who may also own shares, or they may be quasi-celebrities such as retired politicians who lend a certain cachet to the board ranks. The board controls the hiring and firing of senior employee ranks, led by the president and chief executive officer, and provides (theoretically) a Senate-like sober stewardship to the business strategies developed by the employees.

The distinction between shareholder and employee is not always so tidy. It's very common, especially in a startup company, for the senior employees also to be major shareholders, in which case they live both inside and outside the box, as salaried employees and as members of the ownership ranks, and may also hold a seat on the board of directors charged with overseeing their activities as employees.

We'll look more at the employee-employer relationship later. For now, it's important only to appreciate the basic structure of the magic box, particularly the arrangement of pipes: revenues come in one pipe, a portion of the profits flows out another one into the pockets of the shareholders. How much profit reaches the shareholders in the form of dividends has long been the fundamental basis for determining the worth of individual shares. The company is like a piece of real estate that generates lease revenues: the price of the property is going to depend substantially on how much income it can produce for the owner.

Publicly listed companies have their shares traded in the aftermarket, the best-known example of which is the stock exchange. Shares change hands through an auction process, which relies on supply and demand to set the price, which can change with every transaction. The basic truth of the stock market is that a stock is worth whatever someone is willing to pay for it at a given moment. But to quantify the appropriate level of a share price, traditionally it is divided by the earnings per share (EPS) to arrive at the price/earnings ratio, or multiple. To do this, total earnings, whether for the preceding year or preceding quarter (called trailing earnings), are divided by the total outstanding common shares to determine the EPS. Then the going price for an individual share is divided by the EPS. Businesses in different industries (mining, transportation, or banking) have traditionally been assigned different P/E ranges. It has long been considered prudent that a company's P/E ratio fall within the norms for similar companies or companies at similar stages of development. If the P/E is too high, the stock is overvalued; if too low, it is undervalued.

P/E is not the absolute measure of an investment's value, however, because not all earnings flow through to the shareholder in the form of dividends; some are retained by the company for operating expenses, expansion plans, reinvestment in technology, and rainy days. To judge more precisely a shareholder's return on equity, then, the dividend/price ratio is considered. If a share fetches $10 on the stock exchange and the annual dividend to which the shareholder is entitled is 50 cents, the dividend/price ratio is 20:1 and the return on equity is 5 percent.

The dividend is supposed to generate the share value because the stock's return on equity must square with available returns from other investment instruments. Basically, the higher the risk of an investment, the higher the return should be, because no rational investor accepts increased risk in pursuit of lower returns. That's why return on equity is expected to be superior for a stock compared to a rock-solid investment such as a government bond. If ten-year U.S. government treasury bonds (virtually risk free) pay the equivalent of a 5 percent dividend, an investor expects a higher return from a share in a publicly traded company, to compensate for the risk level. It's easy to forget that, while a share in a company is a token of ownership, in practical terms a share is a demand on earnings that comes far down the food chain. Before a shareholder can receive a dividend, governments receive their taxes, banks their loan payments, preferred shareholders (who do not have voting rights) their dividends, employees their wages, and suppliers their payments for goods and services. If there's not enough money to go around, the dividend is reduced or suspended.

No one should be willing to spend $10 on a share of a public company with a return on equity of 5 percent when government bonds are offering the same rate of return. Thus, for the return to improve without an increase in the dividend, the stock price must drop. If government bonds are paying 5 percent, a stock trading at $10 with a dividend of 50 cents is theoretically overpriced. The market may decide that an acceptable return from the riskier stock is 7 percent; as a result, the price should come down to $7.14. Simply put, from the perspective of income production, $10 a share is much too expensive for a stock with a 50-cent dividend.

Well, that's the way the market is supposed to work, but market theory also says it doesn't work exactly that way. Present-day prices of stocks are not based on their return on equity as dictated by the most recent dividend payout: stocks trade at values that anticipate future earnings. In other words, stock markets are forward looking. Their pricing is speculative.

Logic might dictate that the market would wait for an increase (or decrease) in the declared dividend and adjust the stock price accordingly. But the general wisdom of market theory is that prices anticipate future earnings, moving in speculative advance of dividend changes. With tech growth stocks, however, there was often little or no earnings and only nominal (or no) dividends to report, and yet share prices often climbed at vertiginous rates. The only rational basis for a steep increase in share price is an anticipation of large future earnings. The share prices that were abnormally high, based on the current dividend/price ratio, meant that buyers of these stocks were massively discounting future earnings. In other words, they were paying for years and years of anticipated—and large—future earnings up-front when they bought the stock. The only way the share price could be maintained over time was if those long-term earnings actually materialized. In the tech stock boom, the profitability horizon became a serious issue. How long would the market collectively wait for its tech-startup darlings to actually produce a profit before concluding that the going price for the stock was unsupported?

Indeed, if profitability was so elusive for tech companies, why did investors bid their shares to record heights when measured by absolute dollar value, earnings per share, and the dividend/price ratio? Apart from buying into the notion that projected future earnings justified huge present share values, the market made a dangerously unsupportable link between growth in revenues and share value. With tech startups, the key to most business plans was rapidly building market share, regardless of short-term profitability. Companies had to be first to market with new technology and grab as much of that market as possible, to leave as little room as possible for competitors. But for too many investors, forecasts of triple, quadruple, and even quintuple-digit revenue growth rates were translated into expectations of correspondingly high growth rates in share value, which in turn translated into a willingness to pay escalating prices for shares that had little or no underlying earnings to justify them.

More revenues do not by any means produce more earnings. General Motors might be able to double its revenues by halving the prices of its cars, but that would do nothing for profitability. Nevertheless, there was a clear expectation among investors attracted to the tech boom that so long as revenues kept going up, a company's share price should, too. There was a semi-rational basis to this. If the big prize for profitability down the road was market share, then so long as revenues were growing, the goal was in sight. But this quest for market share did not address the question of what a company was supposed to do with it once it got there. Now that it had market share, how did it become profitable when it had never been before? And how secure was that market share? Was it anything tangible or sustainable? If a company like Nortel dominated 80 percent of the "long haul" optical market, what use was that for the future? How did it translate into higher profits in the future? Would changing technologies make illusory any notion of "share" being somehow proprietary and exploitable down the road? Certainly, market share was a more persuasive concept with a retail venture like Amazon.com, which through dominating its niche could build long-term customer loyalty and with sufficiently high sales might be able to reduce costs based on scale of operation. But if the market share was defined by a particular technology, what good was it? It might reflect a company's dominance of a particular sector, the way Nortel did with optical network backbones and Cisco did with IP routers. But it was not so clear that strong sales automatically meant strong customer loyalty, or that technical dominance in a fast-evolving industry could be counted on to continue.

As tech company revenues grew, dragging share prices along with them, the connection between price and earnings and dividends became dangerously elastic, stretched to unprecedented proportions. By January 2000, average dividends even for S&P 500 companies were only 1.4 percent of the average share price, well below the historic average of 4.7 percent.[11]

It was a shockingly low return on equity when measured purely by dividend returns. By then, the stock market clearly was operating on a different economic model than the one many theorists had long insisted was in effect. Cold-fusion economics was ruling the roost.

At this point, cold-fusion economics should have been exposed for the junk it was, because the market was failing a simple test of risk that made it no less inconsistent with reality than the failure of Pons and Fleischmann to generate massive radiation from their simple apparatus. As we've seen, investments have an irrefutable logic of risk and return: the higher the risk, the higher the promised return must be to make an investor take the greater risk. Conversely, investments with extremely low risks can be offered by their issuers with extremely low returns, reducing borrowing costs, for example, for the highest rated bond issues. By that standard, U.S. government money instruments are supposed to offer the lowest rates of return, and quality corporate bonds follow—ahead of shares from the companies that issue these debt instruments, because debt obligations always have to be paid before shareholder dividends, and in the event of receivership, debtors have a higher claim on assets. Yet, by 2000, the stock market's degree of risk, when measured by D/P, had fallen *below* that of the most secure government debt instruments. How could this be possible? How could a stock be more secure than a U.S. treasury bill?

Of course, it wasn't possible, but that didn't stop market apologists from thinking hard about it. Already, the research by Shiller and Campbell showing historically low D/P values since 1983 was being explained away by references to improved corporate efficiency and the average investor's increasing confidence in the equities markets. A surge in future dividends would prove the current nosebleed share prices to have been correct. But how could investors be more confident in corporate America's abilities to make dividend payments than they were in their own federal, state, and municipal governments' abilities to make good on bond interest and principal? It was the very definition of irrationality.

Some market experts were bold enough to suggest that the D/P value was right—that Mr. and Mrs. Typical Investor were right in their conviction that the U.S. economy was so strong that the future earnings of its companies were a better bet than the civilian administration and the Federal Reserve system. Rock-bottom D/Ps were just a patriotic vote for capitalism. And Shiller identified an accompanying absurdity with high P/E levels. Prices can go higher than prudent P/E levels would suggest if investors decide the risk in equities is lower than is normally thought. And as prices go higher, the dividend yield drops as well. Thus, the higher that a stock price becomes when measured by P/E and D/P, the "safer" the investment is somehow judged to be.[12] This was a seeming recipe for disaster when combined with low interest rates, as low bond yields further encouraged toleration of low D/P—and encouraged investors to borrow money to buy stocks.

But there were other explanations for the ability of cold-fusion economics to survive its glaring failure of logic. One was that the market was completely irrational, the domain of ill-informed investors who didn't resemble in the least the Rational Man investor of the rational markets theory. While research by Shiller and Campbell suggests that investors have not been properly using basic concepts like present discounted value (PDV, which attempts to determine how much money must be invested today to realize the value of a stock and its cumulative dividends at a future date) to gauge share prices, it's more likely that investors haven't been considering present discounted value *at all*. Just look at Shiller's own description of the calculation for PDV's component, dividend present value, in the endnotes to *Irrational Exuberance:*

> To compute the dividend present value for any given month, one sums over each subsequent month the present discounted value for the given month of the real dividends paid in that subsequent month. The present discounted value in the given month of a real dividend paid in a subsequent month is the real dividend divided by $(1+r)^t$, where r is the monthly real discount rate and t is the number of months between the given month and the subsequent month.

While the concept could be explained more eloquently (and Shiller surely would have if he wasn't consigning it to an endnote), the sheer density of the concept makes it highly unlikely that the average investor in the bull market of the 1990s was paying much if any attention to DPV or PDV. There is plenty of evidence that investors were doing shockingly small amounts of due diligence on their investments in the 1990s tech boom. Never mind calculating PDV or bothering to read a company's balance sheet—some even failed to verify if they were actually investing in the proper stock.

Take the strange case of MCI Communications and Massmutual Corporate Investors. MCI Communications, the telecommunications giant that grew out of the pioneering independent long-distance carrier service of 1969, was involved in merger negotiations with a number of telecom firms through 1996–97, eventually being bought by WorldCom. The company traded on the NASDAQ under the symbol MCIC. Research has shown that on noteworthy news days for MCI Communications, the entirely unrelated stock of Massmutual, trading on the NYSE under the symbol MCI, experienced spikes of trading volume and price movement that can only be explained by overeager day traders reacting to newswire items on MCI Communications and blindly piling into a closed-end mutual fund on an entirely different exchange.

In early December 1998, Ticketmaster-Citysearch Inc. was preparing for an IPO on NASDAQ, an event duly noted by a number of on-line media outlets, including Yahoo!Finance and ZDII, which unfortunately carried a Reuters item that incorrectly reported the company's ticker symbol as TMCO instead of TMCS. TMCO belonged to Temco Services Industry Inc., an unassuming building maintenance and security services company that traded on the bulletin board market. The resulting confusion was a brilliant demonstration of how people made investment decisions purely on the strength of an on-line news item.

Part of the problem was that the Ticketmaster IPO was priced a day earlier than expected, accelerating the rush to own shares. Nevertheless, on hearing of the Ticketmaster IPO, gung-ho investors mistakenly began gobbling up Temco shares when the markets opened on December 3. December 2 had been another sleepy day for Temco—3,500 shares were traded, and the stock had closed at $28³/₄.

Temco shareholders and management had a major surprise on the third. So many misguided would-be Ticketmaster investors charged into Temco in the first half hour of trading that its share price was driven up to $65. Meanwhile, the shares they actually wanted were reaching a high of $56³/₈ before settling down to $40¹/₄. By the time wayward investors in Temco realized their error and bailed out of TMCO so they could get into TMCS, 69,000 Temco shares had been traded and its price was driven down as low as $23 before finishing the bewildering day at $25¹/₂.

An ironic note. Investors who drove Ticketmaster's price above $50 on December 3 lost more than 80 percent of their investment by February 2001, when shares fell below $10. Temco, on the other hand, was still trading steadily around $26. Although Ticketmaster reached the low twenties by February 2002, Temco shares were still worth more.

It was that kind of volatile investment climate. The idea that things like D/P, PDV, DPV, and EPS were in any way to be taken seriously was a charade of normalcy, behind which the smart money played the market for what it was: a Ponzi scheme.

Charles Ponzi is the patron saint of investment confidence men. He worked his imperfect magic in the United States in the 1920s. Over the course of seven months, he pulled in 30,000 investors with notes totalling $15 million in value, using the cash acquired from one round of investors to pay off the investors from the previous round, and so on and so on, until there was no one left to tap to compensate the last round and the scheme collapsed. It's the operating principle behind all pyramid schemes, including chain letters. In the stock market, it is known as the Greater Fool Theory. As a stock price escalates, enough participants know the increase is irrational, but they aren't worried in the slightest about all those valuation ratios. They're counting on the fact that there are enough participants who haven't the sense to realize the price is irrational. The object is to buy at a low price and sell at a higher one, to someone ubiquitously known as the Greater Fool. Sooner or later, the price run-up runs out of fools, and the last one gets left holding the bag as the price support collapses.

The prevalence of the Greater Fool Theory helps explain why so many investors were willing to ignore the analytical evidence of Shiller and Campbell that, by 1996, the American markets were irrefutably overvalued. Their conclusions didn't matter, if enough fools were around to keep the market marching upwards. The smart money just had to know when to get in, and get out. And so long as you understood that there was a large supply of fools driving the market ever higher, and that you weren't going to be the greatest fool, there was no reason to get out of the market. This meant that the market could be driven ever higher by a mass of fools who were sure they weren't going to be the ultimate fools. And one of the criticisms of Shiller and Campbell's work from the investor perspective is that had investors listened to them in December 1996 and bailed out of an overvalued market, they would have missed out on several years of double-digit gains. Of course, those gains would only ever be realized if they also knew just when to get out.

A bull market is about capital appreciation, not about profitability. Stock prices are supposed to be rising in advance of increased dividend income, but as Shiller and others have shown, even when dividends do rise, the increase in market value is usually far greater than the dividend increase warrants. The market gets ahead of itself, and the dividends never do catch up. In the meantime, the traditional measure of stock returns is thrown for a loop. Investors normally realize most of their gains through dividends, which is why the dividend yield is considered so essential to assessing appropriate stock price levels. Capital gains are considered important, but are secondary to the dividends. In a bull market, the dividends take a back seat in the rush for returns on equity. Stock values are climbing at a rate far higher than the dividend yield (in fact, the yield often drops), and investors begin making the bulk of their gains by buying and selling the stocks and not worrying particularly about the dividends. Ordinarily, the market is speculative in the sense that stocks are priced in anticipation of changes in dividend payments. In a raging bull market, speculation becomes a step removed from the underlying role of predicting changes in dividends. Trading becomes a speculation in whether the stock itself is going to go up or down. Most people probably think that this is what playing the stock market is about, anyway, which helps explain how disconnected investors have become from the purported objective of generating income on dividend payments.

Speculation in the stock price, and not future dividends, is a runaway phenomenon in a bull market. As we've seen, the stocks are priced aggressively high in anticipation of future, higher dividends. The trading value, when measured against present dividends, results in a depressed yield. Investors looking for dividend income are distressed to find that the market overall is pricing stocks so high that dividend-based investing offers discouragingly low returns—returns at or below the rate of inflation. Whether they like it or not, investors are buying stocks in the expectation that capital gains from increasing share prices will deliver them adequate returns.

But there's an important difference between dividends and capital gains. Dividends don't require the liquidation of the shares for the shareholder to realize the income. With capital gains, unless the shares are sold, the profits are strictly paper ones. To realize actual gains from appreciating stocks, they must be actively bought and sold. Even in a bull market, timing purchases precisely is not easy. You have to get to a stock before the rest of the smart money does, ride the price increase, and then jump off at the right time. The earlier you try to get in on a winner, the more speculative the investment is, because you're implicitly buying something the rest of the market has supposedly undervalued, and the odds are that they're right and you're wrong. It turns out that there are far fewer sure bets in a bull market than people who follow the steady upward progress of an index like the S&P 500 or the TSE 300 might think. These indexes are weighted: the more shares a particular stock has available for trading, the more influence an increase in its share price has on the index level. Consequently, in a smaller equity market like the TSE, a few stocks can have an enormous influence on the index level, as Nortel in particular overwhelmingly demonstrated. Most of the stocks in the TSE 300's boom years actually performed indifferently.

The ascent of a bull market demands an important distinction between investing and trading that too few neophyte stock purchasers make. Investing is a long-haul exercise that involves a diversified portfolio. In addition to dividend-producing equities and some that also promise capital gains, there will be debt instruments like government and corporate bonds, perhaps some real estate, art, and antiques, even some more sophisticated security instruments like derivatives that hedge against downside risks. Risk levels will vary within the portfolio, and there is certainly room for speculative ventures that hope to yield quick and handsome capital returns, but the portfolio has checks and balances to avoid a major reversal.

Buying and selling stocks is not investing: it's trading. It might be a component of an investment strategy, but nonetheless it's a speculative exercise, accepting higher risks in the quest for better than average returns. Unfortunately, many people in the last bull market confused trading with investing, a confusion abetted by members of the securities business, who assured them their purchases were long-term income generators, that there were definitive "floors" to prices of certain stocks, below which they would not fall. Cold-fusion economics was their triumph and their undoing. When cold-fusion economics went stone cold, many of its believers were staring at portfolios full of Nortel shares.

8

Fiscal Optics

Unstructured and undisciplined, "pro forma" financial disclosure starts by rejecting the bedrock of all our financial disclosure requirements—Generally Accepted Accounting Principles.
—SEC Chairman Harvey L. Pitt, November 29, 2001

When the Telecom Act of 1996 cross-pollinated with the rise of the Internet to produce a huge appetite for bandwidth, Nortel was perfectly positioned to exploit the demand, particularly for the "backbone" installations of existing and startup long-distance carriers. It had done its R&D homework and had not only competitive fibre-optic networking products, but solutions no other company could match—especially not Lucent.

Nortel's technology coup could not have come in a better sector of the networking business. The overall optical systems market was predicted to enjoy a compound annual rate of growth of 35.8 percent from 1999 to 2003, according to research by RHK and Pioneer Consulting, cited by Epoch Partners in its initial coverage of Nortel released December 12, 2000. In December 1999, the fibre-optic trade publication *Lightwave* published an article predicting that the global fibre-optic market would reach $15.8 billion in 2000. Incredibly, the author, Jeff Montgomery, chairman of ElectroniCast Corp. of San Mateo, California, hazarded that the global market would reach $738 billion in 2025. That was not all. "Fiber-optic components plus electronic and other components plus software will combine to support global-communication equipment valued at several trillion dollars in 2025," Montgomery promised. So much fibre-optic cable was going to be laid per year that one had to wonder if there was going to be any room left for pedestrians on sidewalks.

Without question, fibre optics was the hot sector in the broadband industry. The rise of the Internet, with increased modem speeds and corporate enthusiasm for e-commerce, was expected to create an overwhelming amount of data traffic. The wireless evolution was going to compound that traffic demand, as existing wireless service, poorly suited to moving large amounts of data with its feeble 14K transmission rate, gave way to third generation (3G) digital wireless, whose 2-mbps speed was considered hefty enough to allow personal digital assistants like PalmPilots and laptop computers equipped with wireless modems to surf the Web. Companies dedicated to laying thousands of miles of new fibre-optic backbone, such as Global Crossing and 360networks, added to the fibre-optic appetites of existing telecom carriers and the local exchange carrier startups.

In the mid-1990s there were two rival standards for moving information through glass fibres. SONET was the predominant optical networking standard. But having been established by Bellcore in 1988, it predated the data-networking explosion of the Internet, and a new standard, called Dense Wavelength Division Multiplexing, or DWDM, had emerged.

The most important thing to know about DWDM is that it is far better suited to handling IP-based traffic. SONET, for all its robustness and reliability, is fairly inefficient in handling data traffic, and DWDM was seen as the future of optics, particularly as IP began to creep toward widespread use in voice traffic as well. SONET was being decried as a "legacy" system, a term used in the computer world for old mainframes and software programs that represented significant capital investment. Purveyors of newer technology have to work their way around a legacy behemoth by either making the case for its complete removal or offering a way to build gracefully upon it. In trying to sell ATM into the corporate networking environment, Nortel had come up against a legacy system of sorts in IP-based Ethernet. Nortel's success in selling SONET systems would be interpreted as either a danger or an opportunity. It was a danger because

Nortel's prominence in SONET left it "exposed" to its obsolescence. On the other hand, the huge installed base of Nortel SONET gear would present Nortel with the opportunity to leverage its customer base with "next generation" SONET products that could build on the legacy systems while accommodating the demands of data traffic.

DWDM was supposed to be a Lucent strength. The company had deployed the first commercial DWDM system in 1995 and showed off a 20-gbps system the following year. Lucent grabbed the lead in DWDM, delivering what it claimed to be an industry-leading number of systems worldwide by May 1998.

But having established the lead, Lucent stumbled badly in late 1998 by missing the timing of the next technology rollout, thus leaving a huge segment of the market wide open for Nortel.

For a while, OC-48, with a bandwidth of 2.5 gbps, was the top of the scale in Bellcore's standards. It was also the widest-bandwith optical networking product offered by Lucent. But Nortel went one better by coming up with ready-for-market networking products for both SONET and DWDM at a new standard of OC-192, which had four times the bandwidth of OC-48—a competition-crushing 10 gbps. For long-distance backbone networks, bandwidth is everything, and when the carrier market made a strong shift toward OC-192 in late 1998, Nortel was ready and waiting. For almost two years, Nortel had absolutely no competition in OC-192 optical networks. Lucent, it was felt, had missed the boat by concentrating on OC-48, which was the standard the Baby Bells were satisfied to deploy. But because Nortel was alone in being able to deliver OC-192 product, it scored major contracts with important customers like British Telecom and Qwest, who simply had no other place to turn than Nortel.

By the spring of 1999, it was becoming apparent that Nortel had scored a major coup with its OC-192 systems. In the third quarter of 1998, when Nortel was taking a beating over the Bay Networks acquisition and the Essex House fiasco, Lucent had held the lead in global SONET sales, with more than 30 percent of the market, according to estimates by Dell'Oro Group. Nortel was about ten points back, and Fujitsu trailed in the low teens. By the first quarter of 1999, the market had been turned upside down by the surge in demand for OC-192 SONET that only Nortel could satisfy. Lucent's share was down to the mid-twenties, and Nortel had taken the lead at around 28 percent. Lucent's fall from grace was astonishing. By the second quarter of 2000, Lucent's share was below 15 percent, outperformed even by Fujitsu, which had been trending around the mid-teens, and Nortel's market share was approaching 40 percent. By the third quarter of 2000, Nortel held about 83 percent of the world market in OC-192 SONET, and about 81 percent of OC-192 DWDM, according to Dell'Oro.

At the same time, Nortel was doing very well in mobile wireless, which was expected to grow at a compound annual rate of 14.5 percent from 1999 to 2003. As Epoch would point out, Nortel probably ranked fourth overall in global market share, but unlike its major competitors, which tended to be specialists, Nortel had strengths in all mobile communications sectors. If Motorola (which was alone in selling products using a protocol called integrated digital enhanced networks, or iDEN) was excluded, Nortel stood third overall.

The buzz over Nortel's OC-192 fibre-optic triumph was largely responsible for the company's quick turnaround in 1999. As it outperformed analyst expectations, its choppy passage through the last half of 1998 quickly fell astern. John Roth had evidently built a networking winner. In August 1999, the absorption of Bay Networks was effectively pronounced complete; Dave House left as president and Roth reassumed the job, in addition to his duties as CEO.

Nortel was defeating the once-vaunted Lucent in high-speed optical networking while still going neck-and-neck with it in the core business of voice switching. Nortel introduced a new switching platform called Succession as a means to move its considerable customer base in telephone voice switching from the old central-office circuit-switching standard to a multiservice network with packet-switching capability. And while opinions were far from unanimous about the wisdom (and expense) of the Bay Networks deal, there was no arguing with the fact that it had given Nortel a strong presence in IP-based networking. By 2000, according to Dell'Oro data, Nortel would enjoy 9.6 percent of the LAN market (a distant second to Cisco's

59.2 percent) and a sector-leading 37.1 percent of the WAN market (its single largest competitors being Lucent, at 20.4 percent, and Cisco, at 17.7 percent).

These numbers all sounded impressive, but for a publicly traded company, the most important number was how much money Nortel was earning for every shareholder. And here, the global leader in high-speed fibre-optics found itself in need of some sophisticated fiscal optics.

As noted earlier, the relationship between share price and profitability is customarily defined by the price/earnings ratio, while return on equity depends fundamentally on the dividend/price ratio. It goes without saying that you can't calculate either ratio without the company earning something. Normally, not having any earnings is a problem for a company and its stock price, because if you're not making money, you're losing it. Cold-fusion economics, however, figured out a way to turn losing money into something actually advantageous to stock values.

Like cold-fusion physics, cold-fusion economics began with recognizable processes. Cold-fusion physics was built on elemental chemistry. Cold-fusion economics was built on elemental processes of speculative industries. There are certain situations in which the market tolerates, even expects, companies to lose money. With start-up companies, it's typical not to have any profits—and even little in the way of revenues—for several years as the business brings its products to market. Technology companies can spend years in the R&D phase of creating marketable products, with virtually no sales to report. Yet their shares can be worth quite a lot, and even grow handsomely in value.

While this may seem counterintuitive to the norm of P/E guidance, the explanation is simple. Tech startup companies are not much different than traditional mining ventures. A mining company may be founded on the basis of promising assays from a prospector at a particular stake. There's no mine yet, and there may not be one for several years if mineral prices do not justify the cost of actually extracting and refining the ore. Investors are willing to gamble perhaps a few pennies per share at the startup phase, betting that, down the road, the company will actually be able to operate a profitable mine. In other words, they can see possible dividends in the future, and since all market pricing is supposed to be based on future, rather than present, earnings, it makes no difference whether the company is making or losing money at the moment. So long as profits can be forecast, a market value can be assigned to the stock.

Companies and analysts can get around the problem of there being no past or present earnings by offering a "future" or "forward-looking" P/E. As the earnings potential increases—perhaps the ore deposit turns out to be larger than originally estimated, or the ore price has increased on world markets to the point that a large and very profitable mine can be built—the share price goes up as well, regardless of the fact that there are not yet any revenues or profits. With typical stocks, this forward-looking P/E is based on the guidance provided by the company and analysts' estimates of earnings for the coming quarters or year. As the earnings picture improves, the stock worth 50 cents jumps to $2. There's money to be made here, despite the absence of earnings, and you don't even wait for the dividends to finally arrive. You just have to buy low and sell high.

While this may seem an obvious point—welcome to stock market speculation—it's important to draw the logical conclusion from it and revisit the magic box we previously inspected. The company, as it is now operating, has an entirely different cash flow system. There's little or nothing coming in the revenue pipe, little or nothing going out the dividend pipe to shareholders. Yet the company is functioning in a new dimension of profitability.

In this new model, the cash flowing in through the revenue pipe and then out through the dividend pipe is entirely secondary to the practical, bottom-line profitability. On a pure accounting basis, the company may be unprofitable—even grossly so—but that doesn't mean there aren't profits to be made by investors. A highly unprofitable enterprise can be extremely profitable to individual shareholders. You might say that the important cash flow has been rerouted in the plumbing.

Let's return to our model of the startup company. For most any new business (with the exception of subsidiaries spun off from companies), there is a departure point at which there are little or no revenues at all. The new venture needs to hire staff, lease things, fund R&D, figure out the manufacturing of a saleable product, and build sales and marketing operations. It all requires startup capital without the revenues necessary to replenish it. The company is going to have to operate at a loss for a foreseeable period (spelled out in its business plan), and that requires a storeroom of cash with which to operate. Generally, the cash cannot be borrowed because there's not much to pledge in the way of collateral. Startups often get going with the personal savings of the principals and some help from an "angel"—a wealthy relative or associate. More formally, venture capitalists come through with the funds to get the startup to the launch pad, taking an equity position in return for providing the money to keep a high-risk investment afloat. The business plan may call for $10 million in expenditures in the startup period, which has a horizon of two years. In the tech startup business, the speed at which money was consumed by these new firms became known as the "burn rate," and in the above example our startup is burning through $27,397.20 a day.

The typical business plan in the tech startup heyday of the 1990s did not envision reaching a profitability horizon before the initial startup capital was consumed. More capital would be required. The company would have to either go cap in hand back to private equity markets for another round of venture capital, or turn to the general investment community with an initial public offering (IPO) on a particular stock exchange. In the go-go late nineties, the IPO route was the favoured one for startups, in part because it allowed the company to access a far broader pool of investment capital. Another reason was that certain industries, especially software, liked the transparency of a public company: disclosure requirements for publicly traded stocks allowed industry members to see the fiscal guts of partners, suppliers, and customers, and be reassured about their viability. To be part of this transparent club, companies were compelled to go the IPO route.

Becoming a publicly traded joint-stock company also brought an enticing new dynamic to the cash-flow plumbing. The stock market entirely supplanted the need for earnings. It didn't expect them from high-growth startups, and it happily replaced earnings (as well as revenues) with speculative returns. And those returns were flowing in unusual new directions. Revenues no longer were the primary source of funds with which to pay employees and reimburse investors. Those funds now came from the investment community, and they were distributed in the form of rapid stock appreciation.

A stock that shot through the roof could bring great, almost instantaneous wealth to several classes of investor. First, the venture capitalists who put up the seed money could make a killing on an IPO if the investment bank handling the deal set the issue price far enough below the price the aftermarket—the exchange on which the stock was to be listed—was actually willing to pay for it. The difference between the offering price and the price established in the first days of trading in the aftermarket is known as the "pop." One of the earliest, most admired pops was by Netscape in November 1995. The offering price, initially set as low as $12, was finally pegged at $28, but that still didn't match the aftermarket's enthusiasm for this early Internet stock. On the first day of trading, it reached a high of $71 before finishing the day at $58¼. When the NASDAQ closed for the day, Netscape co-founder Jim Clark had a paper worth of $566 million, while junior partner Marc Andreessen clocked in at $59 million—a pretty good one-day fortune for a young man who had been paid $6.85 an hour while helping create Netscape's forerunner, Mosaic, as a graduate student at the University of Illinois.[13]

As San Jose *Mercury News* journalist David Plotnikoff would reflect, "On Wall Street and in Silicon Valley the news [of the Netscape IPO] was tantamount to a messenger riding at a full gallop through San Francisco in 1849 shouting 'Gold! There's gold on the American River!'"

IPOs with a lot of pop brought instant, massive capital gains to those privileged enough to hold shares at the offering price. These included the original venture cap folks, company principals, and any entity close enough to the investment bank to be fortunate enough to get on the distribution list. Best of all, the huge paper profits didn't come out of the pockets of anyone who mattered. It was the stock market that put up the cash. There was a significant downside to such a pop, however. An IPO was meant to raise capital for the company. If the IPO was seriously underpriced, every dollar of profit made in the aftermarket by those on the distribution list was a dollar that didn't go to the company treasury in a properly priced offering. Sometimes this was unavoidable, because it was hard to read the mood of an irrational investment climate. But if you were one of the people being made fantastically rich by the pop, you probably didn't much care about the IPO undershooting on the offering price. Which should have been a bad sign, because it meant people directly involved in running the company cared less about its long-term viability than did the investors who paid for their popped shares in the aftermarket.

Getting that pop, and sustaining the increase in share price, didn't actually require broad acceptance by investors that the traditional magic box plumbing wasn't important any more. They just had to be shown a new way of calculating earnings. One strategy possible under Canadian GAAP was to get as many expenses as possible off the income statement and squirrel them away on the balance sheet—the tally of assets and liabilities—where they wouldn't have an impact on present earnings. The number of items that can go in either place is practically endless. Interest expense, overhead, management salaries, to name a few, can be removed from the deductions normally applied against revenues, assigned a capital value, and turned into an asset on the balance sheet. Canadian GAAP permitted this in a number of situations: for example, if the company was starting up a new enterprise, if it was doing development-type activity, if it was researching the possibility of going into an area of business that would be of future benefit. Basically, it was permitted in situations where the company could argue that the costs were dedicated to earnings that would show up in the near future.

In the United States, the potential for abuse had long been recognized with this type of accounting—that is, deferring reportage of actual expenditures to improve the company's profitability and cash-flow picture. U.S. GAAP prescribed that, when in doubt, a cost must show up on the income statement. Canadian GAAP, however, was far more lenient, leaving it up to the company and its auditors to do the right thing.

While shifting costs off the income statement was open to abuse under Canadian GAAP, it was at least a GAAP-permissible strategy. When it came to the big-ticket deduction items, however, there was no way to make them disappear completely under any GAAP scheme. Fortuitously, companies began using their own custom calculations of income, which showed a profit where GAAP would never permit.

Public companies in Canada and the United States could not supplant GAAP figures on their income statements, but they could use their own earnings numbers in communications with the press and investors. As we've seen, these custom income calculations were mainly variations on EBITDA, and their proliferation was undoubtedly encouraged by the problem in comparing profitability when one company was using pooling and the other the purchase method in acquisitions. Defenders of this pro forma type of reportage say that stripping away certain costs, particularly one-time charges, can give an investor a much better picture of a company's performance. Pro forma type accounting is well suited to placing corporate performance in a historic context, by setting aside non-recurring revenues and expenses. A single acquisition, for example, can obsure a company's core performance for the year and make it impossible to draw reasonable comparisons between one fiscal year and another. But once companies like Nortel, Cisco, and Lucent went on massive acquisition binges, the very idea of acquisitions (and divestitures to raise cash) being "non-recurring" began to defy logic. Pro forma accounting also allowed tech companies to "reach" profitability long before they were actually profitable. By removing fundamental business costs such as interest, depreciation, amortization, and taxes from the income statement in calculating their own versions of earnings and earnings per share, companies also conditioned investors to think that those costs actually didn't matter and somehow didn't even exist. In the case of Nortel, custom accounting made almost all the costs associated with its acquisition binge magically evaporate.

Nortel's diversification into the cutting-edge world of bookkeeping began with the 1998 annual report, released on February 25, 1999.

On page 12, the company provided something it called "Supplementary measure of net earnings." As Nortel explained:

> The supplementary measure of net earnings, which excludes the amortization of the Bay Networks intangible assets and purchased in-process R&D from other acquisitions, and one-time gains and charges, for the year ended December 31, 1998, represents year-over-year growth in net earnings per common share of 21 percent for 1998 compared to 1997, and of 28 percent for 1997 compared to 1996.

Supplementary measure of net earnings? What on earth was that? We might assume that Frank Dunn, having been in the post of chief financial officer for about a month when the report was released, had discovered a hitherto unknown form of cost management. But Nortel's customized accounting cannot be considered in isolation, for its benefits extended beyond Nortel's financial statements to those of BCE. Jean Monty had turned over command of Nortel to John Roth in 1997 as he took charge of BCE, which then held about 52 percent of Nortel stock. Monty was hailed as Canada's CEO of the Year as he vacated Nortel, an accolade lying in wait for Roth as well. Both men then embarked on ambitious expansion schemes for their companies; in Monty's case, it was to turn BCE into a diversified communications holding company, with investments in telecommunication carriers, technology suppliers (through Nortel) and content providers. As we shall see, the way Nortel cleaved away acquisition costs with its "supplementary measure of net earnings" was critical to the way BCE came to present its own profitability. For now, it's important to recognize that Nortel had come up with something as revolutionary as cold fusion. Pons and Fleischmann had managed to create energy without radiation. Nortel had managed to create earnings without expenses.

The "supplemental measure" in no way replaced Nortel's use of GAAP in its formal statement of operations. Instead, this new measure was something offered up by the company to give what it presumably considered to be a more enlightening snapshot of the company's fiscal health. And what a snapshot it was, for not only did the company have positive earnings where none existed under GAAP—those earnings were actually increasing in the form of something called "net earnings per common share."

This was a fascinating use of terminology, because in the normal accounting scheme of things, "net" is considered to mean

> Obtained after deducting all expenses, losses, taxes, etc.; distinguished from *gross: net* proceeds . . . To earn or yield as clear profit.[14]

It's hard to square the word "net" with a measure of profitability that leaves billions in legitimate costs in a lonely box in a corner of the finance department. Nortel would take another shot at its terminology, but for the time being the company had introduced its new method of presenting profitability and performance. While the income statement—or statement of operations, as it was labelled in Nortel's financial statements—would faithfully adhere to GAAP principles, Nortel was going to offer up a supplementary version of its performance that it clearly preferred to be accepted as the actual measure.

On the opening page of the 1998 annual report's financial section, the company presented three bar-chart graphs tracking what it intended to be the three most important measures of its performance for the past five years: "revenues," "supplementary measure of net earnings applicable to common shares," and "supplementary measure of earnings per common share." Nothing whatsoever about GAAP earnings. Arrows helpfully pointed out how the first was up by 14 percent, the second by 32 percent, the third by 21 percent. Imagine that: earnings growth was outstripping revenue growth!

The "supplementary measure of net earnings" was able to turn a $569 million GAAP *loss* into a $1 billion profit. And if that didn't make people happy, Nortel also threw in the EBITDA profit of $2.6 billion.

EBITDA was nothing new to tech industry investors. But this "supplementary measure" was a neat stunt. Nortel explained it with the following footnote:

> Net earnings from operations applicable to common shares is
> defined as reported net earnings applicable to common shares
> before Acquisition Related Costs (the amortization of Bay
> Networks and Cambrian Systems Corporation intangible assets
> and purchased in-process research and development from other
> acquisitions).

Cambrian Systems of Kanata, Ontario, the tech suburb of Ottawa, had been acquired by Nortel in December 1998 for $231 million in cash and the assumption of $17 million in liabilities. (All acquistion figures in U.S. GAAP.) The deal was greeted with far more enthusiasm by analysts than the one for Bay had been. Cambrian was an emerging-technology company whose OPTera product would allow Nortel to offer a high-speed product for moving optical traffic between Internet backbone networks and metropolitan level (or "metro") networks.

What were the "acquisition-related costs" in the Bay and Cambrian deals that Nortel saw fit to leave out of its calculation of supplemental earnings? Pretty well everything Nortel had paid for, except for tangible assets, of which Cambrian happened to have none. "Intangible assets" consisted of three things: the goodwill on the purchase, the acquired technology, and the in-process research and development (IPR&D). Goodwill, as we have seen, is the surplus of the purchase price over an acquisition's net asset value. "Acquired technology" is, as Nortel described it, "the value of the proprietary 'know-how' which was technologically feasible as of the acquisition date, and is charged to earnings on a straight-line basis over its esti-mated useful life of three years." IPR&D (again to quote Nortel's report) is "the value of the acquired R&D which was not technolog-ically feasible as of the acquisition date and has no alternative future use, and is charged to earnings using an accelerated amortization method over its estimated useful life of six to nine months."

So Nortel was saying to shareholders and possible investors: we're making a supplemental calculation for you of something we still call "net" earnings, for which we're ignoring entirely the majority of expenses associated with acquiring the companies whose ability to make us money is reflected in our revenue figure. We know this makes it look like we got these companies, their technology, and their revenues where applicable practically *for free,* but that's the way we'd prefer to present it.

The idea that it somehow was informative for investors to ignore the intangibles associated with its acquisitions was particularly puzzling with Cambrian. For starters, this was not an acquisition that used Nortel shares. Any argument that goodwill in this case could be ignored because it didn't represent "real" money was indefensible. With Cambrian, Nortel spent real dollars. Yet it was somehow okay to remove the actual use of those dollars in purchasing IPR&D ($204 million, amortized over six months), not to mention $48 million in goodwill being amortized over five years.

That wasn't the only cash Nortel had spent on acquisitions in 1998. Before the huge Bay acquisition, Nortel had made several lesser deals (in addition to the investments in Juniper Networks and Avici). On January 9, it had acquired Broadband Networks Inc., which gave Nortel emerging technology in broadband wireless networks. The $433 million price was met with $149 million in cash and 5.6 million common shares. Only $29 million of that purchase involved tangible assets. IPR&D came to $329 million and goodwill to $75 million.

On April 22, Nortel had acquired Aptis Communications Inc., a Massachusetts startup with remote-access data-networking know-how. The price was $286 million. Up-front, Nortel paid with $5 million in cash and 2.5 million in common shares. Another $37 million in cash and common shares were to be paid to Aptis security holders over three years; in 1998, $3 million had been paid out (Nortel didn't say how much of that was cash or shares). And there was a contingency of a further $71 million to be paid if performance milestones were met. Aptis had only $11 million in tangible assets. IPR&D came to $203 million and goodwill to $72 million.

On June 8, Nortel's subsidiary Entrust Technologies had acquired the Zurich-based security and encryption company r3 Security

Engineering AG. The $24 million price was met with $4 million in cash and about 1.1 million Nortel common shares. IPR&D came to $20 million, goodwill to $4 million.

Finally, on December 22, Nortel had paid $18 million in cash to Bell Canada for the remaining 30 percent ownership of Nortel Technology Ltd., as Bell Northern Research had been renamed. In total in 1998, Nortel laid out at least $407 million in cash in the deals for Aptis, Broadband, r3, Cambrian and Nortel Technology. Leaving aside Nortel Technology, that cash had purchased just $40 million in tangible assets. (With Cambrian, tangibles had been swallowed by assumed liabilities, producing a "liabilities net of tangible assets" of $4 million.)[15] What is so strange about this calculation strategy is that, in the cases of r3, Aptis, and Broadband, Nortel specifically targeted IPR&D—and not goodwill—for removal from its customized earnings figure.

The big hit Nortel avoided with its supplementary earnings calculation was all the IPR&D it booked with the 1998 acquisitions. Because Nortel was writing these assets down on a six-to-nine-month basis, most of the hit on revenues came under GAAP in 1998—$1.24 billion in all—whereas goodwill was being amortized over a period of several years. For Cambrian, Bay, r3, Aptis, and Broadband, IPR&D came to $1.76 billion in total. But with Nortel's new supplementary earnings numbers, that $1.24 billion IPR&D amortization for 1998 didn't exist. Nor would the remainder of the write-down be accounted for in future supplementary earnings figures.

To understand Nortel's decision to obliterate the amortization charges for IPR&D and acquired technology in its custom figures, it is necessary to understand a problem with intangibles at the very heart of GAAP. As the Financial Accounting Standards Board explained when it launched a new project to study intangibles recognition in August 2001, formal accounting only required companies to recognize intangibles—that is, place a value on them and show them as an asset—when they were acquired, either separately or as part of a business combination. Intangibles generated internally by a company weren't recognized as assets at all. And because acquired intangibles were written down so rapidly, they quickly vanished into the unrecognized internal intangibles.

This meant that, in comparing one company with another, investors had no real way of knowing how much in the way of "internal" intangibles one company had versus another. The new knowledge economy was based on assets that good old GAAP couldn't get its head around. Assets to GAAP were things like buildings, machinery, and inventory. Assets to new-economy enterprises were things like patents and trademarks—the know-how stuff. Investors could only see the acquired know-how stuff, not only in the list of assets but in the writedowns, which showed up as a charge against revenues.

To level the playing field for comparison purposes, tech companies like Nortel, in creating their supplementary earnings figures, chose to delete the charges suffered against revenues for their acquired intangibles. As the FASB put it, "the comparative procedure available now is to subtract all recognized intangibles, which allows investors to compare adjusted amounts that ignore all intangible assets." But as the FASB concluded, "In view of the increasing importance of intangibles, that approach is suboptimal."

More than "suboptimal," it made no sense when subtracting all recognized intangibles actually meant subtracting the cost of acquiring them. Even if GAAP methods did not show an asset value for internally generated intangibles on the balance sheet, they at least showed the costs of creating them on the income statement. Those costs ran through the income statement: in the various charges against revenues for salaries, R&D expense, in the fees paid to outside agencies that created trademarks like corporate logos and to patent lawyers to register proprietary discoveries, and in an array of costs associated with operating research campuses, from the bricks and mortar to the cleaning staff. Removing intangible acquisition costs from the income statement because the value of internally generated intangibles weren't represented over on the balance sheet was a prima facie case of throwing away an apple to account for the absence of an orange. Nevertheless, companies went right ahead and did it, in part because the practice was consistent with the desire to show a company's "cash basis" performance.

Once a company started stripping away these acquisition charges for comparison purposes with its competitors, and everyone began thinking of the resulting bottom line as the measure of the company's real performance, a serious discrepancy cropped up in the relative expenses of in-house and acquired know-how. The company that bought its know-how and then took the costs out of the income statement for comparison purposes looked more profitable than a company that produced its own know-how. When something purchased becomes free in an accounting methodology, it makes infinitely more sense to buy it rather than develop it internally, where a charge against earnings results from the day-to-day activities of the R&D department.

This was the crux of the argument against customized earnings numbers. They started out as a tool to compare one company with another, particularly in an acquisition-mad economy with imperfect accounting rules. But this solution to the apparent inadequacies of GAAP warped the value of purchased know-how. Customized figures no longer served to get around the asset discrepancy between acquired and internally generated know-how. They now effectively argued that know-how should be purchased. When supplemental earnings figures became the basis for assessing corporate performance, then operating on the basis that acquired intangibles were free, whereas intangibles generated in-house had an unavoidable impact on EPS, was practically unavoidable. Consequently, so was growth through repeated acquisitions.

Presumably the reason Nortel bought all these firms was to get hold of the knowledge Nortel itself lacked, and presumably that knowledge made a measurable contribution to Nortel's operations. This was particularly obvious in the case of Cambrian, for which more than 80 percent of the purchase price was represented by IPR&D, and its expertise was considered fundamental to Nortel cracking the metro optical markets. Yet what Nortel's supplementary earnings figures proposed was that all that expertise cost nothing. Nortel hadn't developed that expertise in its own R&D efforts, and now a whole bunch of fresh expertise—$1.76 billion of IPR&D, to be charged against revenues under GAAP through 1999, and another $2 billion in acquired technology from Bay, to be written down over three years—had shown up, free of charge. To appreciate the sheer scale of this free know-how, Nortel's own R&D expenses were just $2.15 billion in 1997 and $2.45 billion in 1998.

It must be understood that the value of IPR&D in its acquisitions was determined by estimating (according to Nortel) "fair value based on risk-adjusted future cash flows generated from the products that would result from each of the in-process projects." Thus, IPR&D's values were implicitly based on their ability to make Nortel money. On that basis, it was absurd not to report IPR&D charges in its earnings-from-operations when that value was directly linked to revenue generation.

There's something else to consider with the write-downs of all the intangibles. Conventional tangible assets are written down over much longer periods, up to forty years. With Nortel's acquisitions, which had little if anything in the way of tangibles, the various intangibles were being aggressively amortized: as little as six months for IPR&D, three years for acquired technology. In addition to acknowledging how quickly R&D and technology became passé, these short write-down periods meant that the companies Nortel was buying were very quickly going to become, for all intents and purposes, worthless. Unless Nortel capitalized quickly on the expertise represented by their acquired technology and IPR&D, either by producing marketable products or effectively incorporating the purchased know-how into its own product development, these expensive acquisitions would be a futile use of hundreds of millions of dollars in cash and billions of dollars in shares.

The impact on Nortel's 1998 losses could have been far higher had Nortel not changed its allocations of the purchase costs in the cases of Bay, Aptis, and Broadband after the third quarter. A total of $579 million was shifted away from in-process R&D and reclassified as goodwill, which had a much longer amortization period. (The goodwill and IPR&D charges already discussed for these companies adhere to the year-end restatement.) The resulting savings in amortization charges reduced Nortel's loss for the year by $385 million.

Once the IPR&D costs for r3, Aptis, and Broadband were behind it, Nortel calculated its customized earnings figures by stripping away the expense of goodwill, IPR&D, and acquired technology in every deal from Bay Networks onwards. All the proper GAAP deductions could be found in its financial statements, and in its announcements of quarterly earnings Nortel was careful to state its actual performance under GAAP. But Nortel always led with the supplemental earnings figures, which when the 1999 first-quarter results were released on April 27, had acquired new labels: "Net earnings from operations" and "EPS from operations."

Apparently, no longer were these numbers "supplementary" in the press releases, although Nortel's 1999 annual report did contain a "supplementary measure of earnings per common share" and an explanatory section called "supplementary measure of net earnings." On the other hand, in the annual report's "selected financial data" section, which led off the earnings discussions and was said to be "prepared in accordance with Canadian generally accepted accounting principles," Nortel offered "net earnings applicable to common shares from operations" and "earnings per common share from operations"—both of which, as footnotes pointed out, left out the heap of acquisition costs. Saying these numbers were prepared in accordance with Canadian GAAP was really stretching things.

Nortel's new terminology sounded like something right out of a standard accounting handbook. As it happened, in its second-quarter 1999 statement of operations, Nortel did label its revenues before interest and taxes as "operating earnings," but this term vanished from subsequent statements, perhaps because it was too easy to confuse with the company's customized earnings numbers.

The April 27, 1999, press release read:

> **Nortel Networks Reports Record First Quarter Results**
> • **Revenues Up 26% to US$4.4 Billion**
> • **EPS From Operations Up 22% to US$0.33**
> BRAMPTON, Ontario—Nortel Networks* [NYSE: NT/ TSE: NTL] today reported results for the first quarter of 1999. Revenues increased 26 percent to US$4.42 billion for the first quarter of 1999 from US$3.51 billion for the same period in 1998. Net earnings from operations applicable to common

shares (a) for the quarter was US$222 million, or US$0.33 per
share, compared to US$140 million, or US$0.27 per share, for
the same period in 1998. Including Acquisition Related Costs
(a) of US$692 million (primarily related to the amortization of
the Bay Networks, Inc. (Bay Networks) intangible assets),
Nortel Networks recorded a net loss applicable to common
shares in the first quarter of 1999 of US$470 million, or
US$0.71 per share, as compared to a loss of US$32 million,
or US$0.06 per share, in the first quarter of 1998.

Nortel's performance was cleverly stated. Yes, the company got
around to noting there had actually been a $470 million loss in that
quarter, but that was because of "acquisition related costs." The
release didn't explicitly say that the numbers in the headlines were
Nortel's own accounting invention and that the figures burdened by
these "acquisition related costs" were the real GAAP numbers.
Footnote (a) explained that "net earnings from operations applicable
to common shares is defined as reported net earnings applicable to
common shares before Acquisition Related Costs (the amortization
of Bay Networks and Cambrian Systems Corporation intangible
assets and purchased in-process research and development from other
acquisitions)." Again, nothing explicitly stating "This stuff is actually
GAAP and that stuff in the headline and at the start of the paragraph
is something with no basis in formal accounting principles that we'd
prefer you to focus on." It was even more confusing in the 1999
report, when the selected financial data were said to be prepared in
accordance with Canadian GAAP and yet included the customized
"earnings from operations" numbers.

With the 1999 first-quarter news release, Nortel had settled on
a consistent way of presenting its performance for the future. By
always emphasizing its "net earnings from operations" figures, it
managed to get investors and analysts thinking of the company from
this cost-eviscerated perspective. Nortel guidance became based on
its net earnings from operations, and so analyst estimates also fell in
line. When investors visited investment Web sites, they would often
find that in the capsule profiles of Nortel the EPS figure was based

not on its GAAP financial statements, but was the "EPS from operations" figure Nortel played up in its communications. Here was proof positive that if you say something over and over again, it becomes true.

The "earnings from operations" concept was a strategic triumph. It established a predominant perception of the company's performance that allowed Nortel to go on an acquisition spree using the purchase method without being burdened by the intangibles that represented most of the expense of those acquisitions. The cold-fusion skeptics would have done well to wonder how Nortel could justify reporting revenues made possible by its acquisitions without deducting the costs of the IPR&D and acquired technology. In a way, Nortel's cold-fusion bookkeeping was more outrageous than Pons and Fleischmann's cold-fusion energy. The two Utah chemists at least included the ingredients necessary to produce their alleged surplus heat. Nortel was creating profits without adding in the acquired technology and IPR&D behind the products it sold. That was like Pons and Fleischmann skipping the deuterium altogether.

Nortel explained the purpose of the earnings-from-operations figures in the 1999 annual report. "As a measure to assess financial performance, management utilizes supplementary measures of net earnings and earnings per common share," the report explained. Note that these numbers were supposed to be a tool used by *management*, not, it implied, by shareholders. For as the explanation added, "Supplementary measures of net earnings and earnings per common share should not be considered as an alternative to net earnings (loss) applicable to common shares and earnings (loss) before income taxes (as determined in accordance with Canadian GAAP)." That said, Nortel still supplied these management-assessment tools to shareholders and the public at large through its financial statements and press releases.

Nortel's use of earnings-from-operations cannot be dismissed simply as some public relations dodge, however beneficial it was in overcoming GAAP-based losses. Nortel's custom numbers didn't develop in a vacuum. Hostility to GAAP numbers during the nineties was widespread; according to Thomson Financial/First Call,

48 companies in the S&P 500 were issuing pro forma type results by 2001, where there had been almost none in 1998. The tech sector's urgent enthusiasm for growth through mergers and acquisitions forced formal accounting methods into a secondary role as companies, investors, and analysts sought to use supplementary measurements that achieved what they argued was a more meaningful measure of performance. That didn't mean such numbers couldn't be abused or misinterpreted. But even when used in good faith, the fact that various supplementary numbers had no consistency from one company to another, no formal review of their methodology by a standards board, meant that the numbers were a precarious basis on which to measure corporate performance and the value of shares.

GAAP was far from perfect. The problems with recognizing intangibles and the ongoing review of pooling and purchase method accounting in the U.S. showed that it required some serious fine-tuning. But at least these principles were a set of rules to be applied equally to all companies, and were overseen by authoritative accounting bodies. The rules could be revised, but they shouldn't be ignored. The key was to understand how GAAP worked, and where its difficulties lay.

In the nineties bull market, however, supplemental figures had largely ceased to be supplemental, becoming de facto accepted by investors as the primary measure of corporate performance. The accounting boards can be blamed for not moving quickly enough to introduce necessary reforms, but as we'll see with pooling, they were facing a lot of resistance from companies benefitting from it. The result, nonetheless, was a dangerous disdain for GAAP at all levels of the public markets: among companies, analysts, and investors. This left investors, the least sophisticated of all market participants, with the enormous task of understanding two different sets of books: the official GAAP level, which was riven with idiosyncrasies and unhelpful opacity, and the supplemental information, which, as in the case of Nortel, raised serious questions about the consequences of following its particular metrics in executing a business plan or in deciding what shares were worth. If management wanted to use supplemental figures of its own creation to assess corporate performance, then it behooved investors to take a hard look at those figures and pointedly ask why they were so much more informative than GAAP, and what the consequences might be of management following them. At the same time, they needed to understand GAAP's considerable foibles.

Nortel's directors and management were using the earnings-from-operations figures to measure the performance not only of the company, as the 1999 annual report said, but of its most senior executive as well. As the company's proxy circular of March 13, 2000, stated, "The 1999 salary, bonus and stock option awards for Mr. Roth all reflected the attainment of record 1999 revenues *and operating earnings and operating earnings per share* [italics added]." Nortel has to be taken at its word here. John Roth's compensation package was directly dependent on how Nortel performed according to the supplementary figures that started showing up in early 1999. Nothing in that sentence in the proxy circular said anything about GAAP.

In this way, one year after the supplementary earnings numbers materialized, Nortel shareholders were informed that the company was using them to decide how much to pay John Roth. The conclusion should have been inescapable. Through his compensation package, Roth was being encouraged to grow revenues by buying other companies without having to worry about how the acquisition costs affected Nortel's profitability under generally accepted accounting principles. Nortel had come up with a new accounting method that allowed Roth to use company shares as money, spend cash when necessary, acquire companies where their technology or R&D was thought desirable, and as long as the revenue figure kept growing, the impact of acquisition costs on profits didn't exist. In fact, if you could buy other companies and get their technology for free, by not recognizing intangibles, why should you spend money in your own labs?

By 1999, Nortel had evolved to a surreal plane of growth. The general wisdom held that companies like Nortel, Lucent, and Cisco had to buy smaller firms and emerging-technology startups to capture the technology necessary for their own growth as networking super-companies. To facilitate this, Nortel had developed a system of customized earnings figures, in which the company was discarding acquisition costs—ostensibly, perhaps, to level the accounting playing field with its pooling-method rivals. It must be recognized, however, that Cisco still did a significant number of acquisitions under the purchase method—$751 million in 1999 and $5 billion in 2000—and took the appropriate hits on its income statement. And under the pooling method, historic earnings were retroactively restated, as if the combined companies had always been together. Under the purchase method, the revenues from the newly acquired company just started showing up in the income statement—albeit with hefty amortization charges. Nevertheless, this meant that a huge jump in topline revenues could be shown under the purchase method that wasn't possible under pooling. Nortel's custom earnings figures combined the best of both the purchase method (big jumps in revenue over previous periods) and pooling (no amortization of intangibles) without suffering from the negatives of either system.

And in using those figures as the basis for the compensation of its most senior executive, Nortel was providing a mighty incentive for Roth to grow the company regardless of the impact under GAAP. The company's own annual report said the supplemental figures weren't supposed to be an alternative to GAAP, but for Roth, that's certainly what they appeared to be. He had a profound disincentive to run the company according to GAAP. Supplementary figures made the company sound more profitable than it was. That made the share price go up. The higher the price went, the fewer shares Roth would have to withdraw from the company treasury to close acquisition deals. And the higher the price went, the more valuable the stock options awarded to Roth and others became. And the better the company performed under the supplemental earnings numbers, the more salary and stock options Roth would be awarded, according to his compensation criteria. And for the investors enjoying the rapid appreciation of Nortel's stock price, what reason did they have to insist that the company stick to GAAP-only financial reporting?

How else could John Roth have been expected to run Nortel?

9

The Day Trader

Any idiot selling this stock should be institutionalized.
—posted to the Nortel bulletin board at
RagingBull.com, October 20, 1999

There was something almost preordained about David Chmelnitsky becoming a major investor in Nortel. Born and raised in Montreal, he had attended McGill University, alma mater of John Roth and Frank Dunn, where he studied electrical engineering. As a boy, he had gone on tours of Northern Electric's wire and cable operation outside Montreal (which was sold off by Jean Monty), where an uncle was a labourer, working on the machines that turned out the enormous rolls of wire for telephone lines. He'd even had a summer job at Bell Northern Research while attending McGill in the late 1980s and, after graduating in 1990, was interviewed for positions at Nortel in Ottawa. But after all these near misses, Chmelnitsky was destined to be an investor, not an employee, a true believer in its strengths and its long-term potential.

"I'd always wanted to go to McGill," he recalls. "It was a question of what I would study." It turned out that electrical engineering was not the right choice. He graduated, but didn't like his chosen area of expertise. Instead, he signed on with Andersen Consulting and became a management consultant. For five years, he worked on major software system projects that individually could run for two years, involve thirty to fifty people, and cost millions of dollars. He was in the business of customizing enterprise resource planning software—extremely complex, LAN-based programs employed by large engineering and manufacturing firms like Canadair and Bombardier to manage the construction of an entire airplane. A phone would ring at, say, Bombardier, and an American airline would have an order. The software would work back from the delivery date for the airplane, scheduling everything from part-order dates for sub-assemblies to the work shifts of individual employees.

After five years at Andersen, IBM Canada came along. Big Blue was transforming itself from a "big iron" hardware company to a service organization, and its consulting business in Canada was in its infancy. Chmelnitsky signed on in September 1995, becoming a management consultant based at its head office in Markham, Ontario, north of Toronto. Nortel's head office was just down the road in Brampton, and it turned out that Chmelnitsky and Roth were on something of a collision course. The impact site was down on Bay Street, where Chmelnitsky was quickly assigned by IBM to work on a major contract with the Toronto Stock Exchange.

The TSE had made what seemed like umpteen attempts to move from a traditional auction-pit format to a virtual market in which all the trading happened within computers, the way it did on the NAS-DAQ. The TSE had just shut down a multiyear project that had cost about $30 million and had gone nowhere. IBM stepped in to finally do the job, cutting the exchange over in 1997 as Roth began ramping up the acquisition-driven growth of Nortel, and then carried on with other improvements, troubleshooting, and upgrades.

Chmelnitsky was assigned to work on the TSE account for what ended up being five years. The securities industry became his daily milieu. He became familiar with the various departments of the TSE, including the regulatory and market surveillance area. He dealt with the Ontario Securities Commission (OSC) and with the IT people from the brokerage houses, got to know some analysts, and spent an especially large chunk of time around the traders, seeing them at work, listening to their wisdom. He'd never really paid much attention to stocks, and working on the TSE account for IBM provided a crash-course in market realities. He'd watch traders track the movement of stocks listed on the TSE 300 in spreadsheets fed real-time data. They were building their own version of the index as the prices changed for every single stock, comparing their results with how index-matched instruments were trading. They could see the discrepancies and capitalize on them, buying or selling options, or getting in and out of a major index stock like Nortel. It showed him how out of their league day traders were, the amateurs trying to capitalize on market movements by following news on the Internet and placing quick buy and sell orders through online brokerages. "Professional traders would laugh at the day traders," he says. "They'd say it was like a recreational hockey player going into the NHL, and coming up against Eric Lindros."

He also understood how subtle yet pervasive insider knowledge was in the functioning of the market. "You'd see a spike in a price at the end of the day, and people would say, 'Is that a company that's reporting this evening?' Big surprise when it was. I talked to a lot of traders at different firms. You started to hear the same kind of comments from them. A great one I heard was 'To be a great trader, you need to be *fairly* smart, but not awfully brilliant. And you need to be cool.' Especially the second one. Because if that's the case, you're going to be part of the 'squawk box' talk, where you're going to hear around three o'clock that Nortel, say, is going to be announcing around 4:30, and it's going to be really bad. And that's a selected group, an inner circle of traders that would know that."

Being around the market every day, seeing people who were fairly smart but not awfully brilliant make a lot of money, David Chmelnitsky inevitably was drawn to making his own investments and even toyed with the idea of becoming a trader himself. He took the derivatives fundamentals course from the OSC, but held off on enrolling in the follow-up course that would make him a licensed options trader. While continuing his duties with IBM at the exchange, he began to buy and sell stocks.

Chmelnitsky was practically a poster boy for the new generation of investors. He was Internet-savvy and used the Web to gather information on stocks, going to sites like WhisperNumber.com to assess the historic performances of potential investments. Through his work, he was exposed not only to the inner workings of the exchange, but also to the nascent communications technology. It was impossible to be involved in a project like turning the TSE virtual and not be aware of the unfolding communications revolution. "I knew a fair bit about the telecom industry, how it worked and where it was going. I took a look at what companies made and how it fit in. I also read analysts' reports. I had a heightened sense that fibre optic was going to be huge, with high penetration everywhere." What was also going to be huge was networking, "the ability to move different types of information. And I realized only a couple of companies could do it."

The rising importance of networking, coupled with the phenomenal potential of fibre optics, drew Chmelnitsky toward Nortel. "One of the key things I remember liking about Nortel was that it compared so favourably to Lucent. I stayed away from Lucent, because it didn't do the transition the way Nortel had from Northern Electric. It also didn't have the global sales presence of Nortel. It was very U.S. oriented." He considered Alcatel as well, but felt "Cisco was the only other competitor." And while he invested a little in Cisco, he ultimately decided to stay out of it, finding it pricey. Ultimately, his one networking buy was Nortel.

The Bay Networks deal clinched it for him. On June 15, 1998, the day the acquisition was announced, Chmelnitsky bought 1,000 shares on the TSE on an account at Nesbitt Burns. The price was $82.55, which meant Chmelnitsky had just sunk $82,550 into Roth's gamble on crossing over into IP networking and challenging Cisco on its own turf. On September 10, he bought another 1,000 shares at $75.10. That brought his total Nortel position to $157,650 at an average price of $78.83. After the September 29 disaster at Essex House, when Nortel fell to a low of $41.65 on the TSE on October 8, Chmelnitsky was down by $74,350, a breathtakingly quick loss. But he didn't panic. He stayed with the stock, waiting for it to recover. On January 5, 1999, Nortel finally closed above his average price, at $86. The stock plateaued around $85, and on January 18, he sold all 2,000 shares at that price. His gain, not including dividends, taxes, or commission, was not enormous:

$12,340. He was not the only investor who, rattled by Nortel's precipitous plunge in the fall of 1998, took the first opportunity to recoup his investment as the stock recovered and declined to ride it any further.

David Chmelnitsky turned his attention to other stocks in the broadband communications realm, particularly JDS Uniphase, the optical components maker with headquarters in both Nepean (another suburban Ottawa tech locale) and San Jose, California, which happened to count Nortel among its largest customers. He also invested in Broadcom Corp. of Irvine, California, which acquired eleven different companies in 2000 in its quest to build its portfolio of video, voice, and data networking products. But despite his absence from the Nortel shareholder ranks after January 18, 1999, Roth's company was not forgotten. His early exit meant that he did not participate in the enormous gains provided by the run-up in the first seven months of 2000. Had he stayed put, Chmelnitsky could have tripled his money at the height of the run. Instead, he found himself holding large positions, some of them on margin, in what turned out to be highly volatile tech growth stocks. When the market went into rapid descent in late 2000, he would turn back to Nortel, looking for a safe haven for the cash in his RRSP account.

Through 1999, while David Chmelnitsky invested his money elsewhere, Nortel's stock went on a tear. Having begun the year on the TSE at $77.90, the stock rode the company's celebrated fibre-optic networking successes to $121.85 on August 12. The stock was effectively split with a one-for-one dividend and closed the next day at $64.05. On October 19, the stock was at $74.70, but began a quick climb as anticipation built for the third-quarter figures. At closing on the twenty-sixth, it was at $83.80. The preliminary results, released after the close, lit a fuse under the shares.

Nortel Networks Reports Strong Third Quarter Results
- **Revenues Up 30% to US$5.4 Billion**
- **Net Earnings from Operations Up 61% to US$380 Million**
- **EPS From Operations Up 33% to US$0.28**

BRAMPTON, Ontario—Nortel Networks* [NYSE/TSE: NT]
today reported results for the third quarter and first nine
months of 1999. Revenues increased 30 percent to US$5.39 bil-
lion for the third quarter of 1999 from US$4.14 billion for the
same period in 1998. Net earnings from operations applicable
to common shares (a) for the quarter were US$380 million, or
US$0.28 per share, compared to US$236 million, or US$0.21
per share, for the same period in 1998, an increase in EPS from
operations of 33 percent. Including Acquisition Related Costs
(a) and one-time gains and charges, Nortel Networks recorded
net earnings applicable to common shares in the third quarter of
1999 of US$1 million or less than US$0.01 per share.

Nortel's customized "net earnings from operations" were still
working their black magic on the company's profitability, but at least
in this quarter Nortel was able to show a GAAP-worthy profit of $1
million. But the idea that this company, while growing its revenues,
might be unprofitable, by and large wasn't sinking in.

"We are extremely pleased with our strong growth in the quarter
which reflected continued momentum with our carrier and service
provider customers," Roth said in the press release. "The strong
demand for our optical, wireless, high-speed access and new Internet
Protocol (IP) offerings further confirmed our leadership in creating a
high-performance Internet with new economics and increased speed,
reliability, and quality."

John Roth was now a star, both at home and in the United States.
The *Wall Street Journal* profiled him on November 1, 1999, as a chief
executive who had what he called "a fabulous problem" on his hands:
more demand for product than he could keep up with. He boasted
how a major customer in the past year had increased an order from
$60 to $90 to $270 million in the space of three weeks. In the week
after the third-quarter announcement, Roth had gone to the board to
request a $400 million investment in Nortel's fibre-optic facility in
Montreal. Approval was received in November.

The *Wall Street Journal* story demonstrated just how successful
Nortel had been in getting its "earnings from operations" figures to

speak for the company's performance. The leading financial news-paper in the United States unquestioningly reported, "In this year's first nine months, the company's earnings from operations soared to $970 million, up 65% from a year earlier." Well, not quite. The ven-erated WSJ had used Nortel's earnings-from-operations numbers without explaining what they were. As Nortel's own GAAP statement showed, for the first nine months of 1999, Nortel had actually lost $614 million, or $0.46 (U.S.) per share. What had indisputably "soared" was the amount of amortized intangibles Nortel was carving away from its losses to create the illusion of profits. Intangibles amor-tized under U.S. GAAP in the first nine months of 1998 were $869 million; in 1999, they had almost doubled, to $1.65 billion. And $1.2 billion of that was purchased IPR&D and acquired technology. Given the company's high-tech focus, Nortel was persisting in its earnings-from-operations numbers with the bizarre logic that the cost of the R&D and technology it picked up through acquisitions shouldn't be factored in, while showing the revenues that the tech-nology made possible was more than okay.

With major business press articles congratulating Nortel on its soaring "earnings" and analysts rallying around the stock, Nortel shares would be up to $145.85 on the TSE by year-end. Someone who started 1999 with a single share worth $77.90 ended up with two shares, each worth twice that much, for a capital gain of $213.80 on the investment. An 800-pound equities gorilla had just been born. Thanks in large part to Nortel, the TSE 300 enjoyed the largest increase of any broad index in the world in 1999. But as much as investors had become infatuated with Roth's company, Nortel was facing a host of serious challenges.

The explosive demand for Nortel optical networking gear, par-ticularly in the United States, had helped fuel much of the company's growth. Sales in its carrier segment were up by 32 percent over the third quarter of 1998, and overall revenues for the same comparative period were up by 39 percent in the United States. But the fibre-optics boom was in danger of being fuelled not by actual user demand, but by runaway expectations of fantastic compound annu-al growth in traffic. The consulting firm Ryan, Hankin & Kent

(RHK) predicted that Internet traffic would increase from 350,000 terabits in the last month of 1999 to more than 15 million terabits per month by 2003. Networks were being built in anticipation of traffic levels that didn't yet exist. Nortel was playing into that anticipation with its own products, promising new gear for the Internet that would allow switching speeds at the terabit level—thousands of times faster than gigabit gear. Nortel was in a race with other companies to roll out such product, even though, at the moment, there wasn't enough Internet traffic to warrant terabit capability.

These were early signs that the networking boom might turn out to be something on the order of the railway bonanzas that struck Britain in the 1840s and North America at the turn of the last century. In unregulated environments, competitors could lay as much track as they wanted—often in parallel, between the same destinations—in a rush to capitalize on traffic volumes that were sure to be just around the corner. In Britain, the gross overcapacity in rail lines caused widespread company failures and the impoverishment of investors. In North America, similar investor losses occurred, and enormous consolidations reduced the number of services—in Canada, this brought about the creation of the modern CNR.

The capacity problems of the optical networks were exacerbated by the increasing amounts of bandwidth being offered. Speed translates directly into capacity. If, in jumping from OC-48 to OC-192, traffic moves through an optical pipe four times faster than before, without an increase in the number of bits, the proportion of total capacity being used falls by three-quarters. Networks become even emptier, and a lot of fairly empty optical networks leads to a price war, which leads to lower revenues for the network operators. Which leads to them running out of money and becoming unable to pay for the equipment they've installed or to order more to continue their planned expansion.

That said, there were gathering signs that the market was poised for major investments in optical networking down at the metro level. Internet traffic was pushing the capacity of the old phone system to the limit, and dropping costs for optical gear, particularly from new players in the market, were encouraging incumbent local exchange carriers to get going with an optical cutover.

Part of the anticipated increase in Internet traffic was pinned on the hopes for e-commerce and the associated phenomenon known as customer relationship management (CRM), in which call centres, customer service, and sales and marketing all came together in a seamless network of communications tools and databases which were increasingly becoming based on Internet tools. By 1999, CRM was attracting an evangelical frenzy among its proponents, and companies were being told if they didn't make the transition from a traditional bricks-and-mortar enterprise into something Web-enabled, more agile competitors were going to overtake them in the emerging new economy.

The arguments were persuasive, but the task of actually executing a total CRM strategy proved daunting. Apart from the expense and the potential disruptions to existing processes, companies were running into major problems getting their legacy databases used in purchasing, accounts receivable, and inventory to mesh with the new stuff that was supposed to allow agents access to vital information while interacting with customers. By the spring of 2000, with the NASDAQ nose-diving as investors lost their patience with price/earnings multiples measuring in the triple digits, the enthusiasm for major CRM undertakings would be in serious decline in corporate America.

Nortel was also beginning to face strong competition in certain component segments from not only Cisco and Lucent, but the new players with advanced product such as Ciena, Corvis, and Juniper Networks. On October 22, 1999, four days before Nortel announced its third-quarter results, the markets warmly embraced a new Nortel competitor in optical networking. Sycamore Networks logged the fourth-largest one-day gain in history for an IPO when it finished its NASDAQ debut 386 percent higher than its opening, which was already 614 percent higher than the issue price. As *Forbes* pointed out, a $40 million venture capital investment turned into a $21 billion market capitalization when the day ended. And Nortel was also starting to lose key employees to rivals who craved their optical networking know-how.

Nortel was learning that the competition played for keeps. Just a week before Sycamore's debut on the NASDAQ, a senior Nortel manager was collected, mid-vacation, in Greece, and flown to California by a venture called Optical Networks, Inc. (later ONI Systems) of San Jose, California. According to *Forbes,* Optical Networks already had some houses picked out for the manager's wife to view, complete with information on each school district. He defected to Optical.

"Optical networking equipment is not something a couple of guys in a garage can create overnight," Corey Ostman, chief technology officer at AlertIPO!, a Los Angeles-based Web service tracking public offerings, told Reuters in a June 1, 2000, story. "It has very high barriers to entry compared to a Web site, for instance." ONI and others were getting around the guys-in-a-garage problem by launching raiding parties on the payrolls of companies like Nortel.

When ONI announced on January 22, 2000, its plan to open a 58,000-square-foot facility in April in San Jose to expand production capacity for its metro optical networking products, it also noted that the man leading the expansion was a new hiring. Vice-president of operations Martin Desroches, a Canadian who was last seen working as the senior manufacturing manager at Nortel's Optoelectronics division in England, had extensive experience in Nortel's optical efforts, beginning with his work as a test engineer.

Employee poaching was epidemic in the tech business, and particularly so in the optical sector. Nortel was considered particularly vulnerable because its optical employees, located in Canada, could be lured south by American dollars, lower taxes, and in some cases far better stock option plans. There was no effort to make a secret of the practice. Over at Cyras Systems Inc. of Fremont, California, a new venture developing data-optimized optical switching systems for metropolitan area network applications, poaching Nortel staffers was a fact of life for CEO Stephen Pearse, a former Norteler himself.

"There is no one in the Valley who knows how to do optical transport," Optical's chief executive officer, Hugh Martin, told *Forbes* in a November 1999 article. "We have to import all of our guys." He noted that so many Canadians were lured aboard that an Optical

Networks hockey team was set up. The tab for the hockey team, and the cost of airlifting the Nortel manager out of his Greek holiday, was covered by Silicon Valley's leading venture capital firm, Kleiner Perkins Caufield & Byers, which was setting up Optical Networks and preparing it for its IPO the following spring. Among the investors rounded up by KPCB was none other than Cisco, whose turf Nortel had invaded with Bay Networks. Cisco had contributed $4.4 million of the $50 million in initial venture capital. What went around came around.

The cost of some plane tickets and ice rink rental time was peanuts compared to the riches to be reaped. With the aid of ex-Nortelers, Optical Networks was developing optical routers that it said would sell for $50,000 to $100,000, about half the price of similar gear from Lucent or Nortel.

Nortel tried to fight the employee poaching by Optical through the courts. On October 27, 1999, Nortel filed a plea in the Superior Court of Montreal in hope of shutting down Optical's recruiting. Nortel charged that it had lost nineteen engineers in the past eleven months, nine of them in the previous two months. All were from Montreal and had been working on the OPTera optical product line, which promised terabit-speed service for the metro markets. "ONI is trying to do in a couple of years what we have achieved in 10 [years] by the shortcut of raiding our people and thereby gaining access to our trade secrets," Nortel spokesman Jeff Ferry said in an item carried by Bloomberg News. "Some of the employees were very good."

The attempt to block the hirings failed, but Nortel was granted an injunction forbidding former employees from divulging knowledge of Nortel's proprietary optical network testing system. In March 2000, as Optical (now known as ONI Systems) filed its IPO, Nortel blindsided it with a lawsuit alleging misappropriation of trade secrets, patent infringement, unfair business practices, and unfair competition. The suit accused Optical of hiring away at least thirty Nortel employees as part of "an ongoing campaign" to acquire its optical technology. Nortel also said the timing of the suit with respect to the Optical IPO was purely coincidental.

John Roth spoke out on the Canadian "brain drain" crisis, arguing that high taxes were responsible for the drift of knowledge workers south of the border. He spoke on the issue often in public, and to federal politicians. He was far from the sole speaker on this issue, but his growing profile as Nortel became a stock market darling gave his words particular weight. However, Roth's devotion to slashing taxes must be seen in the context of his own company's particular problems with both established rivals like Lucent, which had better stock option packages, and with upstarts like Optical raiding its fibre-optic ranks. There certainly was a brain drain going on, and it consisted of Nortel employees lighting out for deals they could not refuse.

Nortel attempted to address its competitive shortcomings with a new employee stock option plan program in the spring of 2000, but the company was handicapped by the distinct way the Canada Customs and Revenue Agency treated the taxation of options-based benefits. In both Canada and the United States, the difference between the exercise price of an option and the fair market price at the time of exercise was a taxable benefit. If employees held options allowing them to purchase company shares from the treasury for $20 per share when the fair market price was $80, they incurred a taxable benefit of $60. In Canada, the benefit immediately triggered a tax bill, whether or not an employee actually sold the shares on the open market to realize the $60 gain. Having to pay that tax could force the employee to sell the shares to raise the necessary cash. Selling immediately also allowed them to avoid the catastrophe of the shares subsequently dropping in value, which in no way removed the taxable benefit of $60. The shares could fall to $10, and they would still be on the hook for the $60 benefit. (If they sold them at $10, they would at least be able to report a capital loss of $70.) It was a tax system that discouraged employees from acquiring a long-term stake in their employer, since the safest route when there was a high taxable benefit was to sell the shares immediately, send the government its share, and bank the net profit.

The U.S. system was very different. With incentive and employee stock options, provided the options were not exercised within two years of their being granted, the difference between the exercise price and fair market price was added to the employee's income for the purpose of determining federal unemployment taxes and eligibility for benefits under social security and Medicare, but was not considered taxable income. Only when the stock was sold was there a tax obligation, and this was based on the difference between the exercise price and the price realized for them on the open market. And rather than being reported as income, the difference was treated as a capital gain—or, as the case might be, a capital loss. The average American employee didn't have to worry about a stock option triggering a huge tax bill he might not be able to afford to pay the moment it was exercised, or being stuck paying that huge bill even if the shares were sold at a much lower profit (or a loss) some time in the future.

In December 2000, Finance Minister Paul Martin introduced amendments to Canada's Income Tax Act that allowed the taxable benefits created by exercising employee stock options to be deferred to the year in which the shares were sold, but that didn't get rid of the possibility of an employee still paying considerable taxes on a benefit they never enjoyed. The Canadian taxation system encouraged the worst possible behaviour by corporate insiders from the perspective of investor confidence. Shares gained through stock options were to be dumped at the earliest opportunity if a large spread between the exercise and fair market price produced a huge tax bill. Should this sort of dumping occur at a market peak, those insiders were going to look pretty ruthless and pretty rich, while regular investors, who didn't have the luxury of buying in at deep discount, were caught playing the role of the greatest fools after a stock tanked. All the explaining in the world about avoiding serious tax losses wasn't going to get these insiders off the hook.

John Roth's call for lower taxes in Canada coincided with the shift in Nortel's political agenda after the Bay Networks acquisition, based on the way it was spreading its donations around. In 1997, the federal election year, Nortel had made $199,290.20 in contributions to political parties in Canada—$98,884.80 to the Liberals, $75,405.40 to the Progressive Conservatives, and $25,000 to the Reform Party. Its contributions to the Liberal coffers in 1997 were among the ruling party's highest, exceeded only by six major financial institutions and brokerage houses: Nesbitt Burns ($120,767.10), Scotia McLeod

($118,995.08), CIBC Wood Gundy Securities ($116,499.38), the Toronto-Dominion Bank ($105,851.41), the Bank of Montreal ($100,575.12), and RBC Dominion Securities ($99,453.04). Nortel outspent CIBC (an aggregate of $84,135.60, not including its Wood Gundy subsidiary), its then majority owner, BCE ($79,006.78— although BCE Mobile contributed a further $25,000), and the traditionally generous Bombardier ($86,069.28).

But after 1997, Nortel immediately began cutting back on Canadian political donations. By 2000, total contributions to federal parties were down to $72,674.26—less than what it had given the Liberals alone in 1997. In all, $37,958.36 went to the Liberals, $16,385.90 to the PCs, and $18,330 to the Reform/Alliance. (Nortel gave $3,500 to the NDP in 1998.) Nortel had slipped far down the list of Liberal patrons by 2000, ranking only 38th. (It's worth noting that John Roth never appears on any list of political contributors to Canadian parties between 1997 and 2000, although regulations do not require specific donors to individual candidates' campaigns to be reported.)

Nortel was spending its political dollars increasingly in the United States as the flow of contributions followed the shift in Nortel's main source of sales revenue. Nortel had a longstanding commitment to donations in the American political arena. In 1990, it ranked sixth in donations among telecom service and equipment companies tracked by the Centre for Responsive Politics. These donations flowed from three sources. Political action committees, or PACs, are political committees organized to raise and spend money to elect and defeat candidates. Most PACs represent business, labor or ideological interests. "Soft money" represents donors to national political committees, rather than individual politicians. Finally, the donations include individuals (i.e. employees) giving $200 or more. In the 1999/2000 election cycle, about 25 percent of donations attributed to a typical telecom and equipment services company came from an individual, and about 62 percent in the form of soft money. Nortel's soft money in that election cycle was a near-typical 60 percent.

Nortel (by which we mean all of the above forms of donors) in 1990 made $32,392 in contributions, 63 percent of them to

Democrats. In the 1992 election year, Nortel was third in the industry, at $124,831, betting heavily on the Republicans, who received 74 percent of donations. Nortel was outspent only by Mobile Telecommunications Technology and Motorola. In the 1996 election year, Nortel was again third in its industry, with $217,191 in donations and again sent most of it (68 percent) to the Republicans. With the 1999–2000 election cycle, Nortel's spending increased to $461,493, but by now it had learned to spread the cash around more evenly, sending 51 percent to the Democrats, 48 percent to the Republicans. Having bet heavily and lost on the Republicans in 1992 and 1996, its evenhandedness in 1999–2000 saw the Republican George W. Bush elected to the presidency.

After the acquisitions of 1998, anchored by the major Bay Network deal, Nortel proceeded less aggressively in early 1999. Nothing of note happened until April 16, when it acquired the privately held Shasta Networks Inc. of Sunnyvale, California, which Nortel said had developed "a new class of service-enabling gateways and subscriber policy management systems at the 'subscriber edge' of Internet Protocol (IP) public data networks." Nortel promised that bringing Shasta's technology aboard would "enable the next generation of IP value-added services for the mass business market."

The $340 million price (U.S. GAAP) was met by using about 9.3 million Nortel common shares. The Shasta deal represented another load-up of intangibles: Nortel reported $5 million in net tangible assets, $180 million in in-process R&D, and $158 million in goodwill. This meant that, with no acquired technology, whatever Shasta brought to the party wasn't yet market ready. Nortel also agreed to pay another $18 million cash if performance milestones were met; $9 million was paid out by year-end and tacked onto goodwill.

On April 29, the company's name was legally changed from Northern Telecom Ltd. to Nortel Networks Corp. Things were quiet on the acquisition front for a few months. Then Nortel made another move aimed at enabling business exploitation of the Internet. On August 24, Nortel announced that it had reached a "definitive merger agreement" with Periphonics Corp., a NASDAQ listed company based in Bohemia, New York. Nortel went after Periphonics to increase its presence in CRM technologies, as the firm offered established technologies in computer telephony integration (CTI) and interactive voice response (IVR)—the voice-recognition software by which some poor soul dialling into a call centre or a business could navigate through menus, among other things, by speaking instead of repeatedly punching a telephone keypad. The deal was closed on November 12, with a price of $481 million. Nortel received what it booked as $66 million in acquired technology, $68 in in-process R&D, and $271 million in goodwill.

Officially, those were Nortel's only two acquisitions of 1999, but it embarked on another one before the third quarter was even wrapped. On October 18, Nortel announced another "definitive merger agreement," this time with Clarify Inc. of San Jose. It was yet another move to broaden Nortel's portfolio of CRM technologies. Clarify was the world's second-largest provider of e-commerce front-office software systems, and at $2.1 billion it represented Nortel's largest acquisition since Bay Networks. Clarify's customer list included British Telecom, E*Trade, and General Electric. It also had strategic alliances with the consulting arms of the major audit firms Ernst & Young, KPMG, and PricewaterhouseCoopers.

Those alliances proved to be a significant corollary to the deal, for the consulting business for these audit firms had been turning to the knotty problems of deploying CRM and e-commerce products in corporate environments. Cisco had a longstanding relationship with KPMG, one of Clarify's strategic alliance partners, and in August 1999 had agreed to spend $1 billion to acquire a 19.1 percent interest in KPMG Consulting, when KPMG became the first big accounting firm to spin off its consulting arm. KPMG Consulting was incorporated on January 31, 2000; on February 16, Nortel was playing catch-up with Cisco by announcing a strategic alliance with Andersen Consulting in marketing CRM and e-commerce products and services, about two and a half years after Cisco had struck its pioneering alliance with KPMG.

The Clarify deal, though announced in October, did not wrap up until March 16, 2000. Nortel again used its own shares to fund the $2.1 billion cost. The premium was markedly high. Nortel received just $210 million in acquired technology, $64 million in in-process R&D, and $28 million in net tangible assets, leaving it with $1.8 billion in goodwill to explain away, or at least write down over three years. After the announcement of the Clarify acquisition was made on October 18, Nortel slipped $3.30 on the TSE, but the market rapidly set aside its equivocations when the strong third-quarter results were released the next week.

Despite the dramatic increase in share price and the general accolades in 1999, as the year unfolded Nortel looked more and more like a company trying to keep up with Cisco and fight off threats from upstarts like Sycamore and Optical Networks. There was a gathering sense, albeit a minority one among investors, that perhaps Nortel had fallen behind the technology curve after capitalizing so spectacularly on its OC-192 optical technology. Having received the board's consent in November to spend $400 million upgrading optical facilities in Montreal, the company would announce a further $200 million in January. The problems posed by the emerging threats in optical systems were underscored by Nortel's decision to make another large acquisition, a $3 billion purchase of a startup that had virtually no revenues. Qtera Corp. offered emerging expertise in long-haul optical networking. It came with $33 million in net tangible assets, no acquired technology, and in-process R&D valued at $559 million. But regardless of the figure attached to it, Qtera's R&D was apparently so valuable that Nortel was willing to shoulder $2.4 billion in goodwill. It was yet another acquisition paid for with Nortel stock when the deal closed on January 28, 2000. And stock, as it would shortly become clear, was the main issue on Nortel's agenda as 2000 began. From David Chmelnitsky to the largest pension funds in the country, Canadian investors would not be able to make a substantial move in their portfolios without wondering if it was time to get into—or to get out of—Nortel.

10

He's So Yesterday

Oh Bliss!

Finally after years of hanging on to losers that sometimes went bankrupt and selling good stocks prematurely for small gains, I have a WINNER in NT

—Nova Scotian living in Florida, posted to the Nortel bulletin board at RagingBull.com, November 3, 1999

On TV, Ross Healy looked so *yesterday,* a guy with a neat fringe of white hair surmounted by a brilliant dome; very presentable and articulate, but not a Central Casting choice as a person who specialized in assessing the value of high-tech stocks. On breathlessly upbeat business news programs like CNBC, the typical "expert" tended to have an evangelical, thirtysomething sheen, which went with a whole new way of thinking about stocks and allegedly measuring their value. Far from being fresh off the farm, Healy had been analyzing stocks in Toronto since 1967 and had cut his teeth on such old economy dinosaurs as steel, paper, and forestry. He also ran a firm called Strategic Analysis Corp., which advised its clients—mainly institutional investors, particularly pension funds—on the wisdom of their portfolio holdings by using a proprietary mathematical system which, when you got right down to it, was based on a stodgy belief that companies had measurable values lurking in their balance sheets that no amount of New Economy hoo-ha could obviate.

By the summer of 2000, Healy was handsomely notorious in certain circles. He had gone on the Market Call segment of the

Toronto-based cable business show ROBTv on June 7, when Nortel finished the day on the TSE at $86.35 after a split in the spring and was on its way up up up, and said that the shares were actually worth $25—or less. The "or less" part was important to Healy, because he didn't actually think they were worth even twenty-five bucks. More like eight bucks. But when a stock like Nortel is so stratospherically high, so widely held, and so widely touted, it's fairly impossible to tell people it should command a single-digit price and still have them take you seriously. So he broke it to the public gently, if that's what you can call a proposed devaluation of 75 percent, and went to work deflating the value even more in an appearance on the CBC in August. Healy finally summoned the nerve to stick an eight-dollar price tag on the nation's glamour investment on the nation's public broadcaster. "By August 2000," he asserts, "an outright collapse of the stock price was in the cards."

Nortel was just coming into the descent of its stock market arc at that point, but eight bucks was still a totally outrageous evaluation. Equally outrageous was his pronouncement that the exciting expansion of global fibre-optic networks on which Nortel was gambling its future was as doomed as the nineteenth-century railway boom, when way more track was laid than there were trains to run on them. Railways! The nineteenth century! Steam engines and iron rivets! He said this in the middle of a debate with another, younger, analyst, and Healy could sense in the body language of his debating partner that he was being written off as an old codger who Just. Didn't. Get. It.

After his first Market Call appearance on June 7, a note was entered in the production file to make him a regular; he was back on the show on July 5, then on August 5, and again on August 17. And on and on. In the post-NASDAQ flameout, someone who was willing to go on a widely watched business show and diss the most important stock in the country, time and again, was if nothing else good television.

Unfortunately, for too many investors who tuned into Market Call or saw Healy on other programs on the CBC and TVOntario, his contrarian convictions were little more than entertainment, a chance to shake one's head at the fellow from the deep past of Bay

Street who hadn't got his head around the realities of the New Economy. "People probably dismissed me as a lunatic," he admits. The public responded to his $25 valuation in June by bidding the stock up to $124.50 on the TSE over the ensuing seven weeks, and it can't be said that his eight-dollar pronouncement in August had a measurable impact on the mood of the average investor. King Canute had better success holding off the rising tide with his broadsword than Healy did in fighting back the surge of enthusiasm for Nortel's common shares. It wasn't just the general investing public who tuned out his warnings. Many of his own clients disregarded the opinions they paid him for. When asked how pension fund managers heeded his advice on Nortel, Healy simply says, "Badly."

Ross Healy was not a lonely voice in the wilderness by the summer of 2000. Al and Mark Rosen (more on them later) were doing a devastating job of picking apart Nortel's financial statements, both in private reports to institutional investment clients and in Al Rosen's occasional articles in the Canadian press. And Paul Sagawa at Sanford C. Bernstein and Co. in New York would release on September 28 a gloomy prediction for capital expenditures on telecom equipment in 2001. But Sagawa's downgrade of Nortel, released the same day, while identifying "considerable downside risk" to the stock, still held out the promise of fairly robust sales for the rest of 2000 and on through 2001. And as brilliantly as the Rosens performed in their largely overlooked work on Nortel's financial statement curiosities, Healy stands out for the simple clarity of his message that the most ill-educated investor could grasp, delivered on television, the medium of the unwashed masses. Eight bucks, folks. Even after Nortel all but handed other analysts the necessary ammunition in early 2001, they still shied from joining Healy in a brutal dismissal of Nortel's worth.

Analysts' reputations are made on both the upside and downside of the market. Just as there are analysts who cherish the memory of how they put investors into blue-chip companies back when they were penny stocks, so there are analysts who savour the impending disaster they flagged with a prescient call. HD Brous & Co., relentlessly bearish through 2000, for example, proudly lays claim to having made the first warning of the NASDAQ crash that spring. Yale University's

Robert Shiller had similar good timing in publishing his book *Irrational Exuberance,* which expanded on the themes of market misbehaviour presented by him and Harvard's John Campbell to the Federal Reserve Board back in December 1996. The hardcover edition hit the stores in mid-March 2000; the NASDAQ composite reached its all-time high of 5048.62 on March 10. By April 14, the NASDAQ had lost a third of its value.

To presume that the dour prediction of HD Brous & Co. or the damning analysis of *Irrational Exuberance* had contributed to the NASDAQ meltdown would be folly. All too often, a gloomy prognosis becomes famous because virtually no one paid it any mind. The hardest thing for an analyst to do in a bull market firing on all twelve cylinders is to go against the logic of the herd. After all, if he's wrong, and a client pulls out of an equity position that ends up going through the roof as everyone else predicted, the analyst has forced a client out of a return the likes of which may never be seen again. Not surprisingly, then, the hardest thing for an investor to do is listen to the contrarian's voice and cash in an investment when still greater returns, according to the wisdom of the majority, lie just ahead. As much he was frustrated by the unwillingness of his own clients to follow his advice on Nortel, Healy understood their reticence. "It's very hard to recover from a wrong bet against a major stock in the index," he says. Healy means from the perspective of portfolio value, but he could as easily have meant the fund manager's professional reputation and livelihood. And so the contrarian tends to be a hero in hindsight, the Cassandra no one paid any mind to, or the prognosticator whose instincts were right but whose timing was terrible. For Healy, Nortel became both his lost cause and his claim to fame.

The laws of probability assure us that, with enough stocks and enough analysts, someone is going to make an against-the-grain call that will impart Nostradamic qualities to the lucky sap when it turns out to be correct. Certainly any fool can make one brilliant call—or, more accurately, a call that turns out to be brilliant, while 99 percent of his advice proves to be dross.

Healy was neither a fundamentals-crunching goofball nor a leftie capitalist basher that the rightie media types kept around for amusement. His résumé provides a guided tour of the most respectable addresses and assignments on Bay Street. Named director of investment research at Merrill Lynch Canada in 1984. Served as president of the Toronto Society of Financial Analysts, the third largest such organization in North America. Served on the board of the Financial Analysts Federation as chairman of the *Financial Analysts Journal* committee, and as chairman of the FAF 1983 Annual Conference in Toronto. (In 1990, the FAF merged with the Institute of Chartered Financial Analysts to create the Association for Investment Management and Research, or AIMR.) A past member of the Financial Disclosure Advisory Board of the Ontario Securities Commission. A past chairman of the Investment Committee and a member of the Executive Committee of Trinity College, University of Toronto, where he led the overhaul and restructuring of the college financial and reporting systems. When Merrill Lynch pulled out of Canada, he became chairman and CEO of Strategic Analysis Corporation. The firm had been founded by the enigmatic Dr. Verne Atrill; while at Merrill Lynch, Healy had helped bankroll it. Atrill already held bachelor's and master's degrees in physics when he earned a Ph.D. at the London School of Economics. When Dr. Atrill died in 1989, Healy took over Strategic Analysis Corp.

In Dr. Atrill's opinion, says Healy, "economics was neither a science nor a discipline." Dr. Atrill set out to change that with Structural Valuation Analysis, a proprietary methodology that uses three ratios of balance sheet information to determine the value of an equity. Formulas are fine—lots of them are around that try to bring a rigorous methodology to stock values and market trends. None of them can replace experience or gut instinct. Healy got his start as an analyst at Midland-Osler Securities (which became Merrill Lynch Canada) way back in 1967, two years before John Roth had a job at Northern Electric, four years before there was such a thing as Bell Northern Research. More than a quarter-century later, when confronting the conundrum of Nortel, that early experience gave Healy what he feels was a critical edge over newer, younger analysts. For one thing, he had already watched Nortel go through its misadventure with the Electronic Office Systems division in 1980. A lot of the analysts crowing about John Roth's can't-miss expansion strategy weren't even in high school when the acquisition streak that led to the EOS comeuppance hit Nortel. By the time the Nortel boom came along in the late nineties, Healy says, "I'd already made my mistakes. I got sucked in by management. I believed their stuff and wrote bad reports. But I made these mistakes when it didn't matter."

Healy thrived by sticking to balance sheet fundamentals and not getting distracted by the techspeak that was such an overwhelming part of the New Economy delusion. More important, he didn't try to hide behind techspeak, using the nomenclature of the communications revolution to obscure a lack of appreciation of bottom-line performance, or of even what the nomenclature meant. "A company like Cisco," he observes, "is too complex for an analyst to understand. You have to depend on the company for information. Analysts haven't a clue what they're talking about. If you've been in the business long enough, jargon doesn't matter. Just show me the numbers."

In the hot tech sector of fibre-optics, where Nortel was trading at stupendous multiples of book level and was sopping up frightening amounts of pension and retirement fund dollars, he found things that mattered "in spades. And when it collapsed, there was going to be blood everywhere."

Healy's failure to turn the market against Nortel was understandable, for he was fighting more than the price performance of one particular stock. By the summer of 2000, he was up against several years of momentum not only of Nortel, but of the entire tech sector. Not even the NASDAQ reversal of April 2000 had been able to drive the message home that the whole New Economy thing was an unholy mess of number fudging, wilful blindness, wishful thinking and, well, irrational exuberance. It was even more than the New Economy. It was people's savings, their pension plans, their dreams of opulent early retirement. Often, frankly, it was their greed. Nortel was like an ace of spades at the base of a house of cards. Flicking it away could bring everything crashing down.

Most disconcerting about the situation was that it even managed to exist; that someone as reputable and old-school as Ross Healy was so isolated among his analyst peers in being forthrightly negative about Nortel in the summer of 2000, when the stock was at its historic height and everybody had to own some. Like every good Cassandra, Healy was, of course, proved correct. On September 5, 2001, Nortel would finish the day on the TSE at $8.77, dropping below $9 for the first time, and in another eight months, as Nortel's debt instruments sank to junk-bond status, the stock fell below $4. It was a long, long way down from the buoyant beginning to John Roth's term as Nortel president, when he and the rest of the senior executives had promised shareholders they were "committed to growing profitably and to both creating and investing in long-term shareholder value."

Healy's suspicion of Nortel's performance long predated his first pronouncements on television in the summer of 2000. It cropped up in his weekly market notes to clients on November 9, 1999, in which a headline asked:

> *Positive Earnings Surprise for the 4th Quarter Ahead!?!*
> SAC wishes to make what we believe is an absolutely safe and guaranteed forecast, namely that Nortel Networks is highly likely to provide a nice positive earnings surprise in their 4th quarter. Best of all, NT is only trading at 68 times 1999 earnings and a mere 54 times Y2K earnings, clearly a bargain at twice the price.

Even at this early date in the demystification of Nortel, Healy's writing displayed the biting sarcasm typical of critics running against the heavy traffic of received wisdom. Stock market contrarians deserve a multi-stage progression toward the psychological vanishing point, much like Elisabeth Kübler-Ross devised for human beings coming to grips with their own impending demise. The final stage would entail sporting a "Marx Was Right" T-shirt and not much else as the wearer flees into bug-infested bush. Few contrarians reach this highest of planes; most level out at the comfort zone of sarcastic contempt while still showing up for work in the morning, business attire freshly pressed. By the fall of 2000, the Nortel analysis published by

Veritas Investment Research Corporation, the analysis service to which the Rosens contributed, would become downright smart-alecky. Like dissidents once crushed under the grey weight of the old Soviet empire, financial professionals who wake up to find themselves unheeded by the masses and even ostracized by their peers tend to take refuge in a bitter strain of humour. If they're fortunate, time is on their side and the predicted gloom at last invests them with sagacity.

An investment pro turning the go-go language of his own profession back upon itself is a wondrous thing to behold, for who better knows its pressure points. The solemnity of serious money is swept aside, as the financial markets become a black comedy staged in a theatre of the absurd.

"Here is a company that has reported a steady diet of good to astonishingly good contracts in recent months," wrote Healy on November 9, 1999, "and indeed, with such ongoing good news at hand, we would have expected that analysts' earnings estimates would, if anything, have been on a steady upwards slope. And yet, as we have reported before, to a large extent, earnings forecasts until recently have been pretty much steady all year. In light of this, it came as a bit of a surprise to us last week when we noted that the forecasts had recently taken a sudden down dip."

Healy had noticed a phenomenon for which he could offer no rational explanation. According to the analyst earnings estimates for Nortel posted on the I/B/E/S service, which tracks analyst recommendations, fourteen analysts had moved practically in unison in lowering their Nortel estimates for 1999 and 2000 following the release of third-quarter results. An average of 11 cents had been clipped from 1999, 10 cents from 2000.

"If we were large institutional holders of Nortel," Healy proposed, "we would have some questions for any analyst who remains positive to outright bullish (and this seems to be the case to a man, if this term is still politically correct, and our sources are to be believed) on a stock which appears to have little redeeming investment value, especially in light of down-trending earnings forecast data."

Healy suggested these institutional holders ask the following:

1. In light of the massive spate of company contract announcements, some pretty large, how is it that a majority of the analysts "suddenly" decided to reduce earnings forecasts recently, not only for this year but for next as well? Does this come as a result of their detailed analysis of the most recent quarter which shows (for instance) that margins are slipping or that more R&D is being spent to produce all of these wonderful products that NT is going to be selling in the future, or what? (We would have said that the third quarter looked pretty good to us, with a 30% increase in sales and 33% gain in earnings y/y.) Or has management quietly slipped them "the word" that NT is not going to meet either their 4th quarter estimates or any of their Y2K estimates? In other words, are these new forecasts what are known as "managed earnings estimates"? And if so, what "added value" are the analysts, except as apologists for the company? Why have 14 analysts in the I/B/E/S survey recently dropped their 1999 estimates to just about dead on $1.00? (Check it out yourself for interest's sake.)

2. Why is a company with an apparent 19% 5-year future earnings growth rate (Zack's 5-year average of longer term earnings forecasts) "good value" at 68 times earnings? We would have thought that the old rule of thumb that the P.E. Ratio should approximate the growth rate for such a stock to be good investment value would suggest that this stock is more than a tad on the pricey side. Even at Zack's highest growth rate forecast of 27%, "good value" is dubious.

3. As a follow-up to #2, if NT can't meet any of the former close-in estimates, why this sudden earnings outlook setback and what, if any, are the implications for the years beyond Y2K?

4. Is the company setting up the market for a "positive surprise" in the 4th quarter and Y2K on reduced expectations and, if so, how legitimate is that "surprise"?

5. Or is something going wrong at Nortel that the company has "neglected" to tell the world about but has confided to analysts?

All we have seen from the company is one "exciting" piece of good news after another and yet the analysts covering the stock are reducing earnings this year and next. Is this shades of Boeing a couple of years ago where the company got so chock-a-block with orders that they started to lose money due to bottleneck problems? Do you want to find out? While you own the stock?

Perhaps we are just unduly suspicious these days. Maybe this is tarring an excellent company with the same brush that Barron's used when they noted that GE is getting its 13% growth rate by schlepping in a load of excess pension recoveries in amounts, which coincidentally, are precisely that which is necessary to maintain that sacred percentage gain. Only in this case, NT is showing an earnings fall-off and the street appears to be buying it, presumably because the 4th quarter will now show a "positive surprise." And anyway, the future is out of sight, isn't it?

We do not, of course, wish to impugn anyone's integrity on matters of this import. We are certain that the analysts can provide you with excellent and well-reasoned answers to all of our questions, and that our concerns could be easily allayed if only we, too, had the inside scoop. We were merely wondering why a company selling up at its Bubble Price (a valuation level which it has not attained in over 20 years, if ever) against a background of fading earnings forecasts and an EER[16] fair market value of $46, continues to hold the attraction for investors that it does. If it were us and we owned NT, we would sell our remaining holdings into the current strength and sell short on a Negative Zone Transition back down through the Bubble price of $96. But then, we have recently been wrong on this stock so what is our opinion worth anyway?

In sum, we find it more than a little peculiar that general investor expectations have been managed upwards by a long series of bullish news releases that by all appearances would seem to indicate improving earnings news ahead, while analyst earnings expectations appear to have been managed downwards both for this and next year. Yet the broad investment public has not seen or heard a single word of any lower earnings potential in the general press from the company. If nothing else, this offers at least a very cynical appearance of news manipulation which the company should correct.

E-mailing messages like this to your institutional investor clients tended not to earn you an invitation to the next spin around the Pocono Raceway track with Nortel senior executives. Healy openly suspected that Nortel was guiding down expectations for 1999 and 2000 in concert with compliant analysts, in order to generate an earnings "surprise" with the release of its fourth-quarter and year-end 1999 numbers in January. This, in turn, would give the stock a nice pop. If this was what Nortel was actually up to, it wasn't anything original. Managing the guidance figures produced by analysts was all in a day's work for the officers of the modern public company.

Healy's suspicions about the guidance movement on Nortel were expressed just ahead of the release on December 22 of a staff report by the Ontario Securities Commission that revealed the extent of canoodling between companies and the analysts that covered them. The OSC had conducted a survey of TSE-listed companies on their corporate disclosure practices. It found that 81 percent of the respondents reported having one-on-one meetings with analysts. That was to be expected; what was illuminating was that 98 percent said that they typically commented in some form on draft analyst reports. In other words, whether they actually met in person with analysts or not, virtually all companies vetted the reports of analysts before they were released in final form. The answer was a bit ambiguous. It didn't necessarily mean that virtually every analyst report issued on their company was vetted by them; rather, that virtually every company surveyed did vet reports of at least some of the analysts covering them before they went to final form. Whether those analysts constituted 1 percent or 100 percent of the ones covering them was another matter. As well, 27 percent of respondents indicated that they expressed "a level of comfort" on analysts' earnings projections. Thus, more than one-quarter of these companies admitted to commenting directly on the earnings projections that analysts proposed, which was more blatant than just handing over their own guidance and trusting the analysts to follow it. "In general," the OSC concluded, "the results of the Survey indicate that the extent and nature of corporate disclosure policies and practices of issuers is not sufficient to reduce the potential for selective disclosure."

Healy wasn't in the habit of showing his reports to companies or asking their opinion of his projected earnings figures, and so wasn't privy to whatever conversations might have transpired between Nortel and analysts who moved with the synchronicity of a line of Rockettes in cutting their earnings forecasts by virtually the same amount at the same time. But he strongly suspected that Nortel was getting a little help from its analyst friends in engineering a pop. Healy didn't say why such a pop was important—beyond the thrill of beating the market's expectations—but the momentum could have been important as BCE prepared to announce the plan to spin off most of its Nortel holding in the spring.

The lowered guidance had no impact on Nortel's share price. It had been around $100 on the TSE when Healy predicted a positive earnings surprise for the fourth quarter on November 9; a little more than two months later, on January 18, as Healy awaited the fourth-quarter results, Nortel was going for about $141. "We are watching with bated breath to see how the market reacts to Nortel's earnings," he wrote in his Weekly Market Notes that day. "As we noted a little while ago, NT carefully—and quietly—directed analysts to reduce 1999 cash earnings expectations (as well as those for Y2K) from the $1.10–1.15 area to smack on $1.00 even. We wondered at the time whether this meant that NT would disappoint or merely meet the previous earnings forecast, which had hardly changed one iota for 12 months running previous to the sudden analyst write down of expectations. If the latter, then the company was clearly trying to get an earnings surprise where none actually existed. Assuming this, how will the market react to a non-surprise surprise? By a hefty jump of 25%, as occurred with Intel, or a ho-hum reaction? If the former assumption that a disappointment is in the works, then the stock at 3 times fair market value (its EER), could be very vulnerable. Stay tuned."

Two days later, after watching IBM execute an impressive guidance manoeuvre, Healy wrote to clients: "With the success of IBM's manoeuvre in lowering analyst forecasts and then exceeding it in order to get a strong market reaction, we would assume that Nortel's efforts in this regard should also pay off nicely."

On January 26, Healy was able to post his reaction to Nortel's fourth-quarter and year-end numbers. He could scarcely contain his amusement or annoyance. Nortel had made good on an earlier promise to begin releasing its financials in both Canadian and U.S. GAAP, but it layered on them its own "earnings from operations" numbers, producing several different measures of its performance. "Depending on how you want to look at Nortel," Healy wrote, "the company either came in with a blistering quarter, or missed its target by somewhere between 18% and 78%. Perception being everything, we will look at it both ways. From the market's reaction in the after-hours market, 'blistering' is the consensus, although the hanky-panky and obfuscation that went on to get the numbers that it did would please and delight the most hard-core of cryptic crossword puzzle fans."

Healy's analysis of Nortel that day is such a rare classic of analyst disdain for a stock, at a time when most of his fellow travellers could not bring themselves to reach a position more dour than "hold" on any security, that it bears repeating in whole:

> 1. Sales: Sales set a blistering pace with the company coming in slightly ahead of what they euphemistically term their "guidance numbers" (i.e.: tell the analysts what to expect because the company is so complex that who can figure it out anyway?). Led by an 80% gain in the fibre optics side of the business as well as several other pretty hot areas, the 4th quarter was a barnburner. And there would certainly appear to be much more to come in the next year or two, although the company did admit that longer term, the "absolute" growth may remain high but the "relative" rate may slow down. We take this to mean that we should not be expecting 22–25% annual gains in sales from now until the next millennium.
>
> 2. Earnings: Ah yes, earnings. Have to have those, don't you

know, or they get a bit shirty out there. I mean, just look at poor old Lucent. Decent numbers, but really. Right out of it. . . . Good object lesson in controlling the news flow is how we look at it at NT, don't you know? Especially when you are trading upwards of around 100 times the trailing earnings per share.

We at SAC were certainly impressed by their earnings numbers. Perhaps not in quite the way that some others are, but impressed nonetheless. So let's see.

For openers, they reported an "earnings surprise" of $.55 per share in the final quarter, which beat the analysts' consensus estimate by a solid $.10, or about 18%. While it is probably tacky to mention it, the analysts wrote down their 1999 estimate by a rough average of $.12 a share (to dead on $1.00 per share) in October/November, presumably under the "guidance" of the company as 14 analysts did so virtually simultaneously (as you will remember we reported at the time). If nothing else, we thought it peculiar, as the estimate of $1.12, plus or minus a couple of cents, had been pretty much in force for an entire year. We said at the time and reiterated last week that the downwards "guidance" may have been provided so as to ensure an earnings surprise, and that was how the numbers were viewed when the after-hours trading crowd got a close look. Using the estimate for the quarter from September, the company actually fell short of expectations, but September is an eon—and 50% away in price—from now.

Actually, how "close" that "close look" actually was is also somewhat open to debate. The tax rate fell during the quarter, which added a good nickel to earnings. But this was clearly a surprise to the company as well; otherwise they would have factored it into their analyst guidance. Naturally, investors normally put a heavier weight on tax-reduced earnings than regularly-taxed earnings because the company gets more and greedy governments don't get as much, which comes under the heading of a "good thing." This is called New Paradigm Thinking.

In light of the current price, a little more baffling, but far more encouraging way, to look at NT is the fact that Dow Jones reported that Nortel's net income in the 4th quarter was US$.12 a share compared to a net loss of US$.11 a share this time last year. "Excluding accounting items [and what better items to exclude, we would add] and acquisition-related expenses, Nortel said it would have posted earnings of US$.43 a share vs. a mean estimate of US$.45." This sounds like an earnings disappointment. Luckily, for current purposes, we appear to have been given the Canadian GAAP earnings numbers, which fortunately do not recognize those accounting items either (and, clearly, a whole bunch of other stuff as well to get to $.55). What is good about the Dow Jones numbers is that the percentage gain which you get when you divide +.12 by −.11 is better than when you divide .55 by .45. What is bad about them is that the trailing PE ratio which arises from them makes Nortel look more like Yahoo! than, say, IBM or CP. At the end of the exercise, the way that we look at Nortel is that they must have earned some money or else the street would not have got so carried away last night, sending the stock up some US$9 in after hours trading. Fifty million investors can't be wrong. Whether the real per share number is $.12, $.30 (after special items), $.43, $.50 (after tax rate adjustments) or $.55, the point that everyone needs to focus on is that sales are up and surely you can't sell $6.99 billion worth of product in a single quarter and $22.217 billion in a year without earning something (unless, of course, you happen to be Amazon.Com or Boeing).

Recommendation: Using our EER to determine the fair market value leaves one a little further out on a limb than some might like. If we take the consensus Y2K earnings number of US$1.24, the fair market value of NT is US$31 and C$47. To be able to place the current price of NT as being its EER Price (fair market value) would therefore require earnings of about US$3.75. Assuming, as the analysts do (and somewhat contrary to what the company has actually said), that the company's earnings will grow at a 25% compound annual rate, that number will be reached in precisely 5 years. As that is much better than, say, Yahoo!'s or AOL's numbers suggest, NT is a clearly better buy than either one at the present time. This is not much of a recommendation, but then investors don't have much to go on either. As a final point of interest, here is a company which 'earns' (using the very best case scenario) less than 5% on sales, about 8% on Total Capital and not quite 10% on common equity. This company is no Dell or Coca Cola whose balance sheets provide a strong natural growth rate due to a powerful ROE. Suitable only for momentum players and speculators who subscribe to the Greater Fool Theory of investing.

Ross Healy's call on Nortel on January 26, 2000, belongs in the Analyst Hall of Fame.

11

The Butterfly Plan

Let the good times roll here. The only draw back of owning NT is that we have to pre-condition ourselves for what lies ahead. A dramatic price increase and multiples of our money to be made.

As Austin Powers would say, "Yeah! Baby! Yeah!" or "I shagged her rotten, Baby."

—posting to Nortel bulletin board
at RagingBull.com, November 5, 1999

On January 26, 2000, the day after Nortel released its fourth-quarter and year-end 1999 results (and as Ross Healy distributed his biting comments to clients), BCE announced its plan to spin off all but about 2 percent of its 39.23 percent ownership in Nortel. There were about 1.4 billion Nortel common shares around at the time; in all, 502.2 million Nortel common shares would be turned loose in the BCE spinoff, allowing it to overtake BCE as the most widely held stock in Canada. The divestment would also be accompanied by a stock split, which would take Nortel's common shares up to three billion in all.

The plan to turn Nortel loose had been coming together since at least the previous October. News of negotiations between BCE and Nortel had begun to circulate after Nortel released its third-quarter 1999 results. By the end of October, Nortel's share price gave it a market capitalization of about $120 billion (Canadian), making it the largest company in the country. And yet BCE's large interest made Nortel an awkward subsidiary of sorts. The offspring was out-growing the parent. BCE's proportionate share of Nortel revenues was greater than the revenues generated by all other BCE properties, including Bell Canada. Where Nortel's revenues in 1999 grew 26 percent, the revenues of BCE's non-Nortel properties increased only 5 percent. While BCE's share price had grown about 50 percent since the start of 1999, by late October Nortel's had shot up more than 130 percent. Jean Monty argued that the stock market was viewing BCE's value too much from the perspective of its major stake in Nortel. Getting rid of Nortel would allow BCE, he argued, to stand on its own merits.

In truth, the relationship between Nortel and BCE's earnings reportage created a Gordian knot of intertwined cold-fusion economics. BCE had its own lexicon of custom accounting terms, and Nortel's custom accounting had a direct impact on BCE's profitability picture, because BCE used Nortel's "earnings from operations" as the basis for recording its proportionate share of Nortel's earnings. BCE as a result stripped away its proportionate share of Nortel's acquisition-related costs and consigned them to something called "special items." In BCE's first-quarter 1999 results, Nortel was shown making a $133 million contribution to BCE's "unaudited baseline earnings." (All BCE figures are in Canadian dollars.) These were earnings before "net special items." These so-called baseline earnings were then used by BCE to proclaim earnings per common share of 57 cents, a 14 percent improvement over the first quarter of 1998, while Nortel's contribution to baseline earnings was shown to have improved by 37 percent. Down in the third paragraph of the press release, BCE admitted it had actually suffered a net loss of 18 cents per share, compared to net earnings of 27 cents per share in the first quarter of 1998, after the special items were factored in. These were mainly Nortel's acquisition-related costs, it said, and an explanatory footnote to its "results by operating group" cited "amortization of Bay Networks and Cambrian intangibles."

It was a nice trick. Nortel got to show a substantial contribution to this thing called "baseline earnings," while the costs associated with the Bay and Cambrian deals were separated from Nortel and dumped in the communal slag heap of charges called "net special items." With this kind of clever presentation, Nortel was able to show a positive contribution to BCE via baseline earnings right through 1999, even as its own GAAP accounting said it was losing money in every quarter but the third, when it scraped together a $1 million profit. (Nortel's actual performance showed up under "segmental information.")

Nortel's contribution to BCE was helped considerably by the GAAP practice of a company showing an income gain when another company in which it held minority interest issued shares and so diluted the investing company's proportion of the outstanding shares. GAAP thus required BCE to show income—a "dilution gain"—from Nortel's use of shares to acquire companies, as if BCE had sold shares in Nortel. This transformed share-based Nortel acquisitions, which consisted almost entirely of intangibles, into income over at BCE. For 1998, BCE got to book a $3.6 billion dilution gain under Nortel's "special items" because of the Bay Networks acquisition, which more than offset its $1 billion share of Nortel's acquisition-related costs. This resulted in Nortel making a contribution of $3.2 billion to BCE's "net earnings applicable to common shares" where there otherwise would have been a loss from its Nortel stake of almost $400 million. In comparison, Nortel's own earnings from operations only came to $1.06 billion (U.S.) (when under Canadian GAAP it in fact lost $569 million [U.S.]).

For year-end 1999, Nortel was shown to have contributed operating earnings of $1 billion to BCE, an improvement of $323 million over 1998. Again, this was BCE's proportionate share of Nortel's own custom "net earnings applicable to common shares" of $1.7 billion (U.S.), which mainly didn't include acquisition-related costs. Even after factoring in the $553 million in special items attributed to Nortel's acquisition-related costs, Nortel still made a positive contribution of $449 million, which was a pretty amazing feat, since Nortel's own 1999 year-end showed it with a net loss applicable to common shares under U.S. GAAP of $351 million (U.S.). Again, dilution gains from Nortel's acquisition activities had come to BCE's rescue. The purchases of Periphonics and Shasta, as well as shares issued under Nortel's stock option plan, had delivered BCE an earnings boost of $591 million.

It seemed counterintuitive for BCE to want to get rid of its hottest subsidiary. While there were concerns among analysts that losing Nortel would cost BCE its largest growth engine, dilution gains aside, the more Nortel shares John Roth issued in his acquisition strategy, the more diluted became BCE's claim on Nortel's customized earnings. And the more acquisitions that Roth made, the more acquisition-related Nortel charges BCE would have to account for in some way, which would impact on its overall profitability picture. BCE no longer received top-line growth from John Roth's company. BCE believed that Nortel's presence in its portfolio was actually overshadowing the value of its other holdings, and that BCE's stock was being underpriced by about $47.

Jean Monty was pursuing his own expansion scheme for BCE in many ways as aggressive as the one being undertaken by John Roth with Nortel. Like Nortel, it wanted to turn itself into an Internet-oriented company. Twenty percent of Bell Canada had been sold to the U.S. telecom giant SBC/Ameritech for $5.1 billion, and BCE had consolidated a variety of properties under the Bell Canada umbrella: the national IP fibre-optic backbone, Bell Nexxia; the wireless service, Bell Mobility; and the satellite television service, Bell ExpressVu. BCE was also offering e-commerce services through BC Emergis and CGI, and Internet access through Sympatico. And it acquired complete ownership of Teleglobe, the Canadian long-distance communications service, and was expanding wireless operations overseas through BCI. Within this strategy was an occasional acknowledgement of the importance to BCE of content, and not just the ability to communicate it on behalf of others. In 2000, BCE would make an aggressive bid to create a Canadian media giant, acquiring CTV, the country's largest private television broadcaster, and partnering with the Thomson Corporation to create Bell GlobeMedia, home to CTV, the *Globe and Mail* newspaper, eighteen specialty television channels, and a wide range of Web-based properties.

BCE brought in Morgan Stanley to advise it on what to do with the Nortel block. They came up with the idea of assigning the 540 million Nortel shares to a publicly traded holding company in which BCE shareholders would hold shares. There were certain tax-deferral benefits to this arrangement, but it meant the shares would not be directly held by individual BCE shareholders. For a number of reasons, Nortel didn't like this idea. One was the issue of how the holding company's ownership stake would affect the composition of Nortel's board of directors, but a major sore point was the possible effect that parking about 38 percent of Nortel's share float in a holding company could have on its share price. Nortel struck a special committee from its board of directors, brought in RBC Dominion Securities as an adviser, and hammered out an alternative plan with BCE, which was announced on January 26, 2000. That plan was for BCE simply to get rid of all but about 5 percent of its Nortel shares.

From Nortel's perspective, eliminating BCE's large ownership block probably couldn't happen quickly enough. Nortel's growth strategy was founded on acquisitions paid for with company stock. As a result, Nortel needed as many of its existing shares available on the open market as possible. So long as market enthusiasm remained high, this increased availability could only help the share price. And of course, the more the shares were worth, the fewer of them Roth had to use in buying companies.

A problem with having so many Nortel shares held by BCE was that it suppressed Nortel's position in the TSE indices. The BCE-held shares were not considered part of Nortel's float for the purposes of calculating its weighting in the TSE 300, for example. Turning loose the shares held by BCE would give a huge boost to Nortel in that index. Nortel would become the single largest stock in the 300, and that would have a considerable impact on how the stock was acquired by investors of all stripes.

A straight offering of Nortel shares on the open market could have brought a huge cash infusion into BCE, but this would have tripped equally huge tax implications. Instead, BCE and Nortel agreed that the 37 percent interest (the exact proportion changed with every share-based acquisition and exercised stock option at Nortel) would be distributed in the form of a dividend to BCE shareholders. BCE would realize no direct financial gain.

The divestment was known as a "butterfly" distribution. A new Nortel legal entity, called New Nortel, would be created. Present common shareholders in Nortel would exchange their shares one-for-one for common shares in New Nortel. BCE common shareholders would receive a dividend payment consisting of 0.78 New Nortel shares for every BCE share they held. The common shares of New Nortel would then undergo a split. When the transaction was completed, the existing Nortel shareholders would hold two shares in New Nortel; BCE shareholders would still have their original shares in BCE and 1.56 common shares in New Nortel for every common share they held in BCE.

BCE shareholders would meet to approve the arrangement on April 26; Nortel shareholders would do the same on April 27. May 5 was the date of record for determining the BCE common shareholders who would receive the New Nortel shares dividend, and a two-for-one split of New Nortel would become effective at the close of business.

While the dividend arrangement meant BCE could avoid the tax impact that would have been triggered by a share offering, with the butterfly plan the tax burden was passed on to the shareholders, and it would influence how Nortel was traded after the deal was done. For U.S. shareholders in BCE, the receipt of the Nortel shares would have to be treated as a taxable dividend, with the fair market value of Nortel shares being included in their 2000 tax return. If Nortel tanked after the divestment, they faced a potentially large tax loss, for they were required to pay taxes on the share's value at the time of the divestment.

In Canada, the tax implications were much different. The dividend did not trigger an immediate tax obligation the way it did in the United States. However, if the BCE shareholder then tried to sell the Nortel shares, they were on the hook for a capital gain taxable at an inclusion rate of 67 percent of their gain. (The inclusion rate had been 75 percent until March 2000.) If Nortel shares continued to climb after the distribution, they would be very reluctant to sell them and capture the value of this dividend "gift," as much of it was going to end up being mailed to Canada Customs and Revenue.

Capital gains taxes in the United States have been cited as one cause of the bubble of the most recent bull market, particularly as investors resisted selling shares in expectation of a future drop in the capital gains rate. In Canada, capital gains taxes certainly could help sustain an elevated price for Nortel after the distribution. Demand might be high for the shares, but with so many of them held by BCE shareholders who were discouraged by tax implications from selling them, the supply might not be able to meet the demand, driving the market price even higher. If John Roth wanted a higher price for Nortel shares so he could buy yet more companies with as few of them as possible, this was a great way to do it. And he certainly was going to buy more companies, at the rate of about one a month in 2000.

There was another reason for Roth to relish a continuing ascent in Nortel's share price. It was making him extremely rich.

Cold-fusion economics made one more adjustment to the cash flow experienced by the pipes going in and out of the magic box of the public company. We've already seen with IPOs how a pop in the after-market delivered riches to those fortunate enough to be among the initial subscribers. But there was still another way for a stock market pop, whether over the short or longer term, to deliver healthy returns to a privileged few, regardless of whether or not an IPO started the valuation ball rolling.

Company insiders, principally senior employees, are routinely compensated with stock options, which permit them to buy stock from the company treasury at a set price within a particular time frame. Stock option terms vary widely, but they generally work along the same lines. An executive is granted the right to purchase 900 shares in his company, XYZ Co., on January 1, 1997, at a price of $12, the trading price on that day, which is known as the exercise or strike price. But the options must still vest—that is, become eligible to be exercised—at a future date. One form is "cliff" vesting, in which all the options become exercisable on a particular date. With our executive, his option grant of 900 shares vests over three years, at the rate of one-third per year. He can purchase 300 shares from the company treasury on January 1, 1998, another 300 on January 1, 1999, and the final 300 on January 1, 2000, each time at the original price. The vesting schedule encourages him both to stick around long enough to exercise the options and to work hard enough to drive up the share price so that the options have some value. If the price of the shares after one year is $18, then he can exercise his 300 shares at $12 and make a $6 paper profit per share (before taxes), or a real profit if his option plan permits him to sell them immediately on the after-market. Should the stock price drop below $12, however, the options go "under water" and are worthless.

At Nortel, employee stock options under the 1986 company plan vested at a rate of 50 percent per year. This was changed in 1997, when Roth took over, to a rate of $33^{1}/_{3}$ percent per year, so that options were exercised in the manner described above for XYZ Co. The number of options granted was based on a formula which tracked corporate and individual performance over a three-year period. Nortel also had an option replacement plan, which granted new options to executives as they exercised their old ones.

Thus, while Nortel was far from an actual startup, the stock option system had a similar effect on the profitability pipeline. Through stock options, a major source of employee compensation was placed in the hands of the stock market. The great thing about this was that the "pay" that option profits represented didn't come out of the company bank account, and so had no impact on profits. A complex calculation called the Black Scholes Method could be used to assess the future worth of option grants, but there was no imperative under GAAP to apply the impact of these grants against corporate revenues. It was as if executive compensation was out-sourced to the investment community.

For the people running a company who were blessed with stock options, the need to build a profitable enterprise as recognized by GAAP became less of a personal imperative. The market was con-vinced that GAAP-type profits didn't matter if the company was in a growth phase, or if hard-to-grasp deductions like goodwill amortiza-tion were creating the GAAP losses. From the GAAP perspective, a company could stagger along but be immensely profitable for the people running it, because their greatest compensation source was often the options on stock being bid to the sky by the market.

The revenue flow was running backwards through the pipes. Money was coming in through the outflow pipe that normally delivered dividends to shareholders. Those shareholders, by driving the share price ever higher, were effectively sending money back up the pipe normally used to deliver them dividends—back into the corporate offices, where it could be enjoyed through stock options by the executive ranks—and not by the company overall. The company was in danger of becoming an operating shell for a capital gains bonanza enjoyed by shareholders making a killing on aftermarket trades and by executives making a killing on options.

Fundamentally, rewarding executives with stock options sounds like a good idea. If their performances increase profitability and the dividends being paid out to shareholders, the stock price should go up and they should be rewarded for it. Detractors will note that driving up the stock price in pursuit of options can produce all sorts of short-term strategies that enrich option holders but damage the company over the long term—chainsawing overheads and staffing levels, cutting back on R&D and other expenses that affect net earnings. But with Nortel, the company's long-term health was arguably being compromised by its stock option plan in an entirely different way. For as we've seen, the company's proxy circular of March 13, 2000 (released in advance of the annual general meeting that would approve the BCE butterfly plan), stated, "The 1999 salary, bonus and stock option awards for Mr. Roth all reflected the attainment of record 1999 revenues *and operating earnings and operating earnings per share.*" (Italics added.) As well, in the 1999 annual report's explanation of how Nortel evaluated the performance of its business segments, the company stated that this was based on "measures of profit or loss from operations before income taxes excluding the impact of 'Acquisition Related Costs' (IPR&D expense and the amortization of acquired technology and goodwill from all acquisitions subsequent to July 1998) . . ." In 1999, that meant overlooking $2.15 billion in amortization of intangibles.

Nortel was plainly very happy with the job John Roth had been doing, based on the above criteria. His pay (in U.S. dollars) had risen from $447,533 in 1995 to $609,624 in 1997, when he became president and CEO. At the same time, his annual bonus rose from $418,716 to $1,175,420. By February 27, 1998, Roth owned 59,056 shares and held options giving him the right to acquire up to 354,000 shares.

By February 26, 1999, when the next shareholder proxy was mailed, Roth held options for 507,332 shares and owned outright 61,164 shares. His salary in 1998 was up to $682,783 and he'd received a bonus of $1,261,248. When the proxy was circulated for the April 2000 annual general meeting, Roth had rearranged his affairs somewhat. He now owned 85,800 shares through a corporation, and another 6,400 jointly with his wife, and held options for 1,486,665 shares. Those options were about to double in number with the stock split of May 5. He had also drawn a salary of $812,500 in 1999 and been rewarded a $4.2 million bonus. On the basis of salary and bonus alone, John Roth's compensation had grown from less than $1 million in 1995 to more than $5 million in 1999.

And so it passed that the company's expansion through acquisitions, paid for mainly with stock, didn't simply continue—it gathered momentum. Nortel began the year 2000 with a minor acquisition, an engineering and business strategy consulting operation called Dimension Enterprises, for which it said it paid about $52 million in cash on January 24, $45 million of which was goodwill, the rest being tangible assets. Four days later, after the fourth-quarter and year-end results were celebrated, the Qtera deal closed. Clarify wrapped up on March 16. Eight more deals lay ahead in 2000. The year was turning into an extraordinarily expensive one for acquisitions. In all, $19.7 billion worth of purchases (U.S. GAAP) would be consummated in 2000, with goodwill amounting to $16.7 billion. Eighty-five percent of the acquisition costs were an unquantifiable premium.

Pension funds are, theoretically, the most risk-averse pools of capital. The security of contributors in their retirement years are at stake. Nowhere are the platitudes of probity and patience with short-term market fluctuations espoused more earnestly than in the pension business. Pension fund managers are a special breed of professional investor who would no more risk the equity of present and future pensioners than they would stick a butter knife in a light socket, and the trust boards that hire them and establish portfolio criteria are so risk averse that even the certainty of the sun rising is an event to be hedged against.

All of which is a crock. Pension funds are not reckless Ponzi schemes, but as major players in the securities markets, they are prone to the same hunches, wishful thinking, and herd psychology as any other sampling of so-called savvy investors. And where greed alone was not sufficient impulse, the unique dynamics of the Canadian pension fund pool was enough to turn legions of pension plan contributors into major players in the Nortel bubble. People who swore off gambling any of their take-home pay in the stock market, particularly after the sobering crashes of the late eighties, nonetheless came to wager a significant portion of their retirement nest egg on John Roth's Big Internet Adventure. Nortel would not bring about the absolute ruin of any pension plan, but its flameout, which began in late 2000, would torch an impressive hole in the assets of many of Canada's pension plans, large and small.

Pension funds put the lie to the traditional notion of the stock market investor as a pinstripe high-roller, reconfigured in the nineties as a dot-com–obsessed Yuppie amassing a personal fortune by speculating on the NASDAQ. The vast majority of investment activity on stock exchanges is conducted by institutional players: pension funds, mutual funds, insurance companies, and the like, with pensions representing the single largest pool of investment capital in Canada. At the end of 1999, the Ontario Municipal Employees Retirement System (OMERS) boasted a portfolio worth almost $35 billion; the Ontario Teachers Federation Pension Plan weighed in at $68.3 billion. And the pool of pension investment capital was set to grow fantastically as the federal government unleashed the captive pension plans of workers in various institutions and Crown corporations. Ottawa has decreed that Canada Post is to move from a traditional defined-benefit pension plan—one in which the employer dictates how much of their paycheques its employees must set aside for retirement—to a direct-contribution plan, in which funds are invested according to the wishes of individual plan members, and the rate of return determines how much participants must contribute, how much they can draw when they retire, and even when they can retire. Canada Post is expected to inject about $7 billion into the securities market when it is fully converted to a direct-contribution program by 2002 or 2003, and waiting to join the 50,000-odd Posties are members of the Canadian Armed Forces, the RCMP, and the Public Service Alliance.

While remarkably underreported and unappreciated, the government's plans for public sector pensions was major news. No Canadian financial professional could overlook its implications in the late 1990s. The much maligned civil servant was about to make a fantastic cash donation to the Canadian equities market. Anyone interested in the liquidity of the exchanges, the viability of new offerings, and the market's ability to sustain record values for its hottest stocks was eager to welcome the Posties and their civil service brethren into the grand fraternity of stock market players.

The tens of billions of dollars in existing Canadian pension funds have already had a profound effect on the liquidity and stability of the equities market. The movement of this capital in and out of particular securities is a bellwether of investor confidence. The sheer heft of funds creates their own particular challenges. Federal legislation limited foreign investments for pension funds to 20 percent in 1999. With the federal budget of February 2000, this was expanded to 25 percent in 2000, and would be increased again to 30 percent in 2001. The increase would help address the fundamental problem of the discouragingly small pool of large-scale, blue-chip investment opportunities in Canada capable of absorbing the contributions of even existing pension funds, particularly when pension funds weren't allowed to have more than 10 percent of the value of their holdings in any one security. As of December 31, 1999, according to Morgan Stanley Capital International, Canada ranked eighth in developed nations by market capitalization, with just 2.1 percent of the world's equity pool, with the United States the overwhelming leader, hoarding 49 percent. The budget revision to foreign investment ceilings for pensions had an obvious eye on accommodating the billions about to enter the market from the liberated public service pension funds.

Canadian pension fund managers are free to have a go with smaller stocks, but their small capitalizations cannot hope to swallow the wads of cash these managers need to place somewhere, in something. With around 30 to 45 percent of a pension fund's holdings typically allocated to Canadian equity investments, fund managers inevitably are drawn to hot large-cap stocks that can vacuum up the billions in pension contributions that are expected to deliver solid returns. Once a fund has invested in a stock, it also tends to be a stabilizing market influence, damping the wild gyrations of the amateurs—provided the funds themselves don't leave a particular security en masse. Interested in long-term results, managers aren't (or weren't) expected to get in and out of particular investments quickly. They were expected to sit tight through market fluctuations and not resort to—and contribute to—panic selling. If they didn't think a company had long-term potential, they wouldn't have bought it in the first place. After Nortel nose-dived in October 2000 on disappointing third-quarter results, pension fund pros were relieved to see fund managers stolidly hanging tough with their holdings, waiting for the inevitable upturn that would come once the rest of the market came to its senses and dutifully returned to the collegial ranks of Nortel stockholders.

A hot stock behaves like a hurricane, generating its own weather. The hurricane draws its energy from the warm tropical waters; the stock sucks in the cash of the rapt capital market. As market enthusiasm—demand exceeding supply—drives up a share price, it by definition increases the company's market capitalization, making more room inside the bubble for investor funds as trading volume increases. Fund managers in search of opportunities for their mountains of money come face to face with a behemoth, a rapidly expanding haven with room enough for all, which they had helped create and sustain. It was hard to find a major Canadian pension fund that didn't have a big slice of Nortel in 1999 and 2000—and in 2001, when the stock fell so spectacularly.

Contrary to their veneer of long-term fiscal prudence, pension funds were simmering under the heat of investor expectations. The professional fund managers were under pressure from the governing boards, who were in turn under pressure from the plan enrollees—the pseudo-sophisticated new investment proles. The bull market of the 1990s had brought record numbers of common folk into the stock market. The country was in the grip of what might be called a prosperity panic. Real wages were hardly growing at the same time that the bull market was providing double-digit returns on equity. The financial services industry had been pounding away at the proles with "Freedom 55" concepts of early retirement bliss. The industry was doing an admirable job of shaking investment capital out of rank and file workers through RRSP contributions, including mutual funds, in part by fomenting widespread concern that the Canada Pension Plan would not be able to take care of them in their golden years. Whatever the merits of the criticisms of the CPP's viability and usefulness, the 1990s saw a remarkable change in the relationship between the average Canadian and capital markets. Where the previous generation routinely experienced working lives of forty to fifty years, the baby-boom generation, later than their parents to enter the workforce as they pursued post-secondary degrees, also wanted to get out of it much sooner. Between leaving school at, say, twenty-five, and retiring at fifty-five, they were planning to cut their main income-generating years to thirty years, ten to twenty years less than the productivity span of their parents. The only way to fund those additional years of idleness was to take some of their income while gainfully employed and invest it at reasonably high rates of return. RRSPs, the grand national tax-deferral scheme, gave the government's blessing to the financial market's determination to access fresh investment capital. Between 1990 and 1998, the value of Canadian RRSP holdings increased from $132.3 billion to $191.1 billion. Much of that new capital was coming in mutual funds sheltered within RRSPs. In 1987, there were about 2.5 million individual mutual fund accounts in Canada, with a market value of $20.3 billion. By 1999, there were almost 46 million accounts, with a total value of $389.7 billion.

At the same time, pension plans overall were changing from the old-style defined-benefit plans to the more transparently market-playing, direct-contribution programs in which enrollees made investment choices. Percolating up from the proles—who, outside their nine-to-five routine, were trying to get ahead (and ultimately out of the office or factory) by stuffing spare dollars into tax-sheltered portfolios—was an increasing demand for their pensions to perform at least as well as the overall market. The old steady-as-she-goes modus operandi was becoming difficult to defend, particularly by the defined-benefit fund managers working on commission, whose efforts were being measured with the same short-term yardstick as mutual fund managers. Annual rates of return that lagged behind the market were becoming less tolerable; pension fund boards were losing their inhibitions about replacing the appointed fund managers on the basis of short-term performance. It was becoming more difficult to defend a pension fund as an investment vehicle that had to be nurtured over the long term, with slow but steady growth instead of meteoric rises that invited equally meteoric crashes. At the least, the pressure on fund managers to deliver short-term returns that outperformed the market were undeniable, a desire that could only encourage a more aggressive approach to investments.

As the decade drew to a close, pension fund and mutual fund managers alike confronted an increasingly daunting adversary: the TSE 300 Composite Index, the benchmark against which their investment performances were routinely measured. Created in 1977 as a broad indicator of market performance, it represented 300 of the largest traded companies on Canada's biggest exchange. The composition of the 300 was rejigged in the spring of 2002, but in Nortel's heyday it was subdivided into fourteen sectors, and those sectors were further divided into industry groups, then industries, then subindustries. It's an indicator of the relatively thin nature of the Canadian equities market that this index, ostensibly an elite sampling of the stocks on the country's largest exchange, actually accounts for about 71 percent of all stocks listed. And while the TSE 300 Composite suggests a widescreen portrait of economic vigour, it is often misleadingly cited as a prognosticator of the Canadian economy, a counterpoint to the Dow Jones Industrial Average, which is drawn from trading on the New York Stock Exchange. Unlike the

Dow, however, it is a float-weighted, rather than a price-weighted, index. An indexed stock is weighted according to its total float, the number of shares hypothetically available for trading. Thus, a stock heavily weighted by the index because of a large number of available shares can have an enormous influence on the value of the TSE 300 Composite if the share price skyrockets. Nortel's ability to boost the 300 gave it unprecedented leverage in influencing activities throughout the financial industry.

For managers of pension and mutual funds, the TSE 300 Composite's performance created serious professional headaches. Unless they were dedicated to portfolios stuffed with riskier growth stocks, and got lucky, it was very difficult for them to beat the 300 Composite when so much of its growth was hitched to the increasingly disproportionate presence of Nortel. Those in charge of actively managed mutual funds had their hands tied because regulations prevented them from including more than 10 percent of one stock in a fund's portfolio. If Nortel was the TSE's hottest stock and represented more than one-quarter of the weighting of the TSE 300, then a fund manager could scarcely hope to match the Composite with its own general-mix portfolio. An investor could do better simply by putting his money in one of the indexed funds that allowed individuals to profit from the performances of one of the various TSE indices that happened to be heavily weighted with Nortel.

The butterfly dividend strategy BCE adopted for shedding its Nortel equity created immediate concerns for the mutual fund managers who played such a large trading role on the TSE. Before the spinoff was announced, Nortel accounted for about 16 percent of the total weighting of the TSE 300. The spinoff would take Nortel's allocation to 26 percent. On the more focused TSE/S&P 60, Nortel was already at 22 percent before the spinoff; post-divestiture, it would reach 36 percent. And the proportions for both indices would inevitably go higher as Nortel continued its use of shares to make acquisitions and so increased its total float.

Mutual funds, as noted, were limited to 10 percent in value for any particular stock, which already made it impossible to match the TSE 300 or 60. One way to beat the cap was to invest in BCE and participate vicariously in BCE's own large holding of Nortel. But if a fund already held BCE and the spinoff delivered it a wad of Nortel shares as dividends, on top of the Nortel shares it already held, the fund could be pushed over the cap limit. Fortunately for these funds, the Ontario Securities Commission came to their rescue and allowed them to stop worrying so much about diversification. On January 28, the OSC passed what was known as the "BCE/Nortel rule." This allowed index fund managers to keep matching the composition of the particular tracked index, even if it meant violating the 10 percent cap. For managers of mutual funds, the cap could also be violated as a result of the Nortel spinoff, but managers wouldn't be allowed to buy any more Nortel stock until its weighting in their portfolio dropped below 10 percent. Which was as good as saying that, if Nortel ever got below 10 percent in their portfolio, they probably wouldn't want it anyway.

Pension fund investment strategies change with time and market conditions and differ from one fund to another, but generally 30 to 45 percent of a pension's funds are invested in Canadian equities, with most of the rest devoted to low-risk domestic debt instruments and a small percentage devoted to foreign equities; larger funds also accumulate real estate.

Pension fund managers loved Nortel and its largest shareholder, BCE. These were blue-chip super-performers in the late nineties, the must-have Canadian equities (along with bank stocks) for fund port-folios. In 1999, Harry S. Marmer, director of investment funds at Frank Russell Canada, penned a not-so-facetious ode to David Letterman with his "Top 10 tips for managing DC [Direction Contribution] plans." Item number 3 was "Offer at least two invest-ment choices: Nortel and BCE."

The Ontario Public Service Employees Union (OPSEU) Pension Trust (OPTrust), which was established in 1995, provided prime evidence of how great a return a fund manager could reap from just Nortel and BCE. The defined-benefit fund finished 1999 with BCE and Nortel ranked 1–2 in its holdings. OPTrust had paid an average of $26.57 per share for its 1.9 million Nortel shares. When Nortel surged to a year-end 1999 value of over $140 a share on the TSE, OPTrust was rewarded with a Nortel nest egg worth $280.5 million. Only the value of its BCE holding (2.2 million shares worth $284 million) exceeded it, but because BCE owned so much Nortel itself, in practical terms the OPTrust fund had Nortel as its single largest holding. OPTrust had paid an average of $33.20 for each of its BCE shares, and they had finished 1999 above $131. The TD Bank holding was a distant third in its Canadian equities portfolio, its 2.7 million shares worth $104.9 million.

Nortel represented a profound dilemma to pension fund managers. On the one hand, the traditional conservatism of fund management said not to go overboard on a particular investment, no matter how good it looked. On the other hand, Nortel was viewed as a solid, respected firm that was rocketing the TSE 300 to new heights at a time that equities were providing the only real growth for pension funds. As the stock markets boomed, bonds were in retreat. OMERS, for example, finished 1999 with $34.9 billion in assets, after increasing its portfolio value $3.6 billion and paying out about $1 billion to pensioners. The portfolio overall had increased 15.2 percent in one year, and that was due mainly to the equities. Fixed income (bond) investments had performed poorly, losing 1 percent in Canada and 11.7 percent in foreign holdings. Its Canadian equities had increased a healthy 27.4 percent, but had been outperformed by the fund's measurement benchmark, a combination of the TSE 300 Composite and the Nesbitt Burns Small Cap indices, which achieved a net 31 percent. OMERS attributed its fund's shortcoming to its "under-weighting" in Nortel.

When the new foreign investment provisions for pensions were announced in the February 2000 federal budget, Nortel and BCE were dominating the index, with a combined weight of about 32 percent. As Peter Muldowney, a principal in the Canadian asset consulting practice of Towers Perrin, pointed out at the time, a fund with 40 percent of its assets in Canadian equities that were invested according to their index weightings would have 11 percent of its assets in Nortel after BCE spun off its interest in May 2000—and even that assumption was based on Nortel remaining at a 300 index weighting of around 28 percent. And Nortel was set to climb much higher in price and weighting, taking the 300 and 60 indices with it. The managers of some pension funds would not be able to resist loading up on Nortel in the name of keeping pace with or even beating the 300 index, and as the company's share price rose, the asset mix of the plans became more dominated by Nortel.

At the end of 1999, OPTrust's Canadian equity holdings totalled $2.87 billion, which represented 30 percent of its total assets. At $285 million, Nortel was right at the 10 percent threshold for its Canadian equities, although overall it represented less than 3 percent of total assets. Nevertheless, it would provide a stern test of OPTrust's commitment to diversification. Three-quarters of the way through 2000, OPTrust seemed to be managing the Nortel gorilla. But the last quarter would provide too much temptation, when a drop in Nortel's price created a fevered bargain-hunting market. OPTrust would not be able to resist stocking up on what it thought was a deep-discount sale on Canada's most popular, most widely held stock—not foreseeing the cratering that lay in wait for Nortel in the next fiscal quarter.

Smaller pension funds tended to risk far greater exposure to Nortel because they didn't have the capital to widely diversify. In August 31, 2000, the pension fund of the Colleges of Applied Arts and Technology (CAAT), an association of twenty-five Canadian post-secondary institutions, would report that it held $399.6 million in Nortel shares. Its next largest Canadian equity holding, CIBC, amounted to only $54.7 million. CAAT's pension had more value in Nortel shares than it did in Canadian and Ontario government bonds and debentures combined—$353 million—and Nortel also eclipsed the total value—$151 million—of its top ten foreign equity investments. Back in March, Muldowney had worried about a pension plan having 10 percent of its assets in one stock. At the end of August, 21 percent of the value of CAAT's Canadian equities and 9 percent of the total portfolio were due solely to Nortel.

When 2000 began and BCE's butterfly plan was announced, there seemed a small measure of hope that pension fund managers might treat Nortel with appropriate trepidation. There were too many questions about its actual profitability and its potential for prospering in a networking industry that was undergoing rapid technology changes, with new players coming out of the weeds with killer technology. While Ross Healy wasn't having much success changing the investing patterns of his institutional clients, some of them at least had the sense to want a closer look at Nortel's financial status and turned to the country's foremost forensic account.

Paging Dr. Al, went the call from the institutionals as BCE announced the Nortel divestiture on January 26. And the good doctor sharpened his pencil and started trying to make sense of Nortel's bookkeeping.

12

Paging Dr. Al

Under generally accepted accounting principles, I can turn a $4 million profit into a $2 million loss and I could get every national accounting firm to agree with me.
— Paul Beeston, Toronto Blue Jays vice-president, 1979

On the thirty-eighth floor of the TD Centre Tower on Wellington Street in downtown Toronto, Dr. L.S. Rosen—better known as Al— enjoys a falcon's eye view of Canada's financial services industry. The banks, insurance companies, mutual fund operations, and brokerage houses are crammed into a few square blocks of the downtown, and beating at their heart is the virtual marketplace of the Toronto Stock Exchange. When you view the streetscape from Rosen's aerie in the southeast corner of the black monolith, the nation's engine of prosperity looks like a big confidence game, with the tiny figures on the sidewalks below serving as runners in a complex sting.

"The most fundamental fraud is a Ponzi fraud," says Dr. Rosen on an unnaturally warm winter day, which has allowed the runners to shed their overcoats and galoshes and run their errands in business suits. "All you're trying to do is call people's capital contributions into the same company. And on that basis, you drag other people in. When you look at financial disclosure requirements in North America, and to some extent in Europe, it's a built-in Ponzi fraud."

Dr. Rosen has become somewhat notorious for saying things like this, things that make the financial services industry and the senior ranks of major public companies sound like havens of connivers and cheats. Pre-Enron, his opinions gained him some notoriety. Post-Enron, he is in strong demand, not only from the media, but from financial professionals looking to increase their own wariness and from the institutional investors he'd already been advising, who hope to avoid an Enron-like collapse in their portfolio. "People are saying to us now, 'Give us a list of twenty to twenty-five problem-free companies in Canada, accounting-wise.'" His only response is a rueful laugh.

"I've had over a hundred requests over the last two months about whether Enron can happen again," he says, as Enron executives parade themselves before a Senate investigation committee, pleading the Fifth. "What the hell are you supposed to say? I can give you *thirty* Enrons that have happened in the last fifteen years."

Al Rosen's signature persona is a hangdog weariness, but the humour that percolates forth as he warms to his subject suggests that he is enjoying himself these days, surrounded by numerical canoodling in the highest reaches of the corporate world. Bre-X was a weird confidence game from the already tarnished natural resources sector that got embarrassingly out of hand. Now, the largest auditing firms are under siege, joining the analysts who have already been roasted in the heat of the dot-com implosion and the captains of industry whose unsinkable ships sprouted leaks you could drive truckloads of subpoenas through. Dr. Rosen lives for financial shenanigans, and he is fortunate to be plying his craft in a golden age of balance sheet and income statement hijinks.

Dr. Rosen is the undisputed reigning champion of forensic accounting in Canada. In 1990, he founded Rosen & Associates Ltd., a firm that specializes in forensic accounting, auditor negligence, business valuations, damage quantification, shareholder disputes, financial and equity analysis, and due diligence. He spends a lot of time in court as an expert witness. He has an M.B.A. and Ph.D. from Washington University, although his business cards for Rosen & Associates and Private Financial Research Corporation don't bother with the M.B.A. After the Ph.D. comes the FCA (a Fellow of the Chartered Accountants of Ontario and Alberta), the FCMA (a Fellow of the Society of Management Accountants), the CFE (a Certified

Fraud Examiner), the AIIC (an Associate of the Insurance Institute of Canada), the CIP (a Chartered Insurance Professional), and the CPA (a Certified Public Accountant, USA). Left off along with the M.B.A. is his CA•IFA (a specialist, Investigative and Forensic Accounting). He has written numerous accounting textbooks and has also taught widely at higher institutions, as an instructor and professor of accounting at the University of British Columbia, the University of Washington, the University of Alberta, and York University. Since joining the faculty at Toronto's York University (part-time in 1970, full-time in 1972), he has served in such roles as accounting area coordinator and director of the M.B.A. program, from which his own son, Mark, who joins him around an office table on this day, graduated in 1998.

The main business is the forensic accounting and its investigative variants. In early 1999, Dr. Rosen decided to expand the scope of the enterprise. The sort of analysis he was doing for forensic cases was well suited to helping institutional investors figure out whether a particular company's stock was worth owning. For accounting misbehaviour to end up in court, somebody generally had to sue somebody else, but there was a wealth of untapped financial sleight of hand out there, waiting to be exposed; it wasn't necessarily illegal, but it had a profound impact on anyone's ability to judge a company's worth. At the least, weaknesses in GAAP allowed companies to employ creative yet permissible dodges to make companies look like they were in better shape, with regard to net earnings or cash flow, than they probably were. Auditing firms were blithely signing off on their clients' balance-sheet inventiveness, analysts with brokerage houses were either hopelessly compromised or too grossly undertrained to understand the tricks of the trade, and accountants who were trained to read the balance sheets couldn't see the forest for the trees, caring only that whatever numbers they were showed adhered to GAAP.

"Most CAs were taught to worship the GAAP stuff," says Dr. Al. "Critical evaluation is not part of the program. They're virtually brainwashed in the desert and it's there for life." As for analysts, who are milling about in this very building, riding the elevators with the Rosens every day, Mark Rosen explains, "They're not paid to do any analysis. They're paid to do sales, and they just don't have time to do serious analysis. They take what a company gives them and say, 'Thank you very much, I'll just make this part of my work,' and they hand it out. It's tough to get paid to do real analysis."

By the fall of 2000, there were several distinct enterprises operating out of the thirty-eighth floor offices. Rosen & Associates continued as the forensic accounting practice, which involves work where court testimony could be required. Private Financial Research Corporation (PFRC) was organized to provide a private newsletter to money managers, pension fund managers, mutual fund managers, and their kind. The newsletter provided general commentary on accounting scams and analysis of specific companies. In October 2000, much of PFRC's operation was transferred into Veritas Investment Research, in which the Rosens held a 40 percent interest and which occupied separate offices on the building's eighth floor. (In March 2002, the Rosens withdrew from Veritas and began producing anaysis for Caldwell Securities.)

The Rosens' corporate analysis eschews the usual price valuations and projections and instead tears a company's financial statements to ribbons in search of the underlying truth about the enterprise's health. In the first two years of the service, they pulled apart the financials of upwards of forty companies. Remarkably, it took almost a year for them to turn to Nortel, at clients' requests. But once they looked at Nortel, they couldn't look away.

Mark Rosen is coming along nicely as Al Rosen 2.0. He is bright and polite, and bemused by fiscal misbehaviour without being snarky or smug about it. Ensconced in this suite of offices in the midst of an industry that causes their clients so much grief, the pair are like two special ops worker bees in a strange antechamber of the hive. (They are not alone, however. Their various firms employ a total of seven full-time people.) While working alongside his father, Mark is pursuing his chartered financial analyst (CFA) and certified fraud examiner (CFA) designations. Father and son did the Canadian Securities Course, administered by the Canadian Securities Institute, in the summer of 2001 in order to meet regulatory requirements for some of their activities. The course demands considerable labour to complete, but both plainly think the content was a little light on practical knowledge. Unfortunately, it's the standard training tool for people who want to sell securities in this country.

The idea of Al Rosen having to complete the CSC assignments and write the lengthy final exam is about as surreal as the idea of making Noam Chomsky participate in a spelling bee before joining a linguistics club. Anyone who has done the CSC knows that it is grounded in rote memorization of scads of ratios and their guideline valuations, and applying them to analysis of financial statements. It must have taken every ounce of Al Rosen's willpower not to write contemptuous, sarcastic comments in response to assignment and exam questions. "People are doing crazy ratio analysis that makes no sense," says the senior Rosen, who despite his triumph in the summer of 2001 has left "CSC" off his business cards. "Working capital ratio, that's still in university texts. It came out with U.S. Steel in 1901. The idea of a two-to-one working capital ratio was based on liquidation values in the period before 1919. It makes no sense at all."

Makes no sense at all tends to come up a lot in a discussion with the two Rosens. Mark has his father's cheerful contempt for much of the financial industry. He's fortunate to be getting in on the ground floor of the new millennia's sudden fascination with corporate misbehaviour, whereas his father has slogged through decades of courtroom drama no one paid much attention to. Even in 2000, as the tech boom rapidly went subsonic, Dr. Al was famous enough to attract pilgrims from the local financial press, but his message was sometimes too scary to penetrate the groupthink of Bay Street. He mentions a well-known financial reporter who came calling in the fall of 2000, after the Rosens distributed a brutal assessment of Nortel to institutional clients. Rosen obviously went beyond the limits of what the reporter was accustomed to assimilating. He wasn't offering the usual P/E evaluation, couched in Internet lingo beloved by tech analysts. He was drilling down through the financial statements, outlining clever GAAP strategies and worrying trends to demonstrate why Nortel's share price was about to go down in flames. "He turned *white*," Rosen says, motioning through a solid wall toward the boardroom where the encounter occurred, as his son nods and smiles with a pleasurable memory of the incident. The reporter went back to the newsroom and never wrote a thing.

The rift between Al Rosen and many of his fellow accountants has several sources. His propensity for saying unkind things about his own profession is one of them. Another most certainly is his experience in the 1980s with a Toronto accounting firm he declines to identify. "With the recession, in 1980 to 1982, companies started to fire auditors for the first time," he says. Audit firms were short on work, and mergers resulted. These accounting companies lost their authority with clients or their willingness to stand up to them. "The audit mentality was, 'Go along with the client, because if I don't have X dollars of fees coming into my part of the operation, they'll fire me.' I was in one of the big firms at the time, and just got sick, watching the big change from the seventies. It wasn't long afterwards that you had the Alberta bank failures and the credit union failures, and it's just gone on and on since."

In Rosen's world view, auditors have let their clients do whatever they want within the flexible nature of GAAP, so long as its principles are technically adhered to. But GAAP, he insists, was (and is) an ineffective tool for ensuring corporate health and protecting a shareholder's interest. And therein lies another source of friction between Dr. Rosen and the accounting hierarchy. He sees considerable flaws in Canadian GAAP, which he says have been exacerbated by the success of the Canadian Institute of Chartered Accountants in making it the accounting standard for all firms, public and private, and charities, too. In the United States, GAAP applies only to publicly traded companies.

Canadian GAAP was originally drawn up for "merchandising and manufacturing" operations, notes Dr. Rosen. "It believes you have lots of inventory, receivables and payables," with a rapid churning of cash. As a result, it's what he calls "an old mule" that's been tinkered with and yoked to unsuited enterprises such as hotels, financial institutions, and natural resource companies. If you have an accounting system that presumes a lot of money is regularly moving through the enterprise, there's an accident waiting to happen if in fact revenues booked don't quickly translate into cash on hand. Cash flow and

GAAP-standard accounting can begin running on different sets of tracks. Things can look fine under GAAP, when in fact a company is headed for major trouble. "You can set your watch and wait for the explosion," he says.

"It gets so the cash is off in one direction and the GAAP and pro forma earnings are off in another direction. If you look at financial institution failures, how were the audited numbers—approved by the securities commission people, hyped by the media—so out of whack with the cash? They were just pissing it away, quarter after quarter after quarter."

Another critical source of the rift is a case he lost before the Supreme Court of Canada on May 22, 1997. The court made a ruling that day of which we can safely say 99.9 percent of Canadian investors still have not the slightest knowledge.

File no. 24882, an appeal from the Manitoba court of appeal, was indexed as *Hercules Managements Ltd. v. Ernst & Young*. It was not a headline burner; it does not trip off the tongue of financial analysts. Nevertheless, this appeal ruling cemented in an overwhelmingly unappreciated way the legal relationship between shareholders, auditors, and public companies in Canada. The 7–0 ruling was a profound rebuke to the movement to hold auditors legally accountable to individual investors for the information that appears in corporate financial statements.

The case stemmed from the 1984 receiverships of two companies involved in mortgage-backed loans and investments, Northguard Acceptance Ltd. and Northguard Holdings Ltd. A number of shareholders and investors in these two companies, including Hercules Managements Ltd., filed suit against the companies' auditors, Ernst & Young, and E&Y partner Alexander Cox, who oversaw the audits in 1980 and 1981 and also had investments of his own in some of the two companies' syndicated mortgages. The action, begun in 1988, alleged that the 1980 to 1982 audits were negligently prepared and that by relying on these audits, the investors suffered financial losses.

Rosen had become involved as an expert witness for one of the appellants, Max Freed, when Rosen was in charge of the litigation group at Mintz & Partners, and then continued with the case when he set up Rosen & Associates in 1990. They got "hammered" in Manitoba, but pressed forward with the Supreme Court appeal. That appeal caused Rosen to be pitted against his own kind, the Canadian Institute of Chartered Accountants, which secured intervener status and lined up alongside Ernst & Young.

To win the appeal, the appellants had to argue for a regimen of fiduciary accountability that virtually all investors in Canada thought already existed, and still do. The individual investor views a company's financial statements as his window on corporate performance and the fundamental basis of his investment decisions. If the statements prove to be in error or deliberately misleading, he expects to be able to hold the outside auditors legally accountable. But the judgment on file 24882 crushed any such notion that this was how the system worked in Canada.

The issues in the *Hercules* case are complex, and it is important only to understand the way the dismissal framed shareholders' rights. In the original ruling against the appellants, Justice Armand Dureault of the Manitoba Court of Queen's Bench wrote: "Shareholders have no cause of action in law for any wrongs which may have been inflicted upon a corporation. . . . At best, if any wrong was done in the conduct of the defendants' audits, it was done to [NGA] and [NGH] and cannot be considered an injury sustained by the shareholders."

The appellants in the Supreme Court appeal attempted to argue that individual shareholders could hold an auditor accountable for financial statements on which they based investment decisions—in effect, bypassing the corporate entity (which in their case had gone under) to take on the auditor directly for personal losses. The CICA and Ernst & Young took a very different view. "The lawyer for the CICA and the lawyer for Ernst & Young both argued that financial statements are not to be used by individual investors for investment decisions," says Rosen. "They're *not*. Instead, they're to be used by all of the investors, together, so that they can evaluate management."

This role for audited statements is very different from the one understood by the typical investor. And to help appreciate what the typical investor thinks about accountants and audits, we need look no further than the CICA, which in 2000 commissioned Kroll

Associates to look into what 2,000 "stakeholders" thought of the job
CICA members were doing. The CICA called the results, released in
August 2001—portentously, right before Enron went blooie—"reassuring and challenging." On the contrary, the results appeared to be
alarming, for the average person plainly thought CICA members
were fulfilling a role that the *Hercules* case four years earlier emphat-
ically said that they weren't. And CICA's own intervener arguments
had helped see to that.

From November 1 to 5, 2000, Kroll conducted telephone surveys
to pick the brains of 1,005 adult Canadians coast to coast, among
them 584 retail investors who owned mutual funds, stocks, or corporate bonds, or combinations thereof. Kroll also surveyed accountants
themselves, members of the media, and corporate executives.

The survey revealed that CAs had the highest rating for ethical
practice among ten professions, scoring a mean rating of 8.2 out of
ten, coming in ahead of actuaries, doctors, and professors, and leaving far behind such human detritus as executives, bankers, editors,
lawyers, brokers, and politicians. And investors ranked the importance of financial statements second only to broker advice in sources
of information for investing. Considering the fact that brokers themselves presumably rely highly on financial statements as sources of
information for the advice they dispense, those statements implicitly
are the most important basis of investment decisions.

The survey also found that only nine percent of CAs thought
Canadian retail investors "understand the role and accountabilities of
the auditor." Retail investors generally begged to differ; nevertheless,
only 49 percent of investors rated their personal understanding of the
auditor's role above a neutral "3" (on a 5-point scale, where 5 is "excellent" and 1 is "poor"). And surveyed journalists "suggest that the
media are not well equipped to inform the public on audit-related
issues. For example, only 40% of journalists rate the business media's
understanding of the auditor's role highly (above a neutral '3')."

In short, the Kroll report showed that the average investor considered an accountant the most trustworthy professional around,
relied highly—even primarily—on the financial statements CAs
produced for their investment decisions, but claimed no more

than a middling grasp of the role an auditor played in preparing those statements.

But when it comes to understanding the auditor's role, the typical retail investor understands it not at all. For example, the survey noted that 49 percent of retail investors "believe auditors' professional obligations extend to full responsibility to detect fraud in audited companies. Investors who believe auditors are responsible for detecting fraud may have a false sense of security and an inappropriately relaxed attitude toward due diligence." That's putting it mildly. Investors generally view auditors as an outside, independent investigative force whose job is to go over management's accounting on a forensic basis and ferret out wrongdoing. Which is wrong. To the average person, the word "audit" makes them think of the tax department taking apart his or her house with crowbars in search of undeclared earnings. With a typical unqualified audit on a company's financial statement, the auditor is there to sign off on the information provided them, so long as GAAP is honoured and the auditor does not know, or ought to know, that the contents are in fact misleading. And despite the fact that the CICA feels investors may have "an inappropriately relaxed attitude toward due diligence," it does not explain how those investors are supposed to perform due diligence if the financial statements are not trustworthy.

The appellants in the *Hercules* case arguably were trying to invest accountants with the responsibilities the general public already thought they had. Investors had got it in their heads that they could read a financial statement such as a quarterly report on which an auditor had signed off and use it as the basis for buying, selling, or holding a particular stock. And if the statement turned out to be false or misleading, they could go after the auditor. Well, they couldn't, and except in the case of a statement included in a prospectus, they can't.

The Supreme Court's *Hercules* judgment, delivered by Justice Gerard La Forest, upheld and reiterated the misunderstood ground rules in the relationship between shareholders, the corporation in which they invest, and the auditors paid to prepare the financial statements:

As I have already explained, the purpose for which the audit reports were prepared in this case was the standard statutory one of allowing shareholders, as a group, to supervise management and to take decisions with respect to matters concerning the proper overall administration of the corporations. In other words, it was, as Lord Oliver and Farley J. found in the cases cited above, to permit the shareholders to exercise their role, as a class, of overseeing the corporations' affairs at their annual general meetings. The purpose of providing the auditors' reports to the appellants, then, may ultimately be said to have been a "collective" one; that is, it was aimed not at protecting the interests of individual shareholders but rather at enabling the shareholders, acting as a group, to safeguard the interests of the corporations themselves.

In case you missed it, Justice La Forest said that financial statements are to be employed by shareholders *as a group* within the context of keeping tabs on management and safeguarding the interest of the corporation. They were not to be used by *individual* shareholders as a basis for investment decisions. And they are not aimed at protecting the interests of individual shareholders. Justice La Forest's ruling explicitly viewed shareholders as a collective, exercising their authority within the confines of an annual general meeting. The financial statements were meant to aid them in exercising that authority, in that time and place. Justice La Forest's ruling made it all but impossible for individual shareholders to identify themselves as legally wronged entities distinct from the corporation itself when it came to financial statement misadventures.

In finding that claims in respect of losses stemming from an alleged inability to oversee or supervise management are really derivative and not personal in nature, I have found only that shareholders cannot raise individual claims in respect of a wrong done to the corporation.

CICA was pleased with the outcome of the appeal. In its own statement on the case, it notes that Justice La Forest was reacting to the problem of indeterminate liability which might arise if individual shareholders or other parties were able to go after auditors without having to act through the corporation. "The policy considerations are pragmatic—open-ended and unpredictable liability would give rise to 'socially undesirable consequences,' including increasing costs of insurance and litigation, reduced availability of audit services, and potential decreased vigilance by third parties.

"Based on this reasoning," the CICA explains, "in a statutory audit, the auditor would owe a duty of care to the shareholders as a group because the audit report is made for the specific purpose of guiding 'the shareholders, as a group, in supervising or overseeing management.' *If a shareholder chooses to rely on the report in making personal investment decisions, he or she does so at their own peril.*" (Italics added.)

This is assuredly huge news to the average investor: Employ financial statements in investing decisions at your own risk. If you've got a beef, take it up with management at the next AGM. Anyway, the statements are only provided to let you oversee management. If a wrong has been done in the form of the audit, it's been done to the corporation, not to you, personally.

In defence of the Supreme Court's learned judges, they were only upholding case law precedent in making their *Hercules* ruling. The real problem with *Hercules* was that, unlike in the United States, in Canada, no statutory liability is attached to what are known as "continuous disclosure" documents—the various communications between a corporation and shareholders, including financial statements. Statutory liability basically means a liability enshrined in a legislative statute. Statutory liability for continuous disclosure documents doesn't exist in Canada because nobody wrote it into key governing legislation like the Ontario Securities Act, except for prospectuses. Without statutory liability, the *Hercules* case was left to be decided in the treacherous swamp of common law, whose principles and precedents are built up through case law.

This was why *Hercules* proceeded with the appellants trying to answer fundamental common law tests. The appellants had to establish that there was a prima facie duty of care on the part of the auditors, which the court agreed there was. "It was reasonably foreseeable by the auditors that people would rely on a financial statement," explains University of Toronto law professor Jeffery Macintosh. "And reliance on those statements would be reasonable, too." But before the issue of reliance was addressed—did the investors in fact rely on these statements?—the court considered just *who* the shareholders were. And case law said that, from the perspective of the use of financial statements, they were a collective using them to oversee the company, not individuals making investment decisions. And so the case never even got to the reliance test. End of case.

Macintosh says the *Hercules* case is far from lonely in Canadian court records. While he says it was an important ruling, "there are zillions of cases just like it." Suing auditors for negligence is fairly commonplace. But without statutory liability, "you have to go back to common law, and common law is really difficult to proceed on. Reliance is difficult because as an evidentiary path, how do you prove you relied on something? You just have to testify. There's nothing objective."

An even bigger problem for Canadian shareholders who think they've been jobbed by misleading or incompetent financial statements is even trying to mount a suit. "As an individual, unless I've got deep pockets, I can't afford to sue," says Macintosh. But to have a class action certified, "there can't be a lot of issues that have to be adjudicated on an individual basis." In other words, the suit must demonstrate substantial "commonality"—issues need to be collective to permit a class action. If too many issues are of an individual nature, certification won't happen. And a major issue for individuals is the fundamental common law one of reliance. With a group of people pursuing a class-action case involving corporate misbehaviour or negligent auditing, each person conceivably had his or her own reasons for investing and relied on unique mixes of information for entering into and maintaining that investment. Maybe some people paid close attention to financial statements. Maybe some listened in to conference calls with analysts. Maybe some listened more to their analyst or broker. Maybe some just read the newspaper or caught a gung-ho analyst pumping the stock on TV. And maybe some didn't pay much attention at all. "Reliance would have to be answered plaintiff by plaintiff," Macintosh notes. As well, if the plaintiffs lose a class-action case, they're responsible for the legal costs of the defendants.

It all adds up to a disconcerting situation for would-be litigants. "Canada is not nearly as good a jurisdiction in which to proceed," Macintosh says, looking south of the border to the promised land of statutory liability.

The *Hercules* case left a black hole at the centre of Canadian investing. Investors attuned to the dominant jargon, logic, and processes of Wall Street overwhelmingly had no idea that there was no such thing as statutory liability for continuous disclosure in Canada. They had no idea that they weren't supposed to be relying on financial statements in making investment decisions. On the contrary, reading financial statements was what duly diligent investors were doing. The situation desperately required a legal remedy. But none, to date, has arrived.

Even as the *Hercules* case was unfolding, a movement (albeit a glacial one) was afoot to bring statutory liability to continuous disclosure in Canada. In 1994, the Toronto Stock Exchange convened a blue-chip panel, the Committee on Corporate Disclosure—better known as the Allen Committee, for chairman Ted Allen—to look into continuous disclosure and other matters of corporate transparency. The committee's report, released in March 1997, supported the introduction of limited statutory liability.

Enacting change in the Canadian securities system is complicated by the fact that Canada lacks a single national legal framework. The United States has the Securities Exchange Act of 1934, which empowers the Securities Exchange Commission. In Canada, securities law is a provincial and territorial responsibility, meaning there are thirteen different securities regulators operating under their own securities acts. All of them do come together under an umbrella organization, the Canadian Securities Association. The Allen Committee's recommendation (already made in an interim report in 1995), coming just two months before the *Hercules* ruling, led the

Canadian Securities Association and member regulators from Ontario, Quebec, British Columbia, and Alberta to form their own task force to move forward on the statutory liability recommendation. One of the task force participants was Susan Wolburgh Jenah, then manager, market operations, with the OSC. In an item called "Dialogue with the OSC," released on October 20, 1997, Jenah wrote that the various chairs of the CSA "determined that it was a top CSA priority to respond promptly to the Committee's recommendations and ensure that the Report didn't become just another Report destined for life on a shelf somewhere."

On May 29, 1998, one year after the *Hercules* ruling, the CSA, along with the OSC and other member regulators, published for public comment a slew of proposed amendments to securities laws, including the introduction of statutory liability. In 1999, the CSA produced draft legislation for the provincial governments, again including statutory liability. "We're not in a position to implement the legislation," says Jenah. "All we can do is say, 'We would like to suggest that this kind of legislative amendment be considered.'"

No government has passed the draft legislation, or anything like it. On December 15, 1999, a number of amendments to the Ontario Securities Act received royal assent, but none of them addressed the fact that, according to CICA, individual investors rely on audited financial statements at their own peril.

Al Rosen hates the *Hercules* ruling and the vacuum in shareholder rights that legislators have thus far failed to address. The idea that financial statements are to be employed by the collective shareholders to evaluate management, and not as the basis of individual investment decisions, is laughable. Auditors are signing off on numbers that management is putting together the way it wants. "Management is setting the accounting! They're picking the bloody rules they want. You have to use *their* selection of *their* rules to evaluate them. You have a situation in Canada where the audited financial statements are rubbish. The auditors are not standing behind them. The directors have their own insurance. Nobody has to seriously stand behind them."

When the *Hercules* appeal was lost, the Supreme Court ruling made it very plain to every accounting firm, and the company directors and senior management whom they serviced, what the rules of the game were. Rule number one was unless it's in a prospectus, don't worry about any investor ever coming after you in court over something they didn't like in a financial statement, because the fact that they lost money in an investment based on something you put in that statement isn't your problem. The statements are for the investors to use at the AGM to measure management's performance and *safeguard the interests of the corporation.*

Oh Nortel. We stand on guard for thee. Average Canadian investors assuredly hadn't a clue that this is what they were supposed to be doing when reading the company's financial statements. And as it happened, the most intriguing Nortel financial figure wasn't found in the formal audited statements at all. It was the new accounting construct called "earnings from operations."

13

Where the Cash Flows

When they passed out *cojones,* most analysts stood in the back
of the line with the gerbils . . .

—posting to Nortel bulletin board
at RagingBull.com, November 3, 1999

"We didn't go beyond GAAP in our analysis," says Mark Rosen of the
work he and his father performed on Nortel in 2000. "We had to go
with what was in the public statements. And what we could tell from
them is that it would be a disaster. We couldn't give people rock solid
proof. We basically had to argue that this 'earnings from operations'
figure is completely unreliable. It's fiction, and for it to be continued
to be used at all, what has to also continue is this insane bull market,
where the price just skyrockets to infinity. Because otherwise, you're
just building this pyramid that has to collapse at some point."

When a company as celebrated as Nortel, run by a president and
CEO as celebrated as John Roth, suddenly falls from grace, there is a
natural instinct for the wronged to seek out scurrilous causes. The
merits of any legal actions will have to wait until they have their day
in court—should that day in fact ever come. But they should not
detract from the fundamental lesson delivered by Nortel. There was
plenty to worry about in the company's own financial statements—
all of it legal, all of it perfectly acceptable under GAAP. The warnings were there to be read by those who were willing to dig beneath
the general cheerleading and question the trends in the numbers. By
following the investigations of the Rosens, and extrapolating further

lessons from their work, which was produced under deadline pressures and without a full set of financial data, it is possible to see how many concerns legitimately should have been raised about Nortel's profitability and the logic of its escalating share price.

The Rosen operation[17] turned its attention to Nortel in February 2000, to satisfy the curiosity of its institutional clients. They had good reason to want to know more about Nortel's books. Already popular with investors, Nortel was a major force in the growth of the TSE 300, and with the impending spinoff of most of BCE's minority stake, the company would become the most widely held stock in the country.

Right away, Rosen was handcuffed by Nortel's leisurely approach to filing full year-end results. Like many companies, Nortel's modus operandi was to fire off a press release first with a handful of selected lines from its forthcoming statement, trumpet the good stuff, and then withdraw to finish working on the numbers. This was perfectly legal under the lax reporting system in Canada. At the time, the CSA was proposing that listed companies be required to file annual statements within ninety days and interim (quarterly) statements within forty-five days of the end of the particular period. Nortel generally took about five weeks for quarters other than the year-end one. It was also proposing that companies be required to file quarterly statements that included a balance sheet (which Nortel already did) and explanatory notes, as well as management discussion and analysis (MD&A). No regulation existed that told the company to be quicker, but in the case of the fourth-quarter/year-end 1999 Nortel report, the company still hadn't released a balance sheet and cash flow statement when the Rosens gave up waiting and released their study on February 25. The annual report with the full financials wasn't released until late March. Waiting almost three months to release financial results took the edge off their timeliness for investors—but then, as the *Hercules* ruling made clear, financial statements in Canada weren't meant to aid investment decisions anyway. Nortel just had to have the 1999 annual report out in time for the annual general meeting in April.

Routine lengthy waits for the release of valuable financial data put a lie to the modern notion that information in the new economy was moving at the speed of light and that investors were reacting almost instantaneously in the markets. Unquestionably, rumour and informed speculation whipped through the investment community in the blink of an eye. But companies were taking as long to file full financials after the end of a reporting period as sailing ships of yore used to require to deliver the mail across the North Atlantic. The flow of information for a particular reporting period was incredibly elongated. With a company like Nortel, "continuous disclosure" for a particular year would begin with guidance issued and then commented on by analysts well back in the previous year, perhaps at the end of the third quarter. Investors would make their buying or selling decisions based on this guidance, the actual results for which wouldn't be gained for another eighteen months, when the annual report was finally released. Meanwhile, everyone was waiting for news of how the current year was going to turn out. Two to three weeks into the new year, the preliminary results for the previous year would be issued. Everyone gave thumbs up or down based on these basic numbers, which emphasized the company's customized numbers. The full financials, which contained the really intriguing reading, would not come out for still another two months. By then, the first quarter was almost over, and interest in the finer details of the previous year's performance were rapidly fading. The senior executives had already made their comments to analysts and investors in the conference following the release of the preliminary results, spinning the numbers as best they could, and the buy recommendations had been issued, with fresh price targets. By late March, the previous year was old news. It would take into April to produce and release a capable analysis of the full financials. The second quarter was under way. Bulletins from a company's corporate communications department that hyped new contracts, new acquisitions, and new guidance were filling the electronic in-boxes of the media. In the case of the spring of 2000, far too few investment professionals could be bothered to make a critical perusal of the GAAP vagaries of a balance sheet and cash flow statement for 1999. Investors, analysts, and executives were overwhelmingly focused on the future, not the past.

In late February, knowing that time was of the essence, Rosen did his best without the missing paperwork. Up-front, he included a forthright caveat: that this report to *private* readers was meant to provide a "forthright discussion of business, accounting and financial reporting issues in the hopes of creating a greater understanding of GAAP and the limits of its usefulness to investors. As such, please do not infer from this report that the company's accounting policies are not allowed within GAAP, or that the policies employed by Nortel were not approved by its auditors."

This was more than a careful legal disclaimer. The fact that the Rosens weren't suggesting that Nortel's accounting decisions were in any way improper was a core message of their report. They were trying to show their clients just how financial statements produced in complete agreement with GAAP could provide valuable information about a company's performance that was easily overlooked by an incurious or uneducated investor. At the same time, GAAP's peculiarities could lead to incongruities, illogicalities, and gaping silences where an inquiring mind demanded far more information about a company's activities. Of course, CICA said that financial statements were to be used for investment purposes at the investor's peril. But as the Rosens' cogent analysis amply illustrated, investors placed their capital in peril by not examining these financial statements. And it must be said that some pension funds were beginning to take their role as significant shareholders seriously and were showing more stewardship, which required a more detailed understanding of the financials. The Ontario Teachers Federation Pension Plan, for example, voted against Nortel's executive stock option compensation plan in 2000, to no avail.

To come to grips with Nortel's performance and its future prospects, Rosen ventured to compare the company's financials with those of its main rivals, Cisco and Lucent. This wasn't easy, as their first Nortel report admitted. "While the reasons for our reluctance to engage in intercorporate comparisons are too many to list here," the report advised, "we will rest our assertion on the fact that each company prepares its financial statements using its own set of accounting policies. Our longer time readers should concur that the disparity of accounting applications are so vast, even within the same company on a year-over-year basis, that any attempt at drawing conclusions based on reported accounting figures may prove ludicrous." Nevertheless, making comparisons was worth a shot. Otherwise, there was no way to gauge Nortel's performance or judge its accounting decisions.

Lucent was the giant of the three: $38.3 billion in sales and $4.8 billion in profits for fiscal 1999 (year-end September 30). Cisco was the smallest, with $12.2 billion in sales and $2.1 billion in profits, although it was the fastest growing, having more than doubled its sales and profits since 1997, and was also the dominant force in IP networking, the high-growth, Internet-driven sector both Lucent and Nortel hankered after. Nortel sat between the two, with $22.2 billion in revenues and, well, how much in profits was a big question.

Early in the report, Rosen made an important decision regarding Nortel's history: forget about the fact that the company can be traced back to 1895. With the purchase of Bay Networks, "the company was essentially reborn as of August 1998. . . . For reasons beyond accounting issues—which we address herein—the Nortel of 2000 cannot be compared to the Nortel of 1997 and prior." For Rosen, Nortel was a virtual startup. "Yet, it is also ironic that a company with a 120-year history should be viewed in such a way. It is critical that investors keep abreast of the business and accounting issues that are currently faced by Nortel before they become potential 'problems.'"

Nortel had almost doubled its revenues since 1996, when it decided to exploit networking convergence in voice and IP data. Rosen was concerned that Nortel's aggressive top-line growth over a short period of time, which had made the company a stock market darling in Canada, could be masking problems in actually collecting the revenues it reported. In particular, Rosen was alert to the classic Canadian GAAP problem: the relationship between receivables and sales.

Nortel was in a business that experienced long collection cycles, which created a disparity between booking revenues and actually realizing them. If this disparity widened too much, it could have a serious impact on cash flow. Here's how it worked. Under both U.S. and Canadian GAAP, it was left to management to decide which receivables were current and which were long-term. "Current" for

Nortel meant anything expected to come in within the next twelve months. And because so much of the company's revenue growth had come in the past eighteen months, approximately since the Bay acquisition, it made sense that most receivables would be current, rather than long-term. But Rosen noted that from 1997 to 1998, long-term receivables as a percentage of revenues had grown from 7 to 11 percent, and advised investors to keep an eye on them. Nortel could be caught in a cash flow crunch, the way Lucent had in 1999. Receivables were a company's primary source of cash, and if too much of them weren't collectible within a "current" time frame, its cash flow could go negative, the way Lucent's had in fiscal 1999 to the tune of $276 million.

There were associated causes for alarm in Nortel's receivables performance with regard to day sales. "Day sales" (or day sales outstanding) are considered to reflect the number of days it takes a company to collect on trade receivables, and they help assess a company's cash generation cycle. With tech companies, it's a common tool for ferreting out evidence of a company hoping to hide weaknesses in its sales performance. For a given year, day sales are calculated by dividing the total accounts receivable balance at year-end by the year-end sales figure, then multiplying it by 365. (For quarterly performances, the quarterly accounts receivable are divided by the quarter's sales and multiplied by 91.) Nortel had the worst performance among the big three networking firms. From 1997 to 1999, Nortel's day sales outstanding (based on the current receivables alone) had dropped slightly, from 118 to 112, while the struggling Lucent's had risen from 74 to 99. But Cisco had managed to chop an already sector-leading sixty-six days to just thirty-seven days. "Considering the fine line that separates the current and long-term receivable classification," Rosen wondered, "could waiting an average 112 days to collect trade receivables not be considered long-term (especially when the two nearest competitors average 68 days)?"

Rosen was skeptical of Nortel's assertion that longer-term receivables (as reflected in day sales) were the norm for the industry, in light of Cisco's ability to reduce an already superior day-sales figure by almost half in three years. At the same time, Lucent's day-sales performance had deteriorated by 34 percent. In any event, longer-term receivables seemed to be the norm for Nortel—day sales had been 120 for Nortel in 1995, and 125 in 1996. Although Rosen didn't say this, perhaps Nortel's high day sales were symptomatic of its client base, the large telcos ordering backbone networking products, which was very different from the IP networking business that was the customer foundation of Cisco. But if this was the case, why were the day sales of Lucent, its chief rival in big telco orders, only about 60 percent of Nortel's back in 1996 and 1997, before they both jumped into the IP networking racket? If the IP business associated with Cisco produced much better day-sales figures, shouldn't Nortel's day-sales have improved significantly as it diversified into this area, especially since Cisco was dramatically lowering its already superior day sales?

Maybe the answer was that the kind of product wasn't to blame, but rather that the kind of payment terms were. Lucent's day sales had been going downhill as it got into IP networking *and* began offering significant amounts of vendor financing. Proposed Rosen: "Has Nortel's late arrival to the optical IP network industry forced it to attract second tier customers and to offer extended payment terms in order to maintain its exponential growth rate? From where will Nortel be able to generate cash to finance its receivables? What are the implications?"

Rosen wondered if indeed Nortel might be going the way of Lucent, with steadily deteriorating cash flow harming its ability to fund R&D and other necessary expenses. In four years, Cisco had quadrupled its cash flow, and in 1998 it represented 34 percent of its sales, proof of the effectiveness of a low day-sales figure. In comparison, Nortel's cash flow that year was 9 percent of sales, and Lucent's only 6 percent. Lucent's operating cash flow had crashed by more than $2 billion between 1998 and 1999 as it went negative. Nortel, it would turn out, was destined to deliver a similar jarring reversal.

Rosen was uncertain about the absolute value of Nortel's operating cash flow. Analysts had liked the fact that Nortel's cash flow from operations had been increasing along with revenues—more than doubling, from $730 million to $1.5 billion from 1997 to 1998. But

Rosen fingered Nortel's treatment of long-term receivables as a significant source of improved flow.

"Cash flow" refers to how cash is employed by a company during a reporting period. It is considered by many analysts a more accurate indication of how a company is doing than earnings, particularly in capital-intensive enterprises that carry a lot of amortization charges, which don't represent actual cash outlays during the reporting period. Mind you, the problem with Nortel was that it wasn't really capital-intensive: it wasn't buying a lot of fixed assets the way cable television companies or telecom carriers were. Most of Nortel's non-current assets, as we've already seen in its goodwill-laden acquisitions, were extremely intangible and were being paid for with shares. But never mind. If things were running fine, the company should have had a decent positive cash flow.

Basic cash flow is determined by taking a company's net income, subtracting the dividend payments to preferred shareholders, and adding back the depreciation charges. The actual cash flow calculations with a company like Nortel are far more complex, but the underlying principle is the same: restore amortization, add back accounts payable and other accrued liabilities, which represent obligations that haven't yet actually drawn down cash holdings, and make adjustments for changes (for the better or worse) in receivables and inventory. If receivables or inventories have experienced a net increase over the previous year, cash flow is affected negatively. If receivables are increasing without a corresponding increase in revenues, they suggest the company isn't collecting cash efficiently, and they will consequently have a negative impact on the cash flow figure. And if inventories are increasing in a similar vein, the company is tying up capital in goods that aren't being sold. At the end of the simple calculations, you're left with cash flow from operations. Cash flow in investing and financing activities are also calculated, and the results of all three can be combined to determine a net increase or decrease in "cash and non-cash equivalents" over the previous year. If an acquisition binge is "unfairly" masking a company's cash-generating ability through hefty amortization charges, the operating cash flow should clear away the accounting fog.

Adding back the amortization charges from its acquisitions indeed made a huge improvement in Nortel's operating cash flow. But another improvement came from the unappreciated way in which Nortel classified its receivables. As we've seen, they were divided into short-term and long-term. Lucent, with a day-sales performance comparable to Nortel's, also had both categories of receivables. But unlike Nortel, Lucent reported under current assets its current receivables, as well as "contracts in process," which represented the balance on its long-term receivables after progress billings for the year.

The qualification of receivables was important, because any increase in current receivables is subtracted from net earnings in working out operating cash flow. The Rosens did not make a direct comparison with Nortel's main rivals. A quick inspection of their financials shows that Lucent deducted any increases in both its current receivables and contracts in process from operating cash flow. But Nortel's long-term receivables, having been capitalized as a non-current asset, had no impact on operating cash flow. Instead, changes in long-term receivables were logged under cash flow related to investing activities—not operating activities.

Only Cisco had something comparable in its financial statements. While it reported no specific long-term receivables of any kind, which was consistent with having such a low day-sales figure, Cisco did have "lease receivables," the net values of which were divided between current and non-current assets. Net change, however, was recorded in investing activities for cash flow purposes. Lease receivables, Cisco explained, "represent sales-type and direct-financing leases resulting from the sale of the Company's and complementary third-party products and services. These lease arrangements typically have terms from two to three years and are usually collateralized by a security interest in the underlying assets." Basically, "lease receivables" were Cisco's repository for vendor financing activities. Cisco, at least, explained what its capitalized receivables were and how they were collateralized. Nortel's financial statements said nothing at all about how it determined its long-term receivables constituted an investment activity.

The way Nortel arranged its bookkeeping, there was a definite benefit to classifying receivables as long-term rather than short-term.

If it had a receivable that might be paid in 360 to 370 days, it made
a lot more sense to let it cross the 365-day barrier and call it long-
term, because there was an immediate benefit in the stated cash flow
from operations. The corresponding increases in "investing activities" expenditures, as represented by long-term receivables, would
cancel out the gains in cash flow from operations when it came time
to work out the company's net increase or decrease in cash and cash
equivalents. Lowering current receivables also negatively affected the
calculation of working capital (current assets less current liabilities).
But on balance it was worth improving cash flow from operations,
because this was the figure that was of greatest concern to investors.
Except that no more cash actually flowed into the company as a result
of Nortel's classification of long-term receivables.

It's important to remember that these long-term receivables represented a portion of revenues already booked by the company. By
perverse logic, Nortel did not have to subtract increases in long-term
receivables from the reporting year's revenues in working out operating cash flow the way Lucent did with contracts in process, because
Nortel's long-term receivables weren't "current." And that meant
more operating cash appeared to be flowing than was actually the
case. In 1998, Nortel's long-term receivables had increased by $356
million, but this change had been steered safely clear of operating
cash flow by allocating it to investing activities.

This treatment of long-term receivables as a non-current asset
that affected cash flow in investing activities was not something that
had cropped up under John Roth. It was a vestigial artifact of the way
Nortel used to book the long-term receivables handled by its vendor
finance subsidiary, Northern Telecom Finance Corporation (NTFC).
On May 1, 1994, Nortel sold NTFC to GE Capital Corporation,
but carried on capitalizing its long-term receivables as a non-current
investment right into the John Roth years. Rosen proposed an alternative cash-from-operations figure for 1998 of $1.23 billion, by sub-
tracting the $356 million long-term receivables increase from
Nortel's stated operating cash flow of $1.59 billion.

Nortel said the rise in long-term receivables was "primarily the
result of a higher balance of customer financing at year end." In the

1999 annual report's risk analysis, the company also said that it "anticipates that, due to the amount of financing it expects to provide, the higher risks typically associated with such financings (particularly where provided to 'start-up' operations or to customers in developing countries), the amount of such financings required to be supported directly by Nortel Networks, for at least the initial portion of their term, is expected to increase significantly in the future." At year-end 1999, Nortel had made provisions for future vendor financing of up to $2.4 billion. While Nortel (and its competitors) had been able to place their vendor financing with third parties in the past, as risks and the costs of capital increased, this option was becoming less available, and these companies faced the prospect of carrying more of such financing on their own. More of Nortel's revenues thus were becoming tied up in riskier credit to customers that could not be collected within a "current" (less than one year) period. But as we've seen, by classifying as a non-current asset the long-term receivables to which vendor financing contributed, the company's operating cash performance actually appeared to improve. And at the same time, day sales improved, because only current receivables figure into that calculation. Lucent's "contracts in process" did not contribute to the day-sales calculation, either, but at the same time they weren't removed from the operating cash flow calculation, the way Nortel's long-term receivables were.

Nortel's treatment of long-term receivables in a way that did not affect operating cash flow made day-sales comparisons between it, Lucent, and Cisco highly speculative, and at the same time made Nortel's own year-to-year day-sales trends unreliable. In Cisco's case, you could argue that its net change in lease receivables should also be factored into operating cash flow, if Rosen was going to deduct Nortel's change in long-term receivables that way. Fair enough, but in 2000, this $535 million increase would have left Cisco's operating cash flow at a very healthy $5.6 billion.

Nortel's accounting treatment of long-term receivables conceivably also could have a corrosive effect on the company's actual cash flow by encouraging certain credit policies. Receivables typically are a company's main source of revenue, and the sooner it can collect them the better. But the way Nortel calculated operating cash flow, it would have made sense to make receivables long-term rather than even medium-term, because doing so removed them from current receivables and improved the cash-flow and day-sales figures. The most obvious way to do this was to increase the use of vendor financing, with long payment terms. At the least, the treatment of long-term receivables provided a good reason to tolerate the risks of vendor financing. The company would pay a price in actual in-the-bank cash flow and in day sales, but so long as the company actually had enough cash coming in to pay the bills, either from its ongoing operations or by selling off parts of itself, and could keep explaining away high day sales as typical of the industry, the GAAP cash flow would look a lot better in the process. Every dollar capitalized as a long-term receivable effectively produced a dollar in operating cash flow. It was all perfectly legal under GAAP. But it was also a recipe for the classic accounting debacle of GAAP going in one direction while true cash flow went in another.

Although Rosen did not explore the issue to this degree, the effect of Nortel's unique treatment of long-term receivables could well have been amplified by the quarterly pattern of its sales. Traditionally, the fourth quarter was the company's strongest. The usual explanation is that the major telco carriers always blew off their capital expenditures budgets in the final months of the calendar year, creating a pig in the revenue python of networking companies. By that logic, Lucent, with a year-end of September 30, should have recorded its strongest performance in its first quarter, ending December 31. This was the case in 1998, when it recorded 28.5 percent of the year's revenues in the October–December period. But in 1999, when Lucent came under pressure to meet guidance and began relying increasingly on vendor financing, it was the fourth quarter— July to September—that came through with the greatest proportion of annual revenues, at 27.6 percent. Cisco's sales patterns also didn't support the wisdom that the fall quarter was the strongest in the networking business. Cisco marked its year-end with the last business day in July, meaning its quarters could not be directly compared with those of Nortel and Lucent. But in 2000, Cisco's fourth-quarter (ending July 29) was by far the strongest, with 30.2 percent of the

year's revenues, while the quarter ending January 29 had only 23 percent. Given the rapid acquisitions made by these companies and their
successive impacts on reported revenues, it's hard to draw a firm conclusion about the relative importance of particular quarters. But
maybe Nortel's October–December bulge was actually just a self-
fulfilling prophecy, as carriers and other customers reaped the generous terms of a networking company full of salespeople desperate to
meet quota. If the experiences of Cisco and Lucent are any guide, the
approach of fiscal year-end, and not calendar year-end, may have
been the most important factor in the revenue spike.

Whatever the true situation, Nortel traditionally came through
with a strong fourth quarter, and in 2000, it accounted for 29.1 percent of the year's revenues. If the bulge was due to a rush to book sales
and meet guidance, this could have had a considerable impact on
GAAP cash flow and day sales. These figures are based on where
receivables stand at year-end. Nortel did not provide quarterly cash
flow data, so it was impossible to know how this vital quarter actually played out. But because cash flow depends on the year-over-year
change in the level of receivables, if increases in current receivables were minimized in the fourth quarter while long-term
receivables ballooned in the quest to close deals, Nortel's GAAP
operating cash flow picture would brighten, as would its day sales,
while overall revenues grew. But none of it meant Nortel was going
to collect the money any time soon.

Except for 1997, observed Rosen, "Nortel's treatment of long-term
receivables as part of investing activities has served to inflate the cash
[flow] from operations figures and illustrates the organization's potentially increased business risk. . . ." While he didn't have the 1999
cash flow statements available at the time of writing (and he didn't
specifically suggest the effect that Nortel's treatment of long-term,
vendor-financing receivables could have on actual cash flow), Rosen
had been right to be concerned about the trend. In 1999, the long-
term receivables recorded in non-current assets (not including the
collectibles provision) leapt by almost a billion dollars, to $1.57 billion.

But all this still left the question of why Nortel even thought it
should treat long-term receivables as a non-current asset, and increases

thereto as an "investing" activity. Investing implies the gathering of equity, not the cash obligations of customers. Nortel provided no explanation. As noted, Cisco had lease receivables which it recorded under both current and non-current assets, and booked the changes in the net value as an investing activity. But these were collateralized, and Cisco at least made an effort to explain them. Maybe Nortel's "long-term receivables" were the same sort of beast as Cisco's "lease receivables," but who could know, when Nortel didn't saying anything about them in its notes?

Rosen thought that Nortel's treatment of long-term receivables might be something entirely novel. "Its rationale could be that long-term accounts receivable are not operating receivables, but rather the result of 'investment' decisions," Rosen proposed. "Thus, Nortel may be classifying certain receivables from sales to startup companies as equity type investments." This made sense, given that Nortel's unique treatment of these receivables dated back to the days of its subsidiary vendor financing operation. When startups became unable to pay for receivables from Nortel, Nortel could elect to convert these long-term receivables into equity in the cash-starved company. And because of the flexible threshold of material significance in financial reporting, Nortel did not have to break down how much equity it might be accumulating in such companies. There were no explanatory notes for the balance sheet's "other" category in investments (which had increased from $167 to $418 to $443 million between 1997 and 1999) or for the "other" category of assets ($421 million in 1999). Between "investments–other" and "other assets," in 1999 Nortel had $863 million tied up in things for which it offered no specific explanation. As we've already seen, it had said nothing about the Juniper Networks investment in September 1997 and had never provided details about its equity financing with Avici Systems. With Nortel's treatment of long-term receivables already optimizing the stated operating cash flow, cash flow risked being overstated even further if those receivables were being paid for with shares in a customer's business rather than with actual cash.

Nortel had also left a lot of other questions unanswered for Rosen. Had it begun to increase its equity investments in startup communications companies? What were its repayment terms for the "long-term" receivables? What criteria did Nortel use to decide how much of its receivables were long-term? Did it accrue any interest on outstanding long-term accounts receivable balances, and if so, how much? The fact that Rosen had to pose those questions to his clients in the report showed how many unanswered questions could be raised by the financial statements of a major public corporation.

What Rosen also didn't know yet, but which would turn up in the annual report, was that, in addition to the long-term receivables shown as a non-current asset having ballooned by almost $1 billion, to $1.57 billion, operating cash flow actually dropped $574 million in 1999. Applying Rosen's previous methodology of determining an adjusted operating cash flow, the figure fell from the reported $973 million to just $65 million. Revenues were growing by leaps and bounds, but cash flow was eroding. As time would prove, this disconcerting trend was not to be reversed. The more revenues Nortel managed to report, the worse its operating cash flow became, even before Rosen's adjustments.

This is one of the impressive incongruities of Nortel's performance: how a company with tens of billions of reported revenues, and with reported gross profit margins of more than 40 percent, could actually end up with such a meagre operating cash flow. The whole issue of revenues and cash flow cannot be left without appreciating how companies like Nortel recorded those revenues.

GAAP is based on "accrual" accounting, which is a system of recording revenues and expenses without regard to how cash is actually collected and deployed from day to day. The three major networking companies circa 1999 had distinctive definitions of exactly when they decided they had sold something and so could book the revenues. Lucent's terms were the simplest: "Revenue is generally recognized when all significant contractual obligations have been satisfied and collection of the resulting receivable is reasonably assured," explained its 1999 annual report. Nortel was similarly firm: "Revenues are recognized, net of trade discounts and allowances, upon shipment and when all significant contractual obligations have been satisfied and collection is reasonably assured." Cisco was a little more ambiguous: "The Company generally recognizes product revenue when persuasive evidence of an arrangement exists, delivery has occurred, fee is fixed or determinable, and collectibility is probable." In other words, Cisco was happy to book revenues when it looked like it could probably collect some money for something it had shipped, even if a contract (as opposed to "persuasive evidence of an arrangement") did not yet exist.

All three companies typically recognized sales of hardware at the time of delivery and acceptance; with service contracts, revenues were booked at the time of performance, which in the case of contracts extending over several quarters or years, were booked proportionately to the particular period.

With general long-term contracts, however, revenues were booked in a critically different way. Generally, accounting regulations don't like revenues to be recognized before a product or service has actually been earned: the earnings process is complete, with all work or deliveries final and accepted by the customer. The revenues must be "realized or realizable"—that is, the cash is in hand, there is a firm claim to cash, or there is something readily convertible to cash as a result of an exchange. With long-term contracts, however, such as the ones networking companies like Nortel signed for large installations, it is permitted to begin booking revenues well in advance of the work's completion. There are many recognition options, but the most common one is "percentage of completion." Calculating the degree of completion, which is hellaciously complex, can be approached from two angles: input and output. "Input" is based on the expenses incurred by the company in executing the contract, while "output" is based on what has been incrementally delivered to the customer. The "input" method is often referred to as "cost to cost" and is the recognition method of choice for contracting and engineering projects.

With revenue recognition for general long-term contracts, there were some important distinctions between the main networking companies. Cisco provided no explanation of how it handled these contracts; Lucent booked the revenues based on the percentage-of-completion method, but might use "units of delivery" (output) or "cost to cost," depending on the contract.

Nortel had long said it followed percentage-of-completion for long-term contracts, but in 1999, when it began reporting under U.S. GAAP, the company added an important clarification to its annual report. Nortel now said it recognized the revenues exclusively using cost-to-cost accounting. At the same time, Nortel was paid on a progress billing basis.

Cost-to-cost allows a company to use its own expenses to claim a proportion of the revenues for an entire project in successive quarters, regardless of what is actually being billed or received. It's meant to better align expenses with revenues for tax purposes, and in the United States the construction trade is required to report revenues on that basis. In a very simplified example, it works like this. Let's say a company agrees to build something complicated like a bridge over a one-year period for $500 million. The company estimates its total costs to execute the contract to be $300 million. In the first quarter, the company attributes $100 million in costs to satisfying the contract, due to a lot of up-front expenses, such as design and engineering. Because that represents one-third of estimated costs, the company can recognize the same proportion of the contract's total $500 million value as revenues in that quarter—in this case, $166.7 million.

But that doesn't necessarily mean the company has actually billed $166.7 million against the contract's value at this point, much less received it. Perhaps they were allowed to bill only $125 million at the end of the first quarter under the progressive billing agreement with the customer. The company wouldn't receive that money for at least 30 days; in Nortel's case, the day-sales figure suggested a lag of about 120 days in collecting on current receivables. If vendor financing was involved, the actual cash might not flow in for months or years.

Cost-to-cost could legitimately permit a company to begin booking revenues on long-term contracts before it had even delivered anything, particularly if those costs involved preliminary design work. Nortel also allowed that it sometimes entered into contracts to provide products that didn't exist yet in market-ready form. A high-technology company in this situation could conceivably apportion general R&D costs against the contract, as well as the costs of IPR&D and acquired technology associated with an acquisition. In this way, cost-to-cost accounting could convert acquisition expenses into reportable revenues. In other words, those acquisitions costs weren't just being amortized as an expense against revenues. They could be used to lever revenues out of long-term contracts so that they could be reported as quickly as possible. We have no idea if Nortel was doing this, but it would make sense that wherever it was permissible, the company would try to show revenues based on the legitimate application of these acquired intangibles to active contracts before those intangibles were amortized away.

Most important, a tremendous disparity could develop between revenues as booked and revenues as received, and helps explain how Lucent and Nortel could have ended up with such large day-sales figures. Revenues were being recognized in the financial statements before progress billing could issue an invoice and collect on it.

Overall, Nortel's revenue recognition system raised some interesting scenarios. In the fourth quarter of a particular year, for example, it could announce a long-term $300 million contract to provide a telco with an optical backbone network. First off, the total value of the contract was an estimate only, which could be revised later. If it later turned out there were losses, they would be recognized in the quarter in which they were identified—in other words, previous quarters would not have to be restated. That meant that, in the event of a downturn, quarterly revenue performances could implode as they absorbed losses that under a different accounting method would be distributed back through previous quarters as a recognition that, based on the unforeseen losses, the previously recognized revenue was too high. Under GAAP accounting methods, Nortel was allowed to book in the initial quarter a proportion of the contract's value that it could justify on a cost-to-cost basis, even though nothing had been billed or paid for yet. Estimating how much of such a contract Nortel could start reporting as revenues was a somewhat arbitrary and flexible process—particularly when technology that didn't yet exist was involved. With the fourth quarter traditionally being Nortel's largest, figuring out how much of the slew of end-of-year contracts should be booked right away under cost-to-cost accounting was a major factor in meeting or exceeding guidance. Nortel's revenue recognition system for long-term contracts was yet another opportunity for GAAP and cash flow to race in opposite directions.

As well, Nortel allowed that, in the case of software revenues, which were recognized when delivered, "it provides extended payment terms on certain software contracts and may sell these receivables to third parties." This meant that in the case of extended payments, revenues would not be received at the same time they were recognized, and if these receivables were later sold to third parties, Nortel would have to accept a discount on the reported revenues.

Finally, there was Nortel's method for reporting revenues on sales through "multiple distribution channels," namely distributors and resellers. GAAP prefers revenues to be recognized when a customer takes delivery and payment is either in hand or imminent. But Nortel recognized revenues for these products "at the time of shipment." That meant the moment the truck left the Nortel warehouse with products for a distributor or reseller, Nortel chalked up the revenue, even though the products may not yet have been specifically ordered by a customer at the other end. GAAP went along with this, provided the company made provisions for returns, which Nortel did. It was left to a company to determine a reasonable provision, based on historic sales, to be made against revenues before they were entered in the income statement. This was another case of revenue appearing in the financials before the cash it generated did.

The important issue with Nortel in all its GAAP-agreeable accounting processes was the disparity between revenues as recognized and cash as received. Nortel was nothing like an airline, a hotel chain, or a traditional retailer. There was a substantial amount of revenue reported that, timewise, could become seriously disengaged from the cash collected, and some of it might not ever be collected— either because of discounts on vendor financing sold to third parties, defaults by shaky customers, or because a long-term contract's value might be revised downward. It was hard to imagine a business more at odds with the traditional GAAP enterprise, which had a high churn rate of money, driven by predominantly short-term receivables that produced a reasonable relationship in every quarter between what it reported as revenue and what it actually brought in as cash.

And once you began to question the cash associated with the reported revenues, the very reliability of the operating cash flow became suspect.

Differences in how acquisitions were treated under U.S. and Canadian GAAP standards were also producing discrepancies that made it difficult for investors to properly compare Nortel with Lucent and Cisco. The Bay Networks acquisition was a primary case in point. Depending on whether you used Canadian or American GAAP made a huge difference in Nortel's financial picture. As we've seen, in the United States, the acquisition cost was valued based on Nortel's shares on the last trading day before the deal was announced, meaning under U.S. GAAP it was a $9.1 billion acquisition. Canadian GAAP used the share cost at the consummation of the deal, and that meant a cost of $6.9 billion. The result was a major disparity in goodwill to be amortized and charged against revenues. As well, $1 billion in in-process research and development (IPR&D) acquired from Bay Networks was treated differently. Under Canadian GAAP, Nortel could list IPR&D as an asset and amortize it over its useful life. U.S. GAAP demanded that it all be written off in one hit. Between the differences in amortized goodwill ($420 million) and the treatment of IPR&D ($890 million) for Bay Networks, Nortel's bottom-line performance on those points alone was $1.31 billion better under Canadian GAAP. Factor in the use of pooling method acquisitions by Lucent and Cisco, and the ability to fairly compare Nortel's overall performance with that of its American rivals was approaching impossible.

Nortel's use of supplementary earnings figures wasn't helping matters. Rosen's anger with Nortel over its "earnings from operations" concoction was just beginning to gather steam. Rosen noted that the title of its January 25 quarterly and annual results press release proclaimed, "EPS from operations up 53% in the quarter and 38% for 1999." This was achieved by applying cost-stripping earnings calculations to Canadian GAAP results. Rosen felt this sort of year-over-year comparison was "perilous" because it captured revenues from acquisitions in the most recent year without 'fessing up to the costs related to acquiring them, including amortization and one-time gains and losses.

A more revealing picture would have been gained by removing the contributions of recent acquisitions from the earnings figures to see how truly ongoing operations had performed from year to year. For as Rosen explained, EBITDA-type earnings figures assume that all revenues come from "operations," and one interpretation of that revenues definition holds that they should be restricted to recurring operations and not include revenues heaped on by purchased operations. But the way Nortel absorbed its acquisitions into its existing operating segments made it virtually impossible to isolate them from the company's pre-acquisition performance and produce an assessment both of recurring operations and, where relevant, of the newly acquired properties. Certainly some of the acquisitions, which were made for technology that had not yet reached the market and would be absorbed into its networking products and services, did not warrant or even permit a separate tracking of performance. But it would have been nice to know how a mature operation like Bay Networks was doing within Nortel. Nortel had vowed to operate Bay under its own identity, by offering BayStack switches, for example, but this entity had no operating numbers of its own for investors to examine. Maddeningly, Nortel was isolating and removing the cost of acquisitions in its earnings-from-operations numbers, while absorbing the additional revenues these acquisitions delivered (or, conversely, any losses they might have been causing) without identifying them by specific source. Investors knew just how much of the amortization of intangibles was due to the acquired technology of Bay, for example, but had no way of knowing how much Bay was contributing to revenues.

At Nortel, acquisitions disappeared into the maw of the greater organization. Nortel's revenues were organized into just two principle segments: service provider and carrier (SP&C), and enterprise. SP&C, which accounted for about 75 percent of revenues, represented all its networking sales to telcos and other service providers, while enterprise, which until the acquisition binge had mainly consisted of PBX-related sales to corporate clients, had come to include a variety of e-business systems, including Internet and data networking products at the corporate level.

Other Nortel financial practices attracted Rosen's curiosity.

14

All Aboard

Gambling suppresses natural inhibitions against taking risks, and some of the gambling contracts, in particular the lotteries, superficially resemble financial markets: one deals with a computer, one receives a certificate (the lottery ticket), and, in the case of the so-called mega-lottos, one participates in a much-talked-about national phenomenon. Having established a habit of participating in such gambling, it would be natural to graduate to its more upscale form, speculation in securities.
—Robert J. Shiller, *Irrational Exuberance*

It's easy to forget that, as January 2000 approached, the biggest threat on the radar screen of the economy was not a tech stock meltdown, but a global catastrophe lying in wait inside computers that controlled everything from payroll records to airline navigation systems to office elevators. The Y2K bug swallowed billions in corporate spending as software code was combed, line after line, for potentially fatal programming flaws that would be set off when the clock struck midnight on New Year's Eve and the two-digit "clocks" within the software turned to 1900 instead of 2000. Nortel was kept busy on two fronts, making sure its software products did not bring down the telecommunications systems in much of the world and verifying that its own internal software tools did not leap back a century, to the days of Strowger switches and the Northern Electric and Manufacturing Company. Like other public companies, Nortel's financial reports became burdened with long disclosures on what it was doing about Y2K and how a calamity could affect the company, its customers, and its suppliers.

As anyone who was around at the time knows, January 1, 2000, came and went without any significant catastrophes, at Nortel or anywhere else. Either the crisis, commensurate with the tech stock mania, had been hyped beyond rational belief, or the consultants who took on the job of ensuring corporate and public preparedness had done a bang-up job. One of those consultants was Terry Blackman, a former IBM employee who had set up his own Y2K debugging business. Working as a Y2K project manager for Sears Canada, the City of Toronto, and the International Order of Foresters, Blackman was kept busy ensuring that the employees of these institutions and their clientele wouldn't have to build bomb shelters and stock up on canned goods and water purification tablets in anticipation of the approaching anarchy. When the crisis blew over, Blackman wrapped up his business in February and retired, far from the madding crowd, to his farm in south-central Ontario's Beaver Valley.

The Y2K contracts had left his company with some money in the bank, so when he wound it up, he looked for a place to park it. Watching ROBTv (the business cable television show that would be part of BCE's new media empire before the year was out), he saw an analyst cheering on Nortel, whose impending spinoff from BCE had been announced on January 26. The analyst set a one-year target price for Nortel of $130 (U.S.).

Terry Blackman was tuning into the investment possibility of Nortel just as the company was poised to make a great price leap forward. After the announcement of the BCE spinoff plan, the markets had become extremely volatile. The implications for Nortel weren't entirely clear, and money was shifting back and forth between BCE and Nortel as investors tried to guess how the spinoff would affect each, and as some surely indulged in a bit of arbitrage, trying to figure out which Nortel shares were the most valued—the ones actually trading under the NT symbol or the ones held by BCE. The BCE announcement on January 26 had knocked Nortel down from a high of $154.80 to a close of $143.45 that day. It bounced around madly for the next few days, with volumes on the TSE gyrating between two and six million shares, closing on successive days at $139.95, $130.75, $137.10, and finally at $134.75 on Tuesday, February 1. On February 2, Nortel's yo-yoing took a dramatic upswing. Around 3:30 on Wednesday, trading was halted in Nortel as unofficial word spread that Nortel's weighting in the TSE 300, 100, and 60 indices would be changed on Thursday. Nortel's weighting would be increased by about half a percentage point on each index, so that it would stand at 15.64 on the 300, 18.17 on the 100, and 21.76 on the 60. Before trading was halted on Wednesday, volumes had surged in both New York (to 9.8 million) and Toronto (to 8.7 million) as the price leapt more than 11 percent. In Toronto, Nortel gained $16 from the previous day's close, reaching $150.75 at the end of trading. After another gain, to a close of $153, on Thursday, the momentum investing kicked in on Friday, February 4, as the stock rocketed $18 to finish at $171 in Toronto. In the midst of this surge of buying, Terry Blackman picked up 200 shares at $158.

The momentum was being driven by several factors. Foremost was the index fund managers, who had to increase their Nortel holdings in order to match the new Nortel weightings. But at the same time, John Roth had embarked on a three-week road show in North America and Europe on Monday, talking up his stock in the wake of the BCE spinoff announcement with analysts and institutional investors. These were still the halcyon days of corporate spin, when an executive like Roth could go behind closed doors and say all kinds of things to key investors and analysts that nobody else could hear. Ross Healy was already convinced that Roth and company had guided down analyst expectations for Nortel's stock the previous autumn and reaped an earnings "surprise" with the fourth-quarter results.

Analyst Paul Sagawa of Sanford Bernstein & Co., who was about seven months away from releasing a devastating report on the future heath of the telecom equipment industry, was picking up vibrations of terrific spin as Roth made the rounds.

Part of the reason for the jump in share price, he told Reuters on February 4, "is just that Nortel is out there trying to pound the table with investors. It seems as though John [Roth] has been very enthusiastic in talking about what he thinks is possible from his organization." Sagawa said that some institutional investors were getting the impression that Nortel could better the projections of 20 to 21 percent revenue growth for 2000 by several percentage points. "That's certainly the way institutional investors have been interpreting those comments," Sagawa said.

An analyst with a major Canadian brokerage house, who asked not to be identified, told Reuters, "They're letting it slip to people selectively that they're increasing the capacity of their optical manufacturing again. Nortel's still in the hands of momentum players and they have to be given an excuse to love it."

Nortel wouldn't comment on what Roth and its other executives were saying in the road show appearances, but vowed that its guidance hadn't changed. "We are sticking to what we said in our earnings [report] for future projections," Nortel spokesman David Chamberlin told Reuters.

Be that as it may, Nortel had found some traction with investors, both institutional and private. The stock price continued to bounce around through February and March, but the price direction overall was upward. On March 23, Nortel broke through $200 and reached a high of $211.35 the next day. Blackman decided to take his profits, selling his shares around $210. His net profit for owning Nortel for less than two months was about $10,000. "This seemed like such an easy way to make money," he recalls. While by selling when he did, he avoided a drop in the next month, Blackman missed out on the post-split run-up that would have taken his shares to a pre-split value of almost $250 by midsummer. When Nortel became affordable again, he would be back.

Although their concerns wouldn't go into print in a report to clients until October, the Rosens were becoming concerned with the relationship between index fund investing, Nortel's share price, the company's penchant for acquiring companies with its shares on what was becoming a monthly basis, and the importance of the share price to executing those acquisitions.

As the issue was explained in a Veritas report, whenever a company like Nortel pays for an acquisition by issuing treasury shares, the number of issued and outstanding shares immediately increases. It's on the basis of issued and outstanding shares that weighted indices like those of the TSE base the weighting of an individual stock. However, the number of shares actually available for trading is routinely less than the number on which a weighting is based. That's because a number of shares used in an acquisition are often held in escrow for a period of time, the average being around eighteen months, which temporarily excludes them from the public float. "Although Nortel may not disclose the exact number of shares that are withheld," read the report, "the shares given to key shareholders of the acquired company are usually held in escrow. In the case of the acquisition of a private company, it would not be unusual for most shares to be withheld."

As a result, whenever Nortel made an acquisition and increased its float, index funds had to buy more Nortel shares in order to match its increased proportion of the weighting. But if too many of the shares in the float increase are actually held in escrow, there could be a liquidity squeeze. Too many index funds trying to buy fewer shares than are really available has a predictable result: the price goes up. "The result is simply artificial momentum for the stock."

The Rosens dismissed arguments that this could not happen with the TSE indices. They were absolutely right. With the benchmark 300, only blocks representing at least 20 percent of a total float that were known to be not available for trading, either because they represented an investment by another company or were sealed up in some kind of investment trust, were removed from the calculation of a stock's index weighting. Otherwise, when a company announced a share-based purchase, the float was adjusted accordingly, whether or not those new shares were to be held in escrow. If the new shares represented at least five basis points (0.05 percent) of the total value of the index, the weighting of the particular stock was adjusted right away; otherwise, the adjustment was left to a quarterly update. In this situation, a company like Nortel could steadily increase its total float by a few percent of its total shares issued at a time and trigger immediate upward adjustments in its index weighting, even if those shares

weren't actually available for trading. "Over the long term, a number of acquisitions [with escrowed shares] at three to five percent
of the float each will add up to a large proportion of restricted
shares," the Veritas report warned.

Was this happening with Nortel? More than likely. We know in
the case of at least one major acquisition, which came at the end of
Nortel's spree, that the issued shares were being held in escrow for one
year. It happened in the case of Nortel's purchase of a pump laser chip
operation from JDS Uniphase, which closed on February 13, 2001.
Nortel had agreed to pay for the operation with 64.7 million shares.
When concerns spread that a disposal of the additional shares by JDS
Uniphase could cause a price drop in Nortel, JDS Uniphase assured
the market that it wasn't allowed to touch the shares for a full year.
Nevertheless, following standard practice for the index, Standard &
Poor's, which managed the 300 for the TSE, automatically increased
Nortel's weighting in the index to reflect the float increase.

As Nortel's acquisition streak gathered momentum, the momentum it triggered in index investing appeared to contain an even greater
pricing danger than a simple weighting increase suggested. Already,
Nortel was a problem because it held such a dominant position in the
indices. Managers of pension and mutual funds were chasing the TSE
300 in particular, trying to outperform it in order to justify their jobs.
Where regulations on investing caps permitted, that meant putting
even more Nortel in their portfolios than were in the 300. But under
the Rosens' scenario, all these fund managers were trying to buy from
a pool of available Nortel shares that was smaller than actually existed.
The indices were forcing them into larger Nortel positions, while
Nortel's true share float, owing to escrowed shares, wasn't really growing at the same rate. That made Nortel especially hot, and even retail
investors, who had no obligation to load up on the stock, were being
sucked into the buying maelstrom.

Having completed the deals on Qtera on January 28 and Clarify on
March 16, Nortel followed through with five more acquisitions by mid-
summer. (Acquisition costs in U.S. GAAP.) Promatory Communications
Inc., which closed on March 23, gained Nortel a developer of digital

subscriber line (DSL) platforms for businesses and consumers for high-speed Internet access. The $771 million price included $60 million in acquired technology, $50 million in in-process R&D, and $659 million in goodwill.

On May 12, the week after the BCE spinoff was executed, Nortel was back on acquisition duties. Photonic Technologies Inc. was developing optical component technology that manipulated and controlled the polarization of light, a key ingredient in wave division multiplexing. Nortel already had a one-third interest and used $32 million in cash to acquire the rest of the company. Goodwill was assigned $29 million, net tangible assets $3 million. Nothing was left of acquired technology or in-process R&D.

On June 2, Xros Inc., a Silicon Valley developer of next-generation optical switches, was had for $3.23 billion, using 52.9 million Nortel shares. It was Nortel's largest purchase after Bay Networks. The cost was allocated as $3 billion in goodwill, just $29 million in acquired technology, and $191 million in-process R&D. Xros had yet to sell anything; it was just starting field trials of its X-1000 switch, which used mirrors to redirect photons from one piece of optical fibre to another. This optical "cross-connect" switch, which would be incorporated into Nortel's OPTera product line provided it came through trials satisfactorily, would give Nortel a presence in the emerging cross-connect market, where it had no technology of its own to offer.

Optical components developer CoreTek Inc. was brought aboard on June 23 for $1.2 billion, which included $946 million in goodwill, $115 million in acquired technology, and $176 million in in-process R&D. Nortel used 14.5 million shares to pay for it. In the deals for CoreTek, Xros, Photonic and Qtera, Nortel had committed more than $7 billion to the cause of keeping pace with advances in optical components and with Cisco's similar optical acquisitions, which had totalled almost $10 billion over the six-month period leading up to the Xros purchase.

On July 1 came the purchase of Architel Systems Corp., which produced or developed software used by Internet service providers in the course of customer service. The price was $472 million, paid for with six million Nortel shares. Goodwill swallowed $420 million, while $17 million went to acquired technology and $16 million to in-process R&D.

It turned out to be the last acquisition for two months, but Nortel had hoped to pull off another one. John Roth was betting much of the company's future on the fibre-optic boom, and in late July word got out that Nortel was attempting the acquisition of Corning.

The optical components business was in the thrall of takeover manoeuvres as companies positioned themselves for dominance in what was still promising to be an area of major growth for the communications industry. The NASDAQ crash in the spring had come and gone without impeding the sector's momentum, and one of the most impressively aggressive players was JDS Uniphase of Nepean and San Jose. In only one year, the company had leapt to prominence through the optical networking boom and its series of acquisitions. On June 30, 1999, Uniphase Corporation and JDS Fitel merged to begin the creation of an optical components manufacturer that supplied virtually every major networking company with equipment necessary to communicating with photons. In addition to Nortel, its single largest client, JDS Uniphase supplied Cisco, Lucent, and Alcatel, among many others. It continued to expand through acquisitions, which had to be performed through the purchase method, thus accumulating its own Nortel-like mountain of intangible assets to be amortized against revenues. Unlike Nortel, however, JDS Uniphase hadn't created a new accounting methodology to eradicate the write-downs. Its stock value nonetheless had increased by more than a factor of twenty in 1999, and reached a closing high of $146.53 (adjusted for a March 13, 2000, split) on March 6, 2000. After a dip in the spring NASDAQ meltdown, it returned to a daily high of $140.50 on July 24 and 26.

No sooner had JDS Uniphase swallowed E-Tek Dynamics at the end of June 2000 than it was outbidding Corning for SDL Inc., which made semiconductor lasers, laser-based systems, and (in JDS Uniphase's words) "fiber optic related solutions." The merger with SDL, again accounted for by purchase method, was tagged at $41 billion when a definitive agreement was signed on July 10, making it the fourth-largest deal in corporate America in 2000—bigger than the Chevron-Texaco merger—and the largest by any tech firm outside the phone companies. JDS Uniphase agreed to swap 3.8 of its shares for every share in SDL. The company estimated that the amortization of goodwill alone would result in a charge of about $8.4 billion annually. The acquisition would require regulatory approval, however, and the consolidation of so much optical technology was of great concern to U.S. antitrust regulators. Securing regulatory approval would end up having JDS Uniphase involve Nortel in a major divestment.

But that was many months away. In July, the various optical parties were still scrambling to make more JDS-like monster deals. And Nortel had a hankering to pull off the biggest deal of all. The plan was to sell Nortel's entire optical business to Corning for a staggering $100 billion. Corning would pay for the unit with its own stock, giving Nortel control of half of Corning. This got the markets even more excited than usual about Nortel. After the split that occurred with the BCE spinoff, Nortel had begun the month of May trading around $78 on the TSE. Not much happened through May, but the stock began to pick up again in June, breaking $100 for the first time on the nineteenth. July 12 conquered $110, and then the news of a possible megadeal with Corning pushed the stock to its all-time high of $124.50 on July 26.

But the deal didn't happen. When word reached the ears of Corning investors, they turned and ran. Since selling off its housewares division to focus on fibre optics, Corning had been tearing up the market charts, its price multiplying by more than 800 percent in two years. Acquiring Nortel's optical business by handing over half its common shares didn't look like a winning strategy. The mass exit from Corning knocked the stock from $283 to $250. Nortel went ahead with plans to sink $2 billion into its fibre-optic business over the next eighteen months to improve its manufacturing capacity, with a strong emphasis on optical Internet.

July 26 proved to be less a peak for Nortel's price than the edge of a broad escarpment. All through August, the stock traded around $120, getting as high as $123.75 on August 25. With some three billion shares outstanding, Nortel had reached a market capitalization of almost $375 billion. That was almost 40 percent of Canada's gross domestic product in 2000. What that meant was that, theoretically, if about 40 cents on every dollar being spent in the national economy was instead rerouted into a big piggy bank, at the end of the year the country collectively would have enough pennies to buy Nortel. And the nation would own a company that had lost almost $1.5 billion in the first six months of 2000 and had generated positive operating cash flow in that time of just $35 million.

As Nortel approached its historic high, the mother of a friend of Terry Blackman's puzzled over the great heap of Nortel shares she'd acquired. As a classic Bell Canada investor—the little old lady with the blue-chip dividend portfolio—this ninety-eight-year-old shareholder, who was born before Western Electric had taken a 40 percent interest in the new Northern Electric Co., had been handed her Nortel holding through the dividend distribution by BCE. The damned stuff had gone up about 50 percent since then. It was at $120 when she decided to unload it all. She owned so much that the capital gains bill was $600,000.

People couldn't believe she'd bailed on Canada's hottest stock. When asked why, she explained, "I got these things for nothing, and it doesn't seem right that they're worth so much."

It was that kind of stock in that kind of company. Management released financial figures that suggested it could acquire companies and their technologies for free by using shares, and a shareholder could walk head-first into a $600,000 tax bill because she couldn't tolerate owning something so expensive that it seemed she hadn't ever paid for.

But a lot of Canadians at that point owned Nortel shares, even if they didn't know it. Their government had bought them on their behalf, billions of dollars worth. And as the failed Cornell deal retreated from sight, the man who had done the buying started to think that he should get out of some of it.

It was beginning to look like a good time to get out, cash in, hedge your bets. In the case of erstwhile major shareholder BCE, a financing scheme ended up providing it with a huge windfall when Nortel finally did hit the skids.

After the distribution of Nortel shares in May, BCE was still holding 2 percent of the float, or about 60 million shares. With Nortel shares trading in the $80 range immediately after the divestment and split, BCE was sitting on a stack of shares worth at least $4.8 billion, and growing. Before the second quarter was out, BCE decided to hedge most of its Nortel holding so that they could be used as collateral in raising some $5 billion in long-term debt financing. Consequently, BCE entered into forward contracts—it bought puts—with several unnamed financial institutions for an undisclosed price that gave BCE the right to sell about 46.4 million Nortel shares within a year for an average price of $90. Andrew Willis would report in the *Globe and Mail* on October 26, 2000, that the three financial institutions were Scotia Capital, Citibank, and Credit Suisse First Boston, and that BCE's chief financial officer had stated in July that the arrangement had saved BCE 2 percent in interest on its financing. BCE also had the option, depending on market conditions, to increase the number of shares hedged to 53.5 million. As Nortel headed for $120 and beyond, Jean Monty took some heat for wasting company money on what seemed like an unnecessarily conservative hedging strategy. It would only be a few months before Nortel's rapidly escalating troubles turned Monty's money-squandering debt financing scheme into a brilliant hedge ploy that would reap his company billions when he did exercise the puts in 2001.

Hedging was also on the minds of the directors at the Canada Pension Plan Investment Board. The CPPIB, a Crown corporation, had been created in December 1997 by the Chrétien Liberals as part of its grand scheme to put pension funds into the stock market. With so many banks and brokerage houses vying for the lead in contributions to Liberal party coffers, the government's affinity with the thought processes of Bay Street was hardly surprising. But the urgency to do something about the CPP was undeniable. As noted, the feds were getting ready to turn the major public service pension plans loose in the public markets, and they and their provincial colleagues had the same ambition for the Canada

Pension Plan, the old-age safety net of all Canadians.

The federal government, which was ultimately responsible for the CPP, wasn't going to let the whole plan ride on the fortunes of the market: just the annual surplus. The CPP drew its income from federal and provincial government securities, and while this guaranteed an annual return, the feds had determined that those returns wouldn't be able to keep pace with demographic demands on plan payouts as the boomers aged. In 1996 the federal and provincial finance ministers agreed that the CPP wasn't sufficiently financed. Created in 1966 when gainfully employed people were plentiful enough to cover off the plan withdrawals by retirees, the "pay as you go" plan was in trouble by 1996. About ten million Canadians were paying $11 billion in contributions into the plan every year, while three million retirees were withdrawing almost $17 billion. An obvious solution would be to increase the contribution payments to close the gap, but the federal and provincial governments had a better idea: let the stock market pick up the tab.

In December 1997, when the CPPIB was created, its assets represented only 8 percent of accrued benefits. The federal and provincial governments wanted to see those assets to grow to 20 percent. And so the CPPIB was set up to see if the government could get a better bang for the public buck in the stock market. Pension plans are supposed to spread their risk around in debt and equity, but with the CPPIB it was reasoned (by its board of directors in December 1998) that the bulk of the pension plan already was in highly secure debt instruments, and so the surplus funds should be treated as a bit of mad money, devoted to equities exclusively in hope of getting the double-digit returns the markets had been delivering in the ongoing bull—returns that no safe, secure government bond ever could. They had no illusions about the volatility of stock markets, but the robust bull market beckoned, and the investment board fund only had to return an average of 4 percent per year above inflation to meet the plan's new funding goals.

The fund began investing the CPP surplus—the money left over from the main CPP portfolio after current payments had been met—in March 1999. The fund was given strict orders for its initial investing years. The federal and provincial finance ministers didn't want to see any fancy stickhandling. Eighty percent of funds would go into Canadian equities, the other 20 percent into the foreign equities markets. Foreign investing matched the Morgan Stanley Capital International World Index, minus the Canadian bits. And the Canadian equities matched the TSE 300. It was an indexing investment scheme that played right to the strengths and weaknesses of Nortel's rise and fall.

The CPPIB had received $11.9 million in surplus in the last month of its first fiscal year. For the new fiscal year, beginning in March 1999, the board received its first significant allocation of CPP surplus, a $1.9 billion portfolio starter kit. For the investment board's first full investing year, which ended in March 2000, things were grand. Thanks in large part to a surge in the TSE 300, which itself owed no small thanks to Nortel, the fund appreciated 40.1 percent. The portfolio was off to a roaring start.

Its first full fiscal year was already underway when the CPPIB got a president and chief executive officer. On June 22, 1999, the board's executive head hunt came to an end with the announcement that it had hired one of Bay Street's best-known figures, John A. MacNaughton, effective September 7. The fifty-four-year-old MacNaughton had been in the investment business for more than thirty years, and in March had retired as president of Nesbitt Burns, a firm that had donated almost $200,000 to the federal Liberals over the past three years. (It's hard to call the MacNaughton hiring a patronage appointment when virtually every major financial institution was making major annual contributions to the Liberals.) What the June 1999 CPPIB announcement didn't say was that MacNaughton was about to be named a director of JDS Uniphase. Although there was no conflict involved, since the CPPIB was placing its investments for now purely according to indices, the directorship did give MacNaughton a prime view of a tech stock market then in hyperdrive.

MacNaughton had served as the president and CEO of the brokerage house Burns Fry Ltd. from 1990 to 1994. When it was merged with Nesbitt Thomson to become Nesbitt Burns, a subsidiary of the Bank of Montreal, MacNaughton had carried on as president of the new entity. In 1996, Nesbitt Burns was the lead manager in the IPO of JDS Fitel, and when Uniphase Corporation and JDS Fitel merged on June 30, 1999, eight days after MacNaughton's hiring by the CPPIB was announced, MacNaughton joined the board of directors of the new JDS Uniphase.

The company's 2000 proxy indicated that MacNaughton was one of four "Class 1" directors and a member of the company's compensation committee. His own financial compensation was not large—$1,500 a year plus $500 for every meeting he attended, plus appropriate expenses. But MacNaughton did receive stock options—a lot of them. In fiscal 2000 alone, he was granted options to acquire 40,000 shares (which split to 320,000) at $20.985 (post split) per share.

In late July 2000, as Nortel attempted its megadeal with Corning, JDS Uniphase stock continued its tremendous, acquisition-driven ascent. With Nortel being JDSU's largest single customer, any deal that was good for John Roth's company was good for JDSU. Having already been boosted by the $41 billion SDL acquisition and cleared $130, JDSU rode an updraft from the Nortel-Corning rumours to move to $140. After the Corning deal failed to materialize for Nortel, JDSU fell back to $130, where it hung in for a few days before dropping to $120.

At which point, MacNaughton made his move. On August 8, he exercised 45,000 of his options to acquire JDSU at $20.985. The fair market value that day was $119.88. John MacNaughton spent $944,325 to buy shares worth $5,394,600. He had just made a paper gain of almost $4.5 million. Under the Canadian tax system, this option exercise immediately triggered a taxable benefit. Half of that benefit was taxable at the top Ontario rate of 46 percent, which meant MacNaughton now had a tax obligation of $1,023,563.25. This was the Catch-22 of stock options: they could generate a larger tax obligation than what had been spent to acquire them, and if the stock then dropped in value, the shares could end up being worth a lot less than the tax bill. And so, on August 9, he sold 31,272 shares, for prices ranging from $121 to $121.07 per share, bringing MacNaughton $3,784,262. Less the taxable benefit obligation, MacNaughton had just made $2,760,698.75. This left him still holding 13,728 shares. As the market slid, he watched them sink through the fall, until, on November 28, he got rid of them for prices ranging from $63.13 to $63.50.

MacNaughton's exercise of his JDSU options provided a textbook example of how lucrative stock options could be for company insiders in the world of cold-fusion economics. In another year, the shares MacNaughton was able to buy for about $21 and sell the next day for about $120 would be worth about $5, and investors on the open market like David Chmelnitsky, whose investing enthusiasm had driven up the price in the first place, would be massacred.

Back at the CPPIB, however, MacNaughton was trying to make sure the Canada Pension Plan surplus that had been entrusted to him wasn't massacred. The board was becoming nervous with Nortel's domination of the TSE 300. Index investing had been good to the CPPIB in the past year, but as the Stock that Ate the Index plateaued at around $120 while reporting a GAAP loss of more than $1.4 billion halfway through 2000, the downside was looming for Nortel and Canadian pensioners as well. The board went to the federal government, requesting that the terms of its investment policy be changed. The CPPIB received approval to split the Canadian equities portion of the fund in half. One half would still follow the 300 index. The other half would be placed in a customized "capped 300," in which Nortel was limited to 10 percent of the portfolio. This was hardly a vote of nonconfidence in Nortel, and a more cautious response to the exposure would have been to convert the entire Canadian portion of the fund to a capped 300. But the fact that MacNaughton and his board wanted to pull back from Nortel at all was a sign that John Roth's ability to drive the share price upward at the same pace as revenues was about to falter.

And even Roth probably realized this. Coincidentally, Roth had begun to lay the groundwork for his departure after more than thirty years with Nortel. On June 27, Roth had announced that the board of directors had promoted Clarence Chandran, president of Nortel's Carrier and Service Provider segment, to the post of chief operating officer. Chandran had joined Bell Canada's Ontario operations in 1973, coming over to Nortel in 1985. Since 1990, Chandran had been based in the United States, and Nortel stated that he would continue to work out of the company's Boston-area offices. Nortel's ties to Canada were becoming more tenuous with every passing day. Chandran was the obvious successor to Roth—or at least, the executive most obviously poised to replace him. *National Post Business* would comment to Roth in his CEO of the Year interview: "There's already speculation that your chief operating officer, Clarence Chandran, is waiting in the wings." Roth replied, "I don't think there's any secret about that. Jean Monty made me chief operating officer in 1995; I became CEO in 1997. I thought the transition was extremely smooth. Everybody has to have a successor, and it shouldn't be a secret. If Clarence performs well as COO, why should he not be CEO someday?" Roth's comment provided easy reading between the lines. If Roth was made COO in 1995 and became CEO in 1997, then investors could expect Chandran to replace Roth in 2002. Certainly nobody was expecting Roth to bolt out the door, or wanted him to, such was his aura with investors, and even with Chandran in the COO position, Roth was not viewed as a figurehead CEO. This company was still his, and so was the responsibility for running it profitably.

Be that as it may, Roth chose the summer of 2000, with Nortel's common shares trading at record values, to give the ripcord on his golden parachute a firm tug. And he pulled it on the same day that John MacNaughton realized the profit on his JDS Uniphase options.

On August 9, Roth exercised a total of 450,000 options, 360,000 of them at $7.735, 90,000 at $11.931. (All figures are U.S. dollars.) He thus spent $3,858,390 at an average price of $8.57, and sold all of them that day, at an average price of $81.02, for a total of $36,460,010.

How much had Roth made? Without taking into account brokerage fees (and the tax bill triggered by the employment benefit on the initial option exercise, which would have been about $7.5 million), the difference between his purchase costs and sales proceeds was $32.6 million. John Roth had become one more New Economy executive to be lavishly compensated by the irrational exuberance of the raging bull market. At his base salary of $1.1 million, it would have taken Roth about 30 years—a lifetime of labour at his peak salary rate—to earn at his desk what stock market investors handed to him with one day of trading. Those who purchased his 450,000 share on August 9 and held on to them, believing in the dream of ever-increasing corporate growth, would see those shares fall to $7.56 on the NYSE in exactly one year.

15

No Safe Harbour

A Wall Street analyst who made an unpopular forecast for the semiconductor sector last week has received death threats as a result, sources close to the matter told CNNfn.

—CNNfn, July 13, 2000

Right through the summer of 2000, John Roth managed to maintain a handsome share value for Nortel and carry on with Nortel's acquisition agenda. Although Corning, the big prize, had got away, Roth had three more purchases in the pipeline.

"Acquisitions are a *strategic* part of being a leading Internet Era company," the company declared in its second-quarter report. "They improve our ability to serve our customers, generate new revenue, and build diversity into our revenue stream—diversity in customers, products, and markets.

"Acquisitions also add to our base of highly skilled people, which is extremely important because our people are our most valuable assets. Business is a human enterprise that gets done through people, and we're blessed with a critical mass of exceptional, high-voltage talent that has the drive, determination, and passion to enable Nortel Networks to deliver on its financial commitments while accelerating our momentum as a growth company and industry leader."

First up was EPiCON Inc., which had a software platform that allowed application service providers (ASPs) to deliver and manage software over the Internet. This was a new area of business-to-business e-commerce, in which complex and expensive software tools, which could cost $1 million, could be leased by users rather than purchased outright. Access to, and control of, these programs, were provided by the ASPs. Nortel had already taken a 9 percent interest in EPiCON back in November 1999. The deal closed on September 5, with Nortel issuing about 4.3 million shares (and assumed about one million stock options) to get the remaining 91 percent. Nortel received just $13 million in acquired technology and $6 million in in-process R&D. How much goodwill was generated depended on the GAAP standard. The Canadian GAAP, using the closing date for the valuation, put the total price at $406 million, with $390 million in goodwill; U.S. GAAP set the price at $284 million, with $262 million in goodwill.

On October 5 came Nortel's largest deal since Bay Networks. Alteon WebSystems Inc. delivered Nortel Web-based Internet switching technology. This was one of the most established businesses Nortel had acquired, as it included $127 million in net tangible assets and $391 million in acquired technology, in addition to $403 million in in-process R&D. Nortel also had to swallow 29 million stock options (valued at $428 million under Black Scholes), and the deal, paid for with 81.9 million Nortel shares, carried a typically hefty premium. U.S. GAAP said the purchase cost $8.05 billion, with $6.7 billion in goodwill; Canadian GAAP put the price at $6.03 billion, with $5.26 billion in goodwill. In either case, Nortel had been able to reduce the goodwill by $110 million by arranging a cash sale of Alteon's network interface card division to 3Com before the deal was closed.

The final acquisition was Sonoma Systems, the developer of a technology to deliver simultaneously voice, video, and data over a single connection. The purchase, using 4.8 million shares, commanded one of the largest premiums based on goodwill alone. In addition to $28 million in acquired technology and $26 million in in-process R&D, Sonoma had negative tangible assets of $18 million and obligations for 1.3 million stock options valued by Black Scholes at $15 million. For this, Nortel paid $462 million under U.S. GAAP, $374 million under Canadian GAAP. The goodwill was, respectively, $411 million and $348 million.

And so, in the quest for diversity in the revenue stream, more high-voltage talent, and accelerated momentum as a growth company and an industry leader, since July Nortel had entered into acquisition agreements worth whatever GAAP statement it was that you read. The U.S. GAAP one said $8.8 billion, the Canadian one, $6.8 billion. The $2 billion difference was mainly due to the disconcerting descent in Nortel's stock price as summer turned to fall.

The critics of Nortel's expansion plans and Roth's helmsmanship were few and far between, but they were beginning to be heard. Ross Healy made his deep-discount reevaluations of Nortel's price on Canadian television in June and August. In May, Al Rosen wrote his first publicly distributed words on Nortel's financial state in *Canadian Business* magazine. He castigated analysts for going along with Nortel's good-news earnings numbers that left out acquisition costs and for overlooking the fact that Nortel was actually losing money. The standards in quarterly reporting in Canada were so poor that it was impossible for Rosen to figure out which of nine recent purchases made an identifiable, dollar-value contribution to Nortel's revenues. "But we do know one thing: these acquisitions aren't free. Most analysts, however, are far too busy cheerleading to bother asking Nortel CEO John Roth how much he's paying to bolster his company's sales revenue. Even if Roth managed to get a real deal on the companies, he could be putting the company in a tough position. Unless Nortel keeps on making acquisitions, it may not be able to maintain an upward revenue trend line. And who knows how much that will cost."

Rosen charged that analysts were "too smitten with Nortel's separately reported first quarter 'operating' results—which exclude the acquisition costs the company incurred to boost its revenue—to be worried about really important matters. All of which makes you wonder if the legions of analysts who are in love with Nortel today will be feeling jilted a couple of years from now." It turned out they would feel jilted in less than a year.

On July 25, the same day that Nortel was releasing its second-quarter results, Rosen contributed a scathing article to the *National Post,* condemning Nortel's use of "earnings from operations" numbers that discarded acquisition costs. "Apparently the key to running a healthy business today is to simply ignore half the costs," he wrote. "You still have to pay them, but mum's the word, should anyone happen to ask."

Rosen's comments got under the skin of John Roth. When the *National Post* reported Nortel's second-quarter results as a "64 percent jump in operating earnings," it also reported Roth's unhappiness with Rosen's July 25 article. "Mr. Roth noted that Nortel reports earnings before and after special items," the *Post* reported, "adding that Mr. Rosen's arguments undermine Canadian technology companies' efforts to secure investment, driving them to the United States where valuations in the sector are better understood." Evidently, if people like Mr. Rosen were going to make a lot of unflattering noise about customized earnings figures, then Canadian tech companies would just have to head south, where interpretive accounting was better appreciated. And while the biting criticism of someone as respected in matters of financial probity as Rosen probably added to a creeping unease about Nortel's share value, no market retreat resulted. It took a growing malaise in the networking business to begin moving Nortel downward in September. But even then, the market was so generally upbeat, what with the strong growth still being predicted in optical networking, that when the next Nortel critic signed in, his message was a genuine bombshell.

On September 28, 2000, Paul Sagawa, an analyst with New York's Sanford C. Bernstein & Co., a subsidiary of Alliance Capital Management, turned himself into perhaps the most reviled figure in the limited pantheon of anti-Nortel forces as compiled by unrepentant Nortel boosters. Sagawa may not have been nearly as brutal about Nortel as Healy and Rosen were—on the contrary, he was actually fairly upbeat, at least for the rest of 2000, and worked within the parameters of Nortel's earnings-from-operations numbers in his analysis. But as a Wall Street analyst he had the attention of U.S. press, and anything negative he said could have a far greater impact on share value than the words of Healy or Rosen. Swimming against the tide of bullish prognostications for Nortel in particular and, most importantly, the telecom equipment sector in general, Sagawa released reports on both that predicted a revenue and earnings reckoning in 2001. By Sagawa's calculation, the party that had delivered such spectacular share values to Nortel in the summer of 2000 was just about over.

A Harvard M.B.A., Sagawa had joined Bernstein as a network and communications hardware analyst in 1996, when the Telecom Act brought competition to the fiefdoms of the Baby Bells and local exchange carriers, and when AT&T had responded by creating Lucent. Before coming to Bernstein, he had been a senior specialist in multimedia at the consulting firm McKinsey and Co. for six years—and before that, a national account executive with AT&T from 1985 to 1988, in the years immediately following the breakup of AT&T.

"I had been an optimist about the sector," Sagawa volunteers, which is to say that he had been very bullish about prospects of the main networking suppliers, and in the summer of 2000 he had Lucent, Nortel, and Cisco all rated as Market Outperform. But as Lucent's fortunes in particular slipped, Sagawa's confidence in the long-term strength of its sector also began to waver.

"In the old days, you'd do the job by looking at these companies and deciding who had the cool technologies," he reflects. "But by the summer of 2000, the bonds of the new telecom players started to collapse." The new telcos, particularly the competitive local exchange carriers (CLECs) who were keeping companies like Nortel hopping with their demands for cutting-edge networking equipment and promised particular growth in DWDM systems at the metro market level, were facing a cash flow crisis. The NASDAQ, on which many of them had floated IPOs, had crashed in the spring. The ratings on their bonds, which they'd issued to fund their expansion, were eroding as the market lost confidence in their ability to meet their debt obligations. Something very worrying, as a result, was going on with the customer ranks of the networking companies. Telecom analysts in general and networking companies in particular were predicting booming sales right through 2001, but Sagawa was beginning to suspect that there would be far fewer sales than everyone thought, simply because the money required to place the orders was running out.

It's a sad reflection on the state of the analyst business that for such a phenomenally important sector of the economy, no one was asking hard questions about how much the customers would be able to spend. And if they were, none had the nerve to publish the results and defy the market's groupthink optimism. Instead, the guidance of Nortel, Cisco, Lucent, and the rest were generally accepted, and analysts chose to debate whether one company had an advantage over another in IP routers or DWDM versus SONET. Sagawa was among the first—if not the first—of the major league analysts to abandon the groupthink, the collective assumption that the telecom sector was going to keep growing ad infinitum, with successive waves of new technologies spurring on ever greater heights of infrastructure spending. Suddenly, in the summer of 2000, Sagawa stopped to wonder if this assumption was a dangerously misleading one.

Sagawa conducted a survey of fifty-nine telecom carriers in North America and Europe in an effort to measure the spending plans of the industry as a whole. A picture would later emerge of Sagawa tirelessly crisscrossing the country, banging on telco doors and interviewing everyone from the janitor to the CEO. In fact, while surveys of telco spending plans were important to his conclusions, the critical work was mainly done by looking over financial statements easily found in the public domain—the balance sheets and cash flow statements of publicly traded companies. It was basic number-crunching that anyone, at any time, could have done. The results were sobering. Telecom carriers had been on an equipment spending binge whose year-over-year growth rate, by Sagawa's reckoning, was about to dip noticeably and in some cases actually shrink. "It was clear they couldn't sustain their spending," he says. "They were burning through too much money."

Sagawa's report portrayed a telecom carrier business whose capital expenditures (capex) were steadily outstripping revenues. The fifty-nine surveyed companies collectively were reporting a revenue increase of about 13 percent, while their capex were growing 38 percent. As a result, the average carrier was dedicating 30 percent of its income to buying stuff from companies like Nortel. Sagawa suspected that the proportion was much higher, because of revenues that were double-counted in the survey. For example, a wireless carrier would report long-distance charges to a customer as retail revenue, but the wireless carrier had to buy the transmission time from the "wire" carriers who actually carried the calls through the conventional phone system, and these carriers reported the income as wholesale revenue. The survey thus ended up counting the revenue from a single call twice. Consequently, Sagawa ventured that real revenue growth for carriers was running around 10, not 13, percent, and that the proportion of industry revenues actually being consumed by capex was approaching 50 percent. It was a trend that couldn't continue, as Sagawa noted that the current rates of revenues and expenditure growth would cause capex to overtake revenues in just six years.

Something had to give. Either revenues had to zoom up, to catch up with (and justify) the soaring expenditures, or the drunken-sailor capex buildout would have to go face-down in the gutter. The telecom carriers took a lot of the guesswork out of the prognosticating for Sagawa simply by reporting that they were easing back on spending growth and in some cases reversing it.

In a lot of cases, they had no choice. Carriers were running out of money.

"Carrier market conditions, which contributed to the huge increase in actual spending vs. expectations, have deteriorated," Sagawa wrote, noting that two competitive local exchange carriers, GST Telecommunications and ICG Communications, had become insolvent. GST, which built its fibre-optic network with Nortel technology, had gone bankrupt, with its assets being bought by Time Warner back in May, while ICG, whose stock had shed 95 percent of its value on the NASDAQ in the previous year and counted Nortel, Cisco, and Lucent among its "technology partners," had crumbled in September, just as Sagawa was drafting his report, and was headed toward bankruptcy. It would file for Chapter 11 protection on November 14 and be delisted by NASDAQ on December 18. Attempts to arrange a buyout of ICG by Teligent, another CLEC which based its service on wireless transmission, had fallen through, and Teligent itself would go under the following spring.

"Stock prices for every category of carrier are down in absolute and relative terms after three years of superior returns," Sagawa noted. "Free cash flows have turned sharply negative." Only four of forty-one U.S. carriers had positive cash flow during the first half of 2000, and his table summary of cash flow for CLECs showed only one year of positive cash flow among fifteen firms since 1995, and that was a slim $2 million performance by ITC Deltacom in 1996, making it painful to fund further capex acceleration without external financing. The combined negative cash flow for CLECs in the first half of 2000 was $5.1 billion; for the crowd of new long-distance fibre-optic "backbones" like 360networks, almost $7 billion; and among the major carriers, AT&T Corp. had gone negative by $1.8 billion for the first half of the year, while Sprint FON Group and WorldCom had each outspent revenues by about $1.3 billion.

Sagawa was portraying an industry that had gone wild on infrastructure and hadn't yet found the revenues to fuel further growth. If these carriers were going to keep building at ever-increasing levels, they would have to finance their capex habit. But in the past year, money had become more expensive as the Fed overnight rate had increased a full percentage point, and bond yields had correspondingly risen 100 basis points. All the networking companies had been providing vendor financing, in particular to small, cash-starved carrier startups—providing the customer with the money required to make a sale and keep revenues coming in, even if this amounted to using their own money to buy their own products and allowing the customer to repay them on generous terms. In good times, the vendors were able to flip the debt to a third-party financier and get the revenues more quickly at a slight discount, but those opportunities were drying up in the face of carrier failures, and those failures were exposing the networking companies to write-downs of bad debts and higher contingency provisions against such losses in their receivables statements. At the same time, as Sagawa explained, "increased scrutiny of equipment supplier balance sheets has made it more difficult to secure vendor financing." In other words, credit agencies and other concerned parties were taking a harder look at the vendor financing habits of the networking companies, and in Lucent's case there had been major trouble. "We believe the carrier industry environment, marked by deteriorating financial performance, bankruptcies, falling share prices, rumored consolidation and increasing costs of capital, is not conducive to the aggressive upward spending revisions observed in the past three years," wrote Sagawa.

Sagawa predicted a noticeable deceleration in spending on networking infrastructure, concluding that global spending would grow 19 percent in 2001 compared to an expected rate of 28 percent for 2000. Europe would be the healthier market, mainly because of the rollout of 3G wireless service. The North American component would be particularly hard hit. U.S. carriers were reporting an overall decrease in planned capex spending for 2001 of 9 percent, with significant variations through the carrier industry. Incumbent carriers were expecting a slight increase in their spending, but the new, big, long-distance carriers that were creating fibre-optic backbones—360networks, Level 3, Williams, and Global Crossing—were planning to slash spending by 25 percent, while the CLECs' spending would be down by 23 percent and the Internet service providers (ISPs) would plummet by 35 percent. Not all these cuts could be translated into absolute losses for the equipment makers. Much of the planned decline, for example, with the fibre-optic backbone companies was attributed to the completion of trenching and cable-laying operations. All the same, Sagawa argued that, while 19 percent spending growth for the global market in 2001 would still be above historical averages, the U.S. industry deceleration of 9 percent "would make it difficult for any sizable competitor to deliver on expectations of accelerating or even sustaining their 2000 top-line growth rate."

Nor would the optical equipment or data networking sectors be immune, as some would argue. Traditional voice telephony, already fading as a significant revenue source, could not be expected to bear the brunt of the downturn, since it was now responsible for only about 20 percent of spending. Sagawa expected the optical and data sectors, which had accounted for 60 percent of projected spending in 2000, to fall to 40 percent in 2001.

Paul Sagawa, Ross Healy, and Al Rosen had taken aim at the widely presumed bullish prospects for Nortel from very different angles. Sagawa had approached the problem from the perspective of customer behaviour; Healy concerned himself mainly with drawing up a reasonable share valuation for a networker like Nortel based on balance sheet fundamentals; Rosen questioned the company's profitability and cash flow, and prodded the financial statements for further signs of trouble. Their approaches complemented one another, but in the end, Sagawa's work probably had the greatest potential to deflate the Nortel bubble. Healy wasn't in New York; Rosen was best known as a forensic accountant, and as such wasn't an oft-quoted Wall Street analyst. Sagawa's work provided compelling evidence that actual sales would dry up, an event that could grab the attention of people otherwise unmoved by Healy's analysis of price multiples of book value or Rosen's complaints about pro forma–type earnings that were not unique to Nortel. As well, Rosen's more complex concerns about Nortel's financial statements were limited to the privileged eyes of his institutional clients, who at any rate were generally unable to bring themselves to leap off the Nortel bandwagon. While Healy's pronouncement that Nortel was grossly overvalued might have served to reinforce Sagawa's prognostication on future revenue streams, Sagawa himself didn't adopt Healy's calamitous tone in drawing his conclusions on how the capex downturn would affect share values in the networking sector. Nor did he criticize Nortel's earnings reportage.

Unfortunately, it was in applying the capex information to his analysis of the main networking companies that the general reception of Sagawa's urgent message was undermined. His methods were sound enough. Sagawa was concerned about how the decelerating demand for optical equipment and data networking would affect the elite suppliers, who had price/earnings ratios more than twice their growth rates. He was particularly bearish about the companies that had price/earnings ratios greater than 40. At the time of the report, Nortel's P/E was 78.1, based on projected 2000 earnings, 64 based on future (2001) earnings. Cisco's 2000 and 2001 P/E values were respectively 88.7 and 68.6. Lucent, on the other hand, was at 24.4 and 21.5, its recent troubles having already blown much of the irrational exuberance off the top of its share price. As a result, Sagawa downgraded Nortel and Cisco from Outperform to Market Perform, leaving Lucent alone among the diversified networking elites at Outperform.

"We recommend reducing investment weight in this sector, and favor low P/E stocks with valuation support," Sagawa concluded.

On Nortel, Sagawa was actually quite bullish for the remainder of 2000, expecting revenues to top $31 billion, an increase of 48 percent over 1999, with earnings per share (which, it went without saying, did not include acquisition costs) of 77 cents versus the consensus of 73 cents. It was more than the company would actually deliver. But he could not see Nortel reaching a 30 percent growth rate in 2001, and so reduced his projected revenues from $43 to $40.9 billion and earnings per share from 96 cents to 94 cents, below the 98-cent consensus.

Sagawa didn't give a price target for Nortel, but if he thought a P/E multiple of 40 was the peak of the comfort zone, based on the projected 2000 and 2001 EPS values, the price should have been between $30 and $38. Considering how dire he predicted the telecom equipment market was going to be in 2001, and how horrendously the year actually played out for Nortel and its fellow networking companies, Sagawa's Nortel downgrade was unusually generous. But that didn't make it any less palatable to Nortel investors when it was released on the same day as his telecom downturn report. On September 28, Nortel opened in New York at 59 and closed at 61³/₄. At best, then, Sagawa was saying Nortel's price should be cut by almost 40 percent.

Sagawa was dismissed by the most ardent Nortel boosters as a Lucent shill, a cheerleader for the spinoff of his old employer. After all, as an AT&T national account manager, Sagawa had once made a living selling Bell Labs products, which would have necessitated telling customers why the Bell Labs stuff was so much better than what Nortel was offering. The more irate ones called Sagawa's office to scream at him. There were death threats. Then Lucent's financials started to crumble, and the Nortel true believers felt better about themselves.

The timing of Lucent's latest travails, from the perspective of the credibility of Sagawa's report, was dreadful. Lucent and Nortel were set to release their latest quarterly results on October 24, as both companies marked the end of their respective quarters on September 30; for Nortel, this was the end of the third quarter, while for Lucent, it was the end of the fourth. Quarterly reports are like the required elements in a figure skating routine. The judges like to see clean execution and no surprises. While Nortel was about to two-foot the landing on its triple-toe Lutz, Lucent hit the ice like it had been thrown head-first from a moving Zamboni.

On October 10, less than two weeks after Sagawa decided to leave his Lucent rating at Market Outperform while downgrading its main competitors, Lucent announced that it wouldn't meet its previous guidance when it released its fourth-quarter results on October 24. In July, Lucent had promised that "pro forma" revenues and earnings per share would increase 15 percent for the quarter. While the company was still expecting a revenue increase of 14 to 15 percent over the previous fourth quarter, Lucent was now warning that the quarter's earnings per share were actually going to decline dramatically, from 24 cents in 1999 to 17 cents in 2000. With Lucent having opened the day on the NYSE at $32¼, the revised guidance whacked almost $8 off the price of the former tech darling, which was rapidly losing credibility with investors. Only a year earlier, Lucent had been a $65 stock headed for $83 just before Christmas. Now it was skidding into the low twenties.

Lucent's fourth-quarter results were scheduled to be released on the morning of Tuesday, October 24. But on Monday morning, Lucent announced that its chairman and CEO, Richard McGinn, had been fired over the company's continuing disappointing performance, and that Henry Schacht, the company's former chairman of the board from 1995 to 1997, was taking over both posts and launching a search for a new chief executive. It also warned that, for the third time in a year, the company would experience revenue declines below market expectations when its fourth-quarter results were released after the close of trading, rather than the next morning as originally planned.

Lucent claimed pro forma earnings per share of 18 cents, slightly better than predicted on October 10, but also declared a net loss per share of 7 cents after factoring in annoying things like amortization of goodwill from some of its acquisitions and a $433 million net loss from the spinoff of its Enterprise Networks Group, which had become Avaya Communications—the company Schacht had been running when he was brought back to replace McGinn. And revenue from continuing operations had only increased 12.1 percent, and not 14 to 15 percent as promised in the revised October 10 guidance.

It got worse. On November 21, Lucent was compelled to report a "revenue recognition issue" for the fourth quarter, which meant its sales had been overstated by $125 million and that 2 cents had to be sliced off its earnings per share. The shortfalls of the quarterly results and the firing of McGinn hadn't really affected the share price. If anything, they raised hopes that Lucent was getting its house in order, and the stock enjoyed a small rally, trading above $25 on November 6. But the November 21 news helped push Lucent toward new lows. Having finished November 20 at $20^{15}/₁₆, Lucent was down to $17^9/₁₆ at the end of the next day, and kept falling. It went below $13 on December 28, before closing out the year at $13½. Since September 28, when Sagawa had chosen it to outperform the market, Lucent had lost 56 percent of its value. During the same period, which proved turbulent for all the networking stocks, Cisco dropped 36 percent—with most of the loss coming in the last two weeks of the year—and Nortel 48 percent.

Lucent's dismal news on October 23 raised expectations for Nortel. If Lucent was doing so badly, and optical networking was going great guns, then surely Nortel was making gains. "Lucent ills great for Nortel" was the headline in the *Financial Post* on October 24. "Investors will find out how much business Nortel has picked up today, when the Brampton, Ont.-based company reports its third-quarter results after the market closes," went the story. "Analysts firmly expect Nortel to beat earnings expectations, but investors will be looking for indications about fourth-quarter sales."

Layered upon Lucent's disaster and the anticipation of Nortel's results was a tremendous change in how companies were allowed to communicate with analysts. The traditionally close relationship between companies and the analysts who followed them had long permitted a company to quietly take those analysts aside and gently persuade them that maybe their numbers were a little steep. It could be left to the analysts to fix things and avoid an embarrassing performance shortfall. Many analysts, after all, didn't want to annoy their own firms, who might be handling or seeking investment banking opportunities from the company, or who had client investors who wouldn't appreciate a sharp shock after hearing so many bullish pronouncements from the analysts. And so the analysts could gently guide the stock price down, saying the right things at the right moments, perhaps about the particular sector or the economy in general, which released the hot air from the stock and allowed the company to release its quarterly numbers without delivering a blunt trauma of sudden disappointment.

But as of October 23, 2000, companies could no longer conduct private, cozy conferences with selected analysts if they failed at the same time to share with the investing public at large any information that constituted guidance. The reason was the SEC's Regulation FD (for "fair disclosure"), which went into effect that day. This was a landmark move to deliver true transparency to the equities markets, to ensure that information of a materially significant nature that could affect a company's share price was available instantaneously to everyone, and not just to selected analysts, their employers, and their clients.

Before Reg. FD, disclosure was highly uneven. A root cause of many class-action shareholder lawsuits was that information in a prospectus for an IPO often wasn't as detailed as comments a company officer would make during the IPO launch to analysts and institutional investors at the road shows meant to pump up enthusiasm for the offering, or in a conference call with analysts after the IPO. Shareholders became outraged when they discovered that the IPO contained one level of information, while company officers were making far more detailed statements in gatherings with analysts and large institutional investors and fund managers. And companies like Nortel held their own private road shows for analysts and selected institutional investors which left the uninvited wondering what was being discussed and how much different the message might be that John Roth was delivering to a privileged few.

The disparity in quality of information was due to the Private Securities Litigation Reform Act of 1995, which, in an effort to reduce the number of frivolous shareholder lawsuits in the United States, had introduced the "safe harbour" concept for forward-looking statements. This meant a company and its officers could make reasonable forecasts of future earnings without inviting lawsuits when the numbers didn't pan out, provided they made clear the risk factors at the same time. However, "safe harbour" was not extended to IPOs, where legislators wanted to prevent excessive boosterism. Company officers thus had far more leeway in a road show than in a prospectus, where forward-looking statements that are proved to be false or misleading can trigger personal liability for a director under Section 11 of the Securities Act. But while companies might have been granted more leeway in the forward-looking statements they made to road shows and analyst conference calls, they were extremely reluctant to make the same statements in public press releases, or to distribute the comments more broadly by opening up the conference calls to the public, as either move would invite liability concerns. While Nortel was among the companies to open up their conference calls to all interested parties before Reg. FD came along, senior officers of public companies generally were operating in several distinct tiers of disclosure: what they said in an IPO, what they said in a quasi-private gathering such as a road show or an analyst conference call, and what they were willing to tell the public, by opening up conference calls to them or by inserting forward-looking information in press releases.

While safe-harbour protection is available to press releases (including material posted on a corporate Web site), claiming safe harbour means burdening forward-looking statements with "risk factor" warnings that can bog down the material. As well, companies face increased legal risks when failing to sufficiently protect oral statements to analysts. Statements made in IPOs, corporate press releases, and SEC filings get a thorough going over from corporate lawyers. When a company executive gets on the phone with a bunch of analysts and starts making off-the-cuff replies to questions, lawyers aren't prescreening the answers. They can end up being quoted in analyst reports or, in the case of a conference call opened up to the public, being distributed in all sorts of uncontrolled ways (not the least of which is the Internet), inviting a slew of lawsuits if their predictions fail to come true.

"Safe harbour" encouraged long preambles to conference calls. The executives seconded to the duty were a bit like priests dispensing purifying incense before a sermon. The conference call held by JDS Uniphase on February 13, 2001, to announce the finalization of the merger with SDL in conjunction with its sale of a pump laser chip operation to Nortel opened with a typical preemptive strike against the litigiously inclined, as JDSU president Jozef Straus momentarily surrendered the phone to chief financial officer Tony Muller:

> **Straus:** Good afternoon, everyone. Thank you for joining us on this happy occasion. I cannot tell you how excited I am with the closing of the merger today. By adding SDL and its industry leading technology into the JDS Uniphase family, I believe the combined company will immediately accrue benefit of greater technological depth and increased ability to serve our customers better.
>
> Before we go any further, Tony will now review the safe-harbour language . . .
>
> **Muller:** We would like to advise you that the discussions we will have today will include "forward-looking statements," as that term is defined under the Private Securities Litigation Reform Act of 1995. What we and the Act mean by forward-looking statements are all statements we make, other than those dealing specifically with historical matters (that is, any statements we make about the conduct of our business, operations, and finances up to this moment). All other statements we make are forward-looking statements. Our forward-looking statements include any information we provide on future business operations including, without limitations, our integration plans, the expected benefits of our supply agreement with Nortel, and guidance regarding the future financial performance of the company. All forward-looking statements mentioned are subject to risks and uncertainties that could cause the actual results to differ, possibly materially, from those projected in the forward-looking statements. Some, but not all, of these risks and uncer-

tainties are discussed from time to time in the press releases and
securities filings of the company with the SEC, particularly in
our Form 10-Q filed today. We undertake no obligation to publicly update or revise any forward-looking statements, whether
as a result of new information, future events or otherwise.

Now I will turn it back to Jozef. . .

For class-action lawyers, tracking down every statement made by a
company or one of its officers and determining whether "safe harbour"
was explicitly secured for it became a fundamental part of building
a case. For executives like Jozef Straus or John Roth, every statement they ever made in a conference call, and every encounter
with a reporter or a microphone, was a potential source of legal
action. It could be argued that, rather than improving the dissemination of valuable information, the Reform Act of 1995 was
encouraging a well-grounded legal paranoia over liability and the
applicability of safe harbour to each and every public utterance,
which in turn was making companies more reluctant to disclose
useful information more broadly.

The different levels of disclosure that persisted following the
Reform Act naturally produced different degrees of investor knowledge. In the established system, investors who wanted access to the
best knowledge inevitably needed access to the wisdom of an analyst
who worked for one of the investment banks or brokerage houses.
Information was a highly marketable commodity in what amounted
to an old boys' network in which investors were left on the outside.
But even when investors had access to a report, it was old news for
the market. Whatever timely information that had been disclosed by
the company to the analyst had been acted on by the analyst's
employer and most important clients long before the information
was digested and presented in a report.

One of the most widely quoted experts on disclosure is Steven E.
Bochner of the Silicon Valley law firm Wilson Sonsini Goodrich &
Rosati. Bochner advises leading tech firms on securities law and lec-
tures on the subject. He wrote succinctly on the problems of disclosure in his article "The Disintermediation of Forward-Looking

Disclosures," published in August 2000 by the Practicing Law Institute:

> Information conveyed to analysts during a quarterly conference call, or communicated orally to a room full of institutional investors on a public offering "road show," is often qualitatively better, and more timely, than that available to the average individual investor in a company press release or SEC-filed disclosure document. By "better," I mean more likely to contain the type of information former SEC Commissioner Breeden called the most valuable information investors could have about a company: forward-looking information.
>
> Forward-looking information, such as comments signaling a positive or negative trend in financial outlook, moves the price of stock. And in today's high price/earnings multiple environment (which, in the case of many new Internet issues, means high price-to-next year's revenue projection multiple), the financial stakes have never been greater.
>
> Preferential disclosure of forward-looking information undermines the premise of our system of full and fair disclosure, creating an investor world with two castes: those in the know and those not. It also tends to make more formal disclosures, such as press releases and SEC-filed documents, a kind of secondary material in terms of what really matters to investors.

The only practical solution to breaking down the tiers of knowledge was to make analysts and companies come out of their hidey holes and talk in front of everybody. The old boys' network was to be broken up as the SEC recognized that millions of investors were now trading on-line, without formal relationships with traditional brokerage houses and their analysts, and were being left out of the loop when it came to important and timely information. Through a company's use of selective or privileged disclosure, information that could have a major impact on a share's price was only getting through to analysts and their clients. At the same time, the SEC viewed this sort of disclosure as an insidious tool companies could use to curry favour with analysts. Analysts who didn't toe the line and flatter a company with upbeat reports could find themselves cut off from valuable information. (Even today, companies routinely include hyperlinks to selected analysts on their Web pages.) With many analysts already compromised by the fact that their pay-cheques were filled by the investment banking activities of their firms, the system had promoted a Darwinian evolution of analysts into corporate cheerleaders. Regulation FD was designed to level the data playing field, salvage the tattered reputations of the analysts, eliminate a natural conduit for insider trading, and bolster public confidence in the equities markets.

"In the old world of regulations, companies talked to analysts privately," Bochner says. "Reg. FD says they can't do that. But the SEC has always considered it illegal to do that." Under the SEC's regulation 10B5 ("fraud on the market"), selective disclosure was not supposed to happen, but to successfully prosecute it, personal gain had to be shown by someone acting on the knowledge. Under Reg. FD, notes Bochner, "you don't have to show personal benefit any more."

Selective disclosure was also illegal under the Ontario Securities Act, but that didn't prevent it from happening. The OSC was in a race to catch up with the reform movement south of the border. Not bringing the TSE, the country's largest financial marketplace, up to the standards of the major American exchanges would invite an even further erosion of confidence on the part of the investment community both at home and abroad. The OSC's compliance and enforcement efforts were notoriously lax, due to chronic underfunding of its investigation branch by the cost-slashing Tories of the Harris government. In November 1998, however, the OSC was turned loose as a self-funding entity, freeing it from the tyranny of budget cuts at Queen's Park. It vowed to strengthen its policing of the market, and a skeptical investment community waited to see evidence of a real change.

On April 28, 2000, the Securities Review Advisory Committee created by Ontario's Minister of Finance released an issues list for public comment. Among the topics was selective disclosure. The SRAC wondered whether the OSC should follow the lead of the SEC in its reforms, which was working toward a final version of Reg. FD at that time. The OSC had also never exercised its power under the Ontario Securities Act to impose its own accounting standards for listed companies. The Act only demanded that financial statements of listed companies ("reporting issuers") be in compliance with generally accepted accounting principles (GAAP) and generally accepted auditing standards (GAAS). The OSC had left the matter of what those standards should be entirely in the hands of the Canadian Institute of Chartered Accountants—who, of course, in the *Hercules* case in 1997, had argued successfully that financial statements were not to be used by individuals as the basis for their investing decisions. "Are traditional GAAP/GAAS financial statements adequate in today's markets?" the SRAC was now asking.

The final version of the SEC's Regulation FD was released on August 15, 2000, with its draft terms significantly refocused. Originally, the regulation was to apply to the dissemination of information to anyone outside the company; to avoid major questions about corporate liability, as well as the possibility that a far-reaching definition of selective disclosure could have a chilling effect on the release of financial information in general, the SEC targeted the final version at "senior [company] officials and those persons who regularly communicate with securities market professionals or with security holders." Let off the hook were lesser employees and, more important, ordinary, course-of-business communications, including pronouncements in the media.

The SEC declared that when

> an issuer, or person acting on its behalf,
>
> (2) discloses material nonpublic information,
>
> (3) to certain enumerated persons (in general, securities market professionals or holders of the issuer's securities who may well trade on the basis of the information),
>
> (4) the issuer must make public disclosure of that same information:
>
> (a) simultaneously (for intentional disclosures), or
>
> (b) promptly (for non-intentional disclosures).

Under the new Reg. FD, companies could still hold special private briefings, including conference calls and Webcasts, for individual analysts, but if anything was said that fell within the domain of guidance (and it was pretty hard not to talk to an analyst without saying something that constituted guidance), then that information had to be made available simultaneously to the investment community at large. And in a case where a "non-intentional" disclosure was made—i.e., the CEO goofed and let something slip—a prompt distribution of the information had to be made.

The leeway for recovering from a non-intentional disclosure is important, because the SEC never intended Reg. FD to be used as a legal bear trap to ensnare accidental or materially insignificant leaks of new information. "In any discussions I've had with someone from the SEC," says Bochner, "they've always said, 'We're not going to use this as a 'gotcha!' Reg. FD is trying to encourage disclosure of public information. FD is the stick, and safe harbour encourages forward-looking disclosure."

Reg. FD is significantly different from overlapping exchange regulations which require prompt public notice of materially significant changes in a company's prospects, financing, or senior management ranks. Reg. FD doesn't simply cover new information that might cause a share price to rise or fall—it also covers any reiteration of information already in the public domain. If a senior executive tells an analyst, "We're sticking by the guidance numbers we released a month ago," selective disclosure has occurred and Reg. FD kicks in.

Bochner says there is a subtle but critical difference in what will or will not violate Reg. FD. "Saying, 'We're not going to update our guidance, but let me tell you what we said earlier' is very different from 'We're still comfortable with our guidance,' or 'There's no change in guidance.'" The first example, says Bochner, does not violate Reg. FD, while the last two, by reiterating guidance in a way that constitutes new guidance, most certainly do.

Reg. FD was a tough new standard for companies and the investment community. If its intention was, in part, to restore the reputations of analysts who could otherwise be manipulated by companies that made selective disclosures to their favourite toadies, in the short term at least, Reg. FD backfired. Already under serious duress because of the investor backlash against cheerleader analysts in the wake of the NASDAQ plunge, the analysts' reputations were cut a further notch by Reg. FD's denial to them of special access to privileged information. No longer "gatekeepers" of valuable corporate news, the analysts appeared even more irrelevant to many investors. And many of those investors believed that, if they had access to the same information (and at the same time) as the analysts, they could make stock calls as good as the pros—even better, because they weren't compromised by a salary drawn from an investment bank.

In truth, there was still an important role for analysts to play in doing what their titles implied: *analyzing.* Sifting through data from various companies, making sense of the fortunes of a particular business sector, weighing the impact of general economic indicators, all required skill and dedication that most do-it-yourself investors simply didn't have. And those investors who thought they could do a better job because they weren't compromised failed to recognize their own compromises. In a bull market, people who invest in a stock in the expectation of capital gains rather than simply dividend income tend to filter news with the unconscious desire to reaffirm their investment decision. Negative news is disregarded or explained away. Any news that might be read as favourable to their investment is given inflated significance. Analysts might be vulnerable to believing their own hype, just as corporate executives were, but it's safe to say that most analysts during the last bull were aware of the compromises they were forced to confront, while on the other hand most independent investors were positively myopic when it came to recognizing their inherent biases.

Nevertheless, investors cheered the arrival of Reg. FD. Nearly 6,000 people wrote to the SEC with comments that were overwhelmingly supportive after the draft version of Reg. FD was released on December 20, 1999.

"The financial services industry needs to change with the times," read one particularly lucid opinion submitted to the SEC via e-mail:

Information is plentiful. Investors are largely educated and intelligent. The financial services industry has its role and provides a valuable service, but information broker shouldn't be one of them.

The proposed regulation would permit part owners of companies—investors—to draw their own conclusions about a company's financial status and future outlook at the *same time* as the financial services firms are making their own assessments. The investor then only has to look past the spin put on the information by the company itself, not try to decipher the motivations of both the company *and* the financial services analysts concurrently.

Fair Disclosure is what the investor wants. Please give us that choice.

Urged another e-mail correspondent: "I see no justifiable reason why some information regarding publicly traded companies should be disclosed only to a select group of analysts. Let the information be disclosed to everyone and allow the gifted analysts to prove their worth without hiding behind a curtain of secrecy."

Both correspondents were Nortel employees.

On October 23, John Hughes, manager of the Ontario Securities Commission's Continuous Disclosure Team, was interviewed by Layth Matthews on the Web site InvestorCanada.com. In the course of their conversation, Hughes was asked about guidance and the pressure companies felt to meet quarterly earnings targets. Hughes replied:

Well there are many aspects to that question. You certainly do hear anecdotally or through other means that we are in a sort of culture where very high pressure is placed on quarterly estimates and companies come under huge pressure both internal and external to make sure that they meet those estimates at all costs.

There have been many examples of course where a company, even a very highly regarded, quite stable company,

missed its estimates by one cent or two cents and was very
heavily punished in terms of the impact on the stock price.

The next day, Nortel missed on the consensus earnings estimate
of analysts for the third quarter by a penny. The rush to dump the
stock was so great that it overwhelmed the TSE.

16

Bargain Hunting

I love Nortel. I own Nortel. I think they have a future. But today's results are a GREAT example of why the numbers don't lie. We can go around with our Multi-Color Optical Glasses all day spouting about the demand for their products, how it is time to buy the bargain rates.

But let's remember that it is still possible to run a good company into the ground (i.e. Sears) and run a good Optical company into the lower mantle (Lucent).

—Post of the day on MotleyFool.com, October 26, 2000

In October, before Nortel released its trauma-inducing third-quarter results, the Rosens' Veritas Investment Research Associates produced another analysis of Nortel. The main concern continued to be the deceptive nature of Nortel's "earnings from operations" figures, but other issues were beginning to accumulate.

The Rosens were devoting a lot of energy to beating down any notion that there might be some logic to Nortel's alternative earnings figures. They refuted the argument that it reflected what the company would look like without all the acquisition-related charges; in other words, that they might provide a window onto future earnings capability, once all the intangibles were finished being amortized. The Rosens didn't buy it. Such an explanation confused different points in time. "Because Nortel continually acquires new companies, it is continually incurring new acquisition-related costs. The 'EPS from operations' figure is essentially like a carrot on a stick: it describes a set of circumstances that can never be reached. Even if Nortel decided to stop making acquisitions today (and the company has said that it won't), it would still be years before the company would no longer have any more acquisition-related costs left to amortize. By then, all the other financial statement inputs would have changed anyway. In short, 'EPS from operations' cannot be described as a window to the future."

Then there was the "amortization charges are just a product of accounting, anyway" theory. That didn't fly, either. "Great, so let's remove from the financial statements *all* of the figures that are based on accounting. And we're left with . . . three blank pages. Hmmm. Origami anyone? The reality is that financial statements are based on accrual accounting. If we want to dispense with accounting, should we also be subtracting accounts receivable from revenue, or are we only interested in adjustments that work to boost the appearance of income? Essentially, there is no logical link that can clearly be explained to investors."

The Veritas report also refuted the notion that it was okay to ignore the amortization of acquisition costs because Nortel was buying these companies with shares, not cash. This simply was not true. Several acquisitions in fact had been done on a cash basis. Cambrian had been acquired for $231 million in cash. Since then, Nortel had also used $32 million in cash for the remaining two-thirds interest in Photonic Technologies and $37 million for Dimension Enterprises. That came to $300 million in cash, used in acquisitions that came with $322 million in intangible assets whose amortization wasn't recognized in Nortel's earnings-from-operations figures.

The only way to accept Nortel's EPS from operations stuff was by also accepting, as the Rosens summed up, that Nortel received $14.6 billion worth of free goodwill from the acquisitions since Bay Networks; that it also received $2.5 billion in in-process R&D and $2.5 billion in acquired technology for free; that it did not incur any special charges, such as severance and restructuring costs, or generate any one-time gains; and only had to pay for the tangible capital assets of its recent acquisitions.

The Veritas report then painted a nightmare growth scenario for its clients in which it suspected Nortel had become trapped. "Suppose your company started buying other companies to gain their technology because your business had fallen behind its peers by recognizing the advent of, say, the Internet five years too late." Zing. In making these acquisitions, the company sets a double-digit revenue growth pattern, quarter after quarter. The market expects this trend to continue, which means the company must go on buying more businesses. "Soon, whenever you come knocking on the door of a potential acquisition, they recognize that you have your back up against the wall because the worst move to make in the market is to let investors think that your company's revenue growth might be slowing down." This gives acquisition targets the upper hand, allowing them to squeeze you harder on premiums above the fair market value. "Now, you could either send a seasoned crack negotiating team to hammer out a fair price for the acquisition, or you could send a monkey. Either way, as long as you use 'EPS from operations' to measure the profitability for your company, the market will not know whether you paid a 10% premium or a 500% premium over the acquisition's fair market value."

The consequence was what the Veritas report called a "huge problem." Since the purchases generally are being made with company shares and not real dollars, does the premium really matter? Well, look at the deal from the other side, it suggested. Because the company being targeted for acquisition knows that the acquiring company is making similar offers to companies like theirs, and is closing deals at the rate of one a month, the targeted company is going to have some concerns about share dilution. And so they're going to negotiate for more shares in the acquiring company than a fair premium would suggest. "The acquiring company is probably more than willing to pay any premium, because all it has to do is go to its basement and print more shares."

The only thing standing in the way of an inflated use of shares in acquisitions and ongoing dilution of the shareholder's equity is the objection of the existing shareholders. But their concerns, the Rosens argued, have been mollified by the EPS from operations figures, which they have taken to reading as legitimate net income. And these investors had also been rewarded in the ascending price of their shares by the mechanics of index fund purchasing, which not only builds momentum into a stock through its position in the index, but may attract more investment dollars than are warranted because escrowed shares in the acquisition deals have made the total float smaller than the index says it is.

The Rosens saw Nortel's acquisition binge as symptomatic of a company compelled, or forced, to acquire its new technology by buying it through high premiums paid for with stock. "We think that taking 60% of sales from products less than 18 months old is a staggering revelation when considered in conjunction with the fact that Nortel seems to acquire a significant portion of its new technology rather than develop it in-house." Indeed, although the Veritas report didn't make this point, it was impossible to separate Nortel's own R&D costs from the acquired technology and in-process R&D it purchased. Canadian R&D tax credits, which are generous, cover a wide variety of activities, not just people in lab coats doing brainy things like discovering the signature background noise of the universe that supports the Big Bang Theory, the way Bell Labs once did. R&D includes activities like shop floor practices and manufacturing innovation. It's stuff that has nothing to do with creating patentable new products. And besides that, who knew how much of Nortel's R&D costs were devoted to welding the acquired technology into their existing product lines? And if in fact it was even going well? Nortel's acquisitions produced long lists of products in development, reported by Nortel with progress expressed as a percentage of completion and target dates for marketability. As with any tech company, it was impossible to know how likely it was that individual products would reach the market on time, or at all. The more you considered R&D, the less certain you could be that there was a large stream of innovation, entirely distinct from the technology and R&D delivered by the succession of acquired companies, coming out of Nortel's various campus facilities.

The Veritas report made the financial case for Nortel acquiring technology rather than coming up with it by itself. In-house R&D cost money, whereas purchased R&D largely required Nortel to fire up the printing press in the basement and turn out some shares. The Veritas report proposed that "Nortel has likely been prevented from conducting much of its R&D 'in house' because it has not had the considerable cash that would have been necessary to pay for the R&D that it decided to acquire. If Nortel could have paid for its in-house R&D with its treasury shares, it likely would have done so."

Nortel's ability to generate positive cash flow was worrying. The Rosens compared Nortel with Cisco and Lucent, showing how Lucent had negative cash flow from operations of $378 million for the nine months ended June 30, while Cisco had positive cash flow of $4.5 billion for the nine months ended April 29. Nortel had just $35 million in positive operating cash flow, on sales of $14.1 billion, for the six months ended June 30.

The Rosens feared that Nortel might be going the way of Lucent, which was evidently having trouble collecting its receivables, based on its high day-sales levels and a failed attempt to sell off $2 billion in obligations that included vendor financing to Winstar Communications. Lucent had discounted the value of the Winstar financing by 10 percent when it included it in the package of obligations. The increasing use of vendor financing was a blight on the telecom equipment sector in general. As the startup long-distance carriers and CLECs ran out of cash and found their borrowing ability either limited or cut off altogether, increased pressure was put on the vendors to supply customers with the financing required to buy their equipment. But the eagerness of the equipment makers to keep closing deals that boosted revenues forced them into financing not just the purchase of their own equipment, but the entire "turn-key" operation created with that equipment. In a way, a company offering total-package vendor financing for a network startup was providing that startup not just with the equipment, but with the operating funds from which it could draw to make the payments on the equipment.

In December 2000, the optical networking on-line journal Light Reading surveyed the vendor financing practices of the major communications equipment suppliers, drawing on company data and SEC filings. It found that Cisco had financing commitments totalling $2.5 billion—"commitments" being the total which could be drawn down. Of that, $625 million had actually been drawn down, and a September report by Morgan Stanley Dean Witter analyst Chris Stix estimated that Cisco would finance 9 to 10 percent of its sales in the coming year with vendor financing.

Lucent had the largest commitment—$7 billion—and had experienced the most trouble with vendor financing. Back in 1998, the company had had a commitment of only $2.3 billion and currently had $1.6 billion of its financing drawn down. Nortel had a commitment of $2.4 billion, of which a healthy $1.4 billion was drawn down, and analysts expected Nortel to increase its commitment in 2001 to $3 to $3.5 billion. Epoch Partners' analysis of Nortel, released on December 12, 2000, showed that its outstanding financing as a percentage of sales over the previous twelve months was 4.6 percent; Light Reading noted that Lucent's percentage of sales consumed by vendor financing in the previous year was 5 percent.

Vendor financing was not only riskier than a straight cash sale—it also promised delays in getting receivables paid and affected cash flow. Nortel's operating cash flow had been deteriorating, suggesting the company was heading into Lucent territory. And Nortel's day sales remained quite high in the first six months of 2000—103, compared to the 110 of Lucent and the 40 of Cisco. While Nortel's day-sales figure had been getting better since 1998, it was still high enough to raise an alarm about Nortel's ability to fund its operations. The company deserved credit for reducing its long-term receivables from $1.4 to $1 billion in the first six months of 2000. Nonetheless, there was still the fact that much of the company's positive cash flow could be attributed to parcelling off bits of its e-commerce security subsidiary, Entrust. Since 1998, Nortel had reduced its ownership of Entrust from 72.9 to 27 percent. It had collected $89 million in 1998 and $76 million in 1999 by selling off chunks of Entrust. In the first quarter of 2000, Nortel realized another $513 million gain, then picked up a further $169 million in the third quarter. In all, divesting about 46 percent of Entrust had contributed $847 million to Nortel's net cash position through "Other Income–Net" gains since 1998. And Nortel had more of this cash-flow-from-divesting in mind, as in September John Roth announced the company's ambition to spin off the entire optical division as a subsidiary company. Although one intention of such a move was to start using a distinct optical operation's shares in acquisitions, rather than those of the parent company, Nortel also planned to sell a portion of its shares for cash.

The Rosens were particularly alarmed by Nortel's insistence on paying dividends in the face of continuing losses. More than $1.47 billion was lost in the first half of 2000, yet the company still paid out dividends totalling $112 million. Worse, for the first time since Roth took over in 1997, the company had a retained earnings deficit. From a retained earnings balance of $967 million in 1999, Nortel had plunged to a deficit of $617 million in the first half of 2000. Paying dividends out of a negative balance, instead of restoring investors' capital, "is vaguely reminiscent of the Ponzi schemes that blighted the capital markets in the early 1990s," the Veritas report warned. "Investors will have to watch this situation closely before reaching any conclusions." By year-end 2000, the retained earnings deficit ballooned to $2.73 billion, even as dividends continued to be paid.

The Rosens also lodged a vociferous complaint that John Roth's compensation was based on revenue growth and the "earnings from operations" figures, rather than GAAP accounting. "Isn't the company really encouraging Mr. Roth to go out and complete any acquisition at any price? It sure seems that way. Not surprisingly, Mr. Roth has already announced or closed 11 acquisitions this year compared to just three in 1999 (and he still has another quarter to go). Is somebody bucking for a fivefold increase in his year-end bonus?"

The Rosens believed that Nortel's stock market price performance was due in large part to its peculiar position in the Canadian market—a "stranglehold" on Canadian equities investing—and not because of the underlying value. If Nortel had been another American company listed on one exchange, its price would never have soared so high. The need of index fund managers to match the index proportions of listed stocks, and of institutional fund managers to at least meet the performance of the index, drew capital into Nortel. "Over the past year, too many Canadian portfolio managers have invested too much money in Nortel not because it is the greatest company ever, but because they have felt a gun pressed to the backs of their necks."

The report came out before the third-quarter results—before portfolio managers took the gun and pointed it at their own heads themselves.

Analysts collectively had been looking for sales of more than $7.5 billion from Nortel in the third quarter, with optical networking sales more than doubling. Instead, Nortel came in at $7.31 billion, with optical sales having increased 90 percent. And having expected earnings per share to come in at 18 cents, analysts were none too pleased by the 17 cents Nortel did deliver.

It was Nortel's first setback since working so hard to regain Wall Street's confidence after the third-quarter debacle of 1998. The impact of the third-quarter results was so astounding that one would have thought that Nortel, and not Lucent, had made the biggest mess of its latest quarter. But Nortel had much farther to fall than Lucent, which had already been beaten up by the markets before the latest round of embarrassments. Nortel had been doing swimmingly up to that point, rebounding from moments of sub-$60 prices on the NYSE since late September to touch $70 on October 23. On the twenty-fourth, the stock managed a high of $68¹³/₁₆. The quarterly results brought the price down by more than $18, to $50³/₄ at day's end, and then the major selloff began.

In Toronto, Nortel volumes overwhelmed the TSE's computers, and trading in Nortel was suspended at noon on the twenty-fifth, sending brokers scrambling onto the NYSE to make deals. Less than 16 million shares had been traded on the NYSE on October 23; on the twenty-fifth, volume fell just shy of 124 million as the price slumped to $44⁷/₈. By October 30 it was at $40—close to where Sagawa implicitly had thought it should be. In Toronto, Nortel had dropped from $102 at close on October 23 to $61.25 just one week later. Nortel had started the year on the TSE at a pre-split price of $137.35, or $68.675 post-split. The entire year's gains had been lost.

As the global leader in optical networking, Nortel's third-quarter performance shortfall sprayed collateral damage through the rest of the communications equipment sector. Investors took Nortel's results as a sign that double-digit growth was no longer in the cards and punished the companies around it. JDS Uniphase dropped 18 percent, Ciena 15 percent. The Nortel correction may have even influenced the value of the Canadian dollar. While the U.S. dollar had strengthened from $1.47 to $1.50 Canadian between the end of August to the end of September, its value had then bobbled between $1.50 and $1.51 for the first three weeks of October. It then went from $1.51 on October 23 to $1.53 on October 30, and had reached $1.56 by mid-November, as Nortel's share price continued its post–October 24 erosion. While it could not have been the sole cause of a longstanding weakening in the Canadian currency, all the highly publicized gloom surrounding the Nortel selloff may have accelerated the decline that fall.

For investors large and small, the October 24 quarterly results were the moment of reckoning, even if they didn't realize it. Nortel's shortfall had surprised even contrarians like Sagawa, who had expected more of the company for the rest of 2000. It would amaze Al Rosen that Nortel missed by a penny on analysts' expectations. With so much leeway in how revenues are allocated to particular quarters, surely Nortel could have found the $30 million necessary to make the analysts happy. The large volumes on the NYSE and TSE suggested a widespread conviction that now was the time to take profits on a stock that had lost half its value since midsummer. The selloff by Canadians may also have been encouraged by the provision in the federal "mini-budget," released the previous week, which dropped the capital gains inclusion rate from 67 to 50 percent. It was a good time for investors to sell stocks and realize losses, which could be applied to gains made earlier in the year.

The stock was so widely held, so fundamental to the welfare of Canadian investment portfolios—from private trading accounts and RRSPs with a few hundred shares to mutual funds to pension funds large and small—that it was difficult to summon impartiality when considering how to react to Nortel's third-quarter disappointment and the ensuing price crash. Perhaps it should not have been surprising that so many people reacted with anger—not toward Nortel, for failing to meet performance targets, but toward analysts who didn't believe in the company's glorious future, and toward investors, both private and institutional, whose ongoing bailout was driving down the share price. This bailout wasn't just mercenary—it was a demonstration of a lack of intestinal fortitude, without which a panic selloff could ruin things for everybody. They also got mad at Alan Greenspan, for allowing interest rates to climb and so make it more expensive for the troubled CLECs and ISPs and all the other telecom acronyms to scrape up the money to buy more networking equipment.

They got mad at the press in Canada, too, for making such a big hullabaloo about the selloff and the price drop. Perhaps the most extraordinary criticism in that vein appeared in the Fall 2000 issue of the *Ryerson Review of Journalism,* published by Ryerson University, home of the country's best known journalism program. In it appeared the article, "Nortel crash coverage was shock journalism at its best." The author was a freelance public-policy researcher named Andrew Reddick.

Reddick was exercised by the "sensationalism" of media coverage perpetrated by the CBC, *National Post,* and *Globe and Mail.* Flaying *National Post's* extensive coverage, he wrote that "the paper might as well have included a graphic listing which bridges were the best to jump from now that everyone's pension plans and mutual funds were in the toilet."

"It is disappointing that news outlets such as the *Globe* and the *Post,* which have strong business sections, resort to only covering such situations only when things gets [sic] really bad," he wrote. "Why weren't their flagship columnists warning about the dangers of Nortel speculation while it was becoming the 'gorilla' it became? Why wasn't there a front-page column by Eric Reguly or Terence Corcoran before the crash warning how dominant the company was in all of the country's mutual funds and pension plans?

"Instead major Canadian newspapers and news shows resorted to shock journalism and sensationalism to try to gain as many viewers or readers as possible."

However, a failure to warn investors about the evils of Nortel before the correction occurred wasn't what actually disturbed

Reddick. On the contrary, what bothered him was that this "sensationalism" was encouraging people to abandon shares in a perfectly good stock. It was the fall of 1998 all over again, according to Reddick, when chief financial officer Wes Scott's performance in New York helped unleash the last big selloff in the company's history. Reddick didn't need to add that Nortel recovered nicely from that indignity. "Nortel hadn't enjoyed such front-page hype until late October when Bay Street—and then the media—freaked out again because of overspeculation," Reddick charged.

It's not clear what Reddick meant by "overspeculation"—was the stock actually overvalued? Was too much speculation going on in the media ranks about Nortel's worth? Were investors overspeculating by bailing out of the stock at the first sign of trouble? Whatever he meant, his main message was that the wrong message had been communicated to the spooked masses in this latest Nortel correction. "Not only did [the media] avoid giving any helpful warnings before October 25 but they also neglected to give any significant attention to the reality afterward: that this was an investor overreaction, that it was likely temporary and that, heck, the stock is now a bargain. The headlines could have read: 'Call your broker, Nortel is on sale.'"

Reddick's "reality" in hindsight was utterly unreal: unreal as a contributor to a publication that prided itself on critiquing the bland corporate nature of mass media castigating this mass media for encouraging people to actually question the security of personal investments and mutual and pension funds that were heavily weighted with Nortel stock. The most widely held stock in Canada had just dropped about $120 billion (Canadian) in market capitalization in one week. At one point on October 25, Nortel helped cleave almost 900 points from the TSE 300 and ended up dragging numerous other tech sector stocks down with it. Apparently this did not merit the bold headlines and pages of coverage—unless, of course, that coverage took care to calm down the proles and stop them from dumping their shares, and even tell them that now was the time to start accumulating Nortel at bargain prices.

Reddick complained that "doomsday-like" headlines on the *Globe and Mail* "basically screamed 'Sell while you can . . . Save yourselves!'"

Which, in retrospect, is exactly what those headlines should have been screaming. Ross Healy had basically screamed it on the Globe's ROBTv back in June and on the CBC in August, well before the correction. Al Rosen had been taking swipes at Nortel's earnings creativity in print since May. But thank goodness for the *Globe's* Kirsta Foss, who wrote about "how Nortel was a great buy" on the front page of the Report on Business section. Reddick also gave the thumbs up to two *National Post* business writers, David Olive and Patrick Bloomfield. Kudos went to Olive for writing (in Reddick's words) that "Nortel was surely going to bounce back and that the drop was temporary." Bloomfield, he cheered, "went a step further, writing that he was 'hopping mad' that investors were so harshly reacting and that he wished the 'media could manage just a few investment facts amid our contribution to the confusion.' He is absolutely right."

Looking back on the coverage of Nortel's big dip, it's hard to see what got Reddick so exercised. The headlines were indeed loud. On October 25, the *National Post's* front pages shouted, "CANADA'S FAVOURITE STOCK TUMBLES" and followed up the next day with "BILLIONS LOST TO NORTEL 'GORILLA.'" But considering the fact that the Nortel spill was the worst day on the TSE in thirteen years, the coverage overall was remarkably restrained and shot through not with panicky disbelief, but a widespread acknowledgement that Nortel had been seriously overvalued the previous summer, and that a correction of some kind had been overdue. There were repeated reminders of the importance of having a balanced portfolio. (The headlines bore no comparison to the loud black type that appeared on the cover of the British tabloid, the *Sun,* following the Black Monday crash of October 9, 1987: "IT'S TIME TO THROW YOURSELF OUT THE WINDOW, FOLKS!")

And Bloomfield had not been at all as bullish, as Reddick had suggested, in his column in the *National Post's* Financial Post section. While he questioned the rationale behind the selloff, and declared that "there was nothing in the latest quarterly report to justify taking it down 26% in a day," he also wrote: "There was no excuse for taking the stock to a high of $124.50 (and a forward price-earnings multiple close to 100)." Bloomfield was weary of the hype around the stock both on the way up and on the way down. "It makes me hopping mad that the smart folk of Bay Street and Wall Street managed to corral so many ordinary investors into this stupid (and self-interested) game." He went on to write, "Having switched from their manic to their depressive phase, the people who give us the good or bad word are now focused on the thought that the crock at the end of the wired-world rainbow does not exist—at least until the telecommunications titans have spent much more money than they can really afford." Bloomfield's column concluded: "The fact of the matter is that the Nortel gravy train was overloaded with investors beguiled by overhyped expectations, making yesterday's derailment of both it and the TSE 300 inevitable."

David Olive, it is true, had taken it upon himself to calm the hordes and reassure them that their money was safe in Nortel. "Nortel is sure to bounce back" was the headline on his front-page column in the *National Post* on October 26. "Nothing in the recent 36-hour panic in Nortel stock changes some essential facts about the company," he counselled, ladling oil on troubled waters. Nortel, he assured the readership, still had a commanding 43 percent share of the "high-speed optical equipment" market, whatever that was. But the optical market, in addition to being in a state of transition with the arrival of new competitors and changing priorities in sector spending, was fragmented into competing and bewildering technologies—SONET versus DWDM, ring topology versus mesh architecture, opaque versus transparent switches, high channel count DWDM versus interface-speed DWDM—and sub-sectors—ultra long haul, long haul, metro, and cross-connect. This "share," wherever it came from, was essentially meaningless for an investor if it was supposed to justify long-term strength in Nortel's share price, particularly when the company's financials contained so many troubling issues, despite Olive's assurances that the "essential facts" about the company (i.e., positive ones) had not changed. And Olive made no recognition of Paul Sagawa's well-founded warnings about an impending downturn in carrier capex spending. While he allowed that "a prolonged slump in Nortel's shares could crimp the company's strategy of using its overvalued stock as 'currency' for takeovers," he nevertheless did not believe this was a cause to bolt from the share-holders' ranks. "Nortel shares have come down, if not to earth, then within spitting distance of bargain-hunting territory. In the mean-time, the company's fundamentals have not changed." He advised that "rebuilding the world's telecommunications network, a project akin to late 18th century railway building, is estimated to be a US$1-trillion job. It will go on for a long time, be characterized by stop-and-go construction, and shower its greatest rewards on the strongest players."

It scarcely seems possible that Olive actually cited the early railway buildout as a positive precedent for Nortel's circumstances, given the widespread impoverishment caused by the railway bubble of the 1840s, but never mind. "For Nortel investors," Olive concluded, "the impor-tant thing to know is that their company, regardless of Bay Street's assessment of it on any given day, is one of perhaps three companies in the world that is capable of acting as a general contractor on the mammoth project to build the next-generation Internet." In all, Olive's front-page column was an extraordinary exercise in investment counselling: thin on reportage, long on received wisdom. Apparently it was exactly what Reddick thought people needed to hear.

Reddick and Olive were far from alone in making the point that the correction was turning Nortel into a bargain. Roth and Nortel launched a PR offensive after the price plummet, using a satellite feed from head office in Brampton to do the rounds of news programs in Canada and the United States. Roth called the price drop "a great buying opportunity." He got a sympathetic reception from *Globe and Mail* reporter Jacqui McNish, who wrote on the twenty-sixth: "Mr. Roth's crime? Nortel's third-quarter results, with a 42-percent oper-ating profit increase that most CEO's would die for, simply wasn't strong enough to keep the telecommunications company's stock price at nose-bleed heights." It was a dark day when an article about the country's most popular stock in the country's largest-circulation business paper confused earnings with revenues, although in these twilight years of the tech boom, the distinction between earnings and revenues persisted as some kind of academic argument for most true believers in a stock's nose-bleed valuation. For it was Nortel's *revenues* that had increased 42 percent over third-quarter 1999. The company didn't have any earnings. While Nortel claimed an "EPS from operations" profit of 18 cents per share, a 64 percent increase from 1999, it also acknowledged a GAAP-based loss of 20 cents. And that was a significant drop from the actual GAAP profit of 1 cent in the previous year.

Commiserating with John Roth's predicament was not the general policy of the *Globe and Mail.* Business columnist Eric Reguly ripped into every available target, declaring that the price correction had turned into "bums" Nortel, the TSE (for having to halt trading), journalists, and, above all, analysts. "Probably the biggest bums in all bumdom were the analysts who retained their mortgage-the-house-and-buy-Nortel recommendations right to the tragic end." He cited Sagawa's work as a rare exception of an analyst actually doing his job. "To be blunt, a lot of [analysts'] research sucks, and you only have to visit the TSE reject bin for proof. There, you will find such former high fliers as Philip Services, Newcourt Credit, Laidlaw, Call-Net, Teleglobe and Loewen Group. All of them carried 'buy' recommendations far longer than they deserved."

Reguly noted that "Nortel was pretty much infallible, according to the research reports. If an analyst expressed doubts about the company's abilities to expand sales at, say, a 40-percent-annual clip forever, there was something wrong with him. . . . One of the analysts' sins is a lack of old-fashioned research, specifically combining research on the company with research on the industry and the economy in which it operates."

Reguly was exasperated by the inability of analysts to produce a "sell" recommendation, even while drastically reducing their twelve-month price forecasts. "The downgrades, such as they were—UBS Warburg, bizarrely, maintained its 'buy' rating even though it dropped its twelve-month price target by almost 50 percent—didn't appear until the bad news was delivered. Thanks a lot, guys."

UBS Warburg wasn't alone in its eccentric pronouncements. Lehman Brothers took its price target down from $100 (U.S.) to $55 and reduced its rating from "outperform" to "buy." Across the board, price targets retreated, but still remained bullishly high, and the positive recommendations were largely reiterated. Scotia Capital dropped its price target from $136 to $122 without offering a rating. TD Securities lowered from $105 (U.S.) to $75 and reiterated its "buy." Merrill Lynch reiterated its "buy" and stayed with $80 (U.S.). Griffiths McBurney & Partners maintained its "buy" and reduced the target from $103 (U.S.) to $80. Dresden Kleinwort Benson Securities reiterated its "buy" and dropped its target from $111 (U.S.) to $96. CIBC World Markets reiterated its "strong buy" and a target of $110 (U.S.). BMO Nesbitt Burns maintained its "market perform" and reduced its target from $110 (U.S.) to $80. And Gerard Klauer upgraded Nortel from "outperform" to "buy" and boosted its target from $75 (U.S.) to $83.[18]

In twelve months, Nortel was trading at $9.25 on the TSE and $5.81 on the NYSE.

The Nortel bargain-hunting theme was supported by Fred Ketchen, Scotia Capital's chief of equities trading. "This teaches you once again that the stock market is the least predictable of all things, for goodness' sake," he told the *National Post* on October 25. "Some people in this situation do panic, but one person's panic is another person's opportunity. I think there are buying opportunities here."

The nineties' bull market had been through corrections of various scale, and despite pronouncements going on four years now by Robert Shiller that the thing was seriously overvalued, the beast kept bouncing back. Even with the NASDAQ in a downward spiral since April, investors had become conditioned to view reversals not as a long-term downward trend, but as a market hiccup to be taken advantage of by loading up on "undervalued" stocks and riding them to fresh heights. It was an unfortunate consequence of the rising popularity of momentum investing. Many market players had put aside any consideration of fundamentals and were acting on hunch and groupthink.

An article whose faith in Nortel rivalled that of Reddick's was written by Kevin Press, editor of *Benefits Canada* magazine, the trade journal of the pension industry. The title of his December 2000 editorial—"Buy Nortel"—catalogued his remarkable struggle to buy shares in the traumatized stock as all hell broke loose over Nortel's third-quarter results. Press swam frantically against the current, trying to get his hands on shares of a company he plainly thought was undervalued by a panicky market.

He wrote how, at ten o'clock on October 25, "Nortel Networks is dropping like a bomb. Something about weak sales in the optical department. *Canadian Investment Review* publisher Lori Bak is the first to utter the words 'buying opportunity.' I like the cut of her jib."

When Nortel fell below $70 for the first time since April around eleven o'clock, Press decided to call his broker and place a limit order at $73 or less. But between the volumes causing the TSE to crash that day and the backlog of buy and sell orders, Press's limit order was cancelled. In the end, he was forced to buy at market value on October 27. The stock opened at $74 and finished at $65.50. Press never said what he paid, or how many he bought. But as he admitted, "I'm now one of those pension plan members obsessed with the stock market. I've had tse.com up on my computer since Wednesday morning [October 25]. I am thinking about worker productivity."

As Nortel's price slid following the October 25 earnings crisis, Canadians who didn't have a lick of money in the stock market stopped to think that maybe, after all, they did. They thought about their pension plans, the defined benefit nest eggs that were left to professional managers to handle for them. At the Ontario Public Service Employees Union (OPSEU) Pension Trust, known as OPTrust, the calls started coming in from the rank and file membership. OPSEU represented people like municipal workers and prison guards, not a demographic given to throwing huge wads of cash at speculative ventures. In its Winter 2001 newsletter, OPTrust soothed fears that Nortel's problems might spill over into the members' retirement funds. "Market fluctuations? Your plan's protected!" read the headline on a reassuring article, explaining the trust's diversification program and the mechanics of defined benefit plans. In a sidebar story that addressed Nortel, the trust indicated that between the end of 1999 and September 29, 2000, the value of the plan's Nortel holding had increased from $280 million to $573 million.

The article explained that the increase in the holding's value

> was largely a result of a 2-for-1 stock split and an increase in the
> proportion of the Toronto Stock Exchange 300 Index represent-
> ed by Nortel. Over the same period OPTrust sold a portion of
> our Nortel shares. As a result, at the end of September Nortel
> represented 5.5% of the OPSEU Pension Fund's total market
> value of about $10.4 billion.
>
> On October 31, OPTrust's Nortel holdings were valued at
> $471 million. The change from the previous month reflects
> both the decline in Nortel's stock price and trading activity by
> OPTrust's investment managers.
>
> Overall, the OPSEU Pension Plan Fund continued to
> grow over the first 10 months of 2000. Final investment
> results for the year will be reported in OPTrust's 2000 Annual
> Report, due out in April. A summary version of the report will
> be mailed to all members and pensioners.

The article was meant to assure pension plan members that everything was fine as far as Nortel went. But a quick bit of work with the calculator would have allowed members to read between the lines. If OPTrust had maintained a steady-state position in Nortel from the end of 1999 through to the split in May 2000, it would have had about 1.9 million shares. Because OPTrust began and ended the year with about 2.1 million BCE shares, it's reasonable to assume that at the time of the butterfly divestment, OPTrust received about 1.7 million Nortel shares as a dividend. Adding those shares to its existing holding and running them through the split should have created 7.2 million shares. But by September 20, the fund held 5.6 million shares, based on the portfolio value of $570 million. OPTrust had evidently done some profit taking, or bailing, shedding 1.6 million shares. And as the article indicated, OPTrust had in fact "sold a portion" of its Nortel holding during this period.

But since September 20, OPTrust had begun accumulating Nortel. By October 31, when Nortel finished trading at $69.10 after the October 25 disaster, a holding worth $470 million represented

6.8 million shares. OPTrust had gone bargain hunting. As the article indicated, plan members would not know how many Nortel shares OPTrust held at year-end 2000 until its annual report was released the following April. By then, it would be far too late to fret about the fund's Nortel strategy. Plan members would learn that, at year-end, OPTrust's Nortel holding had grown to 7.6 million shares—two million higher than in late September.

Buying shares in a respected stock when its price weakens generally is a good idea, if there is reasonable hope of a price recovery. But when an investor already holds shares in a dropping stock, buying more as the price slides is known as dollar-cost averaging. Intuitively, it seems like the wrong thing to do. After all, if the price drops even more, you've thrown more good money after bad and will suffer absolute losses on the later purchases, just as you will on the earlier ones. But in the accounting logic of portfolio management, dollar-cost averaging *reduces* losses, by lowering the average cost of its overall holding.

If you own 1,000 shares for which you paid $50 each, and the price drops to $30, you've lost $2,000. If you buy another 1,000 at $30, you've still lost the $2,000 on the original investment, but your average holding price has dropped from $50 to $40. From that perspective, you're only $10 down from your average share cost. The drop looks smaller. And if the share price keeps dropping, to $20, by having invested more at $30, you've "reduced" your per-share loss from $30 to $20. Of course, at the same time, you've increased your absolute loss, from $3,000 on the original investment of 1,000 shares at $50, to $4,000 on the net investment of 8,000 shares at $40.

If the share price rebounds above $40, you'll break even sooner than you would have, had you stayed with the original investment at $50. And nothing helps a portfolio measured on a year-to-year performance basis more than finishing one year with a nice stash of shares with a cheap net cost. But dollar-cost averaging can magnify losses if the price just keeps going downhill. You end up throwing good money after bad, over and over again, trying to reduce your net holding cost. With each purchase at a lower price, the average share cost gets better, but in real terms your portfolio losses keep mounting as the price slides further south.

The fourth quarter of 2000 proved to be an investment sinkhole for many Nortel investors. OPTrust wasn't the only pension plan loading up on Nortel. CAAT increased its portfolio by about 600,000 shares between September 30 and December 31. Bargain hunting also brought in investors who didn't yet have any Nortel shares, setting them up for a major loss. Dollar-cost averaging by existing investors brought down net costs, but only exposed them to much greater losses.

However, while OPTrust might have appeared to be dollar-cost averaging in the fourth quarter of 2000, on a year-over-year basis it actually increased the average value of its Nortel shares. By the end of 2000, OPTrust's Nortel holdings had doubled, from a split-adjusted 3.85 million shares to 7.63 million shares, and their average cost had more than doubled, from $13.28 to $28.97. OPTrust's total investment in Nortel was also up, from $51.1 million to $221 million. And while this didn't reflect any gains OPTrust would have made on selling off Nortel shares in the summer of 2000, it also didn't reflect the damage done to the value of its BCE holding by the Nortel spinoff.

As noted, OPTrust had about as many BCE shares at the end of 2000 as it did at the beginning: around 2.1 million. Its per-share paper gain—the difference between its investment cost and the market price—was $97.98 at the end of 1999. By the end of 2000, the gain was down to $25.83. The per-share drop was $52.15, and the market value drop of the total holding was $195 million. We've already seen that OPTrust must have unloaded about 1.6 million Nortel shares between the May divestiture/split and September 20. If it sold every single one of them at the very height of trading ($124.50, an unlikely but best-case scenario), they would have been worth $199 million. It's more than likely that any gains on divesting Nortel were amply offset by losses in the value of BCE.

Going into 2001, then, OPTrust had twice as many Nortel shares as it started 2000 with (owing in part to the BCE divestiture) and had paid on average more than twice as much for them. The buying activity in the last quarter had served to up-average OPTrust's holding in Nortel. Its break-even point was now far higher, and its exposure to losses was also greater, with the value of the Nortel holding having increased from $280 to $368 million.

By remarkable coincidence, if Nortel went into a real skid, OPTrust would hit its break-even point of $28.97 at almost exactly the same time that the rest of the market encountered its John Roth Loss Threshold—the point at which shares fell below the split adjusted value of $13.31 that the stock enjoyed when Roth assumed Nortel's presidency in 1997.

17

What Logic Dictates

Apparently, if the majority of analysts are wrong at the same time it's somehow acceptable.
—Larry Barrett, Staff Writer, CNET News.com,
November 10, 2000

To stem the bleeding of its share price after the release of its third-quarter results, Nortel went on the PR offensive. The word out of Brampton was relentlessly positive. In addition to a steady barrage of press releases, announcing one new sales agreement after another, on November 1, Nortel confirmed the guidance for 2000 and 2001 it had issued with the quarter's results. According to its SEC filing:

The Registrant continues to expect its percentage growth in revenue and earnings per share from operations in 2000 over 1999 will be in the low 40's. The Registrant also expects its revenue and earnings per share from operations in the fourth quarter of 2000 will be in the range of US$8.5 billion to US$8.8 billion and US$0.26 per share on a fully diluted basis, respectively. Overall, the Registrant expects continued strong growth in Optical Internet, Wireless Internet, Local Internet and eBusiness solutions. The Registrant continues to expect its Optical Internet revenues to grow in excess of 125 percent in 2000 over 1999, to exceed US$10 billion.

Looking forward to 2001, the Registrant continues to expect the overall market to grow in excess of 20 percent. The

Registrant also continues to expect to grow significantly faster than the market, with anticipated growth in revenues and earnings per share from operations in the 30 to 35 percent range. For the first quarter of 2001, consistent with historical profile trends, the Registrant expects its revenue and earnings per share from operations will be in the range of US$8.1 billion to US$8.3 billion and US$0.16 per share on a fully diluted basis, respectively.

The reiterated guidance brought no solace to the Rosens. Notwithstanding David Olive's reassurances in the October 26 *National Post* that nothing in the panic selloff of Nortel shares changed "some essential facts about the company," the Rosens were unable to relinquish their morbid curiosity with what those facts actually were. On November 9, Veritas Investment Research released a report on Nortel, authored by Mark Rosen. "Nortel's recent price correction was hung largely on revenue expectations retreating from dreamland," he wrote. "What will happen when the market realizes that the company's 'earnings from operations' figure is inherently illogical?"

In pursuit of the answer, Rosen decided to conduct a thought experiment. The reason so many people, including accredited analysts, seemed willing to go along with Nortel's supplementary earnings figures—believing, for starters, that the company did not lose $2.1 billion in the first nine months of 2000—was that most of those acquisition-related costs had been paid for with shares, not cash. The implication was that the amortization charges triggered by the value of the shares used didn't reflect an actual expense.

The cost of any share-based acquisition was, admittedly, somewhat arbitrary. The differences in U.S. and Canadian GAAP in the case of the Bay Networks deal produced two very different prices— $9.1 versus $6.9 billion, with the difference affecting the amount of amortized goodwill. But, for the Rosens, that still didn't justify Nortel removing the amortization charges for in-process R&D and acquired technology from its earnings-from-operations calculations.

The displeasure of the Rosens with Nortel's decision to award itself free technology and R&D in its earning-from-operations numbers doesn't require elaboration. Mark Rosen was determined to make the company pay for it somehow. The easiest way to impose the cost on Nortel was simply to add back the amortization charges for IPR&D and acquired technology to the company's earnings-from-operations figure—in effect treating these costs as if Nortel had conducted the R&D work itself, and recognizing them as part of Nortel's usual deduction of R&D expense. But this, as Rosen explained, didn't work. Adding back the "fair value" of IPR&D and acquired technology (as determined by Nortel in accounting for the total acquisition costs) would not properly reflect what it would have actually cost Nortel to conduct the same activities itself.

Elaborating, he noted the differences between U.S. and Canadian GAAP in dealing with in-process R&D. Canadian guidelines allowed a company to capitalize IPR&D—to turn it into an asset and put it on the balance sheet, and amortize its expense over time. U.S. GAAP, on the other hand, required a company to expense the entirety of acquired IPR&D at the time of the acquisition. It was never capitalized, never amortized. "We think that the U.S. requirement is a fairer reflection of the transaction because the company has essentially acquired expenses. That is, if the company were to have conducted the R&D itself, the costs would have likely been expensed."

Mark Rosen emphasized that the "difference between cost and fair value also has to be addressed. If a company does not undertake research and development itself, it almost always has to pay a premium in order to acquire the R&D. The premium is represented by goodwill and usually reflects the difference between the fair value of the R&D and what it cost the acquired company to conduct the R&D." This meant that Nortel would have to pay a premium, as reflected by goodwill, for acquired R&D, whether it used cash or shares to pay for it. Therefore, some of the true cost of that acquired R&D was reflected in the goodwill charge.

And whether a company used shares or cash to purchase IPR&D had a big impact on total goodwill. Buying a company with shares instead of cash immediately means a deal's value goes up, because the seller demands a higher price when inherently riskier Nortel shares rather than American dollars are used as currency—and the greater the waiting period for some or all of those shares to come out of escrow, the higher the risk becomes and so the higher the premium will be. You might say there were in fact two premiums at work in Nortel's acquisitions: the base premium, as reflected in the excess value of IPR&D cost over fair value, which was embodied in the goodwill, and then the premium on the premium, or "premium premium," which inflated goodwill when Nortel used shares instead of cash for the acquisition.

Mark Rosen had reasoned his way to the position where he could accept working out Nortel's true profitability (rather than the GAAP one) if the base premium could be determined on its many acquisitions. In other words, what would Nortel have paid for all these acquisitions if it had used cash instead of shares? If Rosen could figure that out, and amortize it appropriately, perhaps he could draw a more honest profitability picture. It wouldn't be as wildly optimistic as Nortel's earnings-from-operations, but it would be a lot better than the GAAP one based on goodwill generated by purchases mostly made with shares.

Rosen had to make a fairly arbitrary decision on the premium value. Nortel had done only a handful of cash-based acquisitions, but in every case the relative goodwill was much, much lower than in the share-based acquisitions. He selected the largest of the cash acquisitions, Cambrian, for which goodwill was 19 percent of the total consideration—in the share-based acquisitions, goodwill ranged from 48 to more than 90 percent. "We ask that readers not get hung up on the choice," Rosen wrote. For as he noted, raising or lowering that goodwill consideration was a no-win situation for Nortel. If it went higher, the company's past performance looked worse, but if it went lower, the future prospects for Nortel's stock dropped with it.

We'll explain why later, but first, let's consider the results of Rosen's thought experiment. By recasting eleven past acquisitions being amortized by Nortel on a cash-basis premium of 19 percent, the total purchase consideration fell from $20.33 billion to $6.2 billion, and goodwill went from $14.56 billion to $1.17 billion. "It seems like a bit of a leap to assume that Nortel could have saved as much as $13.39 billion of its share currency had it just used cash for its acquisitions, but let's run with it for a moment."

By recasting Nortel's most recent third-quarter results, assuming a "cash" cost for IPR&D, Rosen achieved earnings per common share of 10 cents—not as good as Nortel's claim of 19 cents under its earnings-from-operations math, but a lot better than the 20-cent loss under GAAP. This was mainly achieved by lopping more than $800 million in goodwill amortization from the GAAP numbers.

But would this slender profit translate into a profitable year? Unfortunately, it didn't look like it. Already, for the first nine months of 2000, Rosen's recalculations produced a 5-cent loss per share, which was still far superior to the actual GAAP loss of 71 cents. And Rosen seriously doubted that, with the Alteon and Sonoma acquisitions closing in the fourth quarter, Nortel could pull off a profit even under his generous accounting option. Were Nortel to allocate a majority of the acquisition costs on these last two deals to acquired technology and its longer amortization period rather than IPR&D (which turned out not to be the case), Rosen could imagine—just barely—Nortel turning an adjusted profit of 10 cents in the fourth quarter for a profit of a nickel per share for the whole year. But that would also mean Nortel was currently trading 830 times above these 2000 "adjusted earnings."

Worse, it wouldn't take much, even with cash-equivalent acquisition charges, for Nortel to go negative with these adjusted earnings. Taking the goodwill on the acquisitions up to the 30 to 35 percent range—far below the actual goodwill proportion of Nortel's share-based acquisitions—would be enough to erase the nickel profit.

"Could Nortel really have paid $13.4 billion more for using shares instead of cash?" Rosen wondered. There was no comforting answer. If you used a low proportion of goodwill like 19 percent to arrive at a real value for the acquisitions in the name of improving Nortel's earning performance, you created a huge disparity between the value of cash and the value of Nortel shares. The bigger the difference between "cash" value and "share" value for the acquisitions, the higher the risk factor that was implicitly attached to Nortel's shares. By insisting on receiving a number of shares that created such a huge goodwill premium, the acquired company's shareholders were massively discounting the value of Nortel shares as set by the current price. That discount said that there was a serious risk of a significant price correction at some point in the not-so-distant future. Escrow periods for acquisitions generally don't extend more than eighteen months—and in the upcoming Nortel deal for the JDS Uniphase property, it would turn out that the escrow period was one year. Consequently, the high "premium premium" suggested that the acquired companies' shareholders had a profound lack of confidence in Nortel's share value over a relatively short time frame. "The higher the premium paid," Rosen noted, "the higher the risk of holding the stock. Therefore, the more we assume that Nortel could have saved by using cash, the more we assume that Nortel's stock price is risky in the long run."

To reduce the implicit risk factor attached to Nortel shares in these acquisitions, you would have to argue that the goodwill proportion should be higher than 19 percent in the cash-reassessed deals, but that just created more goodwill charges and drove Nortel's earnings back into the red. By Rosen's argument, investors could not have it both ways. They could not plead that the amortization charges in goodwill that put Nortel in the red were unfair because they weren't real cash, because the moment you started considering the alternative of using cash for those acquisitions, the disparity between a cash price and the share-bought price cranked up the risk level of the stock. And the more you tried to reduce the implicit risk, the more unprofitable you made the company.

Although this wasn't specifically addressed in the November 9 report, investors and analysts who liked to think of the shares issued as not really being cash weren't being logical. The fact was, Nortel had issued what became hundreds of millions of shares to buy these companies. Its shares traded on the major markets for the actual prices on which the cost of the deals were calculated. Treasury shares were being issued that diluted an individual share's claim on earnings. Apologists for the share-purchase spree had to think of those shares in a different but perfectly reasonable way: what if Nortel had sold those same shares on the open market and received actual cash for them instead of mounds of intangible assets? Capital would have been available for Nortel to buy all the startups it wanted (at lower premiums) or to fund research in-house.

There had to be a measurable consequence to pumping millions upon millions of shares out the door. But investors had fallen into a strange mindset—based on Nortel's earnings-from-operations numbers and a market that just kept driving up the share price, no matter how much money Nortel actually lost under GAAP—which held that things really were free. Shares weren't real money, and intangibles like R&D and technology could be had for nothing. And if billions of dollars in goodwill was created at the same time, well, that was free too. Or at least it didn't really exist.

One way to defend Nortel's earnings-from-operations accounting was to argue that it was entitled to overlook IPR&D and acquired technology because those costs didn't represent expenses incurred by present revenues. While the company itself made no claim to this, this had a compelling, if troubling logic, because pro forma-type earnings are meant to strip away charges that mask a company's "true" profitability. But if you accepted this as the rationale for Nortel's earnings-from-operations, then you also had to accept that the billions in acquisitions from Bay Networks onwards hadn't yet made a significant contribution to revenues commensurate with their expense. This was impossible to quantify because Nortel had absorbed its acquisitions into its existing operating groups, making their individual contributions untrackable. Rosen suspected that these acquisitions, consistent with Nortel's custom accounting, indeed hadn't done much for revenues. "The issue we are confronted with most by investors is that the majority of Nortel's current revenue does not come from its recent acquisitions, but rather from its proprietarily produced 10-gigabit and other optical technology," Rosen noted. "So the question that not enough people are asking is why has Nortel made all of its recent acquisitions, if the acquired technologies have not added anything to the bottom line." While most people, observed Rosen, believed that Nortel expected the acquisitions to produce abundant future revenues, he proposed that perhaps Nortel bought them just because it could. A high share price allowed it to use its shares as currency and buy companies where cash reserves would never have allowed. And why? Maybe it was merely to keep these companies from being bought by somebody else.

Rosen didn't elaborate any further, but he had made the plausible case that the recent acquisition spree was in effect part of a grand chess game between the major networking companies, each of them swallowing up companies not only, or even necessarily, to enhance their own technology portfolios or add critical strategic assets, but to stop a rival from owning them. For all the controversy about the value of the Bay Networks acquisition, for example, it cannot be weighed without considering the fact that by acquiring it, Nortel cut Lucent off from a major supplier and prevented Lucent from making the purchase itself.

So how many of Nortel's recent acquisitions had it really needed? Did it make any sense that Nortel was steadily divesting itself of Entrust, an e-commerce security outfit, while at the same buying Clarify, a purveyor of front-office e-commerce software? Wasn't some hallowed synergy being lost in the process? And after surrendering billions of dollars' worth of common shares to acquire a slew of technology companies without a marketable product, what hope did it have of actually coming out with a marketable product that justified the acquisition cost? Ironically, in these deals with extreme levels of goodwill, it was the seller who was being compensated for risk by being issued such generous numbers of Nortel shares. The risk to Nortel shareholders—that the company might not be able to turn acquired technology and IPR&D into a profitable product that justified the share dilution—wasn't addressed at all. Of course, if Rosen was right, and Nortel, Lucent and Cisco were acquiring companies just to keep them away from each other, then coming up with marketable product was an afterthought.

On balance, Nortel generally seems to have been in pursuit of technology it legitimately desired, and there had been some undeniable successes. The Shasta acquisition in April 1999 allowed Nortel to offer the Passport line of ATM switches for wide area networks (WANs). It quickly leapfrogged the market domination Lucent had enjoyed through its acquisition of Ascend earlier in 1999 to claim a

37 percent share of the global market, ahead not only of Lucent, but of Cisco as well. The Qtera and Cambrian purchases would also be labelled a success by Epoch Partners in its December 2000 coverage of Nortel, as they had given Nortel valuable heft in the long-haul and metro-optical networking markets. But in the case of Bay Networks, as we've seen, the hoped-for high-speed optical Internet router hadn't materialized, and Nortel had to resort to a partnership agreement with Juniper announced June 29, 2000, that let it sell the Cisco-killing M160. Clarify's software presented numerous problems in the effort to adapt it to Nortel's total-solutions e-commerce offering. And repeated delays in producing an optical cross-connect switch with the technology acquired in the $3.25 billion Xros deal would prove increasingly distressing to investors.

Nortel was beginning to develop a reputation among its detractors as a company that had lost the ability to develop cutting-edge products in-house, without buying them through expensive acquisitions. And even then, turning those acquisitions into marketable products had in some cases proved difficult or impossible. It was by no means a disease unique to Nortel. All the networking companies that had decided that buying, rather than developing, technology was the cheaper way, were beginning to find themselves vulnerable to the successive waves of startups. Competitors like Juniper, Corvis, and Ciena were presenting a serious threat. There came a point when there were just too many good startups for the established players to hope to buy them all, either because of their numbers, or because after the recent acquisition sprees, the networking giants couldn't go back to the printing press in the treasury department for enough shares. And the pooling method of acquisitions so effectively exploited by Cisco and Lucent was on track to be outlawed by the Federal Accounting Standards Board in 2001.

Mark Rosen raised the provocative if unhappy possibility of how profitable Nortel might have proved to be, even under GAAP accounting, if it hadn't gone on its recent acquisition binge. "If Nortel's recent acquisitions really haven't added to the company's revenue, we estimate that Nortel could be reporting 2000 net income of roughly [U.S] $1.50 per share [under U.S. GAAP]." To be fair, not all those acquisitions could be completely dismissed. Some, like Shasta and Cambrian, had unquestionably contributed new technology that was already realizing revenues for Nortel, albeit at a considerable acquisition cost. But Rosen's point was well worth considering. How much better off would Nortel shareholders be if John Roth hadn't launched such an aggressive, all-encompassing acquisition program and had focused on Nortel's core strength of optical networking, making more selective acquisitions, spending more money in-house on R&D, and striking strategic alliances (such as the recent one with Juniper Networks) rather than buying entire companies at premiums inflated by the use of shares as currency?

"The truly sad part of our analysis is that the more we tried to make Nortel's adjusted performance look better by discounting the premium that was paid for with shares," Rosen concluded, "the worse Nortel's long-term outlook appeared. Basically, any argument that Nortel's losses should be ignored because of the generous use of its share currency, is inherently illogical. Thus, Nortel pundits better act quickly to come up with a new justification for the company's share price, or else the recent correction could seem mild in comparison to what logic dictates is coming down the road."

At Nortel, logic dictated no such thing. Twelve days after the Veritas report was released, Nortel opened its annual investors conference in Boston on November 21. In advance of the conference, Nortel released a statement announcing that it would "emphasize gains in customers and market share for its end-to-end Internet solutions across its key markets. Nortel Networks continues to see strong demand for its city-to-city Optical Internet capabilities and is extending this leadership position into new high-growth opportunities such as high-speed Optical Internet within cities and Wireless Internet. Overall, the Company is accelerating to new levels of leadership in the Optical and Wireless Internet market. The Company will also emphasize its strong outlook and guidance for the fourth quarter of 2000, fiscal year 2000, the first quarter of 2001, and fiscal year 2001."

In the statement, John Roth was quoted as saying, "We continue to expect that our percentage growth in revenue and earnings per share from operations in 2000 over 1999 will be in the low 40's." He also said, "As we enter the final month of the quarter, we are very confident in our previously stated guidance of revenue and earnings per share from operations in the fourth quarter of 2000. . . . Overall, we expect continued strong growth in Optical Internet, Wireless Internet, Local Internet and eBusiness solutions. We continue to expect our Optical Internet revenues to grow in excess of 125 percent in 2000 over 1999, to exceed US$10 billion."

Roth also reiterated Nortel's guidance for 2001. The overall market would grow in excess of 20 percent, but with "our strong market position and leadership in high-performance Internet solutions, we continue to expect to grow significantly faster than the market. . . ."

The release also explained that in presentations at the investor conference, Nortel executives would "emphasize the company's strong outlook based on robust demand and market share gains." According to Roth, "The Internet revolution and bandwidth demand curve have just begun. Our leading capabilities spanning Optical, Wireless, Local Internet and eBusiness, represent a broad, balanced high-growth portfolio. Our growth in these areas is supported by our leadership in, and the strong demand we are seeing for, our city-to-city Optical capabilities in North America, Europe and now Asia. Our first-mover advantage in 40/80 Gbps Optical Internet, Wireless Internet and high-performance eBusiness solutions, and the growing demand for high-speed Optical capabilities within cities across all geographies are also contributing to our momentum."

The executives also emphasized that Nortel would continue to grow faster than the market "by focusing on high-growth areas, driving profitability and streamlining operations for efficiencies. The company is uniquely positioned to balance supply with demand and take advantage of one of the most powerful supply webs in the industry. Executives will also point to robust global demand. Nortel Networks is building 34 of 40 major fiber optic network projects underway worldwide, including the first four 10Gbps networks in the People's Republic of China (PRC). Also in the PRC, Nortel Networks has won wireless networks contract awards in 17 of the 31 provinces. The company is also maintaining its first mover advantage in 3G Wireless in

Europe with recent wins with BT Cellnet, Xfera and Airtel."

It was impossible to reconcile Mark Rosen's glum view of Nortel's imminent future and the company's own aggressive self-confidence. One of them would be proven spectacularly wrong, in a spectacularly short time.

By selling out of his Nortel position before the May split, Terry Blackman, the retired Y2K specialist, missed out on the summer high of $124.50. He watched the stock make its heady ascent without him, and then saw it begin to retreat in September, trading regularly below $100. "There did not appear to be any reason for the drop, as the analysts were still setting target prices up to $200 Canadian, so I bought another 500 shares at $96," he says.

When the third-quarter results sent Nortel shares reeling, Blackman tried not to become part of the panic selling. "I watched patiently as they dropped to $70, then $50. I sold 300 at $53.50, much against the advice of my broker, who had just bought some at $59." In two months, Blackman had lost about $12,000, thereby erasing the quick $10,000 he had made on Nortel in the spring. And he still had 200 shares, purchased for $19,200, on which he had a paper loss of $8,500. He hung in with them, waiting for the turn-around the company's reassurances seemed to promise.

For David Chmelnitsky, who was investing in broadband stocks while toiling at the TSE for IBM, the market's slide as year-end approached was both an ordeal and an opportunity. He had been doing some of his investing on margin, no more than 5 percent of the total portfolio, but as investments like JDS Uniphase and Broadcom fell like bricks from their summer trading highs, he learned how a seemingly small proportion of margin investing could trigger large losses. Broadcom, which had been above $270 (U.S.) in August, was below $150 by October and was headed for less than $30 by the following April. JDS Uniphase, which had been above $150 in March, was down to $50 by the end of October. As share prices went into free-fall and the calls came in from his broker, requesting that he cover the margin, he was forced to sell out of positions, locking in major losses.

As Nortel fell, however, at least he had no position in it, and like so many other investors he was encouraged to view the fourth-quarter drop as a buy opportunity. At the time, his RRSP had a large cash position. He could have taken the money out of it and covered the margin on his trading losses outside the RRSP account, but that would have triggered a tax bill. Instead, he swallowed the margin losses and looked for new opportunities within his RRSP. With plenty of cash, he was well equipped to get back into Nortel and any other stock that looked like a year-end bargain.

"I was like a kid in a candy shop in November and December. Everything had been demolished. Nortel's sitting at $45 to $50 and I'm talking to friends who are traders. They're saying, 'A good rule of thumb is, don't get caught up in all the hype, don't buy then. You wait for the 10 percent up-rise, and pull the trigger. That's what I'm doing.'"

So he waited, resisting the temptation to buy into what could turn out to be a dead-cat bounce—a fleeting rally in a stock or a market index that's only going to plunge further. He was cautious because he knew he wasn't a pro like the traders he spoke with every day at the TSE. He didn't have the day-trader's illusions of having all the answers. "I remember thinking, 'I'm not a trader. I'm not going to fall into that trap.' I know enough at the TSE to know this is not a game. As an investor, I was average, if not below average. A novice. Originally, I had thought, 'I'll do this because I'm making money on it, and it's fun. And I'm buying stocks that I don't mind owning if they tank. I don't want to have to bail on them. Am I comfortable owning Nortel from an investment perspective? Yes.'"

He had at least made a fair bit of money selling call options on shares when prices were buoyant. He might have a stock currently trading at $120. Chmelnitsky would sell calls on his shares at $125 for $4,000 that would expire in a few weeks. If the stock went to $122, the call wouldn't be exercised and he'd made $4,000. If the stock went to $128 and it was exercised, he would be forced to sell at $125, but at least he'd get some capital gains from the shares and also have the $4,000. He never attempted the far riskier activity of trading in options themselves. At the same time, he didn't consider hedging his investments, buying puts to protect the downside risk. His downside risk management consisted of "If the stock drops, so be it. I'm in for the long haul. It's not like the ones I pick are going to go right through the floor."

His patience with staying out of Nortel lasted until December 11. Nortel's recovery appeared well established. From its post-third-quarter low of $49 on November 17, the stock had recovered into the high fifties and low sixties. On December 8, Nortel made a significant jump, after Nortel issued a press release noting encouraging words from the consulting firm RHK. A new study indicated Nortel had passed Ciena as the market leader in wave division multiplexing in Europe. RHK also refuted the gloom, encouraged by the Sagawa report back in September, that the optical market was going to be in trouble in 2001. "As indicated in our report, we see no signs of a slowdown in the optical communications market and expect carriers and service providers to continue spending on high-capacity transport systems," Stephane Teral, director, European optical transport for RHK, was quoted as saying in the Nortel release. "In fact we have slightly increased our forecasts."

Nortel, which had closed at $58.80 on the TSE on December 7, finished December 8 at $65.45. After the markets closed for the weekend, Nortel opened at $65.70 on December 11. Nortel issued another press release, announcing it would be building an ATM data network for Mexico's Telefónica Data. Nortel got as high as $69.85 before finishing at $65.

On his first day back at work at the TSE after the weekend, David Chmelnitsky was sure the dead-cat bounce was behind Nortel. Volumes, which had been as low as 2.1 million back on November 23, had almost doubled, from 7.2 to 13.6 million, between December 7 and 8 as prices moved upward. On December 11, Chmelnitsky pulled the trigger, buying 2,000 shares at $67, thereby betting $134,000 in retirement savings on John Roth's assurances that the company was heading for an even better year than the last.

He had bought back into Nortel just in time to hear that John Roth had been selected as Canada's Newsmaker of the Year by *Time* Canada, which bookended nicely with Roth's selection as Canada's

CEO of the Year, an award co-sponsored by *National Post,* the Caldwell Partners International, CTV, and RBC Dominion Securities. And in two days, Chmelnitsky lost $20,000 on Nortel.

On December 14, Nortel reiterated its guidance. On December 19, John Roth contributed an op-ed piece to the *Globe and Mail* on Canada's competitiveness in the new global economic order. "Our market capitalization," Roth boasted of Nortel, "even at today's bargain-basement prices, puts us in the top two or three global tele-com companies, ahead of others including Motorola, Lucent, Ericsson, and Alcatel—not too shabby for a Canadian startup."

In three weeks, Chmelnitsky lost $40,000. In nine weeks, he lost $70,000. And it kept going from there.

18

Always Teletruth

What passes for research on Wall Street today is shocking to me. Instead of providing investors with the kind of analysis that would have kept them from marching over the cliff, analysts prodded them forward by inventing new valuation criteria for stocks that had no basis in reality and no standards of good practice.

—Mutual fund manager Robert A. Olstein, quoted in the *New York Times,* December 31, 2000

The year 2001 began badly for the North American markets. On the very first trading day, Tuesday the second, investors were blindsided by an unexpectedly grim result for the National Purchasing Managers Index (NPI).[19] Released on the first business day of every month, the NPI is based on a survey of purchasing executives at about 300 industrial companies in the United States. In part because of its timeliness, it's considered the bellwether indicator of how factories are performing, and index movements are felt immediately in the markets. The "bellwether" analogy is apt, for this is the ram that wears the bell and leads the flock wherever it happens to wander. The sheep of the investment community instinctively fall in behind the NPI. And on January 2, 2001, the NPI was headed into recessionary territory.

The neutral baseline for the NPI is 50: any value above it is an indication that industrial production is expanding; any value below it indicates it is contracting. The December 4 NPI report, at 47.7, had indicated that manufacturing had continued to shrink in November—the index had gone negative in August, when it measured 49.5—but the Chicago-area component of the NPI then had given hope of a rebound when it showed an increase for December when released on December 29. Thus the dip to 43.7 for December in the national NPI, when released just after ten in the morning on January 2, came as a major shock to the markets. The index hadn't been this low since April 1991, when the economy was in the grip of a severe recession.

Losses were felt across the board, as the DJIA fell by 145 points from opening to close, but the technology sectors were particularly hard hit. The NASDAQ Telecommunications Index fell 7.4 percent; the Morgan Stanley High-Technology 35 Index dropped 6 percent. Cisco, which marked a 52-week low as it lost 12.9 percent of its value, dropped from its $38^{1}/$_{4}$ close on December 29 to $33^{5}/$_{16}$ at the end of trading on January 2. Nortel, in comparison, came through relatively unscathed, easing from $32^{1}/$_{16}$ to $30^{1}/$_{4}$ on the NYSE. Overall, however, the TSE suffered more than the NYSE, and in the process betrayed the fundamental dependence of Canada's largest stock market on American, rather than Canadian, financial news. While the S&P 500 fell 2.8 percent over the day's trading on January 2, the TSE 300 Composite dropped 3.6 percent on news of an industrial slowdown south of the border.

With the poor performance by the NPI and the resulting downturn in the equity markets, all eyes turned to Alan Greenspan and the Federal Reserve Board's Federal Open Market Committee for some sign of relief. After the shock of the FOMC's failure to cut interest rates on December 19, the NASDAQ, the NYSE, and the TSE had all then staged improbable end-of-year rallies, despite the fact that over the next two weeks the risks to the U.S. economy identified by the FOMC dramatically multiplied. U.S. retail sales had failed to meet expectations during the Christmas season, auto sales were sluggish, and uncomfortably high inventory levels underpinned a weakening in the manufacturing sector. "Business confidence appeared to have deteriorated further since the December meeting amid widespread reports of reductions in planned production and capital spending," the FOMC would shortly note. When the December NPI for manufacturing shocked the markets on January 2, the call went out for Greenspan to act on interest rates before the next scheduled FOMC meeting on January 30–31.

Greenspan evidently listened. On the morning of January 3, a rare telephone conference call was arranged for FOMC members, who quickly agreed to ease reserve conditions in order to nudge the Federal Funds rate down 50 basis points, to 6 percent. Coaxed by a quarter-point drop in the discount rate, the Fed Funds rate, whose previous weekly average had been 6.48 percent, promptly crashed to 5.88 percent before settling, as planned, in around 6 percent.

This rapid, unscheduled move to drop the Fed Funds rate broke with precedent. The FOMC hadn't made an inter-meeting cut since the fall of 1998, when the Asian economic crisis and Russian debt default compelled swift action. Even at that, the FOMC's customary pattern for inter-meeting cuts was to wait for the monthly unemployment figures, which in January 2001 would be released on Friday the fifth. But the FOMC obviously didn't think it had the luxury of waiting two days, and its cut hit the markets like a megavitamin injection in the gluteus maximus. The boost was augmented by an expectation that the FOMC would move against the funds rate again at the regular meeting on January 30–31, as the FOMC promised it would cut the discount rate another quarter point if the twelve regional Federal Reserve banks so requested. Since the January 3 quarter-point cut in the discount rate was meant to move the Fed Funds rate down by a half point, it seemed reasonable to hope that another quarter-point cut to the discount rate at the end of January would produce a further half-point cut in the Fed Funds rate. In all then, a full point could be sliced from the Fed Funds rate by the end of the month.

The markets overall really, really liked this. The NYSE set a new single-day volume record of 1.88 billion shares as the S&P 500, which had fallen 2.8 percent on the second, rebounded 5 percent on the third; on the fourth, a new opening-hour volume record of 489 million shares was set, and January overall would set a new single-month volume record: 27.8 billion shares. The TSE 300 broke even—having lost 322 points (3.6 percent) on January 2, it regained 326 points the next day.

As with the disappointment of December 19, it was the NAS-DAQ that experienced the greatest volatility. The once-glittering tech market was coming off a horribly painful year. After the initial crash in the spring, when the NASDAQ Composite was brought to heel from its 5,000 breakthrough of March 9, the index had struggled to stay above 4,000 all summer. On September 8, it gave up and plunged rapidly downhill, bottoming out when the FOMC's inaction of December 19 pushed it to 2,333 the next day. It had then enjoyed its little end-of-year rally, up to 2,474 at the opening on January 2. When the NPI figures hit the market, the NASDAQ Composite essentially went into shock, recording a 7.4 percent decline with what provided to be the lowest trading volume (1.5 billion shares) for the entire year. The very next day, with the cut to the Fed Funds rate, the NASDAQ made a tremendous 16.1 percent opening-to-close rebound—at 325 points, the largest in its history—on a day that also set a new all-time record for share volume (3.2 billion).

The NASDAQ's back-to-back exhibitions of comatose despair/raging euphoria was a perfect exhibition of the market's precarious convictions. One day, the economy was going to hell and taking the stock market with it. The next day, a rate cut, which most everyone agreed would take months to show real results in the economy, was the cause for record-setting volume and index increases and a return to the hopeful rally that the NPI numbers had so rudely interrupted. Never had the conviction in Alan Greenspan's ability to tweak the direction of the economy been so forcefully expressed.

All markets participated in a remarkable rally in defiance of what by all appearances was a troubled economy, and it sent tech indices in particular skyward over the next few weeks. The new-year rally was a creature of converging expectations and wish fulfilment. On one level, it was a grand exercise in denial, as investors preferred to read the rate cut as the sign that earnings and revenues could actually continue increasing in the networking sector—all Greenspan had to do was lop a point off the Fed, and the telco carriers would continue the capex spending spree that analysts like Paul Sagawa had warned was about to dry up. On a much broader level, the markets were poised for the swearing in of president-elect George W. Bush on January 20. While Clinton had been no great enemy of business and had enjoyed two terms in the thrall of the century's greatest bull market, Bush was a Republican who had made election promises of tax cuts, had close ties to the energy biz, and was sure to uphold his party's traditionally hands-off approach to regulation and market meddling.

Not everyone was buying into the long-term strength of the rally, however. "Stocks' euphoria will be short-lived; earnings numbers will keep slowing," predicted Dr. Ian Shepherdson, chief U.S. economist at High Frequency Economics, in his daily report on January 4.[20] But the Fed's rate cut on the second business day of the new year was also perfectly timed to conjure a self-fulfilling prophecy of a continuing bull market. The January performance of the S&P 500 index was traditionally viewed as a key indicator of how the entire year would play out. Strong numbers from the index promised a strong year overall. Merrill Lynch stoked the optimism with a research note from its chief U.S. investment strategist, Christine Callies, which told clients that historically, within three months of an initial rate cut the S&P 500 made a gain of about 10 percent, which grew to 19 percent within six months and 23.6 percent after a year. The note also pointed out that in each of the past three "easing" cycles in which rates dropped (1989, 1995, and 1996), the S&P 500's price/earnings ratio grew about three points within six months of the first rate cut.[21] This meant that stock prices grew ahead of earnings as market sentiment shifted from pessimism to optimism.

Such historic analysis reverse-engineered previous booms and fingered the rate cut not as a component of a general economic and market rebound, but as the underlying cause. In other words, rather than seeing that a rate cut accompanied a rebound, the data was read to imply that the cut actually caused it, and from there it was a short hop to the notion that simply cutting the Fed Funds rate, regardless of all the other economic data, could turn the economy around and send the market soaring. The market, of course, could soar simply on the basis of investor expectations, but maintaining that rebound was another matter.

With the sudden, unexpected early rate cut from the Fed, the markets were vulnerable to being sucked into a feedback loop. The rate cut gave the markets a boost, and investors could then point to the rise as evidence that the economy was back on a roll, that the January rally was under way, and if the January rally was under way, then the year was going to be a good one for equities, and if the year was going to be a good one for equities, now was the time to buy equities, while they were so cheap. And as investors rushed in to buy equities, because they were going to go higher, they indeed rose higher, on the simple mechanics of supply and demand.

For tech stocks, the feedback loop of the January boom was amplified by a tendency of institutional investors in particular to place riskier bets at the beginning of the year, to ride the wave of high returns should the more speculative picks pan out. If they didn't within, say, the first quarter, there was plenty of time left to bail out and salvage the portfolio's performance for the year. The FOMC's rate cut jump-started a new-year's speculative binge, with the techs leading the way as the large pools of investment capital controlled by institutionals flooded into their shares. And within the techs, those in the networking and telecom sectors roared out of their late 2000 doldrums.

Having begun January 3 at 32^{9/16}$, Cisco soared to a close of 41^{5/16}$ as 162 million shares were traded. It was a day-trading bonanza: the investors who bought in at the opening low scored a one-day return of 27 percent. The next day, Cisco edged up to 41^{7/8}$ as another 109 million shares changed hands. Nortel, too, recovered from the January 2 dip, reaching 36^{1/4}$ on the NYSE by the close on January 4, but Nortel had been unable to command the enthusiasm that had pulled American investors into Cisco. Investors had swapped 271 million Cisco shares on the NASDAQ over the two days, increasing its price 28 percent. A total of 96 million Nortel shares had been traded on the NYSE and TSE over the same period, with a price increase of about 20 percent. Between the closings on January 2 and 4, the spread between Cisco (on the NASDAQ) and Nortel (on the NYSE) jumped from 3^{1/16}$ to 5^{5/8}$, for no other reason than the FOMC had targeted the Fed Funds rate for a half-point cut. For the American investment community, Cisco was still the flagship stock of the networking biz, not to mention a darling of the NASDAQ as a whole. Cisco's dominant position would become increasingly frustrating to Nortel investors as the new year unfolded.

Ross Healy and Strategic Analysis Corp. marked the new year with a traditional review of how 2000 had played out, and what 2001 had in store. "We could hardly conclude a year-end discussion without making mention of one of our favourite short sells, Nortel Networks," Healy wrote to his clients on January 2. "Nortel has certainly performed well for us during 2000 despite an unanticipated rally from its opening price of around $70 up to $126 [actually $124.50] before cratering back down towards its fair market value. We suspect that the stock is not only going lower but potentially a lot lower as the fundamentals for the fiber optic aspect of its business (into which it has poured much of the company's resources and far too much of its balance sheet) come more or less unglued.

"Since the disastrous foray into truth-telling in 1998 which certain executive members of the company blame for the massive dip which the stock took that year (C$100 down to C$43), the company has followed not only a policy of telling nothing but good news, but also it has followed a policy of blitzing the media with any and all good news that it can muster. Their reporting has got to the stage that it feels a little like Hudson's Bay Company reporting the sale of every 31 inch television set. The problem with all this good news is that the general investing public hasn't heard anything else but, and is more than highly likely to be quite taken aback should anything else emerge. And, in our experience, eventually bad news does tend to emerge.

"We do not think that the public may have too long to wait before something other than stellar results appear. While we are unwilling to argue with management's assertions that it will hit its targets for the last quarter of 2000 and the first of 2001, we would also point out that in the short term, that is not all that hard to do for a company which is in the contracting business as there can be some arbitrariness to revenue recognition. However, from all that we can glean, it appears as if the fiber optic side of its business may be in the process of slowing down, if not worse."

Healy cited the case of ICG Communications, the CLEC which had gone bankrupt two weeks earlier. He was confident that it had to owe Nortel *something* in unpaid receivables. But there was no way to prove it. Companies weren't obliged to report on the status of every single customer account—that was privileged information any competitor would wish to have. Still, Nortel had been touted, along with Cisco and Lucent, as one of ICG's "technology partners." ICG's SEC filings indicated only one significant vendor financing deal, with Cisco. It second-quarter 2000 report noted two vendor financing arrangements with Cisco totalling $180 million, of which $99.1 million had been drawn down by June 30. The first-quarter report had also mentioned a vendor financing arrangement with Lucent, but provided no details. The report did, however, say: "The Company has entered into various other equipment purchase agreements with certain of its vendors."

Healy had no doubt that ICG had been on the hook to Nortel. Cisco, for its part, announced additional provisions against bad receivables in December, but Nortel said nothing. The definition of what constituted "material significance" was so broad that Nortel was well within its rights not to say anything, even if millions of dollars might go unpaid by ICG. But the ongoing troubles of networking customers suggested to Healy that there might be unpleasant surprises ahead with regard to receivables. "With the stocks of the network builders in steep plunges everywhere we look, the trifling issue of how some of the contract payments are going to be met when one can neither raise equity nor debt is another question which Nortel has not seen fit to address.

"If things turn ugly in this side of the business," Healy continued, "and heaven knows the world does not need more fiber optic systems when the current ones are operating at a miserable 7 to 14 percent of capacity depending on whom one listens to, then there is another niggling detail about Nortel which concerns us. What will the company do with all of the nice Goodwill which it has laid in, Goodwill which it got when it bought up other companies in the fiber optic supplier business by paying $billions for $millions in sales. Some 60 percent of the Nortel balance sheet equity position is nothing but Goodwill, and, using the newly proposed FASB standards, once one recognizes impairment of Goodwill, it should be then written down (or off). That would be some shock to the public perception of infallibility that Nortel has recently won.

"All in all, as Nortel edges closer and closer to having to 'fess up, we have to wonder just what the ultimate market reaction will be. Despite the plunge from $126 [*sic*] to the close for 2000 of $48, that is still well above its Super Growth Price of $43 which in turn is no screaming bargain at all compared to the past 20 years of valuation history. In fact, that tends to be the high, or close to it, rather than the low. Throw in a potential writeoff of Goodwill, a reversal of a few already-booked profits, and some of the oldtimers will be reminiscing about the last Nortel fiasco in the 1970s." That was the late 1970s acquisition-driven expansion that led to the 63 cent per share loss of 1980. Most investors wouldn't have had a clue what Healy was talking about. "If we are even close to being on track," he concluded, "it'll be like déjà vu all over again."

Ross Healy sat back to watch the fun.

The Internet had created a new class of investor: tech-savvy, intimate with the internal machinations of the companies in which they invested, employing the very technology that drove these companies to trade in their stocks. They were a third way of investing, an alternative to the institutional players and the private investors working through traditional brokerage houses. Analysis from Wall Street and Bay Street was next to useless, in their mind; with good reason, they viewed the mainstream analysts as hopelessly compromised, their incomes reliant on the business drummed up by their firm's investment bank division from the very companies on which they were supposed to pass impartial judgment. Even the SEC was uncomfortable with the implicit compromises faced by the typical analyst and warned investors of this in its online resources.

With confidence in professional analysts seriously eroded, the third-way investors had one less reason to trade through a traditional brokerage house. It made more sense to them to execute their own trades through a cheap on-line discount brokerage and do their own research. There was all kinds of it posted on the Web—precis of full reports by the big houses, full reports from some houses looking for publicity, and much-condensed versions reported in the business press as they were released. Pretty well all the filings required of public companies (except for insider trades) were available on-line, for free, from the SEC. The third-way investor could gather as much traditional analysis as he felt necessary at no cost, and through a bulletin board share news, analysis, and hunches with likeminded market players.

The Internet represented a phenomenal revolution in investment. Investors used the Net to do their trades and gather their research, and the experience was so transforming, so liberating, that when it was combined with other Internet-driven changes these tech-savvy investors experienced in their personal and professional lives, they inevitably came to believe that Internet-related stocks marked the path to riches. After all, the information revolution was unfolding all around them, and investors new to the scene need only look at the already phenomenal performance of the NASDAQ and individual stocks and tech indices on other exchanges to be convinced that the future of communications was also the future of wealth.

Congregating at the electronic bulletin boards that hosted discussion groups dedicated to individual stocks, third-way investors occupied a virtual world of virtual personalities, logging in under pseudonyms and rarely revealing their proper names. Through bravado, casual asides, or authoritative opinion, they could reveal themselves to be war vets, retired telecom engineers, corporate insiders, or former stockbrokers who knew where the bodies were buried. If they so chose, they could construct for themselves any past or present that suited them. The bulletin boards offered a grand game of deception in which spammers could drop in on a bulletin board and tout a favourite stock in hope of driving up the price—or conversely, sow doubt in the bulletin board's stock in hope of encouraging a selloff that would benefit their short position.

"Spammers" were universally loathed, while "shorters" had a

more mixed reception. Shorting a stock is a legitimate investment strategy—you are simply speculating on the stock falling in price, rather than rising—but the bulletin boards tended to be dominated by true believers, investors who were in a stock to make money on the upside. Shorters were no more guilty of talking a stock down than true believers were of talking it up, but with the majority of a bulletin board's participants urging a stock to greater heights, negative opinions were not always tolerated. Part of the majority's aversion to the presence of shorters was the sort of postings they often flung at the board: loud, insulting posts, hammered out in caps, that belittled the optimism of the true believers. It was easy to become annoyed with these people, to filter out their comments by adding their log-in name to one's "ignore" list. But a persistent heckler could just come back under a new log-in name on these free services. Besides, even some of the brighter true believers were guilty of launching their own raids on the bulletin board groups dedicated to other stocks, to taunt their members on the misfortunes of their favourite shares.

The annoyance factor aside, a major reason shorters received such a cool reception was that their doom-and-gloom messages were not the sort that the majority were inclined to or prepared to hear. Stocks encouraged messianic followings on these boards; the true believers were the market's biggest cheerleaders, more emphatic and unwavering in their support of a company than the most disparaged up-tempo analyst. They had made significant emotional and capital investments in their favourite stock, and their personal security was so dependent on the good fortune of their investment that they could become blinded to signs of lurking misfortune, quick to explain away troubling rumours and contrary data. For all the abuse heaped on analysts for failing to accurately forecast the price collapse of stocks like Nortel, many investors were equally to blame in not at least heeding the possibility of a serious reversal. They failed to diversify sensibly, becoming caught up in the groupthink of ever-increasing returns from a single stock. Sometimes they confessed to being unable to help themselves, taking what prudence was telling them was a risky, overweighted position. The farther they got out on a limb like Nortel, the less inclined they were to listen to people trying to tell them that cracks were appearing back at the trunk.

The bulletin boards varied widely in quality. Among the worst were the boards at Yahoo! Finance, which seemed to serve little more purpose than to provide a forum for profanity-laced, one-line flames. Among the best were the ones at RagingBull.com, which set more stringent guidelines on foul language and general etiquette and encouraged far more thoughtful, even inspired, discussions. Like most other bulletin boards, the ones at Raging Bull were essentially public spaces. Membership was free, and all messages were posted for any visitor to the Web site to read. Because of their relatively high level of discourse, public availability, and long-term preservation (all messages are archived and easily retrieved), Raging Bull's postings represent an unmatched record of investor sentiment as Nortel's dramatic rise and fall unfolded.

The dynamics of the Nortel bulletin board at Raging Bull invite a long-term study by a cultural anthropologist. Over the winter of 2000–01, about 600 people contributed to its discussions. Participants were invited by Raging Bull to voluntarily disclose their position on the stock, and this disclosure would appear at the bottom of every message they posted, to provide context to their comments. Those professing to be in Nortel for the long haul outnumbered the contrarians by about fifty to one. A typical declaration for Nortel was

Voluntary Disclosure: Position- **Long***; ST [Short Term] Rating-* **Hold***; LT [Long Term] Rating-* **Strong Buy**

For many board participants, this disclosure remained resolutely unchanged, regardless of the wobbles in the company's fortunes.

As on other bulletin boards, contrarians—the ones admitting to shorting the stock—received a mixed reception on the Nortel board at Raging Bull. Obnoxious postings didn't help, but while some true believers advocated listening to the negative postings, others simply had no time for them. For them, the upward march of Nortel was a done deal: it was a matter of figuring out how high, how soon.

After the setback of October 25, 2000, many true believers had been herded into a defensive huddle. They had unequivocal faith in the company: in its management, its products, its research and development, its global marketing reach, in its all-round superiority to the competition. There was a widespread sentiment that investing in Nortel was a zero-sum game: that the misfortune of a competitor should naturally benefit Nortel and be reflected in a better share price. They were contemptuous of the struggling Lucent, unimpressed with Cisco, and some board members were convinced that the American analyst community generally had it in for Nortel: that they were preternaturally disposed to looking favourably on their domestic stars, Lucent and Cisco. Rightly or not, this conviction that Nortel was not properly appreciated by American analysts led some members to block out the rare voices that had been questioning Nortel's long-term attractiveness.

The members of the Raging Bull Nortel board were a typically eclectic collection: Canadians, Americans, a few Europeans, some of them making trades on a daily basis, others holding long-term positions who just like to chat, still others with no position but monitoring the board, either for their own amusement or to gather a sense of a good time to jump in. Among the Canadians on the board was Michael Hollander, who posted messages under the name "hollam." By training he was a programmer analyst, but he was staying at home with a three-year-old daughter. His wife's job paid the basic overheads, but provided no extras. The rest came from Hollander's investment activities, and he was hoping he could make enough money from dividends, interest, and trading in his investing activities to allow him to continue as a stay-at-home dad for their preschooler.

Also on the board was Wayne Schmengrum, who, like Hollander, was a technology professional. He had earned a bachelor of science in electrical engineering at the University of Waterloo, after which he spent eight years as a design engineer in broadcast video equipment. He had also sold semiconductors for five years and had then moved back into product development as a senior designer. His knowledge of the telecom industry was mainly drawn from his marketing days, and like so many others who contributed to the bulletin board dialogue, he hoped to use his industry knowledge to make profitable investments in the tech boom.

"Back a couple of years ago (during the time we all lost our minds and became fools), I really was still evolving in my investment experiences and learning," Schmengrum reflects.[22] "The boards (message & chat) were rich with characters and we were all willing to clap one another on the back (so to speak) with the paper profits we were making (or more accurately put, seeing). Many (including myself) could envision early retirement and a life of leisure (or perhaps early poor living habits, leading to a premature death . . . LOL[23]). Today, I have discovered that much of what is posted is pure bunk. Over extended, over exposed small investors thinking they will gain some sort of insider edge, rather than those simply seeking to exchange insight and opinion."

Compared to most Nortel investors, Schmengrum was an early adopter. He had got into the stock back in October 1998, after the Essex House fiasco gutted the share value. "I saw what I believed to be an undervalued company with respect to its peers, Lucent and Cisco. I thought their Bay Networks acquisition was a brilliant move at the time." He viewed Nortel as a company with strong sales that was poised to grow, whose stock was at a bargain-basement price. "Looking back now, what I failed to see was the overlapping transitional effects of sales. Old technology was still being purchased while new technology was in demand, causing a blip, bubble, or what ever."

He stuck with Nortel until November 1, 1999, when he sold his entire holding, which had consumed 60 percent of the value of his RRSP portfolio. (Schmengrum declines to say how much he held.) He thought the stock's value at that point had got ahead of itself and moved his money into pipelines. He then watched in amazement from the sidelines as Nortel made its tremendous run to $124.50. As the stock returned to earth, Schmengrum continued to monitor it, watching for the right reentry point. In January 2001 he was still watching, while continuing to contribute comments to the Nortel board. He was one of the more lucid members of the board, knowledgeable about the securities business, able to counter politely the wilder ravings and conspiracy theories of other board members. "I am an engineer by training, so most of my market investments are guided by my understanding of technology more so than finance. I am only self taught in economics and accounting—boring reading, but critical, I think, if you want to self direct your own investments."

He plainly enjoyed participating in the exchanges on Raging Bull's Nortel board, but says he didn't let them direct his decisions—a moot point, since he managed to stay out of Nortel for about fifteen months. "In my view," says Schmengrum, "bulletin boards (as well as chat rooms) are an electronic form of a coffee shop, gym, bar or other casual social place to exchange insights. Yes, one gains familiarity with those that frequent the place, however, one knows relatively nothing about the others, other than their track records on specific statements (this is where bulletin boards have an advantage as they are recorded!!!). I myself, frankly, have a lousy track record (LOL). I have met people, in person, from the Yahoo stock chat rooms (we had dinner and took in a comedy show). Our time was spent discussing non-stock related items though. I have e-mailed many in this fashion."

Michael Hollander was firmly entrenched in the ad hoc community that was the Nortel board. It was, by and large, populated by bright people like Schmengrum, and the group seemed to be self-organizing, different members fulfilling different practical roles, rather than just mouthing off. Articles from news organizations, transcripts of conference calls, gleanings from SEC filings—all made their way onto the board. Hollander agrees with the idea of its self-organizing nature, "since people have different skills that they bring to the group, and they perform the actions that they like to do. Some like to surf the net for articles so they post them when they can. I like mathematical analysis, so I would post PE ratios and trend analysis. I think it comes down to people's desire to feel appreciated and useful."

The Raging Bull board was just one source of information for him. He also kept tabs on the Yahoo! board, which Schmengrum frequented, as well as other Internet resources, such as Silicon Investor, Motley Fool, and StockHouse. "I relied on BBs for opinions on particular stocks and as an alternate source of news and analysis on those stocks. The links that people come across are often very useful, pointing to new sources of information on stocks as well as different analyses, charting tools, etc. I continued to rely on newspapers and 9:30–4:00

CNBC and ROBTv coverage as well, since they are professional and come in with breaking news all the time. I did not subscribe to newsletters or even have a financial advisor."[24]

While these were all important sources of information, he wouldn't say they had a "fundamental influence" on his trading strategy with Nortel. "The strategies were mine; the BBs were means of obtaining information no different than obtaining info from newspapers and TV. Where the BBs were different was that they were interactive and allowed me an opportunity for adult discourse while I was looking after my toddler-age daughter during the day!"

He never met any other board member in person, and while his relationship with a number of the regular participants was warm and respectful, he generally remained wary of the quality of the advice. "I never take anyone's word on anything. That applies to anyone regardless of how long they've been on the board. I also treat newspaper reports with a good dose of skepticism. How better to effectively analyze anything than questioning everything? The best way to be sure is to get multiple opinions from multiple sources before deciding on anything!

"After a while you do see who makes sense and who is a paid hypster. It takes a couple of months to do that. But again, I would still never take anyone's word on anything no matter how long they had been on the board. Sometimes this can hurt: for example when Teletruth decided to sell all his NT at 3:49PM on February 15."

Oh, yes, Teletruth, eleven minutes before closing on the fifteenth. The message you could not forget, when you knew what happened right after closing. Teletruth was one of the great characters of the board, anonymously posting wisecracks out of the ether, taking great relish in his triumphs, bantering with the other members on almost a daily basis. He'd joined the board in June 1999 and had posted over 1,000 messages by January 2001. He spent his time almost exclusively on the Nortel board, dashing off to the Lucent and Cisco boards about a half-dozen times each to rub the members' noses in their misfortunes. He was (maybe) the Vietnam vet among them— who knew, really, in the pseudonymous world of the boards? He had a running joke going about Nortel, in which Nortel was Frostbite

Falls, John Roth was Rocky, Clarence Chandran was Bullwinkle, and rival companies took turns being Boris and Natasha.

For all his wisecracking good cheer, Teletruth was serious about making money on Nortel, and he traded aggressively, making moves on a daily or weekly basis. Like many traders, he considered himself "long" on Nortel, but he strove to make quick profits in rapid day trades on a portion of his holding. He'd had his ups and downs, but in the new year, Teletruth was hot. It was like he had sandpapered the ends of his fingers and cracked the safe. His entries and exits on short-term positions were exceptionally well timed in the midst of volatility. The trade he announced in that 3:49 P.M. message on February 15 was one for the record books, the one that thousands upon thousands of investors large and small would wish they'd had the sense to make. Michael Hollander watched him make it, didn't follow it, and then saw his dream of staying home with his daughter vaporize before dinner was on the table.

19

The Best Job I Ever Had

Analysts are morons.
If they are so smart, why are they still working?
—posting to Nortel bulletin board
at RagingBull.com, January 12, 2001

"It was the best job I ever had," says Kirsten Watson of her time at
Nortel. Unfortunately, the best job she ever had lasted only five months.

She had been hired by Nortel in August 2000 to work in Ottawa
in its Extreme Voice division, which produced IP-based voice switching products. It had not been easy for her to get aboard. Nortel lived
up to its longstanding reputation for hiring only the best people,
cherrypicking the cream of the workforce. "The interview process
was insane, with the background checks and everything." But it was
a badge of honour to have made the grade: "You knew you were good
if you got in."

Watson was working in what she calls a "separate cell" of the
company, an operation "on the outer edge of the core focus." Away
to the southwest was the company's headquarters in Brampton, the
monolith Kirsten and her fellow employees affectionately dubbed the
Mothership. Her division, she says, was on track for being spun off
as its own company. In hindsight, Extreme Voice represented one
more opportunity for Nortel to turn a piece of its business into a cash
injection. Nortel had been talking about turning the entire optical
division loose with its own tracking stock and was also planning to
spin out Netgear. The former Bay Networks division, which made

Internet equipment for small businesses and homes, had been set up as its own enterprise in May 1999, with Nortel holding 69 percent of the stock. Nortel hoped to reap $130 million in a Netgear IPO. Extreme Voice never got the point of having a price tag put on it.

Watson couldn't have been happier. "Nortel had the whole blue-chip feeling. They really treated you well, and the work was great. We were working on cutting-edge things." But suddenly, on Thursday, January 11, she was no longer working on cutting-edge things. She was no longer working at Nortel. She was en route from one meeting in La Jolla, California, to the airport so that she could attend another meeting the next day in San Francisco, when her cell phone rang. It was her boss back in Ottawa, telling her that Nortel had axed her entire division. In essence, she says, Nortel had declared, "We are no longer in the business of Internet call waiting."

"My layoff was clean, professional, and orderly," she says. "We were the beginning of the landslide."

Nortel had not released any statement about the elimination of 4,000 jobs worldwide before word of cuts began to trickle into the media. Granted, at its annual investor conference in Boston on November 21, Nortel had promised it would be "focusing on high-growth areas . . . and streamlining operations for efficiencies." And getting rid of jobs was nothing new for Nortel—it had axed about 4,000 in the previous year, half of them through outsourcing, in the course of increasing its overall workforce. Besides, anything that might be construed as bad news was not its communications forte. As Paul Sagawa says, "I always thought Nortel was a hear-no-evil, see-no-evil, speak-no-evil company." Better to ignore it, and just react to it if necessary. Nor did it file an 8-K, a notice of material change, with the SEC, as it plainly didn't consider this adjustment to be of material significance. By the end of Wednesday, January 10, the media was awash with rumours of Nortel job losses. The economic picture was jittery, and news of cuts, however strategic they might be, now came with a frisson of fear. The CBC aired a news report that night on expected cuts of about 800 Canadian employees, and both the *Wall Street Journal* and the *Globe and Mail* carried stories in their Thursday morning editions. *Globe and Mail* reporter John Partridge wrote,

> Canadian high-tech giant Nortel Networks Corp. has quietly
> begun a round of layoffs that industry sources say will result in
> at least 5,200 people, or 6 per cent of its employees around the
> world, losing their jobs in the next three to four months.
>
> The sources say the first targets for the cuts, which the com-
> pany insists have nothing to do with any recessionary panic,
> include about 750 employees in Ottawa and another 200 in
> Toronto, who got their walking papers on Tuesday.

Kirsten Watson, away in California, was one of those employees
who weren't formally notified until the day of the *Globe and Mail*
story. Nortel's response was masterful. The markets opened on
Thursday to a blitzkrieg of good-news items from Nortel and its customers—the kind of stream of announcements that Ross Healy had
equated with a department store trumpeting the sale of every single
television set. On this day, they did double duty as frequency jam-
mers, drowning out the bad news of layoffs. The company had won
multimillion-U.S.-dollar contracts from China Telecom's regional operators, Qingdao Telecom and Hebei Telecom, for the delivery of high-
performance local Internet. Then GiantLoop Network, Inc. of
Waltham, Massachusetts, "the leader in Enterprise Optical Networking
services," announced "an Enterprise Optical Networking alliance
with Nortel Networks," and that as part of this initiative, the two
companies were co-sponsoring a "five-city seminar series, entitled
'business at light speed' that highlights the importance of managed
optical services for enterprises," to begin January 22. Then came the
announcement that Nortel had won a two-year, $100 million (U.S.)
contract to design and build an Internet protocol optical backbone
network in the United Kingdom for 186k, the telecom subsidiary of
Lattice Group.

Nortel got another dollop of good news into the media courtesy
its former parent, BCE. Its subsidiary Bell Mobility chose Thursday
morning as the perfect moment to reveal it was about to spend $100
million (Canadian) to expand its digital wireless service coverage in

Ontario and Quebec, using technology from Nortel and Sierra Wireless. And to top it off, the *Ottawa Citizen* carried an item on how Nortel and WorldCom had connected New York City and Washington, D.C., "with the fastest high-speed Internet connection currently in service worldwide."

Amid that blizzard of good cheer, Nortel refuted the numbers in the *Globe and Mail*'s story. According to an item carried by "CBS MarketWatch" that morning, Nortel spokesperson Vicki Contavespi said, "The numbers are not correct. We continue to recruit in our high-growth segments and we want our workforce to remain flat this year. We'll do that through attrition and retirements." At the same time, Contavespi refused to supply any numbers on reductions.

"This isn't indicative of any type of slowdown," Contavespi told CNET News.com in an item posted Thursday afternoon. "It's re-jiggering the work force, aligning it with our high-growth areas such as fiber-optic networking and wireless equipment. The way we'll remain flat in 2001 is because a lot of the elimination of jobs will be due to normal attrition or retirement."

Nortel finally issued a press release that went out on the newswire at 2:24 P.M. It began: "Nortel Networks today indicated that it expects its overall number of employees to remain unchanged in 2001." From there on in, there wasn't a chance that Nortel was going to utter the word "layoffs."

After first noting that Nortel's employment had increased from about 83,500 at this time in 2000 to 94,500 by year-end, Nortel explained that "while the company expects to continue to hire in 2001 to address customer needs and drive leadership in high growth markets, the company estimates that approximately 4,000 regular full time positions will be eliminated in the near term through streamlining and realignment activities. The number of affected employees is expected to be minimized as a result of normal attrition, including retirement."

There followed a bit of techspeak bafflegab from chief operating officer and Roth heir-apparent Clarence Chandran. "In 2000, we added critical resources to further enhance our responsiveness to customers and laser-like focus on the high-growth areas of their businesses, where demand is most robust. In 2001, hiring to address high-growth markets will remain a priority."

With a laser-like focus on emphasizing that the so-called cuts were strategic, the news release continued: "By focusing its workforce and product portfolio on the high-growth areas of its customers' businesses, Nortel Networks will further fuel its multiple growth engines of Optical and Wireless Internet, Local Internet and eBusiness. This will result in the ongoing alignment of its business and workforce with high-growth markets, stemming initiatives and organizations that are not in line with this direction.

"Affected employees will be notified in writing and will be offered appropriate termination arrangements including severance and out-placement services."

Well, at least Nortel used the words "termination" and "sever-ance." But in their statements to the press, Nortel spokespeople made sure the media got the message that the workforce would net out at the same size—thereby overcoming the basic news that Nortel was embarking on a series of actual job cuts. Nortel's ability to spin the story was a textbook example of how a major enterprise could get the media to accept its rationale. But while the job cuts were irrefutable, Nortel's assertion that it would replace these jobs during the coming year had to be accepted entirely on good faith. And it generally was.

According to a CBC news item posted to the network's Web site at eleven that night, the job cuts in Canada were part of "a larger realignment." As the CBC put it:

> A Nortel spokeswoman said the company will "exchange" the jobs of people in certain divisions to open new positions in what the company considers to be higher-growth areas. The downsizing is part of Nortel's plan to move away from its traditional voice telecom switching products to the data side of telecommunications. The company plans to "aggressively" add staff to divisions such as optical and wireless data transmissions, e-business solutions as well as voice-over-IP applications, said David Chamberlin, another Nortel spokesman. He added that Nortel's total workforce will remain stable this year.

This invited the question of why, if Nortel was planning to "aggressively" add staff to cutting-edge divisions, including those developing voice-over-IP applications, it had just obliterated Kirsten Watson's entire Extreme Voice division. To be fair, Nortel had noted that pure voice products were under siege. But if the future in telecom was IP-based products, losing Extreme Voice was a perplexing retreat.

The loss of Extreme Voice was not going to be a subject of analyst or investor debate, however, because like most companies, Nortel did not share detailed information of its various operating segments with the market—and, by extension, with competitors. Extreme Voice represented about one-tenth of 1 percent of the entire Nortel global workforce. It never showed up in a financial statement or annual report. It came and went without being noticed at all by the greater investment community. And the investment community appeared to be ready to go along with Nortel's good vibe. According to the CBC, "Analysts said it was only a matter of time before Nortel focused on areas that held the most promise."

On the Raging Bull Nortel board, investors mulled over the meaning of the job cuts, exchanges, or realignments. There were rumours of a hiring freeze until January 22. "From what I hear," read one posting, "only certain parts of the company are frozen, the high growth stuff is rather hot." Another investor, pleased with Nortel's statement, crowed, "JOB CUTS UNTRUE PEOPLE!"

Observed one board member:

> I worked for Nortel in R&D for 15 years+, and we had a freeze nearly every year, usually from 4Q into 1Q. It was routine to help keep costs down as we tried to make our numbers for the year. . .
>
> Regarding layoffs, they are happening, as I stated they would earlier in the week. You decide if it's a positive indicator or not - I haven't been able to.

Read an approving posting:

Nortel is merely being proactive. Looking forward into a challenging year, it is cutting lower priority projects in order to focus on higher priority projects. Not all of the people being laid off are being fired. Some will be redirected into the high priority areas.

Nortel prunes staff every December. Because of the general state of telecom this coming year, it is also pruning projects. Should this be surprising or shocking? One should prune the projects BEFORE they affect the bottom line, not after. Nortel is NOT Lucent.

And it is not much different than what John Chambers suggested was happening at Cisco yesterday.

While Chambers hadn't said anything about job cuts, he was working furiously to maintain investor confidence in his company. Cisco had been downgraded from Buy to Hold on Wednesday by CIBC World Markets analyst Steve Kamman, who doubted Cisco's ability to continue its strong revenue growth percentages and predicted that Cisco was likely to experience a slowdown in the next six months.[25] Compounding the negative effect of Kamman's pronouncement were the troubling words of Chambers himself, delivered that same day to a Morgan Stanley Dean Witter investment conference in Phoenix. Chambers said the current quarter was proving to be "a little more challenging" for Cisco and sent a chill through investors with the observation, "Is the economy slowing? Absolutely." Moreover, it was happening "at a faster pace than people realize."

These were remarkably prescient words. Chambers tried to take the edge off them by reiterating Cisco's expectations of strong fiscal performances. "Let me say this directly: Our customers' business is slowing, not our business with customers." He also stated, "We are not immune, but we won't be as affected as some segments of the IT [information technology] community. If we can execute as we have in the past, I'm more comfortable about our future than we've ever been."[26]

This was a common pleading of the tech sector in the face of the networking slowdown. Sure, customer spending is slowing down, but *our* share of it is still growing. Nortel had already made this argument in its guidance that predicted its sales growth would outpace the increases in the telecoms' budgets.

Investors were so rattled by the Kammen downgrade and Chambers's intimations of economic gloom that they knocked 10 percent off Cisco's daily high in frenzied trading on January 10, before regaining their composure and allowing the stock down about 2 percent on a volume of more than 213 million shares.

Nortel investors appeared to be cut from different cloth. Overall, the knee-jerk reaction of the markets was to applaud Nortel's culling of the herd, rather than read it as a possible sign of looming problems. Investors loved lean and mean operations, and loved it even more when a company chopped jobs in preparation (it said) to aggressively redeploy in cutting-edge, high-growth, high-profitability areas. No one seemed to be aware that an entire cutting-edge growth area in Ottawa had just been whacked. Having opened on the TSE on January 11 at $46.70, Nortel's stock shot up almost 9.5 percent on heavy volume of more than 15 million shares, to close at $51.10. In successfully arguing that its job cuts were really part of a strategic redeployment designed to increase profitability, Nortel deftly avoid a pricing meltdown as the January 18 release date for its fourth-quarter 2000 results approached.

But the evidence was mounting that there was more going on than strategic redeployment. Nortel was tightening its belt; managers in some areas were confronting instructions from up top to make cuts to their operations of 10 percent. The word of layoffs was rapidly spreading. Wrote one Raging Bull board member:

> There are many layoffs also. I've personally been contacted by many senior managers, directors, and vp's at NT in [Raleigh, N.C.], who are being terminated. They seem to be hitting the switching division here the worst with a target of 10% head-count cut from that group by end of February from what I've heard. This of course is the main underperforming division so it makes sense that the biggest group will come from that one. Some of these folks are from the enterprise group so they are hitting that one also.

But this was easy enough to stomach. Underperforming divisions. Slow growth areas. Who needs them. At the same time, Nortel was undoubtedly doing the right thing, paring down costs in sluggish operations, making managers who were too liberal with their budgets behave themselves, as the wild and crazy growth of 2000 receded. That said, this was still a company promising 30 to 35 percent revenue growth in 2001.

News was filtering out through unorthodox channels of a company in the throes of widespread cost cutting, which involved not only ditching a division like Extreme Voice, but ordering managers to reduce costs by culling their respective departments. Some of the evidence was piling up on what amounted to a tech industry Internet scandal sheet called FuckedCompany.com.

FuckedCompany.com was a lark that had turned into a serious source of insider scuttlebutt for the tech sector. Founded as an Internet-based game in which participants could vote for their favourite inept tech company, it had turned into a popular bulletin board for industry employees keen to share gossip and insider knowledge, and help each other avoid nightmare jobs with nightmare firms.

Any company as large as Nortel is going to have its share of misfits, and while its hiring practices were rigorous, it also acquired a large number of employees whom it did not hire itself but who came with its many acquisitions. That lack of employee quality control and the libellous nature of many of the postings (made in the appropriately named Happy Fun Slander Corner) make much of what is preserved in the FuckedCompany.com archives unprintable. But at the same time, the testimonials of current and former Nortel employees that began to accumulate in the wake of the worldwide layoffs painted a picture of company managers struggling to execute rapid and at times arbitrary reductions according to orders from on high.

In early February, a series of posted exchanges began, as someone looked for advice on whether to interview for a Nortel job. Despite the site's relish for flaming witless dot-com enterprises, Nortel attracted many positive comments about its quality as an employer. "You could do worse than working for Nortel," went one reply. "I was with them at their Brampton, Ontario headquarters for about two years and I gotta tell you, they are the best company I've ever worked for. They know how to motivate and keep good people." Wrote another: "Yep, Nortel's a pretty good company to work for. I enjoy the hell out of it, even more now that I didn't get laid off. Sometimes I wished I got laid off, 'cause I hear that they have sweet severance packages. I would like to reiterate that any division other than wireless and optical may be a bit dicey until March. They may be hiring, but the voice from on high may tell them to trim off some fat by next quarter."

There were a few layoff horror stories. "Here's my favourite lay-off story here at Nortel in Ottawa:—[name of manager deleted] used his RIM plaything from the beach in Florida to notify all of his pee-ons BY EMAIL that they no longer had jobs. I had to laugh when this new guy arrives a day later at the office for his first day of work. He has Tech support install his new workstation and configure his Outlook e-mail application and the first message he reads is his lay-off notice (I'm not making this up!!) He's in Ottawa and his fucking furniture is 800 miles away in a moving van enroute from fucking VANCOUVER!!"

Whatever the misadventures, Nortel has received generally high marks for the way it treated outgoing employees, who were routinely given sixty-day notices to allow them time to land on their feet. And having Nortel as the most recent job on their résumé was widely considered to be a major asset. "People still have a sense of pride in having worked at Nortel," Kirsten Watson said, a year after her dismissal. "Nortel hasn't cast a shadow on them. A lot of people would want to go back there." And in the immediate aftermath of being let go, Kirsten had no qualms about the health of Nortel—or more specifically, its once high-flying shares. "I had complete faith in Nortel stock. Even after being laid off, I bought stock in the company."

That faith was shared by the Raging Bull true believers. The stock had finished January 11 on the NYSE at $34^{1}/_{16}$, up from a daily low of $30^{3}/_{4}$. At 11:29, a Nortel board member had coached: "Don't sell under 34$." The optimists rapidly responded.

ferncuc: why would anyone sell at $34.

open200: my thoughts exactly. $34??? more like $44 or $54.

ferncuc: how about 94.00

duduk100: $44 within a few weeks, $54 within a couple months, and $94 within 12 months

Just think: a return on equity of almost 200 percent over 2001, in a period the company was only promising to increase its revenues 30 to 35 percent. And John Chambers, at the helm of Cisco, was saying that the economy was slowing more quickly than anyone realized.

But never mind that. Nortel was on the rise again, and it was time to accumulate. As one Raging Bull posting coached on January 12 , "There is going to be a SHIT load of RRSP money coming into NT within the month. Buy while you can."

As investors awaited Nortel's fourth-quarter report on Thursday, January 18, Juniper Networks' own year-end results, released after the market closed on Tuesday, fed the speculative fever. The IP router company had beaten analyst estimates and even raised its revenue guidance for 2001. Better yet, its pro forma income per share of 53 cents was not horribly far off its actual net income of 43 cents. Juniper was one of the last great NASDAQ Internet superstars, continuing to trade at improbable multiples. As StockHouse.ca reported, "At Wednesday's closing price of US$136³/₈, Juniper is at 317 times current earnings per share (EPS) and about 173 times projected 2001 EPS. In this type of market, these multiples demand perfect performance." Juniper's bold increase of its guidance figures pretty well eliminated any possibility of beating analyst forecasts over the next year. With such high multiples, the stock had a high risk of tanking if the company didn't meet expectations. And in September 2001, Juniper would make its first dip below $10.

But for Nortel investors, Juniper's surprise news served up a full buffet of food for thought. The niche player in high-end Internet routers had been steadily increasing its market share, mainly at the expense of Cisco, which didn't yet have an OC-192 compliant router on the market. Its net revenues had leapt from $102.6 million in 1999 to $673.5 million in 2000. According to the investment community's zero-sum rationale, because Nortel had struck an agreement to sell Juniper's optical router the previous summer after its own attempts to produce an OC-192 optical Internet router had yet to bear fruit, whatever damage Juniper was doing to Cisco was automatically good for Nortel. And if Juniper was increasingly optimistic about its future revenues, this provided further promise of strong growth for Nortel. After all, if Juniper was making hay with its OC-192 router, the M160 and Nortel dominated the OC-192 standard fibre-optic telecom backbone into which Juniper's routers tapped, then it followed that strong sales could be expected from Nortel as well.

Of course, there was another way to look at it: maybe Juniper was just continuing to take market share from Cisco in IP routers, which had nothing to do with whether the OC-192 standard networks Nortel had been building would themselves be a source of further revenue growth. Nine months later, Juniper's CEO, Scott Kriens, would address this scenario during his conference call with analysts after releasing his company's third-quarter results on October 12. While not disputing the belief that the carriers had overbuilt their infrastructure, he would argue that the carriers would need IP routers long before they put in more orders for infrastructure. If telecom carriers had excess capacity, they needed to spend money on things to bring in traffic, not to create yet more empty network. That was, implicitly, good for Juniper and even its router rival, Cisco, potentially bad for Nortel.

But back in January, investors in general chose to read Juniper's most recent financial news as good for Nortel. The American markets had been closed on Monday the fifteenth for Martin Luther King Day, and after Juniper released its results on Tuesday, Nortel lunged forward. Having bounced between $31 and $35 in New York all month, the stock jumped from $31^{15}/$_{16}$ on Tuesday to a high of $35^{1}/$_{4}$ on Wednesday before closing at $34^{3}/$_{4}$. The Juniper results had hardened expectations that Nortel would come through with a solid year-end report on Thursday and hold with its repeatedly bullish forecasts for 2001.

For the most part, the analysts were lining up behind Nortel with their sound bites of advice as the moment of the year-end report release approached. The Raging Bull members tracked their positions. Thomas Astle at Merrill Lynch called Nortel a Near Term Buy on the sixteenth. On the seventeenth, Buy pronouncements were reiterated by Ken Leon at ABN-AMRO Inc. in New York and Dayle Hogg, technology analyst at Griffiths McBurney & Partners (GMP) in Toronto. And on the eighteenth, with Nortel's numbers set for release at the close of trading, Gus Papageorgiou at Scotia Capital Markets in Toronto weighed in with a Strong Buy, and Mark Lucey at TD Securities with a Buy. Wojtek Uzdelewicz at Bear, Stearns was more equivocal with his Attractive, while Eric Buck at Wasserstein, Perella was offering a more pessimistic Hold.

Lehman Brothers was particularly bullish, calling Nortel an "Aggressive Trading Buy," predicting it was headed for $39 to $40 and that earnings might increase by a cent per share. Lehman was encouraged by the positive news from the enterprise and infrastructure sectors which Nortel serviced, as represented by the recent good cheer from Juniper as well as IBM. "Big Blue" had bucked the recent trend of poor performances by computing stalwarts Hewlett Packard, Apple, and Intel by exceeding analysts' expectations with its fourth-quarter performance, released on the seventeenth. IBM CFO John Joyce told analysts that the company was entering 2001 with "confidence" and predicted that, so long as the U.S. economy remained strong, IBM could post revenue growth in the high single digits. IBM's reputation as a master masseuse with its numbers didn't stop its report from raising spirits in the tech sector. Lehman Brothers ventured that perhaps the slowdown in Internet infrastructure spending hadn't been as grave as had been thought.

The market went with the optimists, with Nortel opening higher on the eighteenth at $35³/₈, climbing to $38. There were a few dissenters amid the good cheer. One posting to Raging Bull Nortel's board, claiming to have been made from Montreal, exhorted investors at 2:41 to "short NORTEL at about 3.45 P.M. My guess based on the street is that not all the news will be good. An apparent slowdown will be visible somewhere in the news release and bingo the stock will drop in after hours trading by about 5.00. Good luck!"

But this was not the day for shorters to be heard. Around 3:30, the Raging Bull board began to hear optimist, if nervous, clamour.

> **jrh72:** Moon, fancy meeting you here. Just bought 500 looking for a bounce after the numbers.

> **moonduckie:** jrh72 you are a brave man.

> **ferncuc:** you mean a smart man!!!
> Did you miss all the buys coming in all week, and huge buys of over 1,000,000 shares.
> Someone knows something.

Pfine responded to ferncuc with an all-or-nothing prediction:

> we won't see the $30'sUS tomorrow, IMO. We will either be in the $40's or the $20'sUS. Like most of you, I am betting/hoping for the $40's. It will take another $1/2$ pt rate cut by the Fed on 1/31 to get us above the $40'sUS, and even then it may not happen until we get "increased visibility" of the current (Jan-March) qtr. Five minutes to close and trying to hold $37US. Fingers crossed, etc.

In the final minutes of trading, the stock slipped slightly, to finish at $36^{11}/$_{16}$ at the closing bell, but that was still an improvement of $1^{5}/$_{16}$ over the opening. Put it another way: a profit of $131.25 on every block of 100 Nortel shares. Not a bad haul for a day trader, and if the imminent year-end numbers and guidance from Nortel delivered the nice pop the board members hoped, there was much more to be made even by the weekend. Certainly the signs were good: a rising share price along with high volume. After trading 14.5 million shares on January 16, before Juniper released its year-end numbers after the close, Nortel had seen almost 80 million shares change hands on the NYSE in just two days as anticipation built toward the company's own year-end. There was nothing to do now but wait for the news to cross the wire.

The wait was short. At 4:11 the first news hit the bulletin board.

chycho: 26 cents met numbers, and confirm future is good. UP UP UP

So began a euphoric string of days for the true believers. John Roth and his management team had come through with a strong fourth quarter and nothing but sunshine for 2001.

20

Loss of Visibility

Remember what I said about the 40s last week. Become a believer! Optical is about to be back in vogue, and NT is king!
—posting to Nortel bulletin board
at RagingBull.com, January 18, 2001

The numbers released by Nortel on January 18 were reassuring, even inspiring. After the debacle of the third quarter, Nortel had capped the year with outwardly impressive figures. The company had delivered as promised: revenues for the fourth quarter were $8.82 billion, a 34 percent increase over fourth-quarter 1999. "Earnings from operations" had reached $825 million, or $0.26 per share. For the year, Nortel recorded $30.28 billion in revenue, a 42 percent increase over 1999, and $2.31 billion in "operating income," or $0.74 per share, a 42 percent jump as well. Best yet, after undershooting revenue forecasts for its optical Internet business in the third quarter, Nortel exceeded them in the fourth quarter, pushing them to $10.1 billion.

Nortel was calling for revenues of $8.1 billion in the first quarter of 2001 and a 30 percent increase in its revenues and customized earnings per share for the new year. This was at the bottom end of the previous guidance of revenues of $8.1 to $8.3 billion for the first quarter and growth in revenues and earnings per share of 30 to 35 percent, but it squeaked in as an affirmation. Nortel had amended its guidance "in light of the current economic environment and tightening of capital within the telecom sector." Nortel had been pretty badly slapped around by missing the analysts' consensus EPS forecast for the third quarter by just a penny back in October, and it had Lucent's miserable example of the consequences of repeatedly failing to live up to your own numbers. Nevertheless, Nortel had made a bold and confident prediction. The January 18 guidance exuded the swagger of a major player making a Babe Ruth–like call of exactly to which seat in the bleachers he was about to dispatch the next ball thrown his way.

The Raging Bull true believers dialled into the conference call with analysts and lapped up the good news.

> How do you spell relief? NORTEL NETWORKS! Just beautiful. . .
>
> Conference call was excellent with solid guidance based on market conditions going forward. Very realistic expectations set for 2001 and all in all a big relief for investors in this company.
>
> Oh yeah, beating the high end of revenue numbers was a huge surprise to me. I expected somewhere in the middle around $8.6 or $8.7 billion.
>
> My hat is off to John Roth and his team at Nortel. This really is a powerhouse to be reckoned with for years to come.

It was also an opportunity to pile on Paul Sagawa for his September 28 reports on Nortel and Lucent. Five different postings laid into the Bernstein analyst with relish.

> Sagawa looking like the moron that he is posted no questions . . . hope he disappears and rejoins LU as a salesman or something. . .
>
> Sagawa was wrong. This is all he can say. Many of us lost a ton of money because of him. The Xsalesman from LU should go back to LU. He belongs to the loser group.
>
> I agree that he is wrong and trying to save his face. Anything Nortel achieves is not good enough for him. glad to see he is the only one, so far!

Sagawa is wrong!! Wrong cost many good people much money in their 401Ks, IRAs, etc. Way to go NT, met the number, good guidance!

Sagawa is wrong, was wrong, and continues to be wrong. The man just doesn't get it. NT is overtaking all competitors - and has become #1. . . . CSCO is on the ropes - NT wins.

But not everyone was dismissing Sagawa. Wrote one board member:

I am not a fan of Sagawa and have stated so in the past. However, as I said before, I do believe in accuracy vs revisionist history. Give the devil his due; he was the first to point out potential problems that have come to pass in the industry. We still need to wait and see if his forecast for 2001 is right. I am betting that an aggressive rate cut program by the Fed will reverse the economic trend that Sagawa saw. We will see who is right soon enough.

It was clear people were misinterpreting Sagawa's message—or hadn't really ever read what he'd written. It was one thing to gloat about his misstep in being bullish about Lucent. It was another thing altogether to ignore his warnings about the capex spending downturn coming in 2001. Sagawa was no longer out on a limb on this. Even John Chambers at Cisco was acknowledging a slowdown, while still insisting that Cisco could continue to grow. And Nortel's prediction that the telecom equipment market would grow somewhere above 20 percent in 2001 was not far off Sagawa's call for growth of 19 percent.

Worse, Nortel had failed to meet the supposedly hostile Sagawa's September 28 predictions for 2000. Sagawa had forecast revenues of more than $31 billion. Nortel reported $30.28 billion. He had predicted optical sales to exceed $12 billion. Nortel barely cleared $10 billion. He had predicted a revenue increase of 48 percent. Nortel reported 42 percent. He had predicted earnings per share of 77 cents,

4 cents above the consensus back in September. Nortel reported 74 cents. In short, Nortel hadn't lived up to a single prediction of the analyst Raging Bull investors considered to be the stock's biggest enemy. Where was the joy in that?

In truth, Nortel's fourth-quarter 2000 results left much to be desired. For beginners, there was the matter of its claim that it had actually earned 74 cents a share. This was based on Nortel's tried-and-true magical accounting, for which it tossed aside all those distracting costs of doing business: acquisition-related costs ("in-process research and development expense, and the amortization of acquired technology and goodwill from all acquisitions subsequent to July 1998"), stock option compensation from acquisitions and divestitures, and one-time gains and charges. In this way, Nortel had been able to turn a 46-cent loss per common share in the fourth quarter into a 26-cent profit. A $1.41 billion loss in that quarter had become an $825 million (U.S.) profit. Not only that, but this "net earnings from operations" profit had increased 24 percent. Not only was Nortel getting bigger, it was making more money! And the accounting magic just got better when the year-to-year comparisons were made. "Net earnings from operations" of $2.31 billion, or 74 cents per share, compared handsomely with 1999's $1.43 billion, or 52 cents per share. That was a jump of 42 percent. But once you applied all those expenses that GAAP demanded, Nortel actually recorded a loss in 2000 of $3.47 billion, or $1.17 per share—a huge increase over the 13-cent loss per common share in 1999.

Nortel dutifully reported both sets of figures, but as usual in the press release and comments to analysts and reporters put the emphasis on the "net earnings from operations" results. Whether investors or analysts cared about the dramatic difference between Nortel's imagined profits and actual losses was another matter. The market overall had been so well trained to view corporate performance through the rose-coloured glasses of "everything but the bad stuff" custom accounting used by Nortel and so many other companies that it was almost unseemly to point out the, um, billion-dollar losses. Revenue growth was king, and those "acquisition-related costs" were ephemeral constructs that the smart money knew best to ignore.

Nortel's full financials wouldn't be released for about two months, and they would contain numerous items to alarm anyone who knew how to read a financial statement properly and cared enough about what was in it.

Take retained earnings, which are the profits a company is supposed to hold in reserve after sending dividends to common shareholders. The surplus is carried forward into the next year, and further surpluses are added to it. With a healthy company, you expect a positive balance to develop. In 1997, John Roth's first full year in command, Nortel had retained earnings of $3.2 billion (U.S. GAAP). In 1998, they were down to $1.53 billion; in 1999, down further still, to $967 million. In 2000, they went negative by $2.7 billion. By Nortel's own calculation, its retained earnings had fallen by a total of almost $3.7 billion since 1999, by almost $6 billion since 1997, and yet it still sent dividends to the common shareholders during the entire period. The fact that Nortel was consistently losing money in its GAAP accounting was the initial sign that dividends should have ceased, but this could have been excused if a positive retained earnings balance was maintained. The fact was, Nortel had incubated an ever-expanding brood of shareholders it remained determined to service with dividends, come what may. In January 1997, right before Roth took over, Nortel's 262 million shares were split. Now there were three billion. About $150 million had been paid out in dividends in fiscal 1997. Since then, as the float increased with acquisitions, more splits, and stock options, the dividends tab kept going up— to $178 million in 1998, $204 million in 1999, and $223 million in 2000. In all, $755 million in dividends had been paid to common shareholders over the past four years, while retained earnings steadily sank. In the first three years, at least, there were still retained earnings left after the dividend payout, despite ongoing net losses, but in 2000, Nortel paid out the dividends anyway, despite the large net loss and steep drop into negative retained earnings.

Cash flow for 2000, which got rid of the impact of amortization charges, didn't make for a brighter picture. Nortel's net cash flow from operations was in steep decline: under U.S. GAAP, it had been $1.48 billion in 1998 and $1.05 billion in 1999. Already, in the first six months of 2000, its net cash flow from operations had trickled to just $35 million. Its results for all of 2000 came in at a pitiable $40 million under U.S. GAAP and had gone negative by $10 million under Canadian GAAP. Nortel drew considerable cash from selling off chunks of Entrust ($682 million) and shedding wholly owned operations ($174 million). While Nortel did invest almost $1.9 billion in plant and equipment in 2000, which affected investment cash flow, the $856 million it collected on the "gain on sale of businesses and investment" was clipped from its operating cash flow. It was also required to slice away $743 million in increased current accounts receivables and a $2 billion increase in inventories. If its net increase in long-term receivables of $693 million was reallocated to operating activities, Nortel's operating cash flow went negative by $653 million under U.S. GAAP.

As for assets, therein lay other concerns. Nortel's noncurrent assets stood at $25.65 billion. Of that, $18.97 billion was intangibles—goodwill and acquired technology. And of that, $17.8 billion was goodwill. Thus, goodwill—the unquantifiable premium Nortel had paid for its string of acquisitions—represented 69.3 percent of its noncurrent assets. And the acquisitions that generated all this goodwill had yet more goodwill in store in the future, as many of them harboured milestone-based "contingent considerations." The deals for Sonoma, CoreTek, Photonic, Promatory, Qtera, and Dimension still had maximum contingencies remaining at year-end 2000 totalling $510 million, $486 million of which was to be paid for with Nortel shares.

As for the rest of noncurrent assets, only $3.4 billion consisted of plant and equipment. Another $1.5 billion was in long-term receivables—money owed Nortel by customers who weren't expected to pay within the "current" receivables timeframe of one year, which Nortel had capitalized and placed on the balance sheet as a noncurrent asset. Given the shaky stature of so many CLECs and other new telecom industry players, investors had good reason to worry about how bankable these receivables might turn out to be. Nortel had made a provision of $383 million—in effect, a write-down—against its long-term receivables to cover off defaults. This meant it considered at least 20 percent of its long-term receivables to be so impaired that it wouldn't show them as an asset.

Long-term receivables (described here before the provision for losses) had become a going concern as the years passed under Roth's command. In 1997 they amounted to just $359 million, which was 2.3 percent of gross revenues. In 1998, they made a discernible jump, to $688 million, to 3.9 percent of gross revenues. In the 1998 annual report, Nortel said the increase in long-term receivables was primarily the result of a higher balance of customer financing at year-end. Thus we can safely assume that the increasing amounts of long-term receivables under Roth, both in absolute dollars and as a percentage of gross revenues, and the increasing risk attached to them, were substantially due to the use of vendor financing. In 1999, long-term receivables (with provisions factored back in) reached $1.64 billion, or 7.7 percent of revenues; in 2000, they were up to $1.91 billion, or 6.3 percent of revenues. And with each year, their risk factor, based on the default provision as a percentage of the total (pre-provision) long-term receivables, had increased: from 7 percent in 1997, to 16.7 in 1998, to 17.3 in 1999, to 20 in 2000. Back in 1991, Nortel's default provision for the long-term receivables assigned to its finance subsidiary was less than 3 percent. In its 2001 annual report's MD&A section, Nortel would provide a specific discussion of vendor financing for the past two years. At year-end 2000, total vendor financing drawn down was $1.51 billion, to which Nortel had applied a "provision" of $433 million. That was an implicit default rate of 29 percent. For 2001, the drawn-down vendor financing would drop to $1.35 billion, but the default rate, based on the provision of $887 million, rocketed to 66 percent.

Moving down the noncurrent assets lists in the 2000 report, one encountered "investments at cost and associated companies at equity," which totalled $892 million. Nortel provided no notes to explain what went into this figure. Nortel simply described the "associated companies" as "entities which are not controlled but over which the Company has the ability to exercise significant influence." Al Rosen had become concerned that some of it might represent equity in customers that Nortel was forced to accept in lieu of payments on uncollectable receivables. If so, it meant Nortel was accumulating equity interest in troubled operations in exchange for bad debts that had contributed to Nortel's increasing revenue figures. Whatever they were, Nortel had incurred a $33 million loss on its income statement because of them.

Evidence of Nortel's dealings with companies lumped into its "investments at cost and associated companies at equity" category was thin on the ground, but a sparkling exception was FiberNet Telecom Group Inc., which was launched in 1994 to provide short-haul optical transport between carrier "points of presence" (mainly hotels and Class A office buildings in major U.S. cities). FiberNet showed that it wasn't necessarily the case that Nortel simply accepted equity in startups in order to address bad debts; it was also willing to actively participate as both an investor and lender in order to get the sales. In July 2001, Nortel put together a four-page promotional document for its OPTera product line that showcased FiberNet as a "success story." "To build these high-powered, carrier-class networks, FiberNet selected Nortel Networks OPTera Metro multiservice platforms," Nortel crowed. "Nortel Networks metropolitan solutions are among the most reliable and robust in the industry," FiberNet president and CEO Michael Liss chimed in. "As of mid-2000, the company had committed to US$260 million in Nortel Networks technology and professional services to expand its fiber networks," the document further proclaimed.

Nortel declined to note either in the document or on its corporate Web site (where FiberNet's use of OPTera was still being touted in June 2002) that Nortel was a significant shareholder through its wholly owned U.S. subsidiary, Nortel Networks Inc. While Nortel had made no mention of FiberNet in its own financial statements, it did make beneficial ownership filings in 2000 with the SEC regarding FiberNet, and FiberNet's own filings filled in the fascinating blanks. In FiberNet's 1999 annual report, the startup (which had no revenues to date) indicated that it would be employing Lucent technology. That was already set to change, however. On December 31, 1999, FiberNet had entered into a $60 million master purchasing agreement with Nortel, which gave FiberNet the right "to purchase optical networking equipment and related services at predetermined volume-based pricing." FiberNet just needed the money to actually pay for Nortel's gear. On April 11, 2000, Nortel signed onto a $75 million credit facility for FiberNet, providing $30 million (the single largest participant), on the condition that at least $18.75 million was used to purchase its equipment and services under the master purchase agreement. FiberNet was then listed on the NASDAQ on April 27. On June 22, the master purchase agreement with Nortel was increased to $260 million and extended to 2002.

Eight days later, Nortel completed the FiberNet hat trick: already both a supplier and a lender of the funds necessary to purchase those supplies, it now became a shareholder. Nortel handed over a total of $50 million by summer's end for preferred shares convertible into FiberNet common. By December 7, 2000, Nortel owned 26.3 percent of FiberNet through common and convertible preferred shares. FiberNet's capitalized assets indicated it spent a total of $31.4 million on Nortel goods and services in 2000. Also on December 7, FiberNet gave Nortel a promissory note for $2.3 million in outstanding receivables, bearing 14 percent interest, with the first payment thereon not due until January 2002. At the height of its brief trading glory, FiberNet closed at $18.75 on July 5, 2000. By the time Nortel converted most of its preferred shares into common ones on December 7, the shares were down to $6, and its 26 percent interest was worth $108.6 million. But by the spring of 2002, FiberNet shares were struggling to stay above a dime, and on May 24 the company made the ignominious announcement that its stock was moving to NASDAQ's SmallCap Market. Nortel's $50 million stake was now worth less than $2 million.

Finally, there was the category of "other assets." This is a fairly murky category, with no specific note to elaborate on what went into it. Nortel did explain, elsewhere in its notes, that it included "pension plan and other benefit assets." In the case of the pension plan, Nortel could book as an asset any surplus in its defined benefit plan's funding, based in part on assumptions of the rate of investment return. The 2001 annual report would indicate that $70 million of the funding for the company's defined benefit plan was assigned to "other assets" in 2000. But most of the contents of "other assets" were a mystery. GAAP required no explanation. Rosen strongly suspected that Nortel was taking advantage of the provisions under GAAP that permitted a company to remove expenses like interest, overhead, and management salaries from the income statement, where they would negatively affect earnings, and park them on the balance sheet, on the basis that they were attached to activities that would be of future benefit. It was perfectly legal, but in addition to sprucing up earnings it also obscured the company's actual operating cash flow. Unlike the amortization charges that Nortel stripped away for its earnings-from-operations numbers, any expenses moved to the balance sheet represented cash outlays that would not be deducted from the current income statement. Nortel's "other assets" had been $495 million in 1997, $438 million in 1998, then increased from $465 to $560 million between 1999 and 2000. In 2001, the amount of defined benefit funding assigned to "other assets" would drop to $25 million, while the category overall ballooned to $893 million.

From the perspective of weighing Nortel's share value, uncertainty over how GAAP reporting affected cash flow was a big problem. Analysts who looked to the ratio of price to operating cash flow as a more accurate indicator of company's worth than P/E were slapping a pricing multiple on a figure that might not reflect Nortel's true ability to generate dollars, because there was a good chance that millions, tens of millions, or even hundreds of millions of actual expenditures had been moved from the income statement to the balance sheet.

The trends that the Rosens had seen in 2000 were becoming painfully clear in the year's full financial statements. Nortel was giving every indication of pyramidic tendencies. Every year, Nortel's need for revenue-based growth called upon it to build a newer, wider layer of income at the base. Achieving these revenues meant buying more companies, and buying more companies meant issuing more shares, creating a newer, wider layer of shares in the accompanying pyramid that was the share float. No one could seriously believe that the company was capable of sustaining successive years of growth of 30 to 40 percent—unless, of course, you believed that the optical networking business was capable of laying more and more cable and installing more and more optical cross-connects and DWDM systems every year until 2025 and beyond. Even John Roth couldn't imagine perpetuating percentage increases on the scale seen in 2000. Nevertheless, despite Roth's ambition to keep using up to 10 percent of the company's market capitalization to make share-based purchases every year, Nortel surely had to reach a point where it couldn't keep issuing enough shares to buy enough companies to fuel the kind of growth it had been experiencing. There would have to be an easing of growth. Which was fine, if it led to real earnings and Nortel could keep evolving its products without having to buy the necessary technology with ten of millions of shares. But if the networking industry hit any bumps on the road to near-infinite growth before the company was able to turn its spate of recent acquisitions into strong and sustained sources of new revenue, Nortel and its shareholders were in for a rough ride. Paul Sagawa had warned about those bumps back in September; he had been sure they would start showing up in the new year. And here Nortel was starting the new year with some crowd-pleasing earnings-from-operations numbers and promises of 30 percent growth, while its full financials, not yet available, provoked a slew of troubling questions.

Investors instead were revelling in Nortel's ability to meet its own guidance, post profits (through its own accounting methodology), and continue to promise strong results for the coming quarter and the year overall. It's doubtful that having the full financials to pore over would have made any difference to most of them. They were enrapt with Nortel's ability to deliver on its own special earnings numbers, and as they listened in to the conference call between analysts and John Roth, Frank Dunn, and Clarence Chandran after the market closed on the eighteenth, they paid careful techie attention to things like the array of technology Nortel marketed and how the new products were going to be rolled out.

People weren't in a mood for negativity. A Canadian Press item that failed to stay on message with Nortel received a raspberry:

Nortel Networks revenue up 34 percent in Q4, company posts $1.4B US loss

TORONTO (CP) The cost of acquisitions and other charges produced a $1.4 billion US net loss for Nortel Networks in the fourth quarter, although the Canadian high-tech giant met its target for revenue growth.

"Just got to love the negativism out there," posted one board member. "How else could this idiot get a headline anyhow?"

Michael Hollander was guardedly optimistic as the board members dissected the results and guidance. "Yes, so far it looks reasonable," he posted. "The revenues just over the top end of the range so the market can't hit the stock for not meeting the top end. :-) The earnings right on the money. If they explain the slightly lowered guidance for the first quarter as just being prudent, we should be OK."

The board was psyched. They liked the numbers and what they heard from Roth and company during the conference call. Among the many posted comments:

> Conference call comment I liked . . . was in response to any possible restating of guidance . . the answer given was: NT is being more conservative than they were last year because of the market environment . . close communication with accounting depts. Sounds good to me.

Enthusiasm wasn't unanimous. The contrarians and shorters cruised through the Nortel board, taunting the true believers.

> Analysts say NT will settle in the mid-20s . . . say what you will, and gamble all you like. I would hold a cash position until such after the [1Q] results, because "What if I am right and you are wrong wrong wrong?" The stock will go below $20, that's what!
>
> Don't get me wrong. NT makes money. But the share value is still way too high, as were all techs. Still more bottom

to come. Go ahead and max out your credit cards and margin
all the way. You'll regret it and wish you had listened.

But there was little energy wasted on them. Wayne Schmengrum,
still waiting for the right entry point on Nortel, wondered:

> Will Rocky & Bullwinkle manage to fend off the evil villains
> from San FranCISCO???
> > Stay tuned to this station. . .

Teletruth was pumped. He predicted:

> . . .mid 30's probably will happen early next week and I'm play-
> ing this YOYO until the string breaks!
> > ($38-$42 by month end . . . IT's ALL GOOD! but only if
> you let the string unwind with the yoyo hanging at the bottom)

The Nortel true believers were primed for a pop.

On January 24, at a public meeting in Norwalk, Connecticut, the
Financial Accounting Standards Board made a tentative decision to
act on several long years of committee work and consultation and
eliminate the pooling method from business combinations. An exposure draft still had to be drawn up, but the FASB was determined that
the favourite acquisition tool of companies like Cisco and Lucent
would be scrapped. All acquisitions would have to follow the purchase method. The premium on the value of tangible and quantifiable intangible assets like IPR&D and acquired technology would
have to be booked.

The FASB had already approved the initial work on the proposed
changes to the accounting rules on business combinations and goodwill and other intangible assets back on September 13. On October
3, a last-gasp counterattack was launched on the reform program by
two members of the California Congressional caucus. Christopher
Cox, a Republican from 47th district (Newport Beach), and Calvin
Dooley, a Democratic from 20th district (Fresno), introduced a bill

in the House of Representatives that would delay the FASB's work on combinations rules. Rep. Cox's Web page explained that the proposed legislation "imposes a one-year moratorium on the elimination of the 'pooling' method of accounting for mergers, and commissions a more detailed study of the economic impact of this proposed change. Because the only other method of accounting for mergers—the 'purchase' method—significantly discounts the value of 'intangible' assets (such as employee knowledge, reputation, copyright and patents), elimination of the pooling option will make it difficult for high-tech start-ups and businesses in other knowledge-based industries to attract investment capital."

The FASB was outraged by this rearguard action from the merger-mad technology industry via the California House caucus. Back in 1994, the tech industry had helped crush FASB's efforts to have the cost of stock options charged against corporate revenues. The day after the legislation was proposed, FASB chairman Edmund L. Jenkins lashed out. "The potential legislation must be seen for what it is—legislative interference with the FASB's ability to do its job," he charged. "The proposed bill would directly hamper the FASB's independence by legislating the timing of the FASB's proposed improvements to the transparency of the accounting and reporting for business combinations. The bill, if passed, would have a serious and negative impact upon consumers of financial information." He added: "To delay the completion of the project on business combinations is clearly a political intrusion into the FASB's mission. Delay would unnecessarily deprive investors of important financial information."

Jenkins and the FASB steamed past Cox and Dooley. But in the process, the FASB came to a decision on the treatment of goodwill that disappointed the critics of the practice of using shares as cash and never having to account for their value. Under the FASB's final plan, which had taken shape in December 2000, goodwill would not have to be amortized against revenues, the way it had been under the old purchase method. Instead, beginning January 1, 2002, the value of the goodwill would be entered on the balance sheet and be subjected to an impairment test. In reporting periods in which the booked value exceeded the fair value of the goodwill, the difference would have to be written off against revenues.

Among the critics of the new approach to goodwill was Norm Strauss, national director of accounting standards and partner at Ernst & Young. "Under this model, you could compare goodwill to a wine that improves with each passing year," he said. "So you could have timeless goodwill, which is never amortized as long as it's not impaired."

The new regulations weren't perfect. Some thought the political rear-guard action again had worn the FASB down and produced a quasi-pooling compromise. But the old pooling system, with no goodwill whatsoever, was unequivocally dead. However, the implications were not necessarily well grasped. Wrote one Raging Bull board member on January 18:

> New Accounting 2001?
>
> New guidelines announced in 2000 by the association of accountants (forgot exact name). NT has always used a conservative approach to "goodwill" and resisted the pooling methods used by CSCO & others.
>
> With the new guidelines, NT and other firms like GE will be able to show much better profits in 2001.
>
> Finally a level playing field.

Of course, Nortel had never "resisted" pooling. It just wasn't allowed to use it. And the new regulations would have no impact on Nortel's profitability in 2001. In fact, under the purchase method, Nortel was carrying billions in goodwill that was already subject to an impairment test. Were market conditions to seriously decline, Nortel would have to take a goodwill write-down, charged directly against revenues. It could create billions of dollars in GAAP losses. The companies like Cisco that had based their acquisitions on goodwill-free pooling would never face such a day of reckoning.

Nortel's January 18 release of results and new guidance coincided with unofficial news, gleaned in Europe, that Nortel was about to buy a Zurich-based pump laser chip plant from JDS Uniphase. It turned out to be true. John Roth was back on the acquisition trail, which had been cold since October.

JDS Uniphase had been wrangling with the U.S. Department of Justice's antitrust people over the merger with SDL, announced the previous June. The deal had not been closed because of concerns about the monopolistic position JDSU would gain in laser power amplifiers for transmitting optical signals over long distances.

These amplifiers, called pump laser chips, came in two types: 1560 nanometre, used in terrestrial networks, and 980 nanometre, used in oceanic cables. The latter were the more complicated and more powerful—and more expensive. They had to be able to push an optical signal several hundred kilometres before the next chip shoved it along. While the terrestrial chips had at least a half-dozen manufacturers, the 980-nanometre market only had two main ones: JDSU and SDL, with SDL the market leader. Buying SDL would give JDSU a lock on an estimated 70 to 80 percent of the 980-nanometre market and leave customers like Nortel with little leverage in purchasing the components necessary to fulfil their network contracts. As much as JDSU coveted the SDL 980-nanometre operation, it was standing in the way of justice department approval. JDSU had no choice but to spin it off.

The Japanese firm Furukawa, active in 1560-nanometre production, was in the running to acquire it, but Nortel outbid it and secured a vital optical components facility that greatly strengthened its overall photonics portfolio, thereby improving the odds of a successful spinoff of the photonics segment later in the year. Photonics could operate as its own business, and Nortel could sell a minority interest for cash. And as with Entrust, if cash flow proved dear, Nortel could always sell more of it. There seemed to be a huge risk for Nortel going ahead with this scenario. John Roth had bet the future substantially on optical networking. If a core business was spun off and Nortel's own cash flow performance failed to improve, the company could end up gutting its equity in an essential enterprise just to keep the dollars flowing.

But for the time being, no dollars needed to flow. The deal, which was not announced until February 6, did not involve any cash.

Nortel agreed to hand over 65.7 million shares on February 13, provided JDSU's shareholders approved the deal on the twelfth. Nortel also agreed to certain purchase commitments for JDSU components, which, if they were not met by December 31, 2003, would mean a further payment of up to $500 million in shares. The precommitment purchase was pegged at $2 billion (U.S. GAAP). The acquisition landed Nortel a production facility in Zurich and an office with eight employees in Poughkeepsie, New York, which once belonged to IBM, where automated processes for manufacturing the chips were designed.

Back in 2000, Roth had ventured that he would like to use 10 percent of Nortel's market capitalization every year to fund purchases. Roth had just found a way to spend a little more than 2 percent of it. The announcement had no real effect on the share price, as the deal had been rumoured for weeks. And the stock had been moving downward without any help from a splashy announcement of yet another trip by Roth to the printing press in the company treasury department to crank out a few million common shares.

On the Raging Bull board, Teletruth was ebullient, crowing, "Rocky and Bullwinkle (JR and Clarence) now have purchased their own 980 nanometer optical pump helmet for Rocky's headgear. Its a good deal . . . and GOOD NEWS for Frostbite Falls :) ($44–48 by month end)."

By February 6, the Nortel true believers needed an infusion of hope for their favourite stock. Nortel had risen above $40 on the NYSE on January 19 for the first time since December 13. The stock had rebounded by one-third since the beginning of the year. The stay-the-course investors had been reassured. The John Roth Value Threshold of $13.31 was a fast-receding nightmare. But since closing at $39⅝ in New York on January 23, the stock had been carried away in an industry-wide slide. By the time the JDSU deal was announced on the sixth, Nortel was down to $35.51.[27] Nortel hadn't helped the share value by announcing on the first that it had just secured $1.5 billion in debt financing—Nortel fell from $38.30 to $36.01 on February 2. The optimistic beginning to the year, which had driven the sector indices into a typical January bounce, had given way to a broad retreat. Nortel was fighting a countercurrent of general economic uncertainty and widespread malaise in the communications sector.

February was unfolding as a series of sharp shocks. Inflation fears were back. After running at under 3 percent for years, the American Consumer Price Index for all urban areas (CPI-U) had made a startling jump to 4.2 percent for the three-month period ending in January, with much of the increase due to major jumps in the cost of fuel (45 percent) and natural gas and electricity (47.7 percent). The market was watching the Federal Reserve Board warily. The Fed had cut its discount rate as hoped by another quarter point on January 31, thereby lowering the Fed rate another half point, to 5 percent, erasing the 1 percent gain of the previous year, but the new inflation figures raised the possibility of renewed rate increases, which were always bad for equities and especially bad for networking companies if customers found it even harder to borrow to pay for their equipment.

While the market was volatile, daily volumes for the DJIA were under 200 million, a comfortable zone well clear of any selloff stampede. But the telecom sector was irrefutably in the investor doghouse, with various dedicated indices marching south. Numerous major companies were attempting to spin off subsidiaries and vacuum up more investment cash, but several IPOs had to be either abandoned, postponed, or have their offering price severely slashed. Nortel had already shelved its plan to use an IPO to spin off its Netgear division, but was promising to use a private placement instead in March. Late on February 14, Motorola's wireless service provider arm, Propel, would announce that it was scrapping a plan for an IPO that had been in the works since the previous June.

The commercial conquest of the Internet was suffering repeated setbacks. On December 18, Breathe.com, Britain's fourth-largest Internet service provider, which had more than half a million customers, went under. Canada's clickabid.com closed the same day. Another on-line auction site, Bid.com, was hammered down on December 27. Iam.com, a talent agency, burned through $40 million in startup capital before closing down on January 23. Bazillion.com, a DSL (high-speed Internet) provider with more than 5,000 customers, went off-line on January 15. Disney yanked its Internet venture Go.com on January 27. Mercata.com, a "group buying" site created by Microsoft multimillionaire Paul Allen, called it quits on January 31. MVP.com, the much hyped sporting goods retailing startup involving John Elway, Wayne Gretzky, and Michael Jordan, was sent to the showers on February 2. On February 5, eToys.com announced it would be laying off its remaining 293 employees and shut down in the spring; it filed for Chapter 11 on March 7. Still to come was the demise of broadband ISP provider ConnectSouth on February 27, Idealab's Refer.com on February 26, and Work.com, after backers Excite and Dow Jones lost faith and began layoffs on March 9.

A frightening disease was spreading through the tech sector, called "loss of visibility." Nortel had repeatedly reassured the market of the strength of its financial forecasts, but other companies were beginning to confess that they were having a hard time seeing how much business was over the near horizon. In December, computer hardware giant Hewlett Packard had been one of the first tech companies to confess to visibility loss. More worrisome were the confessions in January to murky visibility by John Chambers of Cisco.

Chambers was working overtime to guide his stock into a soft landing, making several distressing pronouncements about the future of networking. In late January, Chambers was hobnobbing at the annual World Economic Forum in Davos, Switzerland, with the likes of Bill Gates and former president Bill Clinton, who had relinquished the Oval Office to George W. Bush on January 20. Chambers had secured an appointment to Bush's education committee, despite the fact that his personal campaign donations in 2000 had been entirely in support of Al Gore. At Davos, Chambers built on the gloom of his comments on January 10 in Phoenix and a further warning to a Morgan Stanley Dean Witter conference on January 24 that investors should be prepared for less predictable revenue growth. In Davos, Chambers volunteered that business had been "a little bit slow" for Cisco in January, according to Bloomberg News. "The business momentum of most of my customers was very tough in December, and equally tough in January." He was also quoted by Bloomberg as saying Cisco might have to delay some expansion plans as it waited out a slowdown that he called a "two-quarter phenomenon." Having made gung-ho predictions of growth as high as 65 percent as recently as December, Chambers was now speaking of revenue growth of 30 to 50 percent, with the possibility of negative growth in some markets. Chambers's comments heightened already acute anticipation of Cisco's second quarter results, which would be released after the markets closed on February 6.

For the companies whose stocks had been swept up by the January rally, the rebounding market and renewed investor confidence were both a blessing and a curse. Certainly, few CEOs would complain about a climbing share price, particularly CEOs like Nortel's Roth or Cisco's Chambers, who used their common shares as currency in making new acquisitions. But as the rally unfolded and then unwound, companies who discovered that the economy was not as robust as either investors or their sales departments had come to believe were caught in a fresh dilemma. How did you temper the market's high expectations for your future revenues and earnings? If you had fuelled high expectations with your own guidance, investors could hardly be blamed for having increased confidence as an event like the initial Fed rate cut on January 2 surprised the market. But as a company began to realize that the market had got ahead of itself and that the firm couldn't live up to the consensus of the leading analysts, action had to be taken before the next quarterly report. The public utterances of Chambers showed that the game had changed, that in the new climate of disclosure created by Reg. FD, companies had to find ways to temper investor enthusiasm without causing panic selloffs. But while Cisco was working hard to engineer a soft landing for its stock price, Nortel was still aiming for the moon.

21

Ramming Speed

It is amazing, the continued complacency of sentiment on this stock. It's like a nice summer day in Nagasaki in 1945. A single airplane lumbers high overhead.
—posting to the Cisco bulletin board at RagingBull.com, Tuesday, February 6, 11:15 A.M. EST

On February 6, the seventy-two-year-old hardliner Ariel Sharon defeated incumbent Israeli prime minister Ehud Barak in an election that heralded the electorate's impatience with the Palestinian intafada, which had been raging since the previous autumn, and with Barak's efforts to strike a peace accord with PLO leader Yasir Arafat and Syria. Peace with the Palestinians had been a keystone promise by Barak when he was elected twenty-one months earlier, and the ensuing negotiations had been a pet project of Bill Clinton. Sharon's election allowed the new Bush administration to declare immediately the Clinton initiative null and void. The Clinton plan had been premature, the Bush people were happy to make known; he had been pushing to the bargaining table parties who weren't ready to make a deal. While the new secretary of state, Colin Powell, would be heading to the Middle East later in the month, the Bush people would just as soon leave it to the Israelis and Palestinians to work things out on their own. Bush was more interested in introducing massive tax cuts than wading into a diplomatic quagmire.

While Bush was hoping that the Middle East mess would just go away and not have to involve him directly, the Street was unhappy with the escalating instability in the region. There was an unsettling correlation between Middle East turmoil and dips in the Dow. The Suez Crisis of 1956, the Six-Day War of 1967, the crisis of 1973, the Iranian hostage crisis of the late 1970s, the Israeli invasion of Lebanon in 1982, and the Iraqi occupation of Kuwait in 1990–91 were all roughly coincident with downturns in the American economy. The Street would prefer that the intafada did not deteriorate into a full-blown conflict, but in the days that followed Sharon's election and Bush's declaration of new American indifference, violence escalated.

The intafada would be cited by many Muslims as a root cause of the devastating suicide attacks on the World Trade Center and the Pentagon that were to come on September 11, but the conflict had already reached American soil via the Internet. Activists on both sides of the Palestinian conflict had been waging cyberwar against each other's sensitive targets, and on November 2, 2000, Lucent had confirmed that it had fended off an attack by a pro-Palestinian group on its corporate Web site. Already reeling from its own financial disasters, Lucent had apparently become the first American corporation targeted in this cyberwar because of its business activities in Israel.[28]

As Sharon took power on February 6, Cisco managed to do more damage to itself than a pro-Palestinian hacker ever could. It missed the consensus earnings forecast by a penny. After twelve consecutive quarters of meeting analysts' expectations, Cisco Systems came up short in its second-quarter results that day. The consensus, as tracked by First Call/Thomson Financial, was for an EPS of 19 cents. Cisco delivered 18. Worse, the $6.72 billion quarterly result was the baseline for the next quarter. Analysts were expecting $7.6 billion, but now they were told to brace for no better than the second quarter, and maybe even 5 percent less. CEO John Chambers forecast a 40 percent growth rate for its fiscal 2001, which fell within its guidance of 30 to 50 percent. But much of that growth had already been banked. "In a postclose conference call, Cisco forecast that revenue growth would grind to a halt in coming periods as the industry's slowdown winds take hold of the networker's mighty sails," reported Scott Moritz of TheStreet.com.

This was very bad for the networking industry. Cisco was the stock that analysts looked to as an old reliable. If Cisco couldn't live up to their expectations, who could? After-hours trading immediately knocked more than $2 off its stock, and investors began bailing on other networking stocks. In three days, Nortel lost $5 and closed at $30.50 on the NYSE on the ninth.

If ever Nortel doubted its own ability to deliver robust growth, now was the chance to share its concerns. Chambers had been publicly softening up the market since January 10 for a slowdown. And on January 24, Corning had released a sobering set of fourth-quarter results. On the one hand, the company had come through with a blistering fourth quarter, exceeding expectations and increasing its revenues by 52 percent over the previous year's quarter. Overall, revenues in 2000 were up 50 percent. But the fibre-optic company was disquietingly cautious about its future prospects.

"We expect the telecommunications market to experience some softness due to ongoing issues with capital availability," said its chief financial officer, James B. Flaws. "Several customers in both our optical fibre and photonic technologies businesses have recently indicated that their order rate may be lower and more uneven than previously expected in the first half of the year. Also, with the weak retail environment, we expect our customers to adjust their inventory levels of finished LCD monitors in the first quarter. As a result, we are widening our pro forma earnings per share guidance range for the first quarter from $0.29–$0.30 to $0.28–$0.31."

This didn't sound like much of an adjustment, but the fact that a company so fundamental to the optical networking bonanza felt it needed to paint a bigger bullseye for earnings in its ongoing quarter and had dared to speak of "lower and more uneven" order rates was a bit of a shocker. It shocked investors into knocking 9 percent from its share price in premarket trading before the NYSE's bells began ringing on the morning of the twenty-fifth. And while they were at it, investors punished JDS Uniphase's price by 7 percent in the premarket as Salomon Smith Barney decided to downgrade both Corning and JDSU.

While Cisco's earning's shortfall and its and Corning's warnings of a bumpier ride in the current quarter were ominous signs of the downturn Sagawa had predicted four months earlier, they wouldn't necessarily translate into similar problems for Nortel. At this juncture in the industry's evolution, it took a bit of a leap of faith, but nevertheless, Nortel could be believed capable of still delivering on its guidance. After all, it had just handed it down on January 18. Surely one week couldn't change everything. And different companies sold different products. Nortel was extremely diversified. Cisco's main strengths were still in the enterprise data networking sector, and it was under pressure from Juniper Networks in high-end IP routers. Corning made strands of glass fibre. A Nortel investor, dazzled by the company's prominence in areas as diverse as wireless networks and e-commerce software, could whistle past the gathering omens.

But there had been at least one sign of possible problems. On January 26, Bookham Technology plc of Oxfordshire, England, issued a press release reiterating its guidance in conjunction with the completion of two acquisitions. Bookham traded on the London Stock Exchange and NASDAQ; it used a proprietary technology called ASOC to manufacture optical circuits using silicon as the base material and sold components for a variety of networking applications. Among its customers was Nortel. Bookham's press release noted: "Lower sales of [Bookham's] mini-DIL products, principally due to a reduction in orders for this product from Nortel Networks as a result of their evolution to a different product mix, was counter balanced by an increase in shipments of DWDM products, which increased to over 30% of total revenues."

It was a cryptic statement that was not easily deciphered by a Nortel watcher. Was Bookham politely blaming slipping sales by Nortel for reduced orders for its mini-DIL products—phrasing it in a way that didn't jump Nortel on its own guidance? Or could the increase in shipments of its DWDM products also be attributed to strong orders from Nortel? Either way, hardly anyone noticed. The Bookham release largely flew under the radar of Nortel investors.

But within Nortel, there was gathering evidence of a company facing a downturn. At the very least, belt tightening was under way, which is what you would expect of a company with negative operating cash flow, regardless of how upbeat its guidance remained. The inimitable FuckedCompany.com postings by current and former Nortel employees in early February, mainly still responding to someone's query about the wisdom of accepting a job with the company, bore testament to the collateral damage of layoffs and ongoing economizing.

February 5

Met a line manager who was having to waste 5% of his group by last Friday. Worse thing was he had to find ANOTH-ER 5% to fire by this Friday. Nortel are taking a crash diet before somebody tells them they are too fat for the party!

—

We just got a royal bitch-out here from our CEO, cut the bonus pool by 25%. . . .

Waaay too much spending last year, seems to be a common theme in the tech world now.

At least we aren't Lucent. . . .

—

Nortel in Raleigh has rescended [sic] some MBA job offers.

—

My girlfriend is a Director for their Optical Divisions. They have, or are about to lay off 4,000 - 5,000

February 6

Many layoffs in Wireless were announced internally a few weeks back . . . Technical jobs in actual wireless technologies are prolly in fine standing but any accessory positions in wireless i would consider dicey.

End of november we had to layoff all contractors and reneg on several offers, even layed off someone on their first day . . . we were given no alternative. it sucked . . . hiree beware.

February 9

Every Friday at 4pm the Santa Clara office has a free beer and winefest for all employees. This has been a very generous offer. Especially for some of the heavy drinkers. Figure if you Knock down 12 beers in a sitting, which many of the visitors do, that is equivalent to a $55 dollar tab at a bar.

From my understanding all layed off people are permitted to attend during the severance period. Thus "If you are a fired employee and need to drink your sorrows away, you can do it on Nortels budget"

Rumor: Someone told me that they will have 2 kegs. 1 will be with premium beer for current employees and 1 will be a cheaper beer for employees who are on a severance. Additionally, the cups will be slightly different depending on your status.

Employees who have not been effected by the layoff will be given 20 oz cups that have the Nortel logo and read "building the high speed internet."

Employees effected by the layoff and considered on severance will be given a smaller 16 oz cup that has the logo "Just getting Drunk"

I am not sure if this is true. Can someone confirm this? Can someone possibly contact Ottawa on this?

February 10

I worked in Ottawa and I was fired by my asswipe manager while at a business meeting in California. The fuck could not even wait until I got home. . . .

February 14

They laid off entire directorates (several departments) in Ottawa that were working on optical efforts. . . . Nortel is still hiring, but they are looking for younger, less expensive talent. The average tenure at Nortel is going WAY WAY down and continues to drop.

In February 2000, John Richards[29] was hired by Nortel as a contract administrator in the supply chain of one of the company's Internet-oriented divisions. In other words, he was in sales. He had received an M.B.A. and had been doing contract work here and there, but found it difficult to find a full-time position through late 1999 as the Y2K scare put a freeze on hirings. Then the scare blew over and Nortel blew into his life. "When I joined, they were hiring 100 to 150 people a week. There was so much work, and you were putting in crazy hours. But people were treated unbelievably well. You were paid overtime and for your meals."

John loved working at Nortel. He still does, having narrowly missed being laid off in the round of cuts that came in October 2001. "A lot of companies I've been with treated people like shit. At Nortel, it was different. Happy people are productive people. As far as hiring people goes, they didn't make a mistake. They empowered people, trained them, and brought in new people that complemented their skills."

In his area, Richards claims that employees were "fully behind the company" on the first round of layoffs that affected them in January, which reduced the headcount by 10 percent. "They were deadwood, or were about to retire, and you were happy to see them go with a good package. The people cut may not have been the best in the field, but Nortel knowledge was marketable." He agrees that there were arbitrary cuts of 5 percent, "but it gave managers a chance to assess employees and rank them." As for wasteful, or at least generous, spending, it did go on, and it had to stop. "Definitely, some managers, like in any company, didn't handle their budgets well. R&D did well, but a handful of people enjoyed the power. We did blow our expense budgets."

And so the first quarter of 2001 was a different Nortel. Leaner, more careful about the discretionary spending. This quarter is traditionally a slow one, but at some point in the early part of the quarter, it started to become clear to Richards that sales targets weren't going to be met. "A lot of people knew we weren't coming close to the number in the sales plan. You know, if you're on a strong team and you're hurting, then a weak team is definitely hurting. In all the groups, there were a lot of people saying a downturn was coming. The ones who weren't saying it were the ones who weren't listening."

But the downturn wasn't necessarily a cause for panic or alarm.

"You've seen little blips before," he says, "and this looked like a little blip." It turned out it was something else. "This was a perfect storm."

In the days that followed Cisco's first earnings reckoning in three years, Nortel was waylaid along with many other technology stocks in what one analyst called "the Cisco malaise." When the big dog went down, the rest of the pack was vulnerable. CIBC World Markets reiterated its "Strong Buy" on Nortel on February 8, on the strength of the deal with JDSU, but investment capital was moving in the opposite direction. Raging Bull board members complained loud and long about the shadow cast over their stock by Chambers' once golden networking outfit. Hadn't Nortel been punished far worse back in October for missing the consensus estimate by the same amount? Now it was taking a second pounding as collateral damage from Cisco's goof.

"Got to love this market," one complained after Cisco's results were posted. "CSCO came in short. Who got punished more than CSCO ? Its competitors, NT and JNPR. NT is eating LU's lunch. CSCO can't get the scrap from the table. Street is upset. Find a scapegoat. NT and JNPR are the ones who did it. Kill them. We'll see if this after-hour nonsense will be carried into tomorrow. If so, brace for the fall." Another member groused over Chambers' comments in his post-earnings conference call. "Talk about a ballet dance for the media— that was one twirl too many for me to swallow. NT on the other hand, merely says 'we will grow 30% this year'—and then scrambles and gets the job done."

Their faith in John Roth and Nortel remained strong. "JR told us 30% growth in '01, and given his history I conclude that to be conservative," read a posting. "And I didn't hear any doubletalk on any subject from the NT conference call."

Some investors had become so enamoured of Nortel that they had begun to behave like outside consultants cheering on the company rather than investors who demanded information unadorned by PR gloss. "Agree with most of what you said," wrote a member in a discussion of analysts, "but I just think that these highly educated professionals have a responsibility and accountability to know

. . .interpret . . .research and predict the potential of a company like
NT. Some salesmanship from NT representatives would not hurt as
you say. Why not create a marketing department that does just that.
Conference calls and media engagements that hype the company!"

They had been, by and large, won over by Nortel's "earnings from
operations" accounting. A new investor and board member asked,
with breathtaking naiveté: "A Simple question. What is NT's P/E? I
found that it has none, why is that?" A quick and accurate reply was
posted. "They have no earnings ($1.17/share loss), so you can't have
a P/E." But this perfectly accurate answer was immediately slapped
down by a board veteran: "Please stop spreading misinformation. NT
has earnings. Operating earnings for last quarter were US$0.16 per
share. Operating earnings for the year are estimated to be around
$0.96 a share. Therefore the P/E for NT right now is $33.6 / $0.96
= 35. Bottom-line earnings show a negative number because NT has
been making acquisitions. However, since they are generally paid for
in NT stock, to subtract the acquisition price from income is very
misleading." No one posted a contrary opinion to this received wisdom. Acquisitions evidently were free. Nortel was profitable. As
Nortel's stock lost traction, the board's basic cheerleading character,
dressed up in detailed arguments of technological supremacy and
market mechanics, became undeniable.

Teletruth, holding out for a pop, urged Roth on in a February 7
posting:

> JOHN . . . NOW IS THE TIME!!. .
>   . . . your company NOW HAS AN EDGE. . . . so make
> it happen!! These employee's will pull heavy on the oars if you
> just pat them on the #### right here and show them the
> opportunity.
>   It's RAMMING SPEED BABY !!

Michael Hollander was trading daily in Nortel on the TSE,
making quick buys and sells in an attempt to make money on the
turbulent movements the Cisco news set off, down-averaging when
the opportunity presented itself. As Nortel's price slipped, you could

down-average till the cows came home. Wayne Schmengrum was still on the sidelines, still looking for the perfect entry point. "Bought at $33 also," wrote one board member. "Looks like it finally hit bottom. Next week we will look like genious [sic]." But Schmengrum didn't see it yet. His lack of a position, along with his good relations with even the truest believers, allowed him leeway in floating contrary opinions.

"I think this was the last holdout to finding a market bottom," he wrote of the Cisco earnings shortfall. Which wasn't to say that the bottom had actually been found yet. "We saw IBM, [Hewlett Packard] and [Microsoft] provide negative sentiment. We saw the i-nut bubble burst. We saw Intel say . . . '[Oh my God], PC sales may be down!' Finally, the last holdout, CSCO, has stumbled. Now, all that remains to be seen is where the turning point is?"

When the week ended on February 9, there was no assurance that the bottom had been found. Nortel dropped a further 6.4 percent in trading on Friday. Its $3.11 loss, to $46.20, on the TSE, contributed 104 points of the TSE 300's 123.1-point decline. The index was down to 8,957.6, just 0.27 points above where it had started the year. The January rally was officially over.

Analysts generally agreed that Cisco was responsible for Nortel's price woes. The "buy" ratings were holding. Nortel was a different animal than Cisco, which was becoming widely criticized for not having cracked the established major telecom carriers that were Nortel's historical strength. "Cisco primarily serves the lower end of that market, including the competitive local-exchange carriers," wrote Angela Barnes in the *Globe and Mail* on February 10, citing the opinion of Mark Lucey, who tracked Nortel for TD Newcrest. "Nortel is more focused on the large, well-funded operations such as the Bell operating companies and the WorldComs of the world, he said." This was a bit of reassurance that would not age well. WorldCom's revenues had grown from $7.8 to $39 billion between 1997 and 2000, and it had been one of the telecom stocks to ride the January rally, improving from about $14 to more than $23. But WorldCom had been sinking steadily through February. In 2002, the carrier would run into a heap of trouble and see its stock fall below

$2. Lucey predicted that "the value will surface in Nortel." The article cautioned, however, that Lucey was "quick to say he isn't suggesting that it will go back to its high any time soon." Barnes's article noted that David Chapman, a technical analyst with Toronto-based Westminster Securities, "said there is good technical support for Nortel around $44 and $45."

The only cheerful news came from the bad-to-worse saga of Lucent. Since late 1999, Lucent had issued no less than four warnings that it would miss earnings targets. It had fired its president and CEO, Richard McGinn. It had been annihilated by Nortel in the market's movement to the 10-gbps optical standard. It set growth targets that had proved to be too aggressive, and in trying to meet them, resorted to revenue fudging that was now causing a whole lot of trouble. On November 21 it had made its announcement that it had overstated its earnings in the previous quarter by $125 million. Then its own internal review revealed that the overstatement was more like $679 million, and on December 21 it had to go back and reissue its fourth-quarter (September 30) revenues as $8.7 billion rather than $9.4 billion. In January, Lucent warned that it would lose between 25 and 30 cents a share in its first quarter, with revenues dropping 20 percent over the previous first quarter. Consensus among analysts was that the loss would come in at 27 cents. Lucent then reported the loss as 30 cents a share, or $1.02 billion on sales of $5.84 billion. In the same quarter a year earlier, Lucent had booked earnings of 33 cents a share, or $1.08 billion, on sales of $8.07 billion. On January 24, Lucent announced it was laying off 10,000 workers and eliminating a further 6,000 jobs as it followed Nortel's lead in outsourcing production. On February 9, Lucent confirmed that the SEC was looking into its accounting practices, although Lucent insisted that the "investigation" was happening at Lucent's own initiative.

CNET News.com quoted Steven Levy, an analyst at Lehman Brothers, as saying, "They broke the company trying to grow too fast." It was a portentous assessment for the networking business in general, and Lucent CFO Deborah Hopkins provided more grist for the mill by asserting that Lucent had come up short on sales in the most recent quarter because the company "walked away from end-of-year bargain deals." It was a good reason to wonder how aggressively Nortel had pursued its own deals in the quest to live up to its guidance.

Late on the night of February 9, as Raging Bull's Nortel clan gathered to lick its wounds, a member posted, "I feel very good about NT. I bought it based on [contributing technical analyst David] Poxon's recommendation at StockHouse, but what makes me feel ~really~ good is all the inside buying. NT is the only company I checked at clearstation that has the officers, directors, vp, etc., buying stock."

"Good eye, my friend," another member responded. "Not the recommendation, but the insider buying. This *is* important. In My Opinion, that is one of the 3 most important reasons for stock confidence."

Insider trading was the most difficult phenomenon for the do-it-yourself investors to track. At the time, it was one of the few SEC corporate filings that weren't made electronically, and so couldn't be retrieved from the on-line database. Investors generally waited for the electronic news services to comb the paper filings and post the information. It was not always accurate, as proved to be the case with Nortel in the first quarter of 2001.

With the company having reached its year-end, senior executives began to receive their stock options. In the cases of both Chahram Bolouri, president of Global Operations, and Bill Conner, president of e-business solutions, options granted to them in January 1996 under the company's key contributor program were fully vested. The program also provided them with replacement options equal to the number of options they exercised (at the market price on that day), provided they did not sell the shares gained under the first set of options. The plan would, however, allow them to sell enough shares to cover the exercise cost, brokerage fees, and taxes associated with exercising the initial options.

In this way, executives could "trade in" existing shares for newer, cheaper ones, by selling shares on the open market and exercising options to acquire treasury shares. That was what both Bolouri and Conner did. Bolouri went first, on January 26. Beginning with

22,499 shares to his name, Bolouri bought 120,000 shares from the treasury by exercising options at $7.74 (U.S.), for a total cost of $928,800 (U.S.). He also sold 43,400 shares on the TSE that day at prices ranging from $55.29 to $57.40 for $2.4 million (Canadian). While on paper Bolouri came out well ahead on dollars, the option exercise triggered a major tax bill on the taxable benefit of $29.76 per share, and the sale of 43,400 shares also created a large taxable capital gain. And at the end of the day's transactions, Bolouri was holding far more Nortel shares than he started with—99,099. Conner made a similar swap of existing shares for cheaper optioned ones on January 31, selling 117,050 at $39.70 to $39.88 per share in New York, and acquiring 240,000 shares by exercising options at $5.62 per share. The sale brought in $4,648,099, the purchase cost $1.34 million, but the options triggered a taxable benefit of $3,571,200. And Conner finished with more shares than he started with: 136,494 rather than 122,950.

These were hugely significant deals. In hindsight, Nortel investors were right to take them as a sign that senior management was optimistic about their company's fortunes well into the first quarter of 2001. If either Conner or Bolouri expected a major dip in share value, they would have been foolish to exercise their options in this way. It locked in a high exercise price for the replacement options, and besides the tax implications, they both ended up with more shares, exposing them to a larger loss in the event of a major price retreat.

The share activities of Bolouri and Conner would be a source of both confusion and misdirection. MSN Money failed to record Bolouri's purchases, only his sales. And in the lawsuits that would arise against Nortel over its first-quarter activities, it would be loudly alleged that Conner and Bolouri had bailed on Nortel, dumping large numbers of shares at personal profit, without noting that they were buying them at the same time. The allegations would infuriate Nortel.

John Roth had also been active. On January 31, 24,217 Nortel shares that were of indirect benefit to him were sold at $58.61 on the TSE. These were shares held in trust by Sun Life Assurance as part of

Nortel's investment plan for Canadian employees, under which employees contributed a portion of their compensation to acquiring Nortel shares, with the company chipping in at levels dependent on seniority. From 1997 to 1999, Nortel had put over $63,000 (U.S.) into Roth's plan. But after selling the investment plan shares on January 31, on February 5, Roth personally acquired 26,000 shares— not by exercising options, but by going onto the TSE and buying them at $53.65.

Roth had simply swapped shares in the Nortel investment plan for ones of about the same value that would be held directly in his name. But Roth's open-market purchase in particular had a major impact on Michael Hollander's confidence in Nortel. "The news of John Roth purchasing another 26000 NT shares at C$53.65/share sure puts the lie to any rumours of NT preannouncing anything negative," he posted on the morning of February 14. "It sure would be stupid of Roth to buy 26000 shares and then have NT announce any sort of problem!" Stupid or not, Roth was just a day away from announcing Nortel had a very big problem when Hollander expressed his full confidence that nothing of the sort could possibly happen.

22

Very Enlightening

The company's common shares have experienced, and may continue to experience, substantial price volatility, particularly as a result of variations between our actual or anticipated financial results and the published expectations of analysts and as a result of announcements by our competitors and us.

—2000 Nortel annual report

On Monday, February 12, John Roth sat down at Nortel's Brampton, Ontario, headquarters for an interview on the state of his business and its industry, and what the future held for both of them. The deal for the JDS Uniphase pump laser chip unit was set to close the next day. The audience tuned in via a Webcast, a video transmission via the Internet. It was not a conference call. John Wilson, an analyst with RBC Dominion Securities, would ask all the questions. The audience got to listen and watch.

This was the first time RBC had ever conducted one of these Webcasts. The company was very close to Nortel. It had served as its adviser in the negotiations with BCE over what to do with the block of Nortel shares that ended up being handed out to BCE shareholders in the butterfly distribution plan. It continued to be bullish on Nortel's stock. And it was a co-sponsor of the CEO of the Year Award that had been conferred on John Roth—Gordon Nixon, deputy chairman, CEO, and managing director of RBC, was one of the award's vice-chairmen.

After welcoming Roth to the Webcast, Wilson got to the point, noting, "Certainly one of the key questions in most of our clients' minds over the past few months has been the ability and the propensity of your customers to buy telecom equipment. I know you and your senior management team spend a lot of time with customers one on one, and maybe you could give us your thoughts as to how their behaviour has changed maybe over the past six to nine months and how you see it going forward."

"Sure, sure," Roth replied. "Well, certainly, our customers have all set their budgets for this year, and generally have set a budget with an increase. But having said that, they're concerned at the access to capital being tighter this year than last year. So they're making sure that every dollar counts, and as a result, they're reviewing the expenditure of each, almost every decision they make in terms of adding capital to the network."

It was a frank admission that Nortel had a bunch of parsimonious customers on its hands, at a time when Nortel was still on record as expecting revenue growth of 30 percent for the current quarter and the year. He also observed, "This is a routine we haven't seen before, and so they're slowing down expenditures of capital like we've never witnessed before."

Wilson asked him if he saw this as a six-month, twelve-month, or twenty-four-month phenomenon.

"Well, right now, they're really reviewing to make sure that each dollar they spend brings in revenue, and this is a routine that almost all the major customers have instituted. What's happening is that the networks really are being pushed to make sure that they're fully loaded. We see that going [on] in many cases right now where people are depleting spares, depleting circuits—networks are really being run up to full capacity. And I think this is a good trend actually for the industry, because there was a concern about capacity levels.

"But having said that, all the customers are moving to this drill to do that. I suspect they'll continue to do it for at least six months."

"The industry was, I guess the best way to put it would be, on fire for the last few years," Wilson observed. "More recently we've seen several of your larger competitors struggling to keep up their momentum, first Lucent and more recently Cisco. Maybe you can give us some of your thoughts as to how you see the positioning of Nortel. Let's start with Cisco, relative to being defensive against some of the challenges facing their growth outlook."

Roth explained how Nortel "could see that networks were going to move from the world of voice traffic to the world of data traffic—Internet, if you like—but Internet and data now all use the same standard, so it's almost irrelevant whether you talk about Internet or data circuits.

"But data traffic now represents about 70 percent of the load of the networks that our customers carry on their networks. That kind of load requires different technology than we've designed the system to be over the last 100 years. This is the world now moving towards packet networks. Nortel spotted that move very early in retrospect. Lucent, I think, missed it altogether.

"Today if you look at Nortel, between our fibre-optic portfolio, we're well positioned to where all our customers are moving. Now, Cisco had not really put in place a portfolio that big carriers need. Cisco, while they're very, very expert in packet technology for small corporations and larger corporations, don't have the technology required to build a network for the big telephone companies, and this is where Nortel excels.

"So we're moving ahead, and we're actually doing quite well, because this transition is carrying on and as it moves on, Nortel gains more and more share each year."

"You mentioned some of the problems Lucent has had—obviously traditionally the largest company in this space," Wilson followed up. "Could you talk a little bit about what kind of opportunity that presents for you now? Their own management has acknowledged that their behaviour in the past maybe has been a little too aggressive in terms of pursuing deals and price discounting and that going forward they intend to be less aggressive to try and right their financial ship as it were. What kind of opportunities does that present to Nortel?"

One of the opportunities, said Roth, "is that confidence in Lucent is really shattered. Confidence in the investor community obviously is shattered because their stock price is very very low. The company is selling off parts of itself, major big chunks of it being sold off. And I have to say that as far as we're concerned, what's really important is that customer confidence has been shattered as well. And the more that Lucent talks about the work they're going to have to do to fix the company, the worse the customers feel about buying equipment from Lucent. So more and more people I talk to are looking to bring in more Nortel equipment, because they know that our company will be around. They see a very, very high [turnover] rate amongst the engineering groups inside Lucent." These customers were left to infer "that Lucent is losing the ability to service their own equipment."

"Well, if we look at who is biggest in the industry today, congratulations," said Wilson. "It looks like it's going to be Nortel Networks, certainly on the fourth quarter, the December quarter. . . . That obviously is a great accomplishment but at the same time presents a number of challenges for you and your management team. Maybe you could talk a little bit about how your management team is managing the corporation in terms of some of the key challenges to keep a company that size growing at the kind of rate that you've been growing at."

"Well, that's right," said Roth. "We've almost tripled over the last, I guess, four or five years, and we realize we've reached a size now where we probably are one of the biggest companies in the industry, if not the biggest company in the industry, and we never really set out to do that. We wanted to be the fastest growing, we wanted to be the most valuable, but we didn't necessarily want to be big, because with bigness also comes loss of speed, and in this industry, being agile and being quick is very, very important.

"So we're looking right now to see what businesses Nortel should de-emphasize, how to reduce the complexity of our corporation to make sure that we focus on the high-value parts of the business.

"Some of the layoff announcements that you've seen Nortel announce earlier this year was a result of getting out of certain businesses that basically are not going to be part of our future and dropping those. We've moved people across but we couldn't even find enough assignments for people to move to, so we've actually downsized a little bit."

Wilson wanted to talk more about downsizing, "which is an unusual thing to see [in] a company that's growing at the rate that Nortel has been growing. Seeing people being let go, are we done with that or would you anticipate that that's an ongoing type of exercise that you'll continue to do—"

Roth jumped in, obviously impatient with the inference that Nortel was somehow shrinking. "Well, certainly, I think we're almost at the end of this particular period, where we did a fairly large one. But what we'd like to do more frequently going forward is to do smaller adjustments and smaller pockets. We were growing so rapidly last year, just trying to make sure we stayed ahead of customers' demands—we grew 42 percent last year—that we should have been doing some of the tidying up as we went along. We couldn't get around to it, so unfortunately, we're having to do it right now. The better discipline, of course, is to do this every day."

"Will the tidying up be generally across the board, or will we see more in the research area or the sales area . . ."

"No, it's right across the board."

Wilson returned to the issue of size and the threat posed by smaller, more nimble competitors. Juniper Networks and other upstarts had shown that they could produce high-quality, cutting-edge products and take market share from the big networking companies. "To what extent do you spend time worrying about big competitors versus small competitors?" Wilson asked. "How much do you worry about the little startups that are coming out of the woodwork?"

"Well, small startups [are] an opportunity for Nortel to buy new product," Roth countered. "If you've looked at what we've been doing, we've bought . . . what, twenty companies over the last three years. We've been bringing these companies in to bolster our portfolio." Roth explained that while Nortel is "very good at doing product development, there's many small companies who are very, very focused and move very fast and they can in a lot of ways do a better job than we do. So, we're saying, 'That's great.

Let's buy them. Let's make them part of Nortel.'

"What these small companies really miss is the ability to take their product and make it robust enough to withstand the rigours of the public [telephone] network—and in the public network, these things cannot go down.

"What we have learned in the acquisitions we've done is that we have tremendous skill in looking at the product and the company we just acquired, going through that and spotting the deficiencies in the design, knowing where those deficiencies will become lethal once it goes in the big networks.

"We look to fix those problems before we deploy these products in volume. And that has really allowed these products to ramp very rapidly and allow their customers to not suffer the agonies that come with [products from small companies] when they hit technology barriers in their product design."

"You've done a number of acquisitions in the past few years, particularly in the optical side of the business," said Wilson. "That's a part of the business where we saw a lot of momentum in 2000. Maybe you could outline for us which product lines are driving a lot of your momentum into 2001 and 2002 and which geographies seem to be the strongest. . ."

"Well, certainly in the optical business, Nortel really did a good [job] in penetrating the backbone networks, or to put it in English terms, that's the network that goes between big cities," Roth explained. "So the technology that connects large cities together, Nortel has really penetrated that market well. We have a clear leadership in the industry and that's an area where Nortel's market share now is very, very commanding.

"That market really grew dramatically in the United States over the last couple of years. It's starting to slow down in the U.S.—big numbers, mind you, so even smaller growth rates on big numbers is still a significant dollar growth. But now Europe and Asia and South America are just getting under way, so we're going to see higher growth rates in other parts of the world for these big backbone networks.

"Now in North America, what's happening is that the major

networks between the big cities are in place, the fibre's there. Now the drive is to get deeper into the cities, because the traffic actually originates in big buildings and the big buildings are not yet connected up by fibre optics. So there's a huge drive now starting to gain a lot of momentum to build these networks deeper into the city and actually hook up buildings, buildings, and buildings, one at a time."

Wilson then asked Roth about adjustments in Nortel's manufacturing process and supply chain. "Maybe you can give us a bit of an update as to how that's going. As the industry has slowed a little bit, are you slowing the rate of expansion? Where do we sit right now?"

"Well, we had to really do a tremendous job of catching up to the demand last year," said Roth, "and there was the demand that we had and there was the demand that many of our competitors actually were not able to service because they didn't have the appropriate product. But we saw a tremendous gain in market share by Nortel because we were able to ramp up our production capacity in time to meet those demands. We've pretty well caught that up."

Roth said that Nortel would add capacity for its European operations. "But between capacity we've put in place and the technology efficiencies we're getting because of going to a new design, we're in pretty good shape that way."

The two then discussed the supply and demand for components, how Nortel was meeting its needs both internally and from suppliers. That led to Wilson wondering how Nortel's plans were proceeding for a spinoff of its optical components. "You have spoken in the past about the potential one day perhaps to make that a separate stand-alone entity, a spinoff, if you would, just to monetize the value if you would. Where do we stand on that process?"

Roth said Nortel was "going down that path. It takes about a year to do this properly. If you look at our financial statements you'll see now that we've broken out that business [photonics] for last year, which is one of the necessary steps if you're going to take an IPO, because you have to establish a history of what this business is doing. So we're now in the process of doing that.

"And we're continuing to march down the path of taking this to a stand-alone company. It'll never be spun out entirely . . . because this is a very, very strategic component for Nortel. A lot of our systems advantage is based on the technology advantage for this unit, but by the same token we would like to be able to use this unit to do some acquisitions using its stock. . . ." Roth noted how "we just acquired the JDS facility," and revealed, "If this company had been IPO'd earlier, we could probably have bought it using that stock as opposed to Nortel's stock."

"Finally, just to wrap up," said Wilson, "pricing. Obviously an environment where people are maybe being more selective on that dollar . . . might have a little more bargaining power . . . To what extent [are we] seeing aggressive price erosion?"

Roth said there was "nothing unusual" in pricing, noting that "in the fourth quarter, margins were actually stronger. They were up almost a point. So [there is] nothing happening in the industry that's unusual at this point in time. So nothing different."

"Across your product lines?" Wilson asked.

"No. The only one that really is I guess experiencing significant pricing pressure right now is in the third generation of wireless for radio systems. Nortel really is targeting the core networks, but the competition between all the vendors for the radio itself is very, very fierce and given that that's financed, we're sort of backing off that and saying, well, we'll do the core, which is the high-margin [part] of the network and maybe take less of the radio business."

"John, thank you very much for sharing your thoughts with us," said Wilson. "As usual, very, very enlightening. Thank you and best of luck."

The interview was over. John Wilson was right. The interview had been very enlightening. It had provided a fascinating glimpse of Nortel's general strategy and the state of its business, as expressed by its most senior executive. His opening statements about capital expenditures by customers, in particular how "they're slowing down expenditures of capital like we've never witnessed before," sounded truly provocative, something completely new from Nortel. And in a note to RBC investors the next day, Wilson wrote, "In our view, Nortel presented a more cautious outlook for growth in the first half of 2001."

Any investor would have wanted to listen in. Unfortunately, the Webcast was a private one, hosted by RBC Dominion Securities for its own people. Incredibly, in the new age of Reg. FD, Nortel Networks, a significant listed company on the NYSE answerable to the edicts of the SEC, had been bold enough or reckless enough to hold exactly the kind of private Webcast that the new rules were supposed to stamp out in the name of equal access to information for all investors. Word of the Webcast did not get out for another week, when the news was broken by Andrew Willis, John Partridge, and Eric Reguly of the *Globe and Mail.*

One other noteworthy event occurred at Nortel on the twelfth, unseen by the rank and file investors. Senior vice-president and chief technology officer Bill Hawe, based at Nortel's research campus in Billerica, Massachusetts, just outside of Boston, had chosen the day as the perfect moment to resign from the company. Hawe had arrived at Nortel with the Bay Networks acquisition in 1998. He had been Bay's vice-president of architecture, held thirty patents in networking and encryption technology, and was considered an industry expert in the realm of Ethernet. On June 14, 1999, one year after the announcement of the Bay deal, Hawe had been made senior vice-president and CTO as Dave House left as Nortel president.

At the time, Roth had said (via a Nortel press release), "Hawe has a critical role to play as the steward of our technologies and ensuring we are delivering the technology breakthroughs that create value for our customers, be they end users or service providers." On February 12, twenty months after getting the big job at Nortel, Hawe was cashing in his chips. He had stock options exercisable at an average price of $13.06. With Nortel shares down to $30.88 in New York on the twelfth, that wasn't a phenomenally advantageous spread, but Hawe had volume on his side. The CTO had 602,398 of the things to exercise. With them, he bought $7.87 million-worth of shares. He immediately sold 302,398 for $9.34 million, leaving him with 300,000 Nortel shares still in his portfolio. While there appeared to be a profit of about $1.5 million, he would have to pay taxes on the $5.4 million difference between the exercise and fair market price on the shares he had sold.

As with Bolouri and Conner, the Hawe options transactions provided another opportunity for misunderstanding and allegations of insider foreknowledge. It was widely reported that Hawe had exercised and then sold all the shares involved in the 602,398 options, that he had walked away with what amounted to a suitcase stuffed with almost $10 million (U.S.), when in fact he had only cashed in half of them, realizing a profit that wouldn't come close to covering the tax bill on the option benefit—and in the process saddled himself with 300,000 shares whose $30.88 value was shortly to prove extremely precarious. But Nortel didn't help matters by waiting more than a week to announce that Hawe had left. The news of his departure wasn't made official until February 21. And by the time Nortel coughed up that news, the company was at the PR battle stations, taking far more hits than it could hope to defend against. A nine-day delay in admitting that a senior vice-president had taken his leave and exercised more than 600,000 options just days before the Big Event was like a gimme for the company's growing ranks of adversaries.

John Roth's February 12 Webcast provoked interminable debate once the news of it was broken. Ultimately, it would play a strictly secondary role in the class-action shareholder lawsuit that Nortel would face in the United States, and debating whether Roth and Nortel broke Reg. FD that day is strictly an intellectual exercise. The SEC never thought it did, based on the fact that no prosecution was ever pursued. One rumour that circulated held that the SEC (which never comments on cases under investigation) was indeed outraged by Nortel's behaviour in the face of Reg. FD, which was just four months old and had been amply publicized. However, the case against Nortel wasn't considered strong enough to risk losing what would be the regulation's first test case. If the SEC was going to fire a shot across Wall Street's bow, it wanted to do so with a slam-dunk incident.

Had Roth really said anything new in the Webcast? With regard to revenue and earnings numbers, no. He hadn't breathed a word about them in absolute terms, and in that respect at least, you can imagine that he had been properly prepared not to wander into the realm of guidance. That said, he had made comments that led John Wilson to issue a note that spoke of Nortel giving "a more cautious outlook for the first half of 2001." Legally, that was just Wilson's interpretation. While Roth was more explicit than he'd ever been about the severity of capex reductions, he never said, "We're more cautious now than we were back on January 18" or "It's turning out to be worse than what I thought a couple weeks ago." And that's what Reg. FD cared about.

Roth spoke of a six-month horizon for the recovery in capital spending. Was this really any different than what he or Nortel had already said? Back on January 18, in the conference call that followed the quarterly results release, Roth had in fact spoken precisely on this subject. Notes taken by a member of Raging Bull's Nortel board, which were then posted for members, read:

> We see economy which slowed from middle of last year. We see it increasing in second half. We have an ability to go after a high percentage of growth potential. We see end demand not going away. Capital markets have tightened. CLECs seeing it. Many customers are working hard to maintain capital. As markets improve we'll see change. Customers see low-cost bandwidth can save costs. So the demand continues.

According to these notes, Roth also said:

> Less visibility in entire sector b/c of economy. Time perspective. 2001 needs fed reserve to take action. Prudent to leave guidance at 30% for year. Expect to see acceleration in second half.

Roth's comments in the Webcast don't seem substantially different from what he'd said in the conference call. But at the same time, Reg. FD applies not just to "new" information in the sense that it is different from old guidance, but to any information that constitutes a reiteration of old guidance. Did Roth reiterate? As Steve Bochner has noted, you can repeat the information in existing guidance without violating Reg. FD. But if you say something like "What I said three weeks ago in our previous guidance still stands," you've given explicit new guidance, and you've violated the regulation. Roth doesn't appear to have gone that far.

It's also worth noting what didn't happen as a result of the Webcast. While John Wilson wrote in his note about the more cautious outlook for the first half of 2001, at the same time he set a very aggressive twelve-month price target of $100 (U.S.) for Nortel, which he announced the next morning as he reiterated his Strong Buy rating. The reputation of analysts is so tarnished that cynics will say this was nothing more than a feint—telling key clients one thing in a note while blowing sunshine at the general investment community. But the evidence doesn't exist for this theory. If RBC thought Nortel was in any kind of trouble on the basis of Roth's comments, the brokerage did precisely the wrong thing. Late in trading on February 14, Michael Hollander noticed that RBC's Nortel transactions produced 650,000 more shares bought than sold on the day. On balance, RBC clients appear to have been loading their portfolios on the price dip. They appeared to be viewing Nortel's price descent as an artifact of the general downturn in networking stocks set off by Cisco's earnings disappointment, not as a reflection of Nortel itself. Roth's message in the Webcast was confident, even aggressively so. It would have been natural to come away from it thinking that, in the medium or long term, Lucent was a has-been and Cisco, so recently wounded, was out to lunch on the big telco front. Spending was going to rebound and Nortel would reap the lion's share.

The case against Roth for violating Reg. FD today looks pretty weak. The SEC must have realized that as well. Again, as Bochner has noted, the SEC didn't craft Reg. FD as a "gotcha" rule. Its investigators weren't concerned with nuance in statements, in creating leghold traps for corporate executives to stumble into. On the other hand, what they were definitely concerned with was fomenting a new environment of transparency in corporate communications. The RBC Webcast was just the sort of thing the SEC wanted to see become a thing of the past. In legal terms, Roth and Nortel probably did nothing wrong—or at least nothing so clear-cut wrong that the SEC felt action was required. But as corporate citizens, they had made a serious miscalculation in holding a closed-circuit briefing for one of the most important brokerage houses on Bay Street at what proved to be a critical time for the company and its shareholders. The chat between John Roth and John Wilson would haunt the company.

23

Does Anyone Know What Happened?

Bend over, once again, fellow investors! We've been had!
—posting to Raging Bull's Nortel board,
5:48 P.M. EST, February 15, 2001

On February 13, Nortel was set to close the deal with JDS Uniphase on the pump laser chip unit. JDSU had its shareholders' approval; now Nortel had to turn over 65.7 million shares, valued at about $2 billion. Before the markets even opened, Nortel injected some good news: nearly $300 million in communications equipment sales to China, with a reminder that Nortel had 70 percent of that country's market for 10-gbps optical systems. "Spending in China is growing," Anil Khatod, Nortel's president of Internet business, told Reuters. "The commitment to grow China's infrastructure is really serious."

Nortel true believers could savour this news while also enjoying the report, carried the previous day by Reuters, that Moody's Investors Service and Standard & Poor's had lowered Lucent's debt rating to one level above pure junk, thereby cutting it off from the commercial paper market.

But the general investment community's eyes were on Washington, where Alan Greenspan was making his semiannual testimony before the Senate Committee on Banking, Housing, and Urban Affairs. Many investors were still angry with him for having raised interest rates in 2000, making money more expensive just when the telecom industry needed capital to buy the equipment Nortel was trying to sell. Rates had eased in January, but to some, the move had come too late. The Fed had created a crisis and then acted too far down the curve to turn it upwards any time soon. With the tech sector being so thoroughly battered in the markets, investors were looking to Greenspan for some sign that the worst was over.

They didn't get it. Greenspan's speech was far from uplifting. Although he did not return to those famous words, Greenspan feared that the irrational exuberance he had identified in December 1996 was giving way to an indecisive immobility that would choke off the spending that kept the economy running. "We respond to a heightened pace of change and its associated uncertainty in the same way we always have," he warned. "We withdraw from action, postpone decisions, and generally hunker down until a renewed, more comprehensible basis for acting emerges. In its extreme manifestation, many economic decision makers not only become risk averse but attempt to disengage from all risk. This precludes taking any initiative, because risk is inherent in every action. In the fall of 1998, for example, the desire for liquidity became so intense that financial markets seized up. Indeed, investors even tended to shun risk-free, previously issued Treasury securities in favour of highly liquid, recently issued Treasury securities.

"But even when decision makers are only somewhat more risk averse, a process of retrenchment can occur. Thus, although prospective long-term returns on new high-tech investment may change little, increased uncertainty can induce a higher discount of those returns and, hence, a reduced willingness to commit liquid resources to illiquid fixed investments.

"Such a process presumably is now under way and arguably may take some time to run its course. It is not that underlying demand for Internet, networking, and communications services has become less keen. Instead, as I noted earlier, some suppliers seem to have reacted late to accelerating demand, have overcompensated in response, and then have been forced to retrench—a not-unusual occurrence in business decision making.

"A pace of change outstripping the ability of people to adjust is just as evident among consumers as among business decision makers. When consumers become less secure in their jobs and finances, they retrench as well."

Greenspan reiterated the already stated opinion of the Federal Open Market Committee that "for the period ahead, downside risks predominate. In addition to the possibility of a break in confidence, we don't know how far the adjustment of the stocks of consumer durables and business capital equipment has come. Also, foreign economies appear to be slowing, which could damp demands for exports; and, although some sectors of the financial markets have improved in recent weeks, continued lender nervousness still is in evidence in other sectors."

While the Board of Governors and the Reserve Bank presidents foresaw "an implicit strengthening of activity after the current rebalancing is over," Greenspan confessed that "the central tendency of their individual forecasts for real GDP still shows a substantial slowdown, on balance, for the year as a whole." Real GDP growth over the four quarters of the year would be an uninspiring 2 to 2.5 percent.

The Nortel board members at Raging Bull were disgusted.

> stupid GREEN$HIT does it again. why doesn't someone put
> this guy away in the bag. What a #######

The prospects for a big rebound in Nortel's value looked a lot less likely. "Hate to say it," posted one regular, "but it could go to 14.00. 30 was a level, let's hope it was only a small slide and not a break through that level."

Nortel had opened strongly at $47.50 in Toronto, but ended up at $45.04. In New York, it fell through the psychologically fragile $30 level, closing at $29.75. The stock had lost almost $9 in two weeks. The idea was beginning to form that Nortel was no longer a "growth" stock, but instead had become a "value" stock, a dreaded transition for speculators. Dividends would drive the price. And that could only bring the current price crashing further down.

Nortel was getting hit from all directions. The Cisco flameout. The sombre Greenspan speech. Misinformation about the JDSU deal was blamed in part for the ongoing drop. Some investors apparently feared the dilutive impact of the 65.7 million addition to the float, not realizing that the shares were in escrow: JDSU said it would not be able to sell any of them for a year.[30]

When the Nortel true believers returned to duty on February 14, they were walloped with more bad news. Bookham Technology released its quarterly results, and unlike its January 26 guidance, this time people paid attention. The results were much less cryptic than the earlier guidance. "The growth in shipments of mini-DIL products was lower than expected principally due to a reduction in orders for this product from Nortel Networks," the report stated. "Lower sales in mini-DIL products were offset by a strong increase in demand for the company's DWDM products." The report then noted: "Revenues from the DWDM products represented 35% of total product revenues (38% including NRE), an increase of 166% on the previous quarter. Nortel Networks remains the largest customer, accounting for 51% of total revenues (46% excluding NRE) down from 56% in the third quarter."

What to make of this? A lot of "lower" associated with Nortel. Its mini-DIL products were down—not just down, but "lower than expected" because of Nortel's reduced orders. In financial report parlance, "lower than expected" generally meant "hit us out of the clear blue." And while Nortel remained its largest customer in DWDM stuff, its share of business had dropped 5 percent since the previous quarter.

The *Toronto Star* carried a front-page article that day on $5 billion in Chinese trade deals signed with Canadian firms that included nine contracts for Nortel totalling $768 million (Canadian), but the markets didn't pay any attention. The volumes in Toronto were disconcertingly high. Michael Hollander watched as 5.8 million shares crossed on the TSE in the first half-hour, while only 4.6 million flowed through New York. Normally, New York did about twice the volume of Toronto.

"I'm not adding to the total, though," Hollander vowed on

Raging Bull. "I refuse to sell NT at these low levels. I have not even logged into my discount broker today, and will not do so until NT is over C$48 again. This selloff is overdone, but of course there is no way to know how far down the sheep will take NT. I remain confident that NT will be going back up at some point, when investors realize that NT will still be racking up US$8 billion in sales this quarter."

He was immediately flamed by a rogue American contrarian:

> canadians r so dumb when it comes to nt . . .
>> the bottom of this pig is 20 bucks u.s. and thats about 30 cana-
> dian loonies. thanks for your gas alberta.

Nortel went as low as $27.51 in New York before closing at $29.55. In Toronto, it fell to $42.46 before finishing at $45.01. Before Cisco ruined the party, Teletruth had imagined Nortel going as high as $48 on the NYSE. Now he couldn't get that much for his shares in Canadian dollars. Rumours had begun to circulate that Nortel would revise its guidance.

"NT has been 'bookhamed,'" complained one post. "That's about it really. Telecoms are passé. I'd sooner fling my money at a good mare at the thoroughbred race sales at Woodbine. Investing is out. Trading and survival are in. NT is a trade. The company is too fat and fat men don't win races." Another member predicted a $25 share price, based on the Bookham news.

Hollander tried to cheer up the board, noting the recent purchase of 26,000 shares by John Roth. "Good Point, Hollam," a board member replied. "Makes me feel better. I can afford to wait for the recovery." But another member warned: "It could also be cheap PR. Now if JR bought 2.6 million shares for his personal portfolio, that would extinguish rumours." No one seemed to understand that this "purchase" was just a reshuffling of Roth's share holdings from indirect to direct benefit. He'd actually come out ahead. The indirectly held shares brought $1.42 million. Buying the new shares cost $1.39 million.

Hollander was adamant that Roth's purchase meant the company was doing fine and would continue to do so. "I find it difficult to believe that Roth would buy any shares for his personal account right before a preannouncement of negative news. It would be even cheaper PR after such an announcement. Therefore, the only conclusion you can really make is that there will be no preannouncement."

By three o'clock, the board members could see conflicting patterns of support and abandonment. RBC purchases were ahead of sales by about 650,000. TD Securities was about one million to the good. On the other hand, Yorkton Securities and Merrill Lynch were both in the sell category by about a million shares each.

At 3:46, Teletruth made a potentially catastrophic posting:

> Frank Dunn reaffirms 1st qtr. . .
>
> . . .said . . . "Considering the current economic environment and tightening of capital within the telecom sector, we are projecting growth in revenues and earnings per share from operations(b) in 2001 over 2000 of 30 percent. For the first quarter of 2001, we expect revenues of US$8.1 billion and earnings per share from operations(b) of US$0.16 on a diluted basis. Our views for the quarter and the year are within the ranges we previously communicated."

He provided no other explanation. It sounded like Frank Dunn had just reiterated the January 18 guidance, the way Nortel had reiterated its third-quarter results guidance in November and December 2000. But Dunn had done no such thing. Teletruth had posted Dunn's comments from January 18. The error was a textbook example of the reliability of bulletin board information. How many board members decided to stick with Nortel on the basis of this guidance is unknown. The mistake wouldn't be noticed until after trading on the fifteenth. And by then it would be too late.

Reuters carried an item that afternoon about the rumours of JDSU dumping its newly acquired Nortel shares, which, as JDSU itself noted, was impossible, since the shares were in escrow for a year. But Reuters also reported the possibility of a guidance revision from Nortel. The news agency quoted a trader who would not be named: "There were some rumblings of them [Nortel] coming out with either a warning or guiding down their growth from the original

25–30 percent to 20–25 percent." The squawk box appeared to be in working order.

"A spokesman for Nortel said the company would only change its guidance through an official announcement, adding the firm would not comment on rumor and speculation," the Reuters item continued, then went back to its anonymous trader: "Even though [Nortel's] stock looks cheap it's because the sentiment has changed. The real downside is maybe the mid-C$30's—I don't think it's going to C$20."

The board members tried to keep the karmic energy positive with more boosterish postings:

> Just picked up 800 more shares - am reaching do-or-die, bet-the-farm status, if I'm not already there . . . I swore I'd diversify more this year, but I just can't resist!
>
> —
>
> Know you are all at the bottom if you're buying today. Nothing but HUGE upward potential from here. 40's by the end of Feb.
>
> —
>
> I think we close 31 dollars [U.S.]. I also see a big Monday for the Naz with NT seeing 34 - 35. I believe today is the bottom. An excellent entry point.
>
> —
>
> Imagine if we have a fed cut tomorrow? Wow. Nortel could see its biggest one day percentage gain ever. You dont need much of a gain when the stock is trading so extremely low right now. Looks good.
>
> —
>
> I came back @ $30 . . . three days ago. . . . rubbing my hands together and lickin my chops. . . .

But the gloom was gathering. Two weeks of descending value, a glum Greenspan, and a rude surprise from Bookham were pressing down on the group.

> All these positive posts are good but the fact remains that NT

is dying. I consider myself an average investor and have tried to hold long. After todays market action, it is plain to see that NT is in trouble. Call it a conspiracy, call it whatever you want, something is wrong.

I have lost a bundle on NT and have now decided to pull out and put my money elsewhere. What is scary is that I'm an average investor and there are a lot more investors like me. Could be a bloody day for NT tomorrow. Fact is NT is being punished for some reason. CNBC just recommended CSCO as a strong buy. Maybe I'll keep half in NT and half in CSCO. Did you see the good day CIEN, JNPR, [Sycamore] and others had? They all had +10% gains. Remember when NT used to follow? This stock is in trouble.

Conspiracy theories circulated on market manipulation. There had been some major activity in Nortel. With 23.7 million shares changing hands in Toronto, it eclipsed all other industrials, with almost twice its recent daily volumes. It also posted the single largest block by share volume and value on the TSE—a 1.15 million share sale at $44.60. It was weirdly appropriate that John Roth could make you think of the Cigarette Smoking Man on the "X-Files." Wayne Schmengrum had a shot at dispelling board members of their black-helicopters notions. When he was criticized for having an opinion without also having any Nortel shares, he brushed off the effort to shun him and warned, "You can try to imagine some 'special' group of secretive people exchanging info and manipulating, or you can try to start to look at the underlying mechanics of market valuation. Old rule of thumb is to always balance your portfolio. Old rule of thumb is that semi's are cyclical. Recent BS told us that those rules were obsolete. Current markets I think are telling us the 'old rules' may not be so obsolete after all. The only 'new economy' I can think of is what occurred during the 1930's, after Keynes published his paper. That one took about 40 years to prove out."

Tomorrow was another day. They would all try again on Thursday the fifteenth. It would mark exactly the halfway point in the current quarter.

On the morning of February 15, 2001, the honour of ringing the NYSE Opening Bell fell to Christos M. Cotsakos, chairman and CEO of E*Trade Group Inc., of Menlo Park, California. A decorated Vietnam vet, Cotsakos was a former Federal Express and A.C. Neilsen senior exec who had been hired by the on-line financial services company in 1996 to take the firm to the proverbial next level. The company dated back to 1982, but the heart of its success was its all-electronic brokerage service, introduced in 1992. For Cotsakos, going to the next level had initially meant taking E*Trade public on the NASDAQ in August 1996 as part of the great Internet stock boom. But now that the boom was a bust, E*Trade was pulling out of the NASDAQ and listing anew on the NYSE. He was on the balcony, poised over the bell button, ready to celebrate E*Trade's first day on the big exchange.

It was a conspicuous defection, because E*Trade's on-line brokerage business was emblematic of the new-economy equities boom: do-it-yourself investors turning to the Internet to make their own trades, their commitment to the idea of the e-commerce revolution leading them to pump dollars via on-line accounts with firms like E*Trade into the runaway equities market. And in the equities boom of the 1990s, the NASDAQ had become the top venue. The NYSE dominated the global securities market through its bond trading, but on equities its neighbour the NASDAQ became the undisputed trading champ. The NASDAQ had passed the NYSE in 1994 on share volume and became the largest U.S. stock market in dollar volume in 1999. In 2000, the NASDAQ churned through $20.4 trillion in equity trading as the NYSE lagged behind with $11 trillion. But with the spring 2000 collapse, the NASDAQ was in retreat. Initial public offerings of small-cap startups, which had fuelled much of the NASDAQ's go-go growth, were drying up as investment capital was both vaporized by trading losses and choked off by a reticence to accept the now-apparent risks of tech startups.

E*Trade for its part had been just ahead of the IPO explosion, which saw 1,649 companies go public on the NASDAQ between 1996 and 2000, raising $316.5 billion in capital. As tech stock values soared through frenzied trading made possible by E*Trade and other on-line services, E*Trade itself rose from less than $15 in January 1999 to more than $70 by April that same year, before beginning a long, steady decline. E*Trade was trading above $30 when the NAS-DAQ collapsed in March 2000 and sent the stock into another skid as its customers swallowed heavy trading losses and lost the nerves and the means to keep the volumes marching ever higher. It was beginning life in a new neighbourhood at $13.05.

Whatever the headaches with its stock, E*Trade had found a special niche in the post-NASDAQ collapse by mocking the Internet euphoria it had managed to survive. Its television commercial, in which Mister Brooks the chimpanzee, wearing an E*Trade T-shirt, sombrely rode a horse named Prairie through a tumbleweed-strewn dot-com ghost town, became an advertising sensation. And just weeks before Cotsakos's appearance on the NYSE balcony, E*Trade had raised the bar once more for irreverence in advertising with its thirty-second Super Bowl XXXIV spot. Mister Brooks was back for twenty seconds of high pointlessness, dancing atop a garbage can in a suburban garage while "La Cucaracha" played on a boom box and two rhythmically challenged white males in plaid shirts clapped along.

"Well, we just wasted two million bucks," the ad then announced. "What are you doing with your money?"

It was an audaciously provocative statement. E*Trade wanted people to think about the brokerage fees they were paying, but the cheeky ad more likely led many investors who had been caught up in the dot-com bubble to wonder how they could have lost their shirts on a stock that chose a dancing chimp as its mute spokesperson. And the entire market, dot-com and otherwise, was nervously wondering what it was doing with its money on that mid-February morning.

To celebrate E*Trade's move to the NYSE, the company transmitted the sight of Cotsakos ringing the Opening Bell to a Jumbotron screen on Broad Street, where Mister Brooks and his faithful steed Prairie were making a special appearance. The mirth was shortlived. E*Trade was knocked down to $12.71 by day's end. By April 4, the stock would be at $5.56. E*Trade may have dropped $2 million on the airtime for their goofy Super Bowl ad, but the slide from the trading high of 1999 on the NASDAQ to the April 4, 2001, close on the NYSE would consume about $24 billion in market capitalization.

As Cotsakos began the trading day, it had been exactly six years since the Dow Jones Industrial Average reached a new all-time high of 3986.17, at the dawn of the strongest and longest bull market in NYSE history. From the present view atop a wounded but still raging bull, that signal event was like some financial Lilliput, a triumph of another age and of lesser men. Dow 15–02–95 was more than 7,000 index points ago. There was no going back, not without a reversal of fortune that would make the crash of '29 look little worse than a bad afternoon of short selling.

Yet if there was no going back, neither was there a clear way forward. The Street—the amorphous zeitgeist of traders, brokers, analysts, investors, pundits, and other interested parties—thrived on anarchic consensus building. It was a herd without a leader, and its shifts in direction were capable of rapidly degenerating into outright stampedes. For the most part, over the past six years the herd had behaved with orderly confidence. The Dow had moved past 9,000 in the summer of 1998 and survived a bad case of the jitters that fall to renew its spectacular ascent. In 1999, with the Dow punching through the 10,000 and 11,000 ceilings, James Glassman and Kevin Hassett published *Dow 36,000: The New Strategy for the Coming Rise in the Stock Market*—a title so breathtakingly optimistic that its promise of a "coming rise" practically relegated the recent rocket ride in equities values to footnote status in the history of the global economy.

Despite Glassman and Hassett's optimism, the market had since plateaued. The Dow all-time high of 11,722.98 had been set about a year earlier, on January 14, 2000, and the index had been gyrating generally between 10,000 and 11,000 ever since. The impressive collapse of the NASDAQ in the spring of 2000, when about a third of its value was wiped out in thirty-five calendar days, had warned investors against expectations of infinite asset appreciation, but the NYSE for the most part had been able to avoid a wholesale meltdown. The American economy was robust, and investors continued to pour money into equities. Psychologically, it was easy to consign the possibility of an investment bubble to the dot-com lunacy of the NASDAQ. Daily trading volumes in the DJIA stocks, which had been 100 million or less as recently as 1999, had moved consistently above 200 million in 2000. About ten times as many shares of Dow industrials were trading on a typical day in early 2001 as they were in the heyday of the 1980s bull market.

The Middle East was providing an increasingly unsettling backdrop to the market's efforts to pull clear of the February downturn. On February 14, two Israeli helicopter gunships stole over the northern Gaza and fired four missiles at the car of the senior Palestinian security officer Massoud Ayyad, whom the Israelis considered a terrorist. The killing of Ayyad, consistent with Israel's policy of assassinating security threats, met with immediate response. The brokers and traders arriving for another day at the NYSE on February 15 read on the front page of the *New York Times* that Khalil Abu Elba, a Palestinian bus driver who had passed a strict Israeli security clearance only two weeks earlier, had evidently snapped, ploughing his vehicle through the Erez checkpoint in the normal course of delivering Palestinian labourers to their jobs inside Israel. Abu Elba's unorthodox attack killed seven Israeli soldiers and one civilian and left seventeen others injured. It was the single largest loss of Israeli lives since the intafada had begun.

The Street was a cold-hearted place. Whatever the feelings of its individual participants, collectively it took no compassionate interest in the fates of the Israelis and Palestinians. It cared only whether the disruptions could make or lose it money. Conflict might be good for certain defence industry stocks, but it was bad for consumer confidence, and if things really got out of hand, oil prices could jump, fuelling inflation and eroding both corporate earnings and disposable income. The Dow had been as high as 11,114.44 on February 13; on February 14, the day of the Ayyad assassination, the Dow sank to 10,683.39—a swing of more than 400 points. The Dow shed more than 200 points during February 14's trading before rallying to end the day at 10,795.41, a drop of more than 107 points from Wednesday's closing.

For Nortel investors, the day rung in by Christos Cotsakos and punctuated by Middle East violence began well and promised to end even better. The stock opened on a high note, at $30.59 in New York and $46.90 in Toronto—on the TSE, the first trade moved 348,866 shares. Standard & Poor's Canadian Index Operations had announced the previous day that it would be increasing Nortel's weighting by about 0.29 percent in the TSE 300, 0.33 in the 100, and 0.37 in the 60 after the day's trading in response to the JDSU deal. The 65.7 million Nortel shares being issued for the purchase, which were actually in escrow, cued the index funds to start accumulating additional shares that weren't available to buy. The Nortel price increase, which had gained momentum in after-hours trading on the fourteenth, had been set in motion by rudimentary supply and demand caused by peculiarities in index weighting that the Raging Bull members recognized not at all. Better than expected financial results from Ciena and Global Crossing gave Nortel an extra shove. Having already opened $1.89 higher than it had closed the previous afternoon, the stock steamed upwards to $48.61. That was $6.15 above its low of the previous day. Premarket news that Scotia Capital was cutting its Nortel price target from $83 (Canadian) to $65 couldn't hold it back.

A board regular, however, had complained before the market had even opened that Jim Cramer, founder of TheStreet.com, had gone on CNBC and commented on Lucent and Nortel being a "mess."

"I haven't heard anything about an NT mess," the board member griped. "LU has a corner on that infamy as far as I know. Anybody here heard something I don't know? JR is buying stock and Frank Dunn is reaffirming guidance. Doesn't look like a mess to me." There was that Frank Dunn guidance again. The guidance that had never happened. And Roth wasn't buying stock, just moving his holdings around. But Teletruth, who had posted the Dunn "guidance," quickly corrected the complaint about Cramer. "Cramer says its a BUY on CNBC. . . . .if he says buy it . . .buy it!! Says the bottom is in."

At 10:19, a board member asked Teletruth, "Where did you see the Frank Dunn reaffirmation? Do you have a link?" But Teletruth didn't answer.

Michael Hollander was in full optimism mode. He disparaged the rumours that had been surrounding Nortel. "Clearly, there are attempts to manipulate prices. However, fundamentals will win out in the end. I believe there is a greater chance that Nortel would come up with a preannouncement revising estimates *upward* rather than downward. Nice German contract today." Bloomberg had carried news of a new German cable network contract from Callahan Associates International with potential total value of one billion euros ($900 million [U.S.]) for a consortium, of which Nortel was a member. "Together with the Chinese contracts, NT has signed over US$700 million in contracts this week. Keep it up, NT!"

He returned to the subject of manipulative rumour with another posting: "The rumour that JDSU would sell 65 million NT shares was clearly a manipulative rumour. JDSU could not sell the shares since they are locked up for a year. The rumour that NT was about to preannounce an earnings warning was clearly a manipulative rumour. NT just gave guidance less than a month ago. Why would they change it so soon after doing so? It would just show that NT management has no idea about how their business is doing! The quarter isn't old enough to give a warning yet. And JR bought shares on Feb. 5. Clearly the rumour was an attempt to drive the price lower."

Nortel kept climbing through the morning and into the afternoon, struggling somewhat against a general sell sentiment from Canadian brokerages. "After some heavy selling pressure after 11 o'clock, NT is starting to move up slowly again," a board member noted at 2:39. "Usually the last half hour of the trading day swings wildly. Wonder what the market will do today. It looks like a nice up day. The only thing I can see is the lack of conviction from Canadian funds. They are still sell[ing] into rally even now. With NT, I am more convinced that the supply from North need[s] to stop before this stock can truly move to its true value."

Suddenly the mood of the bulletin board shifted. At 3:19, a Raging Bull member noticed that a huge trade, 850,000 shares, had crossed the NYSE board at 2:51, a sell order at $30.50.

Large blocks in fact had begun moving after one o'clock, but the price had remained above $31. The 850,000 sale helped trip the price downward. A 69,000 block at 2:53 went for $30.60, but after that, Nortel common was in descent.

"I have lost total faith with this stock," a board member confessed. Teletruth was fried. At 3:31 he posted:

> John, Clarance. . .
>
> You boys need to wake up and learn to play the game. I know hind site is 20–20 but I'll offer this for the future . . .
>
> . . .all knowing that CSCO was going announce negative (or at least the possibility) you two should have jumped on the horn and reaffirmed NT guidance 1 or 2 days prior to CSCO earnings announcement. This way YOU MAYBE WOULDN'T HAVE BEEN SUCKED DOWN THE RAT HOLE LIKE YOU'VE BEEN.
>
> Teletruth
>
> (Oh Well, Live and learn . . . at the expense of the share holders)

The blocks of 50,000 shares or more crossed the NYSE board in daunting succession, whizzing past like transport trucks packed with equity on the way to who knows where, driven by who knows whom. As they flashed by, they dragged the price below $30. In those block trades alone, beginning with the 850,000 monster, about 2.6 million shares moved through New York in the final sixty-nine minutes. The gains of the day were being consumed by a huge and rapid selloff. The price drooped to $29 around 3:30, then began to recover slightly.

There was nothing on the TSE to compare with the NYSE movement. In addition to the opening trade, there had been several large blocks, one of 431,888 at $47.01, another of 586,029 at $48. But these came at the higher end of the day's trading range, not in a late-day selloff. While Nortel was the most active industrial on the day at the TSE, with 13.9 million shares traded, it did not produce a block trade in the top ten by volume or value.

The Raging Bull board members did not know it, but out on the Pacific Exchange, a feeding frenzy had developed for Nortel options. The $30 February Nortel puts, exercisable on Saturday the seventeenth, were set to expire at the end of the next day. Puts gave the bearer the right to sell the stock at $30. If Nortel stayed above $30, they were worthless. But if the stock went below $30, the volatile value of these contracts would begin to increase. With the deadline looming and the stock drifting toward, and then below, the $30 mark, the options market came alive with trades in the Nortel puts. In the last hour of share trading in New York and Toronto, volumes surged on all four U.S. options exchanges, but most particularly, and for no particular reason, on the Pacific Exchange. Before 2:28 P.M. CST (according to CBS MarketWatch), only 130 Nortel February 17 $30 put contracts had been traded during the day on the Pacific Exchange. After that, demand drove the daily volume to 3,630. With the stock price just barely below $30, the level of interest in Nortel puts seemed unusually high. If Nortel's price crashed before the end of trading on Friday, however, the value of those puts would increase multifold. Did the put contract buyers know something the rest of the market didn't? Or did they know something that was also driving Nortel shares across the NYSE board in megablock after megablock?

At 3:42, as the share price lost altitude, a member posted, "This stock makes no sense?????"

At 3:48, 50,000 shares went by on the NYSE at $29.35. At 3:49, 60,400 commanded $29.45.

Just then, Teletruth announced that he had bailed:

> I dumped it (NT) all of it. . .
>
> . . .I'm out . . . way too weak . . . no support . . . no strength and with no news coming until Fed meeting in March . . . this goes way into the dumper.
>
> Teletruth
>
> (even contracts don't matter . . . may get back in low 20's) good luck to you all.

Two minutes later, 100,000 shares fetched $29.30.

A true believer had lost the faith. It was an appalling moment for those who thought the rally had finally come through, that salvation was just around the corner. Something else was.

A board regular played his own hunch, diving in at the close to gather more shares, just before the last block, a 303,800 whopper, squeezed in before the Closing Bell in New York. "It's amazing what can happen in 15 minutes. Tomorrow will be interesting; expecting wild swings and big surprise during last half-hour (like today) . . . 66% chance it will be on upside. [By the way], NT closed up . . . on to afterhours."

The final price: $46.15 in Toronto on a trade of 11,400 shares, better than the previous day's close by $1.14. In New York, Nortel went its own way, unusual for such a closely tracked stock. Its closing of $29.75 was only 20 cents better than the previous day. A bizarre end to a bizarre afternoon.

At 4:03 came the news.

"Halted," a member reported. Trading had been suspended in Nortel in the after-hours market. He asked Teletruth, "Did you dump too soon?"

He had not. He had dumped with the timing of a Swiss watch. Nortel was lowering guidance. The current quarter would end with a 4-cent *loss*, not a 16-cent profit. And that was on Nortel's "earnings from operations" figures.

"Tele, you must have the instincts of a . . . cat!!!" Wayne Schmengrum exclaimed.

"Hollam . . ." a member posted to Hollander's attention. "I guess some rumours are true."

Over on the Nortel board at Yahoo!, the predictable hell was breaking loose. It was a less erudite and mannered crowd. From 4:07 on, the messages erupted in primal screams.

EARNINGS WARNING!!!!!!!!!!!!!!!!!!!!!

—

HALTED!!!! MY GOD WE'RE SCREWED

—

Pre-announce . . . knew it. Now I wish all you monkey asses paid more attention when a million shares gets dropped before they ask. hold the bag while I run will ya?

—

NT is a BITCH about to get slapped!!

—

FUKKKK NT!!!!!!!

—

Err, Oh-OH! No longer a Rumor. Hope you didn't lose much.
May god have mercy on us all.

—

this is a bunch of bull—i want the sec to look at every block trade
after 2:30 pm new york time. these people need to go to jail. end
of story—and where was the nyse—why did not they halt it
when they saw those large trades on the stock—-really call nt—
everyone and demand—that the sec investigate every sell of any
large amount. this is criminal since the sec changed the rules.

Some of the Yahoo! board members didn't know what was going
on or what had hit them. "I just put my retirement fund all in NT
@ $31 today," someone actually posted at 4:17. "Do you think it'll
be OK?" The enthusiastic reply, appropriately from a board member
named loudheckler, was "you're screwed!!!"

"Well, I was wrong," Michael Hollander wrote to his fellow Raging
Bull board members at 4:27, as Nortel sank toward $20 in after-
hours trading in New York. "I apologize to the board for posting my
opinion that NT would not warn." Some of his board members,
according to their postings, had lost literally hundreds of thousands
of dollars in a matter of minutes. Hollander's chances of staying
home with his daughter much longer had vanished.

Teletruth, who had dodged the bullet with his brilliant trade,
rushed to Hollander's cause:

Hollam . . . NO WAY you need to apologize. . .
    . . .your calls are strong and I will always continue to read /
listen to your input. You've helped me to make money when I
wouldn't have so. . .
        Don't ever stop
        Best Regards
        Tele

Wayne Schmengrum was close behind him.

> hollam, welcome to the club. . .
>
> Personally I hold more respect for those who admit their mistakes and the fact that they can be wrong in there opinions. I have always enjoyed reading your posts and many taught me something. So . . . I agree with Tele. . .

They were, for the most part, shellshocked. Some tried to imagine that this was actually good news, that with the bad stuff out of the way, Nortel could get on with being great again. "We accumulate at better prices. Same great company, same great future. Remember this is NO LU, more like a LU killer," one member cheered.

But few were cheering. "Was afraid to look until I fortified myself. Maybe I'll open that blue felt sack and drown the bottle of Crown Royal, But what do I know?"

Oh, how many of them raged. At the insider trading, which surely must have been going in the afternoon in New York, as all those shares high-tailed it in five- and six-figure blocks. At Nortel, for making them look like such chumps for believing so much that this company wasn't another Lucent. And at John Roth and his fellow senior execs, for issuing such catastrophic guidance just twenty-eight days after saying, as they had been saying since the previous October, that 2001 was going to be a great year, that the future of networking belonged to Nortel.

"I don't get it," one member confessed. "Roth bought 26,000 shares at 35 on Feb. 5th. What was he thinking?" Posted another: "Mr. Roth has misinformed the investors by repeatedly denying any problems and all of a sudden HUGE warning. He should be demoted to the janitorial division."

"Am I understanding this right?" a member posted at 5:39. "They lowered from .16 profit to -.04 loss for the first quarter. Also they lowered their revenue growth from 30–35% to 10–15% for the ENTIRE year. I don't even want to see this for a couple of months. What happened from 1/18 to 2/15? Does anyone know?"

Answering that question was going to take years, inasmuch as it ever could be answered. And the process began just a few minutes after the opening bells rang the very next morning, when Nortel opened at $19.90 in New York and at $30 in Toronto, when news of the first of more than a dozen class-action shareholder lawsuits was delivered by the newswires.

Epilogue

The summit of Nortel's share value, the $124.50 high set on July 26, 2000, overlooked a treacherously greasy south face. When the stock's price started skidding, legions of investors large and small refused to believe that this enormously celebrated company and its enormously celebrated president and CEO were falling headlong into a bone-jarring slide, dragging the shareholders with them. The few contrarian voices had already been largely disregarded. The belief that Nortel would rebound—maybe not to $124.50, but surely to some fresh and profitable height—swept up capital in an avalanche that ran long and hard. Many investors refused to sell out of their positions; many others were carried away in the bargain hunting that followed the third-quarter 2000 debacle. But even after the February 15, 2001, guidance reversal, which was the first unequivocal sign from Nortel and John Roth that things looked very bad indeed, more investors scrambled right into the slide, hoping to ride the boulders across a gulch, as it were, and right up another mountainside to another peak. Instead, they were buried.

The persistent enthusiasm of so many investors was a fitting tribute to the job Nortel's in-house PR operation had done in convincing the public and even investment professionals, by dint of its ceaseless barrage of good-news contract bulletins, that the company was an unstoppable powerhouse, a potent cross-pollination of New Economy tech and old-fashioned blue-chip reliability. However, the news of February 19, 2001, that Nortel had won U.S.-based *PRWeek*'s Corporate Team of the Year Award, was a colossal example of mistimed PR. Coming at the start of the week that followed the guidance retreat, the award's accolades paid embarrassing tribute to a core reason for Nortel's run as a hot stock—a run that was now over.

PRWeek approvingly noted that Nortel's reworked corporate communications strategy "focused on just one message: Nortel as a global technology leader. 'Message discipline' was used to drive this home. It helped that Nortel unleashed a massive news flow in 2000 . . . The result, among other things, was a 300% increase in media coverage."

Indeed, "massive news flow" brought to mind another natural catastrophe: a river in flood that swept up everything in its path. This flow had served to persuade investors that Nortel was growing, growing, growing, and that by the measure of its earnings-from-operations accounting, the company was profitable, and increasingly so. Nortel's PR machine spread the received wisdom throughout the land and, as with a river in flood, there was a certain helplessness felt by the contrarians who tried to stand against it. The bulletin board messages on Raging Bull indicated how every new contract announcement by Nortel had indeed served to reinforce the optimism of investors and kept them believing that Nortel and Roth had the right stuff, that this company was a cut above Lucent and Cisco—the rival firms John Roth had trash-talked back on November 30, 2000, during Nortel's celebratory day at the NYSE.

But now the awful truth was sinking in. Nortel wasn't better than the beleaguered Lucent. Nortel was turning into Lucent. The dispiriting message "NT = LU," posted on Raging Bull, was a bumpersticker realization that, for Nortel investors, the future was freighted with one quarterly disappointment after another, as contracts entered into in the heady days of 2000 withered, long-term receivables became more impaired, and new business in 2001 was severely scaled back. The networking sector was succumbing to capital expenditures shock, just as Paul Sagawa had predicted the previous September.

In the second quarter of 2001, as business continued to sour, the company was forced to take a $12.4 billion write-down for the intangible assets associated with its acquisitions of Alteon, Xros, Qtera, and the JDS Uniphase pump laser chip operation ("980 NPLC Business"). The write-down, along with other special charges for ongoing layoffs and the abandonment of leasehold properties, amounted to $13.6 billion; coupled with operating losses and other charges, Nortel's second-quarter loss came to $19.4 billion. The bad news drove Nortel's stock still lower. It had already closed on the TSE at $13.06 on June 18. The John Roth Value Threshold—the point at which Nortel's shares became worth less than they were when Roth assumed command—had been crossed.

It had taken about four months for Nortel's $2.5 billion (including contingencies) purchase from JDSU to be declared worthless, as the revenues flowing from the optical networking pipeline were reduced to a trickle. Almost half the company's employees were shed by the end of 2001. The company's optical segment bore the brunt of the 2001 sales slowdown, as revenues fell from $9.2 to $2.8 billion. (Wireless sales, on the other hand, actually increased.) Needless to say, Nortel scrapped its plan to spin off its photonics operations. Photonic Technologies, the $32 million cash purchase of May 12, 2000, was shut down. Nortel also sold off many of the elements of other recent acquisitions at fire-sale prices. On November 28, 2001, for example, the assets associated with the Clarify purchase were sold to Amdocs Ltd. for $200 million; Nortel had paid $2.1 billion in treasury shares for Clarify on March 16, 2000.

Rather than reaching revenues of $40 billion in 2001, as Nortel had been predicting up to February 15, sales retreated to $17.5 billion. But Nortel was still striving to put the best possible spin on its calamitous performance. Although the "earnings from operations" term was gone from its "financial highlights" summary in its 2001 annual report, Nortel was applying the same accounting magic to what it now called its "pro forma net earnings (loss)" results. Nortel defined this in part as its "Reported net earnings (loss) from continuing operations before the after-tax impact of Acquisition Related Costs (in-process research and development expense and the amortization of acquired technology and goodwill from all acquisitions subsequent to July 1998)." While it conceded in a footnote that "this pro forma measure is not a recognized measure for financial statement presentation under U.S. GAAP," it turned a $24.3 billion net loss from continuing operations into a loss of only $4.5 billion.

Nortel explained that the pro forma measure was provided "to assist readers in evaluating the operating performance of Nortel Networks['] ongoing business and each of the items listed above were excluded because they were considered to be of a non-operational nature in the applicable period." In addition to the acquisition-related costs already mentioned, Nortel's pro-forma figure also excluded "stock option compensation from acquisitions and divestitures, all

special charges (which includes restructuring), any gain or loss on sale
of businesses, one time gains associated with certain investment sales,
any associated items included in the income or loss of our equity
accounted investments, and the loss from discontinued operations."
While these omissions were consistent with the SEC's prescribed use
of pro forma where divestitures and discontinued operations are
involved, Nortel had just admitted that every acquisition it had made
since 1998 for which it was still amortizing intangibles in 2001 was
in truth "non-operational" by year-end. The expansionary Roth years
had summarily been declared a total write-off.

Nortel had been a veritable *Titanic*: enormous, seemingly
unstoppable, commanded by men brimming with hubris. The economic downturn that others in the networking industry were beginning to fret publicly about in January was like a great icefield into
which Roth and his fellow senior executives had steered with apparent unconcern, convinced the great ship's own momentum could
carry it through.

And when the fatal collision occurred, Roth did not go down
with the wreck. Nor was he tossed overboard, the way Richard
McGinn had been at Lucent the previous October. As the ship began
to sink lower in the water, Captain Roth was bundled into a lifeboat
stacked with the proceeds from his stock option exercises, and he
pulled clear while shareholders milled in confused panic on the main
deck, unsure of whether to jump in the water or stick with the limp-
ing vessel. Although Roth received no bonus in 2001, the contents of
his pay envelopes actually increased 28 percent, to more than $1.4
million (U.S.) for the year (by year-end his per annum salary was
$1.5 million), even as sales bled away, the share price fell into single
digits, and his company eliminated almost half its global workforce.

Few besieged corporate heads have enjoyed so graceful an exit. In
April 2001, Nortel announced that in preparation for Roth's retirement, they would begin looking for his replacement. His heir apparent, Clarence Chandran, had been given long-term medical leave, the
company said, for injuries related to a stabbing incident in Indonesia
in 1997. On November 1, the great headhunt found the perfect head
right in the company's existing senior management. Chief financial

officer Frank Dunn took over as president and chief executive, and the following February was forced to reclaim his old job of CFO when his successor, Terry Hungle, was caught raising and lowering the number of Nortel shares within his long-term investment (401K) plan in advance of corporate news that moved the stock price to the advantage of his shufflings.

With the promotion of Dunn (who was paid $850,000 to Roth's $1.5 million), Roth went on a one-year paid leave of absence that would segue directly into his retirement, when he would begin to collect a pension that would pay him, according to Nortel's compensation tables, more than $600,000 annually. For three months Roth also served on a newly created "office of the chief executive," comprising himself, Dunn, and chairman of the board Lynton "Red" Wilson, which was supposed to ease the transition from Roth to Dunn.

Having exited 2000 as a certified executive genius, with his CEO of the Year and Time Newsmaker of the Year awards buttressing his reputation, his personal esteem suffered a remarkably quick devaluation after the February 15 reversal. Roth was very much like Nortel's own stock: overhyped on the way up, then ruthlessly disparaged on the way down. He was the bull market personified. Commentators thereafter crafting diatribes against the stock market, greedhead corporations, and whatever other reviled aspect of capitalism came to mind, began to treat him like the sprig of parsley a middling restaurant lays alongside the roast beef, green peas, and mashed potatoes: the predictable garnish required in any broad denunciation of the bull market's excesses.

Although critics like Patrick Bloomfield had already disparaged Roth's penchant for hyping his own stock back in October 2000, Roth's boosterism became his foremost alleged failing. This widespread trait of New Economy CEOs had been a striking departure from the old etiquette, in which corporate leaders acted as if their stock didn't even exist: talking publicly about share values was considered unseemly. Their job was to run the company prudently. The market's job was to figure out what it wanted to pay for the shares. The CEO didn't tell the Street what to pay for shares, and the Street didn't tell the CEO how to run the company. In contrast, the CEOs of the tech boom, with their compensations so dependent on stock options, couldn't shut up about share price. They behaved like mayors of cities who peppered their speeches with references to property values rather than the local standard of living or quality of the schools. But given the way Nortel chose to assess and compensate Roth's performance, it would have been extraordinary for him to have behaved otherwise. After the downturn, Roth was disparaged for having done exactly what the company said he was being paid to do: grow the company's revenues without worrying about the GAAP-based costs, and pump up the stock price.

Nevertheless, Roth's Icarus-like plunge was a striking comedown from his few brief years as a New Economy poster boy. Management guru Tom Peters paid an unfortunately ill-timed tribute to Roth in his article "Leadership Is Confusing as Hell" in the March 2001 issue of *Fast Company*, which would have gone to press before the February 15 reckoning. It was one of the last times the scalded media, so many members of which had fawned over his ability to ratchet Nortel's stock price skyward, would have anything nice to say about him. Noting that "leaders like to work with other leaders," Peters quoted Roth as having once said, "Our strategies must be tied to leading-edge customers on the attack. If we focus on the defensive customers, we will also become defensive." Peters then explained that "leaders are known by the company they keep. If you work with people who are cool, pioneering leaders who have customers who are cool, pioneering leaders who source from suppliers who are cool, pioneering leaders — then you'll stay on the leading edge for the next five years. Laggards work with laggards. Leaders work with leaders. It really is that simple."

Well, it turned out not to be that simple. The pioneering leaders of the communications revolution like Roth didn't have five years of leading-edge coolness to look forward to. They were turning into laggards overnight and finding leadership confusing as hell. Their problems were remarkably similar and had nothing to do with failing to elect themselves to a special clubhouse of testosterone-charged go-getters. Investors had bought into their similar visions of geometrically expanding revenues and had bid up their stock prices to delirious heights. The pioneering leaders, whose charisma and vision the investors had swallowed, hook, line, and sinker, became obscenely rich by exercising lucrative stock options and then offloading the shares in the enthusiastic marketplace. Now their business plans of escalating growth had turned into ones of diminishing revenues, widespread layoffs, and punishing losses, and the shares were now worth a small fraction of what they were when the pioneering leaders flipped their exercised options into instant personal fortunes. Whatever losses these cool leaders may have incurred on the shares they still owned were usually more than offset by the profits on the shares they bought and sold through options. And any capital losses they had on retained shares offset for tax purposes the gains on the ones they'd sold.

In June 2002, Nortel's price dropped below $3 on the TSE. It had fallen 97 percent from its July 26, 2000, trading high. Nobody's holding a tag day for John Roth, but the approximately 750,000 Nortel shares he directly or indirectly owned as of March 2002 had fallen in value from $93.4 million at the July 2000 trading high to $1.9 million by June 2002. And of the 6.3 million options he held, only 880,000—400,000 exercisable at $3.72 and another 480,000 at $5.96—held much near-term hope of actually proving to be valuable.

The 5:39 p.m. Raging Bull posting on February 15, 2001, had asked, "What happened from 1/18 to 2/15? Does anyone know?" This was the central mystery to Nortel's comeuppance. Investors—some of whom were suing the company and its principals, including Roth—found the abrupt reversal in guidance too incredible to believe. How could a company this big be proved so wrong in so short a period?

The events of the week of February 12 to 16 had raised a host of concerns about the possibility of improper behaviour by Nortel, by Nortel insiders, and by investors with inside knowledge of what Nortel was up to. Fifteen months later, nothing official had come of those concerns. No regulator in Canada or the United States had taken any action on the private RBC Dominion Securities Webcast given by Roth on February 12, on the strange trading patterns in Nortel common on the NYSE on the afternoon of February 15, or on the unusual volumes in Nortel puts on the Pacific Futures Exchange as the guidance reversal loomed.

More than a year after the February 15 reversal, however, Nortel did not believe that the regulatory magnifying glass had been removed from its past activities. In its 2001 annual report, released in March 2002, Nortel advised, "Securities regulatory authorities in Canada and the United States are also reviewing these matters." And "these matters" were the numerous allegations of impropriety presented in the various class-action lawsuits that sprang out of the February 15 guidance reversal.

Immediately following that reversal, suits in three different Canadian securities jurisdictions (British Columbia, Ontario, and Quebec), and more than a dozen separate suits in the United States, were launched against Nortel and its senior officers. Because of the more amenable legal climate in the United States, the main action has been south of the border. The American lawsuits coalesced on October 16, 2001, into a single action under co-lead counsels Milberg Weiss Bershad Hynes & Lerach and Weschler Harwood Halebain & Feffer. Milberg Weiss is the American securities litigation industry's big dog; with more than 170 lawyers on staff, it is involved in at least half of all shareholder class-action cases in the United States. It had been one of the first out of the blocks on Nortel, issuing a press release on its suit after trading closed on February 16. Milberg Weiss initially set the beginning of the class period as January 19, the day after Nortel's year-end 2000 results were released and its guidance for the first quarter of 2001 and the year overall were substantially reiterated. By the time the many U.S. suits were consolidated, the class period had been stretched back to October 24, 2000, when Nortel released its third-quarter results and guidance for the rest of 2000 as well as 2001.

In addition to opening the door to far more participating plaintiffs, the expanded class period cranked up the maximum losses suffered. According to Stanford Law School's Class Action Clearing House, the suits against Nortel, as they stood at the end of 2001, represented the largest "disclosure dollar loss" of any securities fraud suit in the United States that year. The $29.3 billion loss represented the drop in market capitalization of the shares over the course of the class period. (Stanford worked from an opening date of November 1, 2000, for the class period, as stated in some of the initial suits. Working from the eventual October 24 class date would have made the dollar loss much higher.) Only six suits that year exceeded $10 billion in disclosure dollar loss, and in securing this dubious honour, Nortel could at least claim to have outperformed Cisco, which ranked second, at $25.3 billion, having inevitably earned a class-action lawsuit of its own for the drop in its share price. (Cisco won, however, on "maximum dollar loss," which is the drop from the highest trading point during the class period to the trading value the day after the class period. Cisco rang in at $330.5 billion, while Nortel was eighth overall, at $77 billion.)

In December 2001, the trustees of the Ontario Public Service Employees Union Pension Trust (OPTrust), represented by Milberg Weiss in the United States and the pension law firm Koskie Minsky in Canada, applied to the U.S. District Court, Southern District of New York, to be the lead plaintiff. The appointment was granted on January 10, 2002.

OPTrust had become trapped in a ruinous dollar-cost-averaging strategy with Nortel, accumulating increasing amounts of the stock from September 20, 2000, onwards, even as the share price steadily deteriorated. Its 5.6 million shares at September 20, worth $570 million, had become 7.6 million shares worth $368 million at 2000 year-end. During 2001, OPTrust boosted its Nortel holding to 8.7 million shares, and at year-end 2001, they were worth $104 million, after a total investment of $247 million. To appreciate the scale of OPTrust's Nortel misadventure, it had spent a total of $251 million to acquire all the shares in its next six largest Canadian equities, which at year-end 2001 were worth $446 million. On April 8, 2002, OPTrust released its 2001 portfolio results, revealing a loss in investing activities of $359 million, with net assets at $9.4 billion. While OPTrust congratulated itself for not having allowed the proportion of its Nortel shares in overall Canadian equities to match the company's position in the TSE 300, its Nortel losses nonetheless represented almost three-quarters of the total fund's decline. In announcing its participation as lead plaintiff in the suit, OPTrust said its specific losses during the class period amounted to $52 million. OPTrust also said all the costs of the suit were being borne by its lawyers.

By the spring of 2001, Milberg Weiss was involved in 457 class-action suits, which targeted not only Nortel, but Lucent, Cisco, JDS Uniphase, Alcatel, Juniper Networks, Bookham Technologies, Corning, Sycamore Networks, Avici Systems, and Entrust, alleging various misbehaviours that were said to have caused the meltdowns in their stock prices. And that list included only the networking gear companies. The actual networks—AT&T, 360networks, WorldCom, Teleglobe, to name a few—had Milberg Weiss suits of their own.

The initial suits against Nortel were thin on specifics and seemed to misfire by alleging insider trading by Bill Conner and Chahram Bolouri, when an inspection of SEC filings showed that the two men were buying Nortel shares at the same time they were supposedly dumping them. Under the "second consolidated amended class action complaint," against Nortel, filed on January 18, 2002, the allegations against Nortel were fine-tuned. Among other things, the company was alleged to have engaged in various improper revenue recognition activities in order to meet guidance numbers for year-end 2000. It had already vowed to defend itself vigorously against the suits that cropped up after February 15. Having successfully beaten off the suits over the 1993 downturn and the 1998 Bay Networks purchase, the company's defiance is not surprising. At the time of writing, none of the various shareholder class-action suits had been certified by a court.

Other lawyers were busy on other fronts. A suit was launched in Tennessee on December 21, 2001, mounted, according to Nortel itself, on behalf of participants and beneficiaries of the Nortel Networks Long-Term Investment Plan which alleged, according to Nortel, "among other things, material misrepresentations and omissions to induce Plan participants to continue to invest in and maintain investments in Nortel Networks common shares in the Plan." The purchase of the JDS Uniphase pump laser chip operation inspired a suit of its own, filed on behalf of investors who purchased JDSU shares between January 18 and February 15. This suit took on Nortel over the precipitous drop in Nortel's stock value that was triggered by the guidance revision, which came just two days after the JDSU subsidiary purchase was finalized. Nortel said the suits alleged "violations of the same United States federal securities laws" as the lawsuits that had been consolidated on October 16, 2001.

Under the JDSU-related suit, Nortel was being accused of deliberately overlooking a deteriorating sales environment after the January 18, 2001, guidance reiteration so that its share price could remain high enough to minimize the number of shares that would have to be used to execute the deal with JDS Uniphase for the pump laser chip operation. The accusation was an echo of the Nortel's Bay Networks acquisition, which had generated a lawsuit that charged the company with suppressing negative information to maintain a high share price in order to execute the purchase on the most favourable terms.

The Bay suit had been dismissed without fanfare in January 2000, and the sort of allegations that arose over the JDSU and Bay deals are standard fare in class-action litigation cases. The very nature of share-based acquisitions tends to drive a price upward toward the date of a deal's announcement and often pushes it downward as the speculative euphoria passes and some investors give the deal the thumbs down. As Mark Rosen had pointed out in his Veritas research, when a company uses its shares for a purchase, it generally pays a steep premium because shares are far more volatile than cash. The seller demands the premium to shield against a possible downturn in the value of those shares, particularly if they are held in escrow. Nevertheless, it was considered suspicious in the extreme that Nortel's drastic guidance revision of February 15, 2001, came just two days after the JDSU deal was finalized. It seemed incredible that Nortel could think that business was great on February 13, then suddenly decide that business was terrible on February 15.

Yet this is the only conceivable defence available to the company: everything fine on Tuesday, everything horrible on Thursday. And it may not be possible to underestimate the role played by the pistol-whipping Alan Greenspan delivered to telecom and networking companies with his dour February 13 speech. According to Nortel, the decision to revise its guidance emerged from a board meeting on Thursday, and in a speech to the Canadian Club on the following Monday, Roth explained, "We run a regular review of our sales force in terms of what the forward view looks like. The review that we had last week disclosed that the orders are not coming in." Roth subsequently told the *Toronto Star* that he responded to the surprising news that the company couldn't meet its first-quarter targets with a heartfelt "Holy shit!" Nortel's best defence in fact may be that it was so big and bureaucratic that the news from its many divisions and regional operations of a net sales slowdown didn't filter through the reporting system to the top management layers in time to avoid an abrupt guidance reversal. Or it may just have been that the decisions among Nortel's customers were so abrupt, so widespread, and so near-simultaneous, as the wobbly optimism of January keeled over in mid-February, that nothing could have been done about it. And considering the numerous other suits against its networking brethren over their share price implosions, failing to properly anticipate the capital expenditures slowdown wasn't a sin unique to Nortel.

Nortel's corporate culture may have set itself up for the guidance shocker—a shocker that was possible even if warnings of a downturn had been accumulating at the ground level for some time. One former Nortel employee suggests a "cry wolf" scenario. Quarterly sales targets would be set, and sales teams would invariably complain that they were too high. When the targets were then revised downward, the sales teams would go out and beat the targets and collect performance bonuses. After several years of quarter-over-quarter revenue growth, it became almost impossible within the company to know if, when some sales teams began complaining about unreasonable targets (as allegedly some had as early as the second half of 2000), management was witnessing yet another bonus-boosting ploy, or if the sales force was encountering a genuine downturn. As employee John Richards has said, his sales team had seen "little blips" before—poor performances within a particular quarter—but that they had been able to pull the quarter out anyway. In the first quarter of 2001, he asserts, Nortel ran into the "perfect storm" of customer cutbacks, as major clients across the board suddenly reined in spending. At the same time, however, he says that while the harsh downturn, "externally, was a big shock, internally, you'd had a feeling. . . ."

"Companies get their sales info from their customers," says Paul

Sagawa. "Nortel's customers were still saying, 'Hang on, we'll still make this work.'" He also points to a phenomenon in these communications equipment companies that he equates with the children's game of "telephone," in which participants sit in a circle and whisper a message in the ear of the person next to them. By the time the message comes back around to the first person, it has been completely altered. Sales people talk to telco contacts at the engineering level to determine what networking equipment is going to be required. "Top management [at the telco] tells the engineers, 'We're not spending any more money.' But the engineers say, 'Keep on sending stuff. We'll let you know otherwise.'" The sales reps in turn pass on to their own manager projected orders that water down the spending slowdown message even further. By the time the message percolates up through Nortel management, the cutback has vanished completely. (Roth would remark while in Calgary for the company's annual meeting in April 2001 that speaking with the treasurers of its largest customers might have saved Nortel from being blindsided.)

"Cisco more or less suffered from the same thing," Sagawa says. "You believe your customers too much, and orders can be cancelled. Information was available from other sources, but companies were not using them." The telcos finally ran out of cash, and no one would give them any more. "The Street told the telcos: 'You're on a diet. No more spending.'"

Another problem Nortel faced was the "spikiness" in their sales. Cisco enjoyed fairly smooth revenue curves over time, because its large volumes of sales were spread among hundreds, if not thousands, of customers, large and small. Although Cisco would experience a serious downturn in early 2001 like every other networking firm, a decision by just a few of its customers to reduce capex spending would not have had a significant impact on the continuous curve. Networking companies like Nortel and Lucent, however, which relied on sales of large, expensive products to a very select carrier customer base, could suffer abrupt dips in revenues if in fact just a few of the big telcos decided at the same time that they were delaying making final commitments to multimillion-dollar, long-term contracts or were scrapping them altogether. It was precisely this spikiness that allowed Nortel to outperform expectations in 1999, when demand surged for its high-speed optical products. Just a few good customers could deliver amazing revenue boosts. The capex crunch showed that spikes could point downward as well as upward.

David Chmelnitsky, for one, has been inclined to believe that Nortel could well have been caught flat-footed by a calamitous dip in orders from its elite customer base. He was just winding up his work on the TSE automation project in mid-February, before moving on to new consulting duties for IBM, when the February 15 reversal hammered his RRSP account. He had other broadband stocks, and he had his ear close to the ground in the networking business and among brokers and analysts. "One comment I heard was that, really, Nortel had twenty customers. That's shockingly low. I think the Good Ship Lollipop was going along, and sales people were starting to get phone calls—'Let's put off this shipment,' or 'Let's cancel this order.' And when that started happening . . ."

While not inclined to defend Roth or Nortel for what happened to his investment, David Chmelnitsky's anger in the face of his mounting losses was largely reserved for the investment professionals he'd got to know around the TSE, and whose wisdom he had followed. Before the February 15 downturn, "I talked to people doing institutional sales and was hearing, 'There's support levels for Nortel at $40. It'll hold there. Don't say anything, because you don't know what you're talking about.' And it went to $8."

"I remember hearing ridiculous explanations, people saying, 'There's no way it's going below this certain floor,'" Mark Rosen recalls. "'There's this close circle of traders that control the stock and they don't want it to go below that figure, and so it won't.' And so people were buying it, based on things like that."

When the stock went to $8 on the TSE, Chmelnitsky was still so confident that the company could turn itself around that he opted to do some dollar-cost averaging, buying another 1,000 shares on September 18, 2001, at that price. The following spring, when Nortel fell below $4 on the TSE, his total Nortel investment of $75,000 was worth less than $8,000.

The Nortel downturn cost him some friendships among the analysts whose advice he'd followed. "I actually told them that if I was so wrong in my job, the TSE trading system would be crashing every day. You claim to be analysts, you did your CFA, and you got it really wrong. For sure, there was some emotion there. I'd never lost any money on Nortel before. Analysts hold everybody else up to such high standards, having to meet EPS targets, and then look at how they perform."

When the bad news on Nortel was released on February 15, investor Terry Blackman was still holding onto 200 remaining shares of his 500-share acquisition at $96 on the TSE. The first 300 had been dumped for $53.50, and the remaining 200 represented a $19,200 investment. At the close of trading on February 15, those shares were worth $9,230. In a matter of minutes, with release of the guidance revision, after-hours trading cost Blackman another $3,200. And still he hung on, coached by a broker who had personally bought in at $59 during the dead-cat bounce the previous autumn. Blackman watched the stock slide until he couldn't watch any more. He canned his broker, opened an on-line trading account, and dumped the 200 shares at $23 about a month later.

Blackman had made about $10,000 buying and selling Nortel in the spring of 2000. But his follow-up foray into the stock had cost him about $20,000. The $10,000 net loss was not appreciated, but the far more catastrophic experiences of other people he knew gave some solace. Some losses were absolute, while others were on paper, but they were nonetheless substantial. He had a neighbour who lost $400,000—"almost all of his retirement fund"—and two friends who dropped $250,000 and $80,000 each. "In these three cases," he says, "two of them had acquired BCE shares through spending their entire working careers at Bell and, in the other case, had inherited BCE shares as part of their inheritance." They had received Nortel shares in the butterfly divestment. "In all three cases, they did not sell at any price because they did not want to pay capital gains tax on the Nortel shares they received when Nortel split off from BCE."

Wayne Schmengrum had sat out the whole roller-coaster ride of Nortel common from November 1, 1999, right through the shocking correction that accompanied the February 15 reversal by Roth and company. "I managed to stick to my convictions on valuation and stayed out of the stock until it started to tumble," he recalls. "I still did not see the fact that the sales bubble had occurred and that future growth would be severely curtailed by then." Relying "simply on technical analysis," Schmengrum made his re-entry—he does not say how much he acquired—after the February 15 announcement whacked Nortel down into the twenties.

All that patience and careful analysis immolated his investment. "I thought that the gap would be filled and a slow reversal would happen at that time. Obviously, it did not." His one consolation was that he had been far less aggressive with Nortel the second time around. Back in 1999, Nortel had represented about 60 percent of his RRSP holdings. This time around, it only accounted for about 6 percent.

Despite their losses, these investors were not lining up to sue Nortel. They seemed remarkably sanguine: angry to varying degrees with how the company and its management behaved, but not agitating for a day in court. The idea of a conspiracy to mislead investors didn't resonate.

"They never really got it going the way they wanted to," suggests Mark Rosen of Roth and his fellow senior execs. "I think they expected it to go on longer than it did. And that's why they were sort of caught off guard in early 2001 by the speed with which it collapsed on them. I think they thought they had a lot longer, more and more quarters, to try and show some numbers from their previous acquisitions. Most of the growth that they showed was not from their recent acquisitions, but was from the strategy they took in '97, '98, with their own products. I think that if they hadn't made a lot of those acquisitions, they would be in a much better position." In fact, when Nortel restated its 2000 revenues to reflect discontinued operations—the recent acquisitions it had written off, shut down, or sold off in 2001—revenues only fell from $30.3 billion to just under $28 billion.

Terry Blackman is contrite about his Nortel misadventure. "In hindsight, I ask myself how I could have believed that a company earning 18 cents a quarter and buying up startup companies for billions of dollars could possibly be worth $200 a share [as some were predicting] when there are about three billion shares outstanding. Live and learn (I hope!)."

"I myself look back and see what a fool I became and it was hard to stop becoming the fool," Wayne Schmengrum says of his days playing the dot-com stocks. "When you can invest in highly speculative equities and see a consistent hit rate above 50 percent with returns well above 100 percent in periods of less than twenty-four months . . . well . . . it does tend to go to your head. I think the old saying 'Everyone's a genius during the late stages of a bull market' is *very* true."

Ross Healy reflects on his experiences with the New Economy bull with very different emotions. The clients who heeded his advice managed to get very solid returns from what he calls "the dull stuff," things like banking stocks and Rothmans. He takes some pride in even having wrenched Nortel insiders away from their company's shares, before the price truly imploded. "I got anonymous e-mails from Nortel employees, criticizing my comments. So I'd send them my analysis. I got a couple of them out in the high thirties."

Healy's public stature increased tremendously after Nortel fell toward his eight-dollar prediction of August 2000 and kept going right past it. He became more of a media regular, showing up not only on ROBTv, but TVOntario, CTV NewsNet, and the CBC. Sitting in the makeup room before one such appearance, someone made the mistake of good-naturedly calling him the "Nortel guru."

Healy blanched at the implication that he was some kind of sage who could do no wrong. "I've made mistakes in the past and I'll make them in the future," he said in return. If people started accepting uncritically everything he said, "I'll be just like John Roth. They'll say, 'He's infallible,' and bet the farm on me."

He shows little interest in the wave of lawsuits over Nortel's fall from grace. "You can't prove chicanery against a company," he says. "All you can prove is investor and analyst gullibility."

He reflects on how angry people became with contrarians like him, people who followed his advice, bailed out while the bailing was good, and then thought they might have bailed out too soon. "You've lost me money!" these people would scream. "You don't understand the twenty-first century!"

On the contrary, the contrarians—"the lone voices in the wilderness," as Healy calls that small circle—understood the twenty-first century precisely. When it came to stocks and investors, it looked a lot like the twentieth century. And the nineteenth. And the eighteenth. And the seventeenth. Take away the optical cross-connect switches and insert railway track or tulip bulbs. Then wind it up and watch it play out before the same hurt and bewildered audience.

Notes

[1] The Toronto Stock Exchange was rebranded as the TSX in April 2002. The old TSE branding, historically correct for the events in this book, is employed throughout the narrative.

[2] The NYSE did not move to decimal pricing, abandoning the "sixteenths" fractional system, for all listed stocks until January 2001.

[3] In contrast, the Federal Reserve Board moved the discount rate downward a record eleven times in 2001 as it fought off an encroaching recession.

[4] In 1999, CHYC's owners, Haliburton Broadcasting Group Inc., received CRTC permission to move CHYC to the FM band, where it now broadcasts as Moose FM 98.9.

[5] The text of this "lost" official history of Northern Electric and Nortel is preserved at www.navyrelics.com/tribute/bellsys/northern_electric_a_brief_history.html.

[6] mirror.lcs.mit.edu/telecom-archives/archives/history/stentor.bell-canada.

[7] As quoted in *Saturday Night Live: The First 20 Years,* edited by Michael Cader (New York: Houghton Mifflin, 1994).

[8] The evolution of the technology industry around Richardson, Texas, is documented at www.telecomcorridor.com.

[9] In 1984, Mitel introduced its first digital PBX, the SX-2000. The company had established a manufacturing plant for its PBXs and semiconductors in Wales in 1983; in 1985, British Telecom took control with a 51 percent interest, and Michael Cowpland set off on a new venture, the software company Corel.

[10] There was another illogic to their cold fusion that was easy to confirm. It had already been proven that fusing two deuterium atoms creates helium. Consequently, Pons and Fleischmann's palladium cathode should have been packed with telltale helium atoms if any kind of fusion, cold or not, was actually occurring. The pair promised skeptics that they would inspect their cathode for signs of helium, but never released the results.

[11] Robert J. Shiller, *Irrational Exuberance* (New York: Broadway Books, 2000), p. 13.

[12] Shiller, p. 192.

[13] "Internet Born with Netscape," by David Plotnikoff, San Jose *Mercury News,* December 24, 1999.

[14] *Funk & Wagnalls Standard College Dictionary.*

[15] Nortel did gain cash totalling $765 million (U.S.) from its 1998 acquisition activities, $721 million of which was in the coffers of Bay Networks. Nortel as a result had a net cash acquisition of $115 million from its various 1998 deals. While someone might argue that this net cash position indeed made the companies purchased with cash "free," it also meant accepting a ransacking of the working capital of the acquired operations—mainly Bay Networks—to make purchases. And to

get that Bay Networks cash, Nortel had to issue about 135 million shares, take on 39.4 million stock options, and assume liabilities totalling $475 million.

[16] Earnings Efficiency Ratio. As Healy himself explains, "It is simply stated the estimated earnings one year out divided by the cost of capital (the 'Hurdle Rate').

"If a company is expected to earn $2 a share and its costs of capital is $1, then the EER is 2. We expect that the price/book that the company sells at in the market will be 2 as well, and the correlation is excellent between these two measures. This helps explain why Coca Cola which is only growing at six to seven percent still manages to sell at nine times book (which otherwise doesn't make any sense).

"When the p/b is below EER, the stock is expensive, and when the EER is greater than p/b, the stock is 'cheap.' In the case of NT, there is really no earnings being forecast at this juncture, and the stock is 'speculative' (that is, waiting for an earnings recovery which may or may not transpire, and the earnings may not be enough to 'support' the price anyway)."

[17] I have used the singular "Rosen" through this discussion to avoid having to make distinctions between the various Rosen operations and individuals, even though, in the case of the operations, they have different ownership structures.

[18] Analyst ratings as reported by *National Post*, October 26, 2000.

[19] The full, official title was the National Association of Purchasing Managers (NAPM) Report on Business: Manufacturing. The NAPM is now known as the Institute for Supply Management (ISM).

[20] "Fed lowers rates in surprise move," Rex Nutting, CBS MarketWatch.com, January 3, 2001.

[21] "Stocks zoom on surprise Fed rate cut," Julie Rannazzisi, CBS MarketWatch.com, January 3, 2001.

[22] Wayne Schmengrum was interviewed via e-mail.

[23] Bulletin board shorthand for "Laughing Out Loud."

[24] Michael Hollander's comments to me were made via e-mail.

[25] "CIBC analyst: Cisco's glory days are over," Tiffany Kary, CNET News.com, January 19, 2001.

[26] "Analyst, CEO comments roil Cisco shares," Larry Dignan and Tiffany Kary, CNET News.com, January 10, 2001.

[27] The NYSE changed from fractional to decimal pricing on January 29, 2001.

[28] "Lucent says Mideast hackers attacked Web site," Erich Luening, CNET News.com, November 2, 2000.

[29] Not his real name.

[30] JDS Uniphase did end up selling 41 million of the 65.7 million shares before its fiscal (June 30, 2001) year-end. Two-thirds of the shares obviously has been released from escrow, perhaps as a Nortel rapprochement to JDSU's disappointment with the abrupt drop in Nortel's share value just two days after the laser chip plant deal was concluded.

Note on Sources

This is a book about investing in a publicly listed company and the quality of information available to investors. Consequently, the narrative relies heavily on continuous disclosure documents of Nortel and other companies, which include annual reports, financial statements, IPO's, insider trading reports, and press releases. These were gathered on-line from the companies themselves, the Ontario Securities Commission and the Securities and Exchange Commission, as well as from online media and investment sites. Pre-1996 Nortel annual reports were examined at the Metropolitan Toronto Reference Library. The most important of the commercial sites were CBSMarketWatch.com and Biz.Yahoo!, which also provided historic stock prices and index values. Some press releases and media reports were also preserved in the archives of the investor bulletin boards, and for retrieving these I relied mainly on the Nortel page at RagingBull.com.

In many ways, this felt like a virtual story. Nortel was a networking company determined to expand from traditional telephony into the Internet, and investors traded on-line, researched Nortel and other companies on-line, and exchanged opinions with each other (and ultimately with me) on-line. Not surprisingly, I spent a tremendous amount of time on-line, striving to retrace the steps of the various companies, analysts and investors. I read a wide variety of media reports in the course of writing this book. Many are cited specifically in the text, but others provided information on the activity of the markets, the economy and the telecom sector. Particularly beneficial were CNetNews.com, Bloomberg.com, TheStreet.com and CBSMarketWatch.com. I also looked to StockHouse, Money.com, Forbes.com, The Motley Fool (Fool.com) and CNN.fn. These on-line articles were often valuable simply for the hypertext links they provided to corporate Web sites, and I'm grateful for the shortcuts they provided. Additional insight on investment and stock market fundamentals were found at About.com, InvestorGuide.com and The Investment FAQ (www.invest-faq.com). My discussions of market and investment theory were informed by Robert Shiller's *Irrational Exuberance* (Broadway Books, 2001). As well, his article "Valuation Ratios and the Long-Run Stock Market Outlook," cowritten with John Campbell, which appeared in the Winter 1998 issue of *The Journal of Portfolio Management,* was most informative and is the subject of my own analysis in Chapter 2. Edward Chancellor's *Devil Take the Hindmost* (Penguin Putnam, 2000) was similarly informative on stock market scams and historic bubbles, and also provided two indirect quotations (John Bowering's recollections of David Ricardo's basic investment strategy, on page 45, and the opening quotation from William Fowler at the beginning of Chapter 6), as well as his own comment on the South Sea Bubble at the beginning of Chapter 7. I also owe a debt to Robert Park's *Voodoo Science* (Oxford University Press, 2001), whose content inspired my coining of the term "cold fusion economics." My discussion of investor confusion regarding Ticketmaster and MCI Communications in Chapter 7 owes a debt to "Massively Confused Investors Making Conspicuously Ignorant Choices (MCI-MCIC)" by Michael S. Rashes, written in November 1999 as part of his doctoral dissertation at Harvard University's Department of Economics.

My account of the interview of John Roth on the RBC Dominion Securities Webcast on February 12, 2001, in Chapter 22 is based on a transcript prepared by and provided to me by a staff member of *The Globe and Mail*. In addition to official information from the Financial Accounting Standards Board and the results of my own interviews, my discussions of pooling versus purchase method accounting were aided by an article from the Finance and Investment Web page maintained by the Wharton School at the University of Pennsylvania ("Plan to Prohibit Pooling in M&A Accounting Causes Tidal Wave of Controversy"), and the article "The Pooling of Interest Rules Changes," by Cassandra A. Camp, posted at the Web site of accounting firm Carlin, Charron and Rosen LLP, (www.ccrweb.com).

For the history of telecommunications and networking, and the activities of individual companies, including Nortel, I have relied mainly on continuous disclosure documents. General information on communications technologies (including standards) were gathered from Telcordia Technologies, Sangoma Technologies, LANTimes Online, Webopedia.com, Business Communications Review, ePanorama.net, TelecomWriting.com, the Internet Society (ISOC), the on-line telecom archives at the Massachusetts Institute of Technology, Tom Farley's "Telephone History" series at Privateline.com, TelecomWeb (www.telecomweb.com) and Lightwave (lw.pennnet.com). Political campaign contribution figures were gathered from Elections Canada and the Center for Responsive Politics (Opensecrets.org). Information on Canadian patents was secured from the Canadian Intellectual Property Office at Industry Canada.

Stanford University's Class Action Clearing House (securities.stanford.edu) was an invaluable source of information on securities fraud class-action cases in the U.S.

Wherever possible, I have striven to secure information at the primary source. In addition to continuous disclosure documents from and about various companies, I have employed official opinions, statements and data sets from a variety of institutions on both sides of the Canadian-American border, the uses of which are mostly self-evident within the text. For the record, other sources I have consulted include the following. In Canada: the Ontario Securities Commission, the Toronto Stock Exchange, the Canadian Securities Association, the Supreme Court of Canada, the Canadian Institute of Chartered Accountants, the Bank of Canada, Statistics Canada and the Canadian Radio and Telecommunications Commission. In the United States: the Federal Trade Commission, Federal Communications Commission, Securities and Exchange Commission, NASDAQ, the New York Stock Exchange, the Chicago Board of Exchange, the Financial Accounting Standards Board, the Federal Reserve Board, the Institute for Supply Management, the Association for Investment Management and Research and Stat-USA (Department of Commerce).

Index